OWEN WISTER

OWEN WISTER

CHRONICLER OF THE WEST, GENTLEMAN OF THE EAST

— *by* —

Darwin Payne

SOUTHERN METHODIST UNIVERSITY PRESS • 1985

LIBRARY OF CONGRESS CATALOGUING-IN-PUBLICATION DATA

Payne, Darwin.
Owen Wister, chronicler of the West, gentleman of the East.

Includes index.
1. Wister, Owen, 1860-1938.   2. Authors, American—
19th century—Biography.   3. Western stories—History and criticism.   I. Title.
PS3346.P39   1985   813'.52 [B]   85-1989
ISBN 0-87074-205-1

For Phyllis,
Mark, Scott,
and Sarah

Contents

Preface

COMPILING THIS LIFE OF OWEN WISTER was for me a thoroughly enjoyable experience, and I shall never look back upon it except in that regard. The subject provided me with a constant source of intrigue, whether my study revolved around his association with his eastern acquaintances or his time on the trail with western companions. To obtain the facts and flavor of his life, similarly, required me to spend considerable time in the civilized libraries of the East and some time as well in retracing Wister's movements in the West. In their very different ways, both of these endeavors were abundantly satisfying.

Although the stature of Wister as an American writer admittedly has diminished with the passage of decades, a considerable body of criticism related to his works and life has appeared and continues to appear in literary and historical journals as well as in books. All of these materials certainly are helpful to a biographer as they were to me, but I determined to form my original impressions, as best I could, directly from Wister's own voluminous papers and from his writings. I envisioned the result primarily as the narrative of the life of an important American who happened to be a writer, rather than as a literary biography with extended criticisms of his writings.

The papers that Wister left are unusually full and engaging. They are found primarily in the Manuscript Division of the Library of Congress, placed there by his daughter, Mrs. Frances K. W. Stokes, in behalf of all the Wister children. Many other letters are scattered in libraries and repositories throughout the nation. Second to the Library of Congress as a source of original letters is Harvard University's Houghton Library, where the papers of so many of Wister's acquaintances are located and where Wister's letters to them may be found. Another important source for Wister material is the University of Wyoming's American Heritage Center, which holds his western diaries and a fine collection of his western photographs. The Arizona Historical Society in Tucson also has photographs Wister took of the West. I am indebted to all these institutions for their cooperation and assistance.

In writing and publishing a book several sets of individuals emerge as being indispensable at various stages. The first set are those involved with the research aspect. Here I refer to the librarians at the institutions mentioned above as well as others at Southern Methodist University's Fondren Library, the Main Reading Room of the Library of Congress, the Dallas Public Library, the Richardson (Texas) Public Library, and the University of Washington at Seattle. During these basic research activities out of town I was accompanied frequently by my sons Mark and Scott and their mother, all of whom happily adjusted to the urban settings of Washington, D.C., and to the campsites of Wyoming.

The writing of the book itself is a solitary endeavor, but the preparation of the manuscript for publication requires the assistance of a new set of individuals. Here I was fortunate indeed. Trudy McMurrin, director of the SMU Press, greeted my work with enthusiasm and served as a source of inspiration as well as of essential assistance; Teddy Diggs, the editor for the book, was an unusually thoughtful and diligent editor who saved me from error and was a thoroughly agreeable partner in our joint endeavor. Indeed, the same must be said about all the staff of the SMU Press.

Others I should like to thank specifically include Marshall Terry of SMU's English Department, who read an early version of the manuscript and gave valuable suggestions; Mrs. Frances K. W. Stokes, who permitted me to see certain restricted materials in the Wister papers and who sent hard-to-find photographs for the book; Mr. and Mrs. George M. West of Seattle, who shared with me their knowledge and materials concerning Mr. West's uncle, Wister's first western friend; Pascal Covici of the SMU English Department; and my wife, Phyllis Schmitz Payne, who provided me with the inspiration to bring this project to completion.

February, 1985   Darwin Payne
Dallas, Texas

Introduction

IMPRESSED upon generation after generation of Americans is a vivid image: the cowboy as hero. Strong and silent. Fearless and honest. Handsome, and gentle with women. The characterization has been repeated in novels, stories, plays, movies, radio serials, and television series. If, in search of the source of this hero cowboy, we go down to the corral, saddle up our favorite horses, and follow separate trails winding over and across hill and stream, we most likely will arrive in the general neighborhood of a novel entitled *The Virginian*. Published in 1902, this book provided a central character who found an emotion in the American public never before revealed. For its writer, the book brought overnight celebrity status and an identification he would never lose.

Owen Wister, the author, was enamored of the West and spent much time there learning and enjoying its ways, but he was not a Westerner. He was the cultured product of the East Coast, a Philadelphian of aristocratic background, the grandson of famed British actress Fanny Kemble, and a direct descendant of Pierce Butler, United States Senator and delegate to the Constitutional Convention. Wister was as comfortable and as welcome in the salons of Boston's finest families as he was in those of Philadelphia, and the same may be said of the welcome he received around the campfires of cowboys and soldiers. As a music student at Harvard he was highly acclaimed for his promising talent, and his dream of becoming a composer of serious music was well under way in Paris before family complications brought him back to America for a false start at a business career. He attended law school and earned his degree at Harvard, but the practice of law did not appeal to him. Throughout most of his life Wister suffered from neurasthenia so severe that he took frequent and lengthy rest cures.

The first such cure, prescribed for him in 1885 by the famous Philadelphia physician-author S. Weir Mitchell, carried him to a Wyoming ranch and changed his life. As an Easterner, Wister was so intrigued by this entirely new society that he determined to record it for posterity. When he found that he could sell his stories to such magazines as *Harper's Monthly*, he gave up his law practice.

When Wister wrote *The Virginian*, seventeen years after his first visit to the West, he already was the author of many stories with western settings. These tales formed the basis for three early books—*Red Men and White*, *Lin McLean*, and *The Jimmyjohn Boss*—which portrayed cowboys, soldiers, Indians, and miners in realistic fashion. In fact, the books were based on real people and actual episodes Wister had encountered himself or had learned about during his travels. The success of these works caused many readers to predict that Wister would be the American Rudyard Kipling. Yet neither their success nor, indeed, that accorded to more than a tiny handful of works in America's literary history could compare to the surge of approval that followed the publication of *The Virginian*. The qualities of the central character transformed the prevailing cowboy, as earlier portrayed by Wister and other writers, from a carefree, one-dimensional figure into a much deeper, more pleasing one. The addition of a romantic side to a serious cowboy made this character appeal to readers of all sorts. "When you call me that, smile," the Virginian's famous comment, became the most widely repeated line ever uttered by a cowboy. Some of the actors who spoke the words in the decades that followed included Dustin Farnum, William S. Hart, Kenneth Harlan, Gary Cooper, and Joel McCrea. Many of the tale's episodes carried sharp and lasting images: the outlaw Trampas giving the Virginian until sundown to get out of town (this on the eve of the Virginian's wedding); the good-natured cattle rustler Steve hanged without rancor from a tree by vigilantes because he had violated the code; the hilarious baby-swapping incident at the dance in the barn; the brutish cowboy committing an unspeakable act of cruelty against the horse Pedro; the Virginian's gentle but persistent courting of the proper schoolmarm from the East, Molly.

The Virginian has sold some 1.8 million copies; more than five decades after its appearance it was said to have been read more by living Americans than any other novel. Millions of people saw four movie versions. Thousands saw the theatrical adaptation on Broadway, performances by national companies (at one point two national companies were touring the nation at the same time), or amateur renditions. Millions more were introduced to the story in the 1960s through a popular television series.

Wister, after achieving his great success, largely abandoned the West as a theme. His own enchantment with the region had declined, and the West that he had known in the 1880s and 1890s was disappearing.

More important to him, he wanted to prove that he possessed the level of literary skills practiced so successfully, but less popularly, by his friend Henry James. In this mood he followed *The Virginian* with a polite novel of manners entitled *Lady Baltimore*. Its setting was genteel Charleston, South Carolina, and the writing style smacked strongly of James. The book sold well, but today it is forgotten. It was the last novel Wister ever completed, although he was not yet out of his forties. He wrote biographies of George Washington and Ulysses S. Grant, and when World War I came he turned his attention to that conflict and its aftermath, writing jingoistic books such as *The Pentecost of Calamity* and *Neighbors Henceforth*. His last book-length work, published in 1930, was a reminiscence of his friendship with Theodore Roosevelt and of their circle of friends.

One of the most pleasing aspects of Owen Wister's life is the group of colorful friends with whom he associated. Most of them are the familiar figures identified with the elite ranks of the eastern seaboard: Roosevelt, whom Wister first met at Harvard and who remained a life-long friend; Frederic Remington, the illustrator for so many of his works; Henry James, close friend to Wister's mother, Sarah Butler Wister, who introduced James to the life of American expatriates in Rome; Oliver Wendell Holmes, Jr., the eminent jurist with whom Wister spent so many convivial evenings; William Dean Howells, who persuaded Wister *not* to publish his first youthful novel; John Jay Chapman, the caustic critic with whom Wister shared artistic and literary ambitions from childhood; Phillips Brooks, Boston's prominent Unitarian minister; Rudyard Kipling, the acclaimed writer to whom Wister often was likened; and even Ernest Hemingway, who shared with Wister a love for the outdoors. On the other hand, not cordial at all were Wister's associations with another writer, the socialist Upton Sinclair, whose views Wister found repulsive.

In sharp contrast to these well-known personages stands an assortment of western friends who knew nothing at all of society but who won Wister's admiration and lasting friendship because of their mastery of western trails. The most significant of these were Charles Skirdin, an Army scout who had learned to cope with the frontier after being abandoned in Arizona as a six-year-old child; Dean Duke, ranch foreman and wit; and George West, who guided Wister on his first hunting trips and probably more than anyone else served as a model for the Virginian.

Not least in interest are the members of Wister's own family, especially his grandmother, Fanny Kemble, who early and to her dismay thought that her grandson would never be a "book man." His mother, Sarah, was a constant source of inspiration and criticism. She was a fascinating intellectual who terrified servants and made life difficult for everyone around her with her demands for perfection. Wister's father, Owen Jones Wister, was a physician who struggled hard to provide stability for his only child and for his artistic and impractical wife. Wister's wife, Molly, was efficient and long-suffering, a civic force in her own right in Philadelphia, and a great-granddaughter of the Unitarian minister and transcendentalist, William Ellery Channing.

During the last half of his life, his preoccupation with the West having faded and his faith in its redeeming effect on civilization now lost, Wister involved himself regularly in controversy. He had a knack for headline-making statements. He blasted American higher education for its intellectual impoverishment; he inveighed at length against the "quack" novels that American democracy had brought; he lambasted the Germans for their viciousness in causing and conducting the war; he insulted President Woodrow Wilson in a tasteless poem; he created ill will in the sensitive issue of whether the nation's dead soldiers should be left in their European graves or brought home; and he debated with those who opposed animal experiments in medicine.

In 1937, at the age of seventy-seven, he defied arrest by appearing as promised on a speaker's platform to protest Franklin Roosevelt's plan to "pack" the Supreme Court. State officials issued an arrest warrant for Wister because his committee had failed to obtain a license for raising funds. Yet despite these publicized animosities, the Roosevelt administration honored Wister shortly after his death in 1938, naming a prominent peak in Wyoming's Grand Tetons for him.

One sees in the single life of Owen Wister aspects of a quiet but intense struggle over the relative positioning of American social classes. The traditional ruling classes, designated by their ancestry and their genteel manners, feared displacement. New classes, distinguished merely by the accumulation of wealth, were beginning to assert themselves in positions of power. Older standards and values were being eroded by commercialism. Wister, his family, and his friends were deeply a part of the old. On the other hand, the commercial success he gained as a writer placed Wister within the new. It was, however, a world against which he struggled mightily.

Part One

THE MUSICAL PRODIGY

Chapter I

A GENTLEMAN BORN
(1860–1878)

LATE SUMMER, 1882. A young American, two spit curls plastered over each side of his smooth, alabaster forehead, sits in Richard Wagner's theater at Bayreuth, intently watching one of the earliest performances of *Parsifal*, the composer's final opera. His clothing and manner pronounce this spectator to be a gentleman. He is accustomed to attending performances in the best concert halls in Europe and on America's East Coast, but he is nevertheless unusually nervous at this moment. The legendary piano virtuoso, Franz Liszt, is sitting with Wagner himself in Wagner's private box at the rear of the auditorium. It is Liszt whom the American momentarily must confront, for inside the young man's pocket is a letter which his grandmother, the widely acclaimed Fanny Kemble, has written to her friend. The letter introduces to Liszt her grandson, whose name is Owen Wister. It will ask Liszt to confirm what the best musicians in America have been saying: that this handsome, brown-eyed youth is on the threshold of a brilliant musical career. And should Liszt decline in the confirmation, the American's youthful dreams will be shattered.

The youth's well-to-do but demanding father, a physician, is not satisfied with the American assessments of his son. Since, after all, it is he who must subsidize musical studies in Europe, he has insisted that his son be examined carefully by knowledgeable European authorities. If they see a spark of genius, then studies on the continent under the finest maestros are assured. Otherwise, a business career awaits. The latter, to Owen Wister, is unthinkable. A favorable opinion from Liszt, the man whose dramatic mastery of the piano and whose innovative compositions and arrangements have earned widespread acclaim, could not be contested. No better judge existed; not even Wagner, whose music—despite Owen's own passion for it—was not acceptable in the conservative Wister household.[1]

Wagner, now in his seventy-ninth year, appears from the American's viewpoint to be cross. He has reason to scowl: he has worked diligently to insure the success of this second festival at Bayreuth, and *Parsifal*, written as a "final victory over life," is his most difficult opera. It has been performed thirteen times, and only two festival performances remain. But Wagner's triumph has been dimmed by problems. Some of the singers he personally chose have quarreled; the crowds have taxed almost beyond belief the modest accommodations of the town; and early in August a sudden asthma attack nearly killed Wagner. (In fact, he now has less than six months to live.) On top of these considerations, this very day marks the beginning of a two-day ceremony in which his daughter Blandine is marrying an Italian count.[2]

Liszt obviously feels much better than his longtime friend. He is strikingly handsome even at seventy-two: shoulder-length white hair frames prominent features and fierce eyes that miss nothing. Twelve years earlier in Munich, Wister, as a boy of ten, actually had been introduced to this great man by his grandmother; perhaps Liszt will remember. But there is no way to know without seeing him, and that moment arrives as the curtain falls. Young Wister summons his courage and, with a last glance at his friends, walks directly to Liszt, thrusts the treasured letter into the genius's uncalloused hands, and then quickly disappears into the crowd to watch. Liszt simply puts the letter, unopened, into his pocket and walks to the huge restaurant next door. There he sits down and scans the letter between interruptions from admirers. When Liszt has finished reading, Wister walks boldly to his table, bows, and introduces himself. To his great relief he sees that there has been nothing to fear, for Liszt amiably greets this grandson of his friend and, speaking in French, insists that Wister visit him the next afternoon after the wedding festivities at Wagner's house, Wahnfried.

The next afternoon Liszt is asleep, not to be disturbed. An hour later Wister returns as directed, and he now is led inside where Liszt immediately begins questioning him as to his musical preferences. Does he like Rossini? No, Wister responds, and he reacts negatively to other great names as well. It is a pattern of disapproval that will remain with him throughout life. Liszt merely smiles at the youthful cocksureness.

Soon Wister is invited to sit down at the piano. He begins to play a piece he composed during his last year at Harvard, *Merlin and Vivien*. He is puzzled at his calmness, for he knows that now, more than any other time, he should be nervous. Liszt, listening from a few feet away, seems to contain a volcano within his aging body. Finally, after a few bars he mutters an approving "Hm!" at a chord he did not expect. He walks suddenly to the piano, reaches over his guest's shoulders, and improvises several bars. "You should do something like that," he says, and then sits down again, asking questions now about the young composer's other works.

They talk for nearly an hour. Afterwards, the elated youth writes to his father that he has won Liszt's "most decided applause." Liszt himself writes to Fanny Kemble that her grandson indeed has "un talent prononcé." It thus seems certain that an intense program of musical study in Europe can commence, and the youthful Wister is filled with visions of grandeur and acclaim.[3]

Owen Wister indeed would become famous for his creative powers. Had a soothsayer foretold the nature of that fame, however, Wister, his socially prominent Philadelphia family, and his eastern friends would have blinked in disbelief. His reputation would come not as a composer of music but as the man most responsible for establishing the cowboy as the folk hero of the American imagination. His western tales, based largely on firsthand experiences, would spawn generation after generation of imitations. Along with his friends Theodore Roosevelt and Frederic Remington, he awakened the American public to the fascination of the cowboy, the soldier, and the Indian. Wister's never-to-be-forgotten hero, the Virginian, would serve as the prototype for a horde of strong and silent cowboys who cavorted for millions on movie screens, on the radio and television, and on the pages of countless western novels. The trail that Wister was to take to that destiny included many fascinating turns.

An early yearning for music was not unusual for one of his heritage. Owen Wister was conscious especially of his mother's family because of the creative fire which marked it. Perhaps the trait had been passed down from his distant ancestor, John Kemble. When that hardy fellow went to the gallows in 1679 for his role in the Popish Plot, he displayed a flair for the dramatic by sharing a pipe of tobacco with his jailer and cheerfully shaking the hangman's hand a moment before the noose tightened around his neck.[4] Six following generations of Kembles, having departed from their ancestor's Roman Catholic faith, gained acclaim through acting and singing, writing plays and books, and composing music. An apogee came in the late 1700s and early 1800s when a triumvirate of handsome and celebrated Kemble siblings reigned in the

British theater: John Philip Kemble of Drury Lane and Covent Gardens, a tragedian; his sister, Sarah Siddons, also a tragedian; and their younger brother Charles, noted for lighter roles.[5] Charles married Maria Theresa de Camp, born in Vienna and named after the royal Maria Theresa. Of humble origin, she displayed talents as a child for singing and dancing which proved so bountiful that, from the age of twelve, she alone supported her family, becoming a famous performer in her own right before she married Charles. This talented couple became the parents of Frances Ann, eventually to be known as Fanny Kemble.[6]

Fanny won acclaim as a theatrical genius from the instant of her childhood debut as Juliet before a crowded and excited audience in her father's Covent Gardens theater. Inaugurating her career at a peak that actresses rarely achieve in a lifetime, she quickly gained fame throughout Europe and America for her beauty and talent. Many men pursued her during a tour in America, but none successfully until a persistent and wealthy Philadelphian of eminent social standing, Pierce Butler, wooed and won her. Butler, grandson and namesake of the Pierce Butler of South Carolina who was a United States senator and delegate to the Constitutional Convention, was so enamored of Fanny that he followed her from city to city. Proper Philadelphia was shocked at the spectacle of this well-bred son clamoring for the attention of Fanny Kemble, who after all was only an actress. But public opinion did not alter the determination of the strong-willed Butler, and the marriage took place.

The wedding vows hardly had been consecrated before a natural clash emerged. Fanny was not merely talented; she was bright, headstrong, intellectual, and temperamental, and she held the then novel notion that marriage was intended to be a partnership on equal terms. Butler, a handsome man of dark, penetrating eyes and muttonchop sideburns, held without apology the traditional view that the male was master. Fanny's viewpoint was incomprehensible to him. Other irritants underlay this basic schism—particularly the widely publicized journal Fanny published that was highly critical of the institution of slavery. It embarrassed her husband especially because he owned slaves himself on his Georgia plantation on the island of St. Simon's.* In the midst of

---

* The plantation had been passed down to him through his grandfather. It was this same property in 1804 that Vice President Aaron Burr, smarting from public criticism after he killed Alexander Hamilton in their celebrated duel, momentarily retreated to under the original Pierce Butler's hospitality. Here in the South, Burr found a much more sympathetic viewpoint concerning his participation in the duel. (James Parton, *The Life and Times of Aaron Burr* [New York: Mason Brothers, 1858], p. 371.)

this continuing marital turbulence two daughters were born. Three months after the birth of the first child, Sarah, Fanny was pleading for freedom from both domestic duties and her husband: "I must again beg you that you will perform your promise of sending me to England, when my child was born. If you procure a healthy nurse for the baby she will not suffer; and, provided she is fed, she will not fret after me." Pierce Butler would not grant such freedom to the mother of his children, but hard as he tried he could not prevent her from taking frequent and prolonged absences from home.[7]

Despite Fanny's seemingly casual sense of maternal responsibilities, she took exceptional care to insure a superior upbringing for the child who would become Owen Wister's mother. Forever seeking to broaden her own mind and determined to do the same for her child, Fanny sought to teach her blond-haired girl to think originally instead of merely to acquire information. But an accumulation of facts, too, was inevitable with a mother who herself had studied Latin and Goethe, and who was friends with Harriet Martineau, Henry Wadsworth Longfellow, William Ellery Channing, William Makepeace Thackeray, and practically everybody else she considered worth knowing. As for Sarah's physical development, Fanny permitted her no sweets and rightfully took pride in her daughter's resulting healthy glow. Sarah and her younger sister Fanny were, their mother later commented, two of the richest girls in America. (Once they were grown, however, their father suffered a financial setback shortly before the Civil War, and the family fortune declined.)

The conflict of personalities between parents inevitably spilled over into the rearing of the children. When Sarah was eight and Fanny five, Butler permitted their mother to return home after one of her frequent absences only if she agreed not to interfere with the routine he had established for his daughters. Fanny acceded, but harmony was impossible. She eventually claimed that her husband made her an unwelcome guest in her own home. Finally, in 1848, when Fanny had been away in England for more than two years, her husband sought at last to give her the freedom she seemed already to have acquired in fact: he sued for divorce on grounds of abandonment. Fanny fought the divorce desperately for fear she would lose her children. The case became a *cause célèbre* throughout America, the frequent charges and countercharges receiving wide publicity. After a year the divorce was granted, and Butler won full custody of the children. Not until seven years later, when Sarah became twenty-one, did mother and daughter resume a relationship.[8]

Sarah was a rare, precious flower. If her character lacked steadiness, it abounded in intellect and culture. She wrote poetry, played the piano with skill, conversed in French and Italian, and displayed all the graces and more than Fanny Kemble, or Pierce Butler, or Philadelphia manners required.

Such a young lady inevitably attracted suitors, and the man who won her hand was a Germantown doctor of distinguished heritage, Owen Jones Wister. He was the great-grandson of John Wister, son of a huntsman to the Prince Palatine in Hillspach, near Heidelberg. John Wister had lived in the Philadelphia area since 1727 when he and his brother Casper emigrated to America. This industrious duo lost little time in achieving prosperity. They established the first long-lived glass works in America at Salem, New Jersey. In 1744 John built the family home Grumblethorp, preserved today as a historical Germantown dwelling. John's grandson, Charles Jones Wister, set up the first telescope and observatory in the United States; he studied botany and cultivated a garden of rare plants; and he corresponded with eminent persons such as Louis Agassiz (who also happened to be a friend of Fanny Kemble's). And John's great-grandson, Owen Jones Wister, proved to be a model student at the Germantown Academy, prospering likewise under the tutelage of Amos Bronson Alcott, brought to the community for a while by solicitous parents. From Alcott's unusual teaching methods young Wister graduated to the study of medicine in the office of a family friend and at the University of Pennsylvania. Upon graduation in 1847 he became an assistant surgeon in the Navy and sailed on a long cruise to East India, where he encountered Chinese pirates and other wonders of the Orient. In a few years he developed a dyspeptic condition which caused him to resign his commission. Returning to Germantown, he built up an extensive medical practice, eventually emerging as a very eligible suitor for the pretty daughter of Fanny Kemble and Pierce Butler. He was meticulous and practical; she, whimsical and artistic. But a match was made. Fanny thoroughly approved, and it would be difficult to imagine any displeasure on Butler's part. The wedding took place in early 1859.[9]

The couple had only one child, a brown-eyed boy born on July 14, 1860, at 5103 Germantown Avenue, just down the street from historic Grumblethorp. Dr. Wister wanted him to be named Daniel; Mrs. Wister preferred Owen. Her choice prevailed. There would be no middle name;

he was called simply Owen Wister. But Dr. Wister's choice—Daniel— would not be forgotten. The child would carry the nickname of "Dan" throughout his life.

It was an uncertain time for the birth of a child. The nation's two great sections were approaching the outbreak of hostilities at Fort Sumter that would mark the beginning of the Civil War. The rift was especially troublesome for the Wister family, for it was split in its sentiments. Sarah held the ardent pro-North convictions of her mother. Her husband, Dr. Wister, felt the same way. But Sarah's sister, Fanny, adopted her father's pro-Confederate views. Soon after the war began, the two sisters, who refused to permit their differences to interfere with their devotion to one another, joined in a common cause: their father was arrested in late summer 1861 on a charge of high treason and imprisoned in Fort Lafayette at the gate of New York harbor. Authorities believed that he had sought to arrange for arms to be sent to Confederates in Georgia. Sarah and Fanny gained permission from President Lincoln to visit their captive father in New York, but they could talk to him only in the presence of an officer. Butler eventually was released after pledging that he would not be active against the North.[10]

While the great war raged, young Owen grew up quite oblivious to the strife. Things more immediate held his attention. He listened to his mother play the piano, and he quickly became aware of his favored station in life. He ordered a little Negro page in no uncertain terms to come back and shut all the doors he had neglected to close; he reprimanded the housemaid by telling her that the floors she had just swept did not look at all nice. Already he was being molded for adulthood, and the push to prepare him was not without its toll. A week before Christmas the three-year-old child cried out in his sleep: "I don't want to grow! I want to stay a little boy!"[11]

Nearby at Grumblethorp lived his paternal grandfather, Charles Jones Wister. Owen toddled over daily to see this aging patriarch, a man who once had conversed with George Washington. Years later Owen would remember his grandfather as an old man with "thick tough hair, a quizzical countenance, and a shrewd twinkle in his eye," who wore a broad straw hat and white-starched summer clothes.[12]

The formality of Owen's surroundings could not entirely repress him. At the age of four he devoured some beans in Grandfather Wister's garden which caused him to retch violently until he was spitting up blood. Two days later he enlivened a friend's birthday party by drowning a chicken in a pond in an effort to see if it could swim. Standing in the middle of the water, he paid little attention to his hostess's pleas to come out. Even a threatened spanking failed to budge him. "You don't whip other people's children," he retorted smartly.[13]

One day the youngster climbed out a window on a landing between the house's second and third floors, then crawled along the gutter to the roof's edge, where his horrified mother saw him. On one side was a steep slope; on the other, a sheer fall of thirty feet. "I was nearly paralyzed not knowing what to do, not daring to call, to stand still or to go away & let him come in by himself," Sarah Wister wrote to a friend. Finally, by speaking softly, she cajoled him to safety. Such antics caused her to describe her son as "so bad & clever & incomprehensible" that she was at her wit's end, convinced that she was bringing him up very badly. One thing especially marked Owen's childhood: his mother's constant travels along the eastern seaboard to visit friends and relatives meant that he spent about as much time away from home as he did there.[14]

Owen's maternal grandfather, Pierce Butler, did not have long to enjoy his grandson. In August 1867 he became ill on his Georgia plantation and died. The only written record of contact between the two is an undated letter in which Butler wrote that he would return from a trip to Sarasota Springs with a bow and arrow from the Indians to give young Owen.[15]

The country place three miles outside of Germantown, called Butler Place, which Butler had shared so turbulently with Fanny Kemble, was willed to his daughters, as was the Georgia property. A Frenchman had built the main house of this estate in 1790, before the Butler family acquired it in 1810. It would remain a prize family possession for some 115 years. Located on York Road, Butler Place was a striking centerpiece for about three hundred acres of farm land. A long double row of maples formed a grand promenade for entering the white, two-story main structure. Expanses of lawn encircled the house; on the grounds were gardens, flower beds, a grape arbor, a duck pond, a spring house, a greenhouse, a sundial, two stone tenement houses, and a large stone barn. Oleander, lemon, and citron trees, brought by Fanny Kemble from her husband's Georgia plantation and planted in red wooden tubs, adorned each side of the driveway.[16]

For a number of years the Germantown estate was occupied by tenants, but after Sarah inherited the property upon her father's death, she and her husband moved there. Sarah Wister ruled regally. Guests who met her own rigorous social, intellectual, and cultural standards were invited there for parties. During Owen's childhood those who fulfilled her requirements included such persons as Matthew Arnold, William Dean Howells, Henry James, Sydney Lanier, William M. Evarts, and Arthur Stanley, dean of Westminster, not to mention many of the most distinguished families from Philadelphia, Boston, and New York. Sarah set aside one afternoon a week from noon until 4:00 P.M. for receiving callers, allowing herself ample time for cultural pursuits in the other hours. In supervising the household servant staff she demanded such meticulous performance that few stayed long.[17]

A second floor "Morning Room," facing the east, was reserved for Sarah's private use. Here she composed essays on music, art, literature, and education; graceful poetry for publication (appearing notably in the *Atlantic Monthly* beginning in the mid-1870s, under the encouragement of editor William Dean Howells); and translations into English of poems by Alfred de Musset. She never signed her published works, for she sought to avoid public recognition, and when Howells once revealed her authorship of an *Atlantic* article she reprimanded him sharply. She played Mozart, Beethoven, Chopin, and Schubert on the piano for her own enjoyment, and she had taught her son to read music by the time he was eight years old.[18]

Aside from her social and cultural graces, Sarah Butler Wister was an unusually beautiful woman, fair-skinned and blessed with a bountiful head of chestnut hair. Her combination of beauty and intelligence meant that her closest associates were frequently distinguished men of the time. One such friend in Philadelphia was a distant cousin, the brilliant physician-novelist S. Weir Mitchell, author of such historical tales as *Hugh Wynne* and *Constance Trescott*, and a pioneer specializing in the treatment of nervous disorders. Mitchell often read his manuscripts to Sarah to benefit from her penetrating criticisms. She was, Mitchell declared, "the most interesting woman I have ever known." She once confided to him that since the age of fifteen the longest, strongest wish of her life had been for death. Mitchell's biographer believed Sarah Wister provided the model for several of the heroines in his works. Mitchell was not the only American novelist to be so inspired, for Henry James would write of her as well.[19]

Dr. Wister barely tolerated his wife's highfalutin ways. He disliked society and rarely accompanied her to Philadelphia or to any other place. Rather, he submerged himself in his medical practice and resisted as best he could his wife's attempts at the grand life. Perhaps he felt compelled to do so for financial reasons, for despite the family's comfortable status he regularly fretted about his expenses. For ten years after the marriage he was said to allow himself no recreation, to belong to no club, to take no holiday, and to let as much as a year pass without venturing even to Philadelphia. He dedicated not only his days but also his evenings to his patients. Friends warned him that he overworked himself, and they were right. Physical symptoms soon underscored their point when Dr. Wister began to suffer from acute dyspepsia. One evening he found himself unable to write even so simple a thing as a prescription. With this ominous warning he gathered up his wife and son in 1870 and left Butler Place for a three-year sojourn in Europe.

Young Owen was just ten years old, but Europe was not new to him. He had been boarded in a Swiss school for three months when he was six. Neither would a change in schools be particularly novel: he already had attended the Cavalry Academy, Miss Mary Stokes's School, and Dr. Shoemaker's School on Manheim Street.[20]

In Europe the Franco-Prussian War was on the horizon. The Wisters' stay was idyllic, however, hardly touched by the conflict which would unify Germany and have such a profound effect on the history of the modern world. Early July found them in Munich, where they attended with Fanny Kemble performances of Richard Wagner's *The Rhinegold* and *The Valkyrie*. These two productions were being alternated that summer to acclaim, attracting devotees such as Johannes Brahms, Camille Saint-Saëns, Joseph Joachim, and Liszt. Yet Wagner's music seemed devoid of all the formalized rules accepted by the Wisters and by Fanny Kemble, and they did not appreciate it. When Liszt called upon them in their hotel rooms, they talked politely in French of art and literature as Owen sat in a corner watching. Later he would recall that his grandmother asked Liszt to tell her the truth about Wagner's music. "Madame, c'est un grand ouvrage," responded Liszt, "un tres grand ouvrage." After he departed, the Wisters and Fanny concluded that Liszt had chosen not to be more specific in order to avoid criticizing his friend Wagner. But as Owen's own musical education progressed, he came to realize that Liszt indeed considered the works to be great and that his parents and his grandmother simply had not been prepared to understand Wagner's innovations. Whether Owen as a ten-year-old child appreciated Wagner that summer in Munich is not known, but as an adolescent and for many years after he championed Wagner and loved his music above all other.[21]

On July 19 the family were steaming up the Rhine, where they saw Otto von Bismarck's locomotives puffing busily up and down the shore with arms, when France declared war on Prussia. The news caused a flutter of excitement among the passengers. The family proceeded to Mainz, failed in an effort to reach Oberammergau, boarded a train crowded with travelers for Lindau, crossed the lake for Romanshorn, and finally arrived safely in neutral Switzerland.[22]

There, Owen was enrolled in a boarding school at Hofwyl while his parents went to Italy for a prolonged stay in the company of other Americans. Owen found himself housed with other students in a long stone house surrounded by trees, a lake, and the village gymnasium. His classmates came almost solely from France and Italy, and since classes were conducted almost entirely in French his knowledge of the language improved dramatically. The daily routine was rigorous. Classes began promptly at 7:00 A.M. with French, followed by German, English, music, mathematics, writing, and a second session in German. Classes in the spring began at 6:00 A.M. before breakfast. Owen performed adequately —an achievement of no small means—but he warned his mother not to expect high marks in his lessons conducted in German, for he did not understand that language well.[23]

The Franco-Prussian War loomed large in the students' daily lives after a French army of 83,000 men, threatened by Prussian forces, retreated to Swiss soil and surrendered to Switzerland. To the amazement of the Hofwyl students, the Swiss government lodged two hundred of the prisoners in the village gymnasium in sight of the school. Every day the admiring boys watched the captives drill. More than fifty years later Wister would recall that the soldiers' faces were "grave, unhappy, little washed, little shaved, their uniforms dingy, their voices, as they responded [to the roll call] rather wild and strange." The boys saw none of this at the time—the captives were entirely thrilling and romantic. One day a prisoner attempted to escape in full view of the students and guards. As the boys watched, he ran along the rim of the lake, a tiny distant figure untouched by the many shots fired at him. Finally he was overtaken by the guards without injury.[24]

Owen's interests increasingly focused on music. "Every day I learn more music and I am getting quite wild about it," he wrote to his mother. His music teacher, Herr Thomas, marked his reports "sehr gut," a

13

compliment Owen did not receive for his other studies. In the spring
Dr. Müller, the headmaster, arranged a special program to entertain the
French prisoners. Owen played three selections on the piano, and he
also acted the minor role of a page boy in a comedy. For his piano solos
Owen sat with his profile to the audience, a position he did not like
because it made him nervous to see spectators from the corner of his eye.
(Liszt had introduced this practice in 1839.) Anticipating a spring vacation with his parents, he told his mother, "I hope you have a piano where
you are for I shall bring my music and play with you, and if you have
not a piano I shall sink into an armchair in profound melancholy." He
expressed to Grandmother Kemble the same desire for a piano duet, and
he also promised to speak with her in French. Already he was writing
occasional letters to his mother in French.[25]

"Truly Hofwyl is a nice place with robbers, blackberries, & wild-
pigeons [sic] nests in the garden," Owen wrote to his mother. Yet a
dozen years later he was to recall his stay there with bitterness. He noted
that he had suffered from homesickness; that he had been "bullied &
teased by the French & Italian sh–ts"; and that he had been a "very
miserable" little boy. In the midst of this agony he pleaded with his
mother to permit him to write her more often. "There is not a single
minute in the whole day that I do not think of you & wish to be with
you & in the night I dream about you the whole time," he wrote poig-
nantly to her. Sarah Wister did not encourage such feelings. She believed
one letter a week to be sufficient, and she instructed her son to write
her no more than that.[26]

Relief came in the summer of 1871 when Owen visited his Aunt
Fanny, recently married to a clergyman of prominent English family.
He was the Reverend James Leigh, son of Lord Leigh of Stoneleigh
Abbey, Warwickshire. Owen successfully prevailed upon his parents to
let him spend the next school year with Aunt Fanny and her new husband. At the Kenilworth School, which he attended as a day student,
he studied Latin, Greek, French, German, mathematics, and, of course,
music. While Owen was not especially diligent in his lessons, the master
thought he detected a particular musical talent. "He bids fair to play
the piano not only with execution but with taste." From his own viewpoint, evidencing his critical nature, Owen felt his piano instruction at
Kenilworth to be inferior. More vigorous interests also arose such as
playing cricket and climbing trees to gather bird eggs for his collection.
Before the school year ended he had collected twenty-seven specimens.

Eager to show them to his mother but realizing her sensitivities, he promised not to bring them on his next visit unless she asked.[27]

Sarah Wister, who with her husband had made Rome a home base, was not nearly so faithful a correspondent as her son. On one occasion, when Owen had not heard from her for three weeks, he told her that he had begun to think she was dead. Upon hearing her excuses, he retorted, "*I* am quite sick and tired of you saying that I do not like long letters and *I* will not write to *you at all* if you say so again for you know quite well that if you would write to me a letter of 50 pages I would be glad." As the Easter holidays approached he had to remind her that both he and the headmaster had to know where he was to go when school recessed.[28]

For all her accomplishments, it was true that Mrs. Wister was notably deficient in human kindness, even to her own son. Fanny Kemble once observed that Sarah was "as fond of her baby [Owen] as I think she could be of any creature too nearly resembling a mere animal to excite her intellectual interest, which is pretty much the only interest in infants or adults that she seems to have." Her remoteness affected Owen deeply, and although he never explicitly mentioned it, the letters he regularly wrote to her throughout her lifetime and his constant effort to win her approval provide abundant evidence.[29]

Sarah Wister and her husband were enjoying a rich life in Rome amidst a large colony of American expatriates who had created the international society that Henry James would soon describe. The Wisters participated fully in a gay round of social affairs and salons, offering a weekly reception of their own and attending those held by other Americans such as the lawyer-turned-artist William Wetmore Story; Luther Terry and his wife, who was the sister of Julia Ward Howe; Mrs. Charles Sumner, then awaiting a divorce from her famous political husband; artist Edward Darley Boit and his wife; Mary and Edmund Tweedy; and Mrs. Henry Russell Cleveland. The occasions were enlivened further by the presence of European intellectuals and socialites who happened to amuse the Americans.

At a party given by Mrs. Cleveland in late December 1872, Sarah Wister met impressionable Henry James, newly arrived from Paris and intent on staying indefinitely in Europe. James, twenty-nine, was writing travel sketches and reviews for such publications as the *Nation* and the *Atlantic Monthly*, but he had not yet published a book. Sarah and James had many friends and interests in common; they were instantly attracted to one another. James readily accepted Sarah's immediate invitation to come to her house two nights later. He was received by the entire family, with both Owen and Fanny Kemble there for the holiday. Sarah proffered another invitation for the following day—this one for James and her alone. They went to the Colonna Gardens, walking and talking for nearly two hours. "A beautiful woman who takes you to such a place and talks to you uninterruptedly, learnedly, and even cleverly for two hours is not to be disposed of in three lines," James wrote to his mother in Cambridge. He accepted further invitations to the Wister house and to other outings. In the process he began gaining early impressions concerning the Americans in Europe which he would soon use to advantage in his novels. "The chapter of 'society' here— that is American society—opens up before me," he wrote home.[30]

Soon Sarah and James were riding horseback together for hours along the aqueducts. Sometimes Dr. Wister went along, sometimes not. The couple frequently visited the Villa Medici to chat with artist friends of Sarah's such as Ernest Hébert. James enjoyed the company of other ladies during this Roman episode, including that of Mrs. Charles Sumner, whom he had met at the Wisters', but with no other woman was he seen as frequently as with Sarah. He thought her hair to be the "handsomest" he had ever seen, but he found her so intense personally that he declared no one could be entirely comfortable in her presence, not even Sarah herself. She "isn't easy," James told his father. Yet he could not escape her, and he did not want to. "Mrs. Wister seems to have marked me for her own—having again bidden me to come to her this P.M. and be walked somewhither by her. She has a fierce energy in a slender frame and has always some social iron on the fire. She rides, walks, entertains, has musical rehearsals, writes largely (I believe) and is very handsome in the bargain," he wrote home. His frequent comments about her in his letters home caused his mother to worry. She knew of Sarah Wister, and she told her son that Sarah was "too conscious of her own charm to be very dangerous I am told—but beware!" Sarah, ever alert to a probing, sensitive, and literary mind such as James's, had found in him an ideal partner for her own intellectual and cultural forays. As James's biographer Leon Edel has observed, the pair were together more than one might have expected for a single young writer and a married woman, but probably not enough to set tongues wagging.[31]

Sarah was warned by James that she no doubt would "recognize an allusion or so" to her in his Roman stories. Both the novel he wrote the next year, *Roderick Hudson*, and a story, "Madame de Mauves," contained such allusions. Yet the best description of Sarah by James came some twenty years later in a short story, "The Solution," in which he limned a "Mrs. Westbrook."

> She was extravagant, careless, even slightly capricious. If the "Bohemian" had been invented in those days she might possibly have been one—a very small, fresh, dainty one. . . . She had a lovely head, and her chestnut hair was of a shade I have never seen since. . . . She was natural and clever and kind, and though she was five years older than I she always struck me as an embodiment of youth—of the golden morning of life. We made such happy discoveries together when I first knew her: we liked the same things, we disliked the same people, we had the same favourite statues in the Vatican, the same secret preferences in regard to views on the Campagna. We loved Italy in the same way and in the same degree. . . . She painted, she studied Italian, she collected and noted the songs of the people, and she had the wit to pick up certain bibelots and curiosities—lucky woman—before other people had thought of them.[32]

At the end of March, after three months of Sarah's socializing with James, Dr. Wister decided that the family should return home. Whether he were jealous of this relationship is not known. Judging from his character, he probably was immune to Sarah's diversions. James himself observed that Sarah was "broken hearted" to leave. Their friendship and regular correspondence would continue over many years, but never would they be as close as they had been in Rome.[33]

Back home at Butler Place, the Wisters' lives resumed with some changes. Dr. Wister forswore the rigorous hours of the past and undertook a more modest medical practice. While headaches and neuralgia ceased to be a problem, his dyspepsia and frequent insomnia would never leave him entirely.[34]

As for Owen, for the first time in his young life he achieved a regular routine. After briefly attending Germantown Academy, he was sent by his parents in the fall of 1873 to St. Paul's, an exclusive boarding school in Concord, New Hampshire. He would remain at this Episcopalian school until graduation in 1878; its impact would be an important and continuing force throughout his life.

St. Paul's was modeled after the English public schools. Its solemn headmaster, the Reverend Henry A. Coit, often was compared to Thomas Arnold of Rugby. Dr. Coit had become rector upon the school's founding in 1856, and his dignified and erudite personage would be the institution's dominating force until his death in 1895. The school's Episcopalian orthodoxy attracted more students from New York, Philadelphia, and New Jersey than from the Unitarian region of New England.

If religion provided the foundation for St. Paul's, its superstructure was a heavy emphasis upon the classics. Dr. Coit was a fine Latin and Greek scholar who taught those classes in demanding fashion. He had a small, neat beard with a clean-shaven upper lip, and he exercised a fearfully rigid behavior code. If students for some reason did not meet the headmaster's personal conception of St. Paul's standards, Dr. Coit was known to dismiss them with the nebulous explanation that they simply were not with "the spirit of the place." For a student to be summoned to Dr. Coit's study seemed no less awesome than Judgment Day itself, and if Dr. Coit did err at times in peremptory judgments, he would not admit it. Many of St. Paul's boys went on to Harvard, and it was implicit that Owen would do so. Dr. Coit himself preferred Trinity College because it was affiliated with the Episcopal church, and he disliked the irreligious influences which seemed all too pervasive at Harvard.[35]

When Wister enrolled at St. Paul's he was one of about 160 students. Considered to be an immature thirteen-year-old by his parents, he proved to be anything but that alongside his American peers, despite an early setback in his decorum. In the first few days he bought a share with several boys in a "punt," and it tipped over when one of the partners stepped in. "The water rushed in & we rushed or rather foundered out[,] the whole of the school in a spasm of laughter watching us." In the classroom he immediately was placed with the advanced French students, and although he found himself at the bottom of his Greek class, he rose to the top in a month. In the October "hare and hounds" race of four miles he finished seventh out of twenty-three runners. That same month he persuaded five other youths to join him in arranging a production of a play, *Enchanted Glen.* When he wrote home to ask his mother for assistance by sending some old clothes for costumes, she misunderstood him and thought he wanted real theatrical costumes. A letter from home reprimanded him for such extravagant demands; Owen, in return, chastised his mother thoroughly for having misread him. Dr. Wister responded personally to his son: "You are an ill tempered ass, and have written your Mother a very silly and impertinent letter. She is offended and, I am sorry to say, hurt by what you have done; and until she receives a proper apology you must not expect to hear from her." Owen apologized, and soon he reported that the play had been a great success.[36]

To Owen's continued displeasure, his mother still did not match his own regularity in writing weekly. "Why do you not write to me?" he asked. "Are you so displeased with my last monthly report that you do not wish to own me?" He asked the same question half a year later. If she were displeased at anything, he thought she had no right to be, "for where do you suppose I am in my form this month? *TWELFTH*!!! a rise of *19* in two months!!!" He also had excelled recently in German, tying for the highest marks and reporting that the master authorized him to say he had done "gloriously" and was the "prize scholar."[37]

During this first year Wister developed a distinct interest in literature that rivaled his dedication to the piano, which he practiced daily. In November he published his first literary creation in the school newspaper, *Horae Scholasticae*. His story described an underwater descent which he himself had made some months before in London. "Down in a Diving Bell" marked the beginning of a long relationship with the school newspaper, culminating in his editorship.[38]

His expanding reading habits included William Shakespeare, William Prescott, Jules Verne, Sir Walter Scott, Lord Alfred Tennyson, Henry Wadsworth Longfellow, William Thackeray, Robert Browning, John Milton, Mark Twain, Walt Whitman, and the reminiscences of Robert E. Lee. He sent his mother a copy of a poem whose author probably horrified her: Walt Whitman's "To a Locomotive in Winter." As for Twain, Owen at first found him "not particularly funny," but his opinion slowly changed until he was won over totally by "The Facts Concerning the Recent Carnival of Crime in Connecticut" appearing in the *Atlantic*. Owen urged his mother to read it.[39]

Sarah Wister thought these reading habits too frivolous; she was reinforced by the strict school standards as to proper reading and ideas. When Dr. Coit saw Owen with a book about emotion in animals and men, he requested Owen to put it away because it was not of a high tone. When Owen boldly commented to a master than Dean Stanley and certain others seemed to think that "The Song of Solomon" in the Old Testament was in truth a love song instead of a theological work, he was reproved for irreverence, and his marks in decorum were reduced.[40]

Fanny Kemble, who frequently lived at York Farm adjoining Butler Place, was convinced that her grandson lacked literary aptitude. She described him at thirteen as "very clever indeed," but not intellectual.

His inclinations seemed to her to point toward a career as an engineer. "That he will be a *book* man I doubt; I think he will never be a hard student of anything but mechanical powers, natural laws of force and motion, and the results to be derived from them as applied to machinery." Such a conception meant that Fanny Kemble was disappointed in Owen.[41]

Actually, she had misread him. Owen's fondness for books was such that it attracted the attention of school librarian Hall Harrison. Harrison put the young student to work as an assistant librarian, and at Harrison's request Owen managed a great coup for the school's growing collection of books. He persuaded his grandmother to sign and donate a volume of Shakespeare's plays, and he wrote to her that he intended "to beg books" from everyone he knew. Before long Owen had procured nearly fifty volumes for the library, many of them from his mother. In the fall of 1875 his work earned him the position of secretary to the Library Association, a rather prestigious job for a fifth form student, since the previous year the position had been held by a sixth former. "I ought to be overwhelmed, but I *ain't*," he wrote home.[42]

He did not fully realize even then that his mother, despite her attempts at anonymity, had a literary reputation of her own. A woman connected with the school asked Owen to obtain some autographs— including that of family friend Longfellow, as well as those of Fanny Kemble and Sarah Wister. Owen could not understand why she wanted his mother's autograph, and he explained to her that his mother was not Fanny Kemble. "She said she knew it, and that you were Mrs. S. B. Wister, and wished I would get *your* autograph. I don't know why she wants it, I'm sure.—Are you famous in any way?" Thus alerted, Owen began reading his mother's articles with new appreciation. (Her work was available regularly in the *Atlantic Monthly*, as well as occasionally in magazines such as *Lippincott's*.) Upon finding that he genuinely liked her writing, he promised henceforth to read everything she did, and he encouraged her to write dime novels for more money instead of so many book reviews for "cake-money."[43]

If Sarah Wister's literary reputation continued to be limited to a small circle, that of her friend Henry James suddenly was taking on new dimensions. When James visited Sarah at Butler Place in October 1875, his first important novel, *Roderick Hudson*—which recaptured the Roman society they had enjoyed together two years before—was being published by installments in the *Atlantic*. James's purpose in the three-day visit was to bid Sarah farewell, for in three weeks he would sail again for Europe. Sarah entertained him by taking him one day to the piazza at a place called Strawberry Hill; by going the following day to an artist friend's home where a forty-mile view offered inspiration; and, finally, by having her mother join them for dinner. On the next day "Mr. James went away," not to return for six years.[44]

Owen's own literary output began to take on larger proportions soon after "Down in a Diving Bell" appeared in the *Horae*. He formed an alliance with a younger student, John Jay Chapman, who already exhibited the contumacious stamp that would forever mark him as a maverick. The even-tempered Wister struck up a genuine friendship with Chapman which endured a lifetime. The two chose *nom de plumes* for their contributions to the *Horae*: Wister became "West" and Chapman was "Grafton." Owen wrote poetry and essays on mountains, winter, and Rockaway Beach, but his most ambitious undertaking was a four-part series on the nation's 1876 centennial celebration in Philadelphia which he had attended faithfully that summer. In this series, he criticized a Long Island boarding house as another in a long list of places in America where one should *not* go. "The boarders are so low a class, with one or two exceptions, that it is quite impossible to distinguish between master and man without watching which of the two waits on the other." Fiction did not appear in the *Horae* until Owen introduced it with a Gothic tale of ghosts and chivalry.[45]

As a fifth form student Owen became editor of the newspaper. With the power of this position he confronted Dr. Coit in a power struggle and, surprisingly, won. The conflict occurred when the headmaster decided that the *Horae* must be reduced in size to four pages because its demands on the editors' time seemed improper. Owen refused to edit such a paltry newspaper, and he resigned in protest. Dr. Coit consequently rescinded his ultimatum and even agreed to enlarge the *Horae* to twelve pages. Owen resumed his service as editor.[46]

Already this youthful editor was looking toward a more ambitious writing project: a novel. He and another youth (unidentified but presumably Chapman) constructed an elaborate adventure plot in which an Italian who had fled his country disguised as a woman fell in love with a French woman who escaped her native land by dressing as a man.[47]

Reading and writing consumed much of Owen's time, but his love for music continued to be even more serious. He practiced daily on his Chickering piano, sang in the choir, and took up the organ, substituting on occasion for his music teacher at chapel services. "The first day I was literally shaking all over with fright, and as I was playing the voluntary, as each boy came in he stared at me for about a minute before he went to his seat, which was horrid." Sometimes in the evenings he pumped the organ for his teacher, James Knox, to play. For more direct musical experience, Owen and some students organized a musical group called Terpsichore. The ensemble boasted of two violins, two cornets, two flutes, a clarinet, and a melodium played by Owen. The musicians performed at the school and at other places in the area, including a nearby insane asylum.[48]

Owen's musical tastes, becoming increasingly discriminating, centered on a worship of Wagner. Since those days in Munich when the Wister family had been unappreciative of Wagner's operas, Owen had grown to recognize the composer's genius. He carefully followed accounts of the first American performance of *The Flying Dutchman*; he already knew much of its music, and he regretted to hear that his mother had not attended. "I am perfectly sure you would admire Wagner a great deal more than you do if you were to hear *Tannhäuser,* or know of it," he assured her. Ludwig van Beethoven was second on his list of preferred composers, and in his sixteenth year he wanted the music to Beethoven's sonatas. He summed up his changing tastes: he was beginning to dislike Felix Mendelssohn because of a lack of originality; he did not appreciate Giuseppe Verdi at all; George Frederick Handel and Christoph Willibald von Gluck were rising in his estimation; and Wagner he continued to like better and better, especially *Tristram and Isolde*.[49]

Together with John Jay Chapman he lamented over the inexact state of music; it seemed to them to be still in a primitive stage of development, corresponding to man's mind. The human mind, they pompously asserted, was insufficiently cultivated to receive music's meaning with certainty. One day, Owen was confident, "a symphony will express to the mind just as clearly as if the composer was talking—of course poetically talking—a distinct story, tragic, comic, moral, or imaginative."[50]

Chapman did not have long to remain at St. Paul's. In the fall of 1877 Dr. Coit asked his father to take him away: he clearly was not in accord with the spirit of the place. Owen, who clearly *was* in touch with the school's spirit, lost his best friend. "There is no boy to whom I can say so much & who understands me so thoroughly as he did; I think we knew each other through and through." Certainly there was nothing "sentimental" about the relationship, he told his mother. "I think of all things I hate most it is sentiment in any shape whatever. It seems to me to destroy a man's capacity for judging soundly about a great many things, and does not really add to his appreciation of poetry or music."[51]

Owen now was composing serious music. He began an opera when he was sixteen, and his librettist was none other than his grandmother, who was faithfully following the directions sent by her grandson. Even his teachers could find little technical fault with his music, although one of them urged him to work harder on "graceful or pretty" music.[52]

One morning in the school infirmary, recovering from a brief illness, Owen hummed a refrain from one of his compositions while brushing his teeth. A boy on the other side of the room overheard it, rushed over to exclaim how pretty it was, and insisted that Owen teach him the melody. The boy played no instrument, Owen wrote home, but "he gave round with it like Mark Twain and his literary Nightmare."[53]

In a more ambitious enterprise, Owen composed the entire score for a minstrel show, organized an orchestra and chorus which he personally rehearsed, and even arranged for the printing of the program and tickets. He prided himself on being a demanding conductor. He showed his overture to the conductor of the Concord Orchestra, who took it, played it through, and praised the work highly.[54]

The minstrels represented just half of the program, the other part being a production of two scenes from *The Merchant of Venice* in which Owen played the role of Shylock. When the students presented the entertainment before the school it was the Shakespearean performance rather than the minstrels that won official praise. Dr. Coit could see nothing funny in such songs as "Old King Coal," a parody of the coal strike. His obvious inability to see the broad humor of the light-hearted minstrels spoiled the performance. His bewhiskered face so clearly registered his shock that the boys "who made the jokes were half frightened out of their wits & brought them out with a trembling whisper." Afterwards, Dr. Coit called the minstrels "vulgarities," and he held Owen responsible for this improper frivolity. While Dr. Coit complimented those who had staged Shakespeare, Owen heard not a word of praise for his work. Nearly two weeks later Dr. Coit still had not spoken a pleasant word to him.[55]

Owen "Dan" Wister was a healthy youth. He bore none of the frailties sometimes attributed—by unthinking students—to those possessing artistic dispositions. He was of sturdy build and good height, and he was handsome with dark eyes framed by prominent eyebrows. On

May 2, 1875, when he was fourteen years old, he stood five feet six and one fourth inches tall; five weeks later, according to his careful measurements, he had grown nearly an inch and a half more. Despite such rapid growth, there was nothing gangling or awkward about him. A classmate said Owen's usual appearance as he walked on campus was that of an "aged form" trudging along with a smoking cap over his brow, barely permitting the escape of "dark and delicate curls hanging in rich festoons" over his forehead.[56]

Owen participated in all the vigorous sports at St. Paul's: cricket, hare and hounds, rowing, skating, coasting, and riding. The collection of bird eggs that he had started at Kenilworth continued to grow, reaching ninety specimens by the time he was fourteen. He owned a pair of climbing irons which enabled him to conquer the highest branches of the tallest tree. His description of a hare and hounds foot race of some thirteen to fourteen miles showed the travails of that school activity. "They took us through marshes, over a brook into which many tumbled, thro' briers in which my trousers (last summer's) were irretrievably torn, and up hills which were so steep and so slippery that it was with the great difficulty one could get up at all." The race had not been required; he ran entirely on "principle" because he had heard that the turnout was to be slim, and he had wanted to help maintain a custom he admired.[57]

During the winter of his last year at St. Paul's, Owen persuaded his parents to permit him to take boxing lessons. He liked them so well that he immediately signed up for a second course. "I don't want to be a 'house-boy,' & have tried hard not to," he wrote to his mother. He had never been on a camping or hunting outing, though, and during his seventeenth year he began to feel that he needed this experience. He announced plans to fulfill this yearning the next summer. "I'm sure it would be a good thing for me . . . which would make me stronger & healthier." His ability to ride horseback, he reasoned, should make the undertaking relatively simple.[58]

When he reached the age of fifteen Owen began to complain of ailments, generally of mysterious origins. Dr. Wister warned his son to safeguard his health above all else, a prompting which elicited a self-examination by Owen which was to occur regularly in future years.

> I don't feel so perfectly strong as up till now have always felt up here. Any violent exercise such as running will give me either a head-ache or else make me feel a little uncomfortable in a way that I can't explain;

I mean uncomfortable not in any particular place but just so; however it does not last any time and I always sleep well, so that otherwise I am all right.

Dr. Wister concluded that his son was spending too much time on editing the *Horae* and on composing his opera. "Hurry and its brother worry are the destroyers of health & life; and in young people are not to be permitted for one day," he advised.[59]

Owen's detailed discussions of music in his letters irritated his father, who did not hesitate to complain. Owen's rejoinder was that "very often" he had nothing else to write about. "It amuses me in a harmless manner," he said. If his father were fretting because he feared his only son might choose the uncertain career of music as a profession, then he worried over nothing. "The idea of making it a profession never entered my head for one moment; I probably have more common sense than you credit me with." Dr. Wister warned Owen that his "success" in music seemed to be causing him to lose his perspective. Owen, of course, denied this, and he assured his father that music never interfered with his studies or his exercise. Owen cautioned his father to keep these points in mind and not become unduly concerned when he took harmony and counterpoint at Harvard the next year.[60]

Contrary to her more practical physician son-in-law, who felt that an artistic temperament was ill-prepared to deal with a harsh world, Fanny Kemble now began to find some favor with her grandson, along with some new faults. The summer of his fifteenth year gave her reason to question her assessment that he never would be a "book man." Upon arriving at Butler Place from school, he had surprised his grandmother by telling her that she reminded him of Tennyson's Mariana in the moated grange. Moreover, he had come home, in her words, "a tall, broad, healthy lad—speriamo!" In disposition he was "amiable, and well disposed, and extremely clever." He bore a remarkable resemblance, she thought, to her uncle, John Kemble, as he had appeared in *Macbeth*. Now, however, she privately expressed disappointment in her grandson in another area—his supposed lack of "animal spirits." A concomitant concern was his alleged predisposition to laziness. "I am afraid he will not work; otherwise, I think he would be a remarkable person."[61]

Some of her doubts were erased the following summer. Fanny Kemble found herself praising the verses he had composed. "I think them remarkably good, because of their simplicity and singleness of purpose." The youngster, she acknowledged, was "unusually gifted" with a lively poetical imagination. She did not yield entirely to her earlier estimation that his "most decided tendency" was toward "scientific objects and mechanics," but she did add an important third dimension to her assessment. "His most remarkable gift is a real talent for music, which seems to me to approach original genius." She realized that his qualities represented a truly unusual combination of different capacities which "cannot fail, I think, to make him a remarkable person in his day." If at present he remained a "very chaotic and heterogeneous *bundle of beginnings*," it also was obvious that his natural endowments were most promising. She frequently joined him in piano duets; it was at this time that she agreed to write lyrics for his opera; and she made no more mention of his laziness.[62]

Owen clearly was becoming an adult. He listened with understanding as his parents lamented over the sad state of moral degradation to which the federal government had fallen in 1876. (Fanny Kemble thought the Wisters would have departed the country in disgust but for their son's welfare.) He agreed with his father when Dr. Wister decided in 1876 to bolt the Republican Party for Samuel Tilden so that the government machinery might be thoroughly cleansed; he heard his parents protest the debasement of culture and manners brought about by crass commercialism; and he sympathized with them over the problems of the southern properties which Aunt Fanny now managed largely by herself. He soon began to join in such conversations around the dinner table.[63]

Owen felt that he was sufficiently prepared to bypass the sixth form and to enter Harvard directly in 1877. If his parents disagreed, he proposed that they send him abroad for a year. They denied both requests, Dr. Wister informing him that he was too immature.[64]

Neither did his parents permit him to follow so many of the other St. Paul's students in being confirmed in the Episcopalian faith. They asked him to delay this decision until college. Again, it was a matter of maturity. Many young people, in their opinion, took this serious step prematurely and with permanently harmful results. Sarah Wister wrote that they did not wish him to take such action before his character and convictions warranted it. "I am well aware that this is not the usual view," she acknowledged, but added that those who conceived early confirmation to be a safeguard for proper moral development often discovered the reverse to be true.[65]

It would not have been surprising, considering such parental restraints, to see the emergence of a rebellious boy. But no such thing happened, and Owen completed his final year at St. Paul's in high spirits despite his initial wish not to return. His last year ended in an unfortunate and gloomy note for everyone. Two students died of scarlet fever and classes were abruptly dismissed for the year in early May for fear of an epidemic. Owen was disappointed at missing graduation ceremonies and festivities, but he looked forward to Harvard.[66]

Chapter II

HARVARD, CLASS OF '82
(1878–1882)

OWEN WISTER ENROLLED AT HARVARD in an age that was—it has been said—devoid of momentous issues. Yet many critical and intriguing questions did exist. Rutherford B. Hayes, having taken his oath of office in secrecy because of dark threats and rumors arising from his controversial election, was the unexpected occupant of the White House. Civil and economic rights guaranteed to former slaves during Reconstruction were eroding rapidly in the South. A fad for buffalo robes caused western riflemen to slaughter bison by the millions, and the rapid decimation of those vast herds which once thundered over the continent brought added misery for the American Indian. The western plains resonated with the musical peal of sledgehammers wielded by sweaty laborers laying steel rails across the continent. Ambitious entrepreneurs, operating out of a public mood of laissez-faire, were extracting great fortunes from the nation's abundant resources and founding industries of far-reaching consequences. It seemed not to matter that not everyone shared in the vast national bounty, for the idea had taken hold that vigorous competition would simply weed out the weak and help society advance more quickly to ultimate perfection. Rather than being a time of blandness, the period was, as historian Howard Mumford Jones has described it, "an age of energy," a critical time for sorting out national priorities for years to come.

It is true that the issues of the day failed to engage the attention of the self-assured freshman from Philadelphia. Neither did they engage the attention of many other young Americans. Wister's own interests extended not much farther from Harvard than across the Charles River to Boston. In this cultural and intellectual heart of the nation lived America's brightest men: writers such as James R. Lowell, Henry Wadsworth Longfellow, Oliver Wendell Holmes, Ralph W. Emerson, and William Dean Howells; ministers such as Phillips Brooks; architects such as H. H. Richardson; and painters such as John Singer Sargent. Pervading the social and cultural fabric were the great families: the Cabots, the Lees, the Higginsons, the Saltonstalls, the Lodges, the Searses, the Lawrences, and the Holmeses. These exalted circles welcomed Owen Wister as one of their own. They knew of him from Fanny Kemble and from Sarah Wister. From the beginning, young Wister felt at home in Boston society.

Harvard, not yet a truly national university, had an undergraduate student body numbering less than a thousand. The faculty consisted of perhaps half a hundred. The institution was changing under the dynamic direction of Charles W. Eliot who, completing the first of four decades as president, was setting a pattern for curriculum which would revolutionize college studies everywhere. Harvard students traditionally had followed the classical pattern of study in which everyone took virtually the same subjects—Greek, Latin, mathematics, and ancient history. Eliot's innovative elective system was changing this. As Samuel Eliot Morison said, the elective system was refuting the idea held since Pericles that an educated man was one who knew *certain* things. When Wister enrolled in the fall of 1878, Eliot had instituted the elective system for all students except freshmen. To be admitted, however, Wister and his 218 freshman classmates (110 of whom were from Massachusetts and two, including Wister, from Pennsylvania) had been required to pass exams in Latin and Greek grammar, Greek literature, English composition, arithmetic, elementary algebra, and plane geometry. Wister's scores were high enough to place him in advanced sections of Greek and Latin. All students still were required to attend chapel services daily (a regulation that would be abolished in 1886), belying Dr. Coit's conviction that the place was too worldly for St. Paul's graduates. The Department of Music in which Wister chose to center his studies consisted of just one man, Professor John Knowles Paine. Paine's appointment to that professorship in 1875 made him one of the first persons in the nation to hold such a position.[1]

When Wister moved into Room 58 at massive, red-brick Thayer Hall in the Yard, he found himself in friendly company. "Everyone is here," he happily exclaimed. In his later years Wister would exaggerate that as a freshman he wandered "obscurely and anonymously" about the Harvard Yard. "Here I knew that I was nothing; and here to me at the bottom of the ladder, the names of those at the top, upper-class men, juniors and seniors, the great ones, began to grow familiar before ever I had seen their faces." However he may have felt inwardly, such a description did not at all fit the outwardly gregarious, confident freshman that his classmates saw.[2]

He plunged immediately into campus activities. When the first issue of the *Crimson* appeared it carried two Wister articles under his old St. Paul's pseudonym, "West." Two months later he won election as freshman editor of the *Crimson*.[3]

Without delay he began paying social calls on the finest families in the area. He attended a musicale at the residence of Mrs. Jack Gardner, the "Queen Bee" of Boston who set an unconventional pace for that city's society with her high-spirited antics; he enjoyed afternoon tea with the Parkman family; he occasionally dined after Sunday church services with the popular Episcopalian minister Phillips Brooks; he visited with Mrs. Louis Agassiz at a time when she was arranging for women to attend Harvard classes for the first time; he went to Professor Paine's house to sit at his feet and hear Paine's overture to "As You Like It" and his renditions of Beethoven; and he attended the opera with President Eliot's family, a rare privilege for any student. While he hardly needed an advisor in social affairs, Frank Cabot, a junior student, saw to it that the young Philadelphian did not languish in his new surroundings. His social calendar as a freshman obviously was one that few people—except by accident of birth—could achieve.[4]

Boston's musical and theatrical events gave added cause for crossing the Charles River bridge. Once, on a bet, Wister and two friends escorted to the Boston Theater a male classmate disguised as a girl, and sat primly with "her" to see the premiere performance of a play about western mining adventures. The escapade apparently fooled practically everyone. "Of course," Wister acknowledged, "the people just near us got at last to suspect the truth, especially since the young lady occasionally forgot herself, & said in quite masculine tones 'By Jour, there's so & so; he'll recognize me sure.' "[5]

Opera demanded and got Wister's more serious attention. After one feverish spell of opera-going he proclaimed it "the most luxurious week I think I have ever spent." On Monday he saw *I Puritanis*; on Tuesday, *Carmen* (with the Eliots); on Wednesday he missed *Rigoletto* to go to bed; on Thursday he attended *Faust*; on Friday, *The Magic Flute*; and on Saturday, *Lucia di Lammermoor*. All of Boston "twice told" appeared to be there for the Saturday matinee. "There were 4500 in the house and all of them in the highest state of enthusiasm; I could not look in any direction without seeing someone nodding & smiling at me, & gesticulating in pantomine of admiration at the various things going on on the stage."[6]

To Dr. Wister news of these activities implied neglect of studies. Two months earlier he had worried over his son's eyes; now he repeated his concern that such events unduly strained them. "Five nights to the opera is rather too much for a mature man; and for a boy who has work to do next day, who particularly, as an individual trait requires a great deal of sleep; who droops visibly during the holidays from too much frolicking, it is utterly bad."[7]

Despite his father, Wister determined to have a piano for his room. If he were to study harmony he simply had to have one. He vowed not to permit the instrument to distract him from his other studies, and he felt entirely capable of dispersing crowds of students who might congregate around the piano. "I hope you will consent," he wrote to his father. "I need not tell you what a crushing disappointment it will be if I can not study Harmony." The importunities succeeded, and Wister selected a Chickering only after he had had all questions satisfied through correspondence with Mr. Chickering himself.[8]

Another part of Wister's education lay in mastering the intricacies of the dance floor. He joined the classes of Boston society's favorite, the Italian count Lorenzo Papanti, a thin and fiery-tempered disciplinarian who had been an institution in Boston since the 1830s. Papanti taught classes at his palatial Tremont Street ballroom, where students not only learned the dignified dances of the day but also acquired elegant ballroom manners. When Wister composed a polka redown which was played for a class dance, he became an overnight sensation. He confessed to his mother that it was "the vilest Strauss-and-water compound you ever heard, & good for nothing but to mark the time." Papanti's class also provided the setting for Wister's first recorded romance—he became enamored of a young lady named Pauline Revere, perhaps a descendant of Boston's noted silversmith. "I came out of Dancing Season not as complete as I went in I'm afraid—a very considerable piece of my too susceptible heart being in the possession of Miss Revere, whom I like better than any girl I know, & this is most alarming," Wister confessed. A problem existed, however; Miss Revere was older. Nevertheless, his candle would burn for her for more than a year before flickering out.[9]

Wister's religious impulses, Dr. Coit's fears to the contrary, deepened during his freshman year. He attended services at the Trinity Church, where Phillips Brooks's magnificent rhetoric had brought Episcopalianism to a social par with the Unitarianism of Boston's finest families. Brooks, who had come to Boston from Philadelphia and who knew Sarah Wister, was a bachelor. He and Wister began to have lunch together with some regularity after Sunday worship services. Soon, Owen's long-desired confirmation as an Episcopalian came about, conducted presumably by Brooks. However, Harvard's student body contained several self-proclaimed atheists who tested Wister's faith. As a result, he confided to a friend that he had decided to avoid all future discussions with atheists.[10]

St. Paul's had prepared Wister well for college—perhaps too well—for Harvard did not pose much of an educational challenge. Toward the end of his freshman year he cynically concluded that "college is not one-tenth the place School [St. Paul's] was." Its tone, beginning with the faculty and ending with the freshmen, was not high. "I am afraid that Harvard is just the World in every respect, except that learning is pursued there. And as I did not expect that College was going to be that, I am disappointed," he wrote to his mother.[11]

It was with such feelings, in the spring of his freshman year, that Wister encountered an upperclassman at a boxing match who did impress him—Theodore Roosevelt. Roosevelt, a junior, had slugged his way into the light-weight division finals of the Harvard Athletic Association's boxing matches. The popular Roosevelt, who had been cheered throughout the tournament by Boston friends such as the Saltonstalls and Lees, now found himself outmatched. Nevertheless, he fought with high spirits and proved his sportsmanship after an unfortunate incident. His opponent evidently had failed to hear time called at the end of a round, and as Roosevelt dropped his guard he received a solid smash to the nose. Blood gushed forth and the crowd instantly began hissing and booing for the late blow. Realizing the innocence of his adversary, Roosevelt immediately motioned to the crowd for silence, told the timekeeper that the student clearly had not realized the round was over, and with bleeding nose walked to the boxer and shook his hand. Here, Wister felt, was a man of character and breeding. He recalled fifty years later that the incident had shown in an instant the "prophetic flash of The Roosevelt that was to come."[12]

Harvard's president may have been convinced that a youth of eighteen years could best determine his own academic needs, and that idea may have been converting institutions of higher learning throughout the land, but such a notion did not sit well with the Wisters. While their son as a sophomore had a technical right to choose his own courses, they would not permit such foolishness. Wister obligingly continued to submit to his parents' direction. In October of his sophomore year he asked for their approval to take Greek, Latin, logic, history, and music (counterpoint). The German that his mother continued to insist he study conflicted with Greek, as did some other courses she proposed. "I am afraid you will have to make a new selection, & that I will have to study German next summer," he informed her. Sarah Wister insisted that he find a way to study German, whatever the obstacles. Wister accordingly located a classmate who knew the language and who would read with him two hours weekly.[13]

A year later Wister expressed concern that his course load of twenty hours, five more than the normal load, would be his ruination, and he told his mother that they *must* confer about it. His mother was unyielding. Mrs. Wister's admonitions naturally included urgent appeals for superior grades, and finally during his junior year Wister became so exasperated that he rebuked her openly. "Let me tell you one thing: *Never* unless I am in danger of being dropped from my Class, write & say you will be dissatisfied if I don't get such & such a %." Such warnings served to depress rather than to stimulate, he informed her. "I don't know whether I shall get 75% or not. I hope I shall, & am trying to, but that is all."[14]

As a sophomore Wister became eligible for participation in the college's elaborate system of clubs. The highest achievement was admission into the exclusive "final" clubs. To be eligible, a student had to be among the first fifty in his class to be selected for the Institute of 1770. This meant membership as well in the Dickey. Failure to achieve such status signaled an end to a student's hopes for Harvard's more elite social circles; selection, on the other hand, "assured social success in College, a lion's role in Boston's debutante society, prompt election to the best clubs of New York and Boston after graduation, and a job at Lee Higginson's or a New York brokerage house."[15]

The happy announcement of inclusion in the Dickey came each fall when members paraded through the Yard and serenaded at the dormitory windows of the chosen few. "On election nights, many a sophomore lay sleepless in his dark bed, listening," Wister recalled. In the fall of 1879 he, too, lay restlessly in his new room in Holyoke during this time of "suspense, wondering, whispering, yearning," straining to hear the shuffle of feet that might stop beneath his own window. Many were disappointed, but not Wister, for joyous singing soon relieved his anxiety. The next week the chosen few found themselves subjected to intensive hazing. One evening the hazing centered on Wister's own room, and Wister and other pledges had to perform a series of nonsensical feats conjured up by Theodore Roosevelt and a handful of other Dickey members. The week of hazing was both miserable and gleeful. When the last ordeal ended, Wister "stood unblindfolded, blinking, damp, embarrassed, deliriously happy, with friends gripping my hands." It was a moment never to be forgotten, and he remembered it vividly fifty years later: "Bless the old merry brutal ribald orgiastic natural wholesome Dickey! Bless the handful of wild oats we sowed there together so joyously!"[16]

The new member's musical talents and literary skills found a convenient form in the Dickey, for the group's theatricals were a regular campus occurrence. No sooner was Wister initiated than plans were made to stage the musical burlesque, *Ivanhoe*. Wister served as musical manager. He borrowed music from Charles F. Gounod, Anton G. Rubinstein, Sir Arthur Sullivan, Jacques L. Offenbach, Alexandre C. Lecocq, and, of course, Wagner; he wrote original lyrics; he privately rehearsed the soloists and the chorus; and he served as accompanist for the performance. Roosevelt, a campus hero, did not escape notice, for Wister rephrased words from Offenbach's *La Belle Hélène* to fit him:

> Awful tart
> And awful smart,
> With waxed mustache and hair in curls:
> Brand new hat,
> Likewise cravat,
> To call upon the dear little girls.

Afterwards, Roosevelt let it be known that he considered the humor to be in bad taste. He was in a minority: *Ivanhoe* earned such praise that the cast performed in Boston and New York.[17]

Harvard's supreme "final" club was the Porcellian. The club had been founded simply enough in 1791 by a group of students who got their name from dining on roast pig, but as the years went by only the most elite could anticipate election to the Porcellian. Wister professed that he did not expect a summons to the exalted club whose members numbered less than twenty. However, in the spring of his sophomore year, a Porcellian named Harry Shaw casually asked him whether he had joined the A.D., Porcellian's competing but slightly less-esteemed social club. Wister said no, adding that he had never dreamed of being asked. Shaw then told him that he stood a "very good chance" of election into the Porcellian if he desired it. When Wister replied affirmatively, Shaw shook his hand warmly and informed him that he already had been elected.[18]

"It was the most unexpected surprise I ever had," Wister wrote to his father. Dr. Wister, however, was irritated. It meant, among other things, additional expenses. Moreover, it appeared that his son had joined the Porcellian without first obtaining consent from home. Restraining an impulse to react heatedly to his father's chastising letter, Wister carefully built up the advantages of membership for his doubting parent. Careful inquiry as to expenses involved and as to the moral and intellectual fiber of the members had proved his own doubts concerning these matters to be unfounded, he assured his father. The initiation fee amounted to just twenty dollars, contrary to popular belief which held it to be far higher, and annual expenses amounted to less than $250. Many of the fellows, Wister claimed, were no richer or pretended to be no richer than he. As far as the rowdy reputation which the class of '77 had bestowed upon the Porcellian, members now were working diligently to rectify that by practicing moderation in every respect. "I believe the library is the greatest feature [of the club]. . . . It numbers at present 7000 & odd volumes," Wister wrote. "The very best men all about Boston have belonged to the Club, Mr. Salstonstall, Mr. Sam Eliot, Mr. Elliot Cabot, Mr. Frank Lee, Mr. Theodore Lyman, Prof. Child, Prof. Lane, Mr. Seargeantt [sic] Perry, and lots more I could mention." As for the possibility that the club might disrupt his studies, Wister said he studied better in the Porcellian library than anywhere. "No one disturbs you, and everything is absolutely quiet." Being a Porcellian, he contended, insured an association that upon graduation became the "strongest tie" to college.[19] The twelve-page letter, surely the longest he had ever written to his father, had the desired effect. Dr. Wister cordially yielded.

Wister never regretted his Porcellian association. He spent hours at the club talking, writing letter after letter on club stationery, exchanging polite toasts over drinks, and forming an intimate circle of friends which indeed lasted a lifetime and tied him closer to Harvard. Nothing, not even the national acclaim eventually brought to him through his writing, ever meant so much to him, he later attested. It was the beginning of a lifetime of associations with clubs where he could enjoy good masculine companionship over a drink or meal.

Among the Porcellian's members was Theodore Roosevelt, and it was here that Wister, then nineteen, and Roosevelt, twenty-one, came to know one another well and to form close ties. Wister was flattered that Roosevelt, nearing graduation and already working on a history of the naval war of 1812, paid him so much attention. He admired the older student for his wide-ranging knowledge, for his moral sense, and for his ease in making judgments. The relationship of mentor to younger disciple emerged from the start, and their lifelong friendship never deviated from that pattern.[20]

The Porcellian Club did not prevent Wister from continuing to devote a considerable amount of time to Boston society. On one spring day he wrote to his mother that "on Sunday I spent the day & night with Mrs. Cabot at Brookline, & took tea with the Lowells, after calling on Miss Bacon & the Saltonstalls." He knew and visited as well such persons as Henry Wadsworth Longfellow, Dr. Oliver Wendell Holmes and his jurist son, and he particularly enjoyed a close association with the Lee and Higginson families. In fact, Boston now seemed much more familiar to him than Philadelphia, and before coming home for Christmas in his senior year he told his mother that he knew "nothing & therefore care nothing about Philadelphia society." Meanwhile, he posted his mother through the mail of their mutual Boston acquaintances, including Henry James: "He called to see me, & I returned his call—but both of us were out. I was asked to dine with him at the [Charles Eliot] Norton's to-night, but am going out of town for Sunday."[21]

To add still further to Wister's wealth of friendships, in 1880 a favorite pal from St. Paul's joined him at Harvard: John Jay Chapman. Since withdrawing prematurely from St. Paul's, Chapman had been tutored at home in New York City. There he had expanded even further his interest in the arts. Intellectually, he remained several steps ahead of his peers. His pugnacious character had lost none of its edge. Wister had kept up with "Jack" through his brother Henry who also was at Harvard. The two rejoiced at their reunion.[22]

In contrast to Wister, Chapman expressed disdain for the affectations of Boston society. "I make it a point to abuse Boston," he wrote, and he did so with alacrity. This had an effect on Wister, who now began privately to criticize society himself. Having developed a close friendship with Bostonian Joe Lee, for example, he confessed to his mother that Lee occasionally enraged him with his snobbish attitude. "His apathy & lack of interest in anything that does not concern a first cousin grows no better. I'm afraid it is incurable—Chapman & I came to the conclusion that the Lees & Cabots had in one week more family business than most people did in 20 years."[23]

Only one thing seemed worthy of undivided attention these days—music. Wister became increasingly serious in his own efforts at composition. In May 1881 he sold to a music publisher for "starvation prices" his composition of a polka redown. The publisher assured him that he would be more liberal in future payment if the work proved successful (which it did not).[24]

For any devotee of music, an exciting event occurred in Boston in 1886. Henry Lee Higginson, a broker and banker of great esteem as well as a good friend to Wister and his family, realized a longtime personal dream by singlehandedly founding the Boston Symphony Orchestra. Conductor George Henschel, only thirty-one years old, directed the seventy-member orchestra that first season in a series of twenty programs which sparked animated debates between Wagnerians and anti-Wagnerians, and which caused many other stimulating discussions as well.[25]

Professor Paine, Harvard's sole music professor and a European-trained composer himself, bolstered the ambitions of Wister, his star pupil, with praise. The relationship between professor and student became unusually close. They discussed music at length and attended concerts together. Professor Paine, however, scorned Wister's infatuation with the frivolous Offenbach and the unconventional Wagner. "Sensuous!" he would exclaim. Still, Wister could not resist including in his own piano exercises "indecorous and scandalous explosions" of Wagnerian harmony. Paine's blue pencil scornfully crossed out these diversions. Yet he did permit them to pass without condemnation in Wister's free compositions.[26]

Paine clearly was convinced that his star pupil had genuine talent. Dr. Wister, though, continued to disapprove of his son's preoccupation with music. In the face of continuing parental pressure Wister notified his parents in October 1881 that for the sake of his grades he had resigned as the acting manager of the Hasty Pudding. Further, he no longer was working on his operatic compositions. His attention would henceforth be riveted on lessons and exercise. Then came the more important statement: "But I am more determined than I ever have been to take up music as a profession."[27]

Still, despite such proclivities to music and study, there remained a robust element in this sturdy Pennsylvanian. He was as apt as anyone to carouse loudly in the dormitory, and he did so with friends such as Charles Sturgis, Robert Paine, and Henry Sedgwick. He served for a while as manager of the college cricket team (maintaining as well a membership in the Young American Cricket Club in Philadelphia), and he was no stranger to the tennis courts. One Saturday he played a marathon round of fifty-eight tennis games. He pedaled a high-wheeled bicycle, took instructions on horseback riding, continued his boxing lessons, and occasionally hunted with a prize possession, a new shotgun. With Henry Chapman he took a long walking tour of the Berkshires. (A photograph shows the two hikers with their knapsacks, a full mustache hiding Wister's upper lip.) He was a football fan, and along with other students stood in rain and ankle-deep mud to cheer the Harvard team in its 1881 match at New Haven with archrival Yale.[28]

Except in music, Wister might not have been termed a brilliant student, but he clearly was a superior one. Under duress from his parents he assumed heavy academic loads. This permitted him to have a double major in music and in philosophy. "Everyone I tell that I have 20 hours exclaims with horror," he said about his junior year schedule. In the fall of his senior year Wister informed his mother that, continuing at his present rate, he would graduate *cum laude*. His average grade for the preceding years was seventy-five, and he stood forty-first in the class of '82. "When you consider that I have taken a very prominent post in many other things besides the occupation of studying my lessons, I do not think you or my Father have call to be dissatisfied." Actually, the academic load did not overburden him. He confessed that except for special occasions he had not found it necessary to study at night since his freshman year.[29]

The constant criticism and direction from his parents often exasperated Wister. No matter what he achieved, he always seemed to fall short of their exacting standards. In one of his regular letters home he included as a surprise for his mother a twelve-line poem that he had composed in French. Instead of expressing her pleasure, Sarah Wister critically studied the poem and found it lacking in quality. She reprimanded her son for dashing off a poem without painstaking care. He was reminded that a thing worth doing was a thing worth doing well. Taken aback, Wister responded: "If the idea occurred to write it, why not write it badly & let it go? There are lots of things that are worth doing for a minute or two that, are not worth doing well, for the pains taken would kill them." As for Dr. Wister's attitude about his college-age son, John

Jay Chapman summed it up by asking Owen on one occasion to remember him to Dr. Wister and to "tell him that whenever I hear of your doing anything particularly amusing or frivolous, I say 'Humble, what would Doctor Wister say to that?!' "[30]

Two days after his mother had chastised him for his imperfect French poem, Wister heard better news about some verses he had composed in English. The news came from Thomas Bailey Aldrich, editor of the *Atlantic Monthly*: "Your poem of two stanzas entitled 'Beethoven' is accepted for publication." Wister's spirits soared; it was his first publication outside Harvard and St. Paul's, and it would be printed in the same prestigious magazine for which his mother regularly wrote. Moreover, there had been no indication that Aldrich knew who Wister's mother and grandmother were.[31]

The preoccupation with his health that surfaced at St. Paul's increased during these Harvard years. Wister seemed especially susceptible to various minor ailments and nervous strains. Perhaps it was pressure from home that caused him to complain so often of illness, or perhaps it was behavior learned from home since both his mother and father had histories of ill-defined nervous exhaustion. Dr. Wister reinforced health worries by constantly urging his son to get adequate rest and exercise. One nagging problem was Owen's eyes, which continued to be a source of complaint.

A severe cold suffered during his junior year put Wister under the care of family friend Dr. Fred Shattuck; he recuperated at the Boston home of Harry Lee. In the daytime Wister discussed theology with Mrs. Lee, but at night his drug-influenced sleep was uneasy. "Last night the opium in some powders I took gave me a ludicrous & dreadful dream," he wrote to his mother.

> I dreamt that Dr. Coit was sitting lecturing to a lot of us on a platform, across which hung a clothes line loaded with pocket handkerchiefs of different sizes & colors. These he explained he had in the course of his life hung upon this line; one every time he committed a sin. He then took them up one by one. Finally he came to two stained with blood. He said, unnaturell [*sic*] & horrible as it was, he, even he, had committed two murders. One was that of the Prince of Wales, & the other of his younger brother Arthur. Every thing then became lurid. Dr. Coit's hair grew long & black like an Indian's; he became more and more agitated; his eyes glared, & finally his long hair flew up all over his head & he shrieked that although there was no substance of the murdered man upon the pocket handkerchiefs, he now saw both of them standing

on the platform in front of him. I looked & saw nothing. It was like Macbeth & Devnian; and I woke up feeling most unpleasant.

The frightening dream seemed to reveal Wister's deep and conflicting feelings about the long and lasting influence exerted by Dr. Coit and St. Paul's.[32]

During his Harvard years, though, he frequently visited St. Paul's on weekends and special occasions, a practice he was to continue throughout his life. Dr. Coit even attempted to persuade him to become a master there upon graduation. "I am flattered but that's all," Wister told his mother, and he declined. A friend who had begun to teach there already was beginning "to dry up," and Wister did not wish that upon himself.[33]

As far as Wister was concerned his career was settled: music. Aside from composing and studying under Paine there was another, more public outlet for his talents—the Hasty Pudding Theatricals. As a sophomore he was the musical manager and accompanist for the Class of '82 spring production, *Der Freischütz,* or *The Bell! The Belle! and the Bullet!* His partner in this venture and in similar ones to come was George Waring, who served as business manager and property manager. Waring, from a prominent New York family, and Wister struck up a friendship that endured a lifetime. *Der Freischütz,* rehearsed fifty-nine times by the company, not only played in Cambridge but also moved on to high acclaim in Boston and in New York City, where the cast performed in the old University Club Theater at Madison Square. Other burlesques followed, including a spectacular one featuring "Queen Elizabeth" entering the stage on the deck of a "steamboat." Another comic opera was *Lady of the Lake.* A photograph of the cast shows Wister, legs crossed and with a banjo in his arms, sitting in front of the other performers. For these old burlesques of English origin Wister had to find tunes to fit words that had been written many years earlier. Thus, the scores he composed contained strains purloined from Gounod, Rubinstein, Wagner, Sullivan, Offenbach, and Lecocq. When Professor Paine composed his own music for a Greek play, *Oedipus Tyrannus,* Wister took a part and found a picture of himself along with his fellow actors on the pages of *Harper's Weekly.* "I am leaning forward left leg bent & right leg out behind, as if I was running; left arm stretched to the chorus & right arm up in a gesture of horror."[34]

When the class of '83 needed assistance for its 1881 burlesque presentation of *Faust,* the talented Wister answered its call. He was repaid with a handsome singing tribute given during the performance.

All hail to thee!
Who did'st thine aid lend
To us when by anxious doubt oppressed,
And may thy name,
With rev'rence grateful,
Fall from the lips of Eighty-three.

Yes, dear Wister, we thank thee,
Our gracious assistant,
Eighty-two's charming orpheus
Whom iv'ry keys obey.[35]

The crowning glory, however, one that would be remembered and even revived in performances years later, was the production in the spring of 1882 of an original comic opera written by Wister himself, *Dido and Aeneas*. It was the first original play ever performed in the Pudding theatricals, and it came about because the old burlesques had been done so often that they had lost their novelty. Wister, inspired by the French operettas then in vogue, *La Belle Hélène* in particular, determined to write a new operetta for the Class of '82. He believed he should write on a subject familiar to all students, and since Harvard students were required to have a knowledge of Greek literature he chose Virgil's story about the pious Aeneas. Without telling the other club members, Wister began writing the operetta in the summer between his junior and senior years. The old burlesques had been written as rhymed couplets; Wister decided to break from that tradition in favor of prose, retaining, however, the familiar abundance of puns. For his music he borrowed from works of Franz von Suppé, Georges Bizet, Offenbach, Lecocq, Sullivan, and Wagner, interposing bits of his own compositions but feeling unequal to the task of creating entirely new melodies to last a full evening.

When he returned to campus in the fall, he revealed for the first time his ambitious plan and won the club's approval to proceed. He began polishing and revising, he formed an orchestra, and finally he rehearsed the full company with great care. Until now Pudding theatricals had been performed to the accompaniment of a single piano. But when the curtain rose in the spring for *Dido*'s first performance, there sat Wister in a conductor's chair waving a baton before a full orchestra. The startled audience laughed at the novelty of it as the prelude began. Wister, with his back to the audience, feared the worst. Not until after the first act did someone tell him that the laughing merely represented the audience's pleased diversion. *Dido*'s opening scene showed

Venus picking up a telephone (which had been invented only six years earlier): "Hulloa! . . . Central office! Give me Juno!" The spectacle of these classical figures speaking in slang and dancing and singing proved little short of a sensation. An impresario who happened to see the performance immediately invited the company to go on tour to Philadelphia, New York, and Boston. Arrangements were readily agreed upon.[36]

In the midst of the triumph, however, Wister's health again failed him: he went to bed with scarlet fever. "I really don't think you've shewn much sense of fitness," John Jay Chapman chided him. "It's not tragic, it's not comic, it's not dramatic—certainly your instinct has failed you." More seriously, Chapman said the play was "too good to lose much even by your absence."[37]

In Philadelphia scores of Wister's friends and relatives saw two performances. Two days later in mid-April, the company performed at Madison Square Theater in New York. The result was a resounding success with encore after encore demanded. For the greater part of the three-hour performance roars of laughter rang out from what one writer described as a "large, brilliant and fashionable" audience. Wister's script was declared to be equal to or better than any librettos save those of Sir William Schwenk Gilbert. "Mr. Wister is a modern writer," declared one newspaper critic, "and his work shows a freedom from all veneration of the past that proves him to belong to the advanced thinkers of the day, and there is no saying where his talents may lead him." While little of Wister's music was original, the highly praised libretto was his entirely. Its success was an early portent of things to come.[38]

The great clamor over *Dido and Aeneas* obliterated in Wister's mind even such memorable events as initiation night into the Hasty Pudding. The week of hazing, the singing of original odes, and the thick, heavy, recalcitrant mush the pledges swallowed could be recalled by an act of will, he later noted, "but Dido and Aeneas recalls itself. . . . It was our great adventure."[39]

Wister's head rang with still other acclaim as his triumphant senior year neared its conclusion. The song he had sold a year earlier had been issued, and the publisher, heartened by acclaim for *Dido and Aeneas*, "earnestly recommended" that he now compose his own comic opera with original music. Wister had no time at the moment for such endeavors, however. And although he now seemed to have little need for her services as his librettist, Fanny Kemble had informed her grandson in October that she must discontinue their earlier collaboration.[40]

43

Wister's literary efforts were capped by yet another successful venture, his first book. As a senior he had written a series of articles for the *Lampoon* satirizing college life at Harvard. The articles now were collected and published as *The New Swiss Family Robinson: A Tale for Children of All Ages*. The book was a takeoff on the popular *Swiss Family Robinson*. A colorful cover adorned the oversized edition. Published by Charles W. Sever and the University Book Store, the effort gained little but local notice, but it did earn a complimentary letter from Mark Twain.[41]

As graduation approached, Wister began planning a grand tour of Europe, a popular adventure of the day for Americans who could afford it. His mother would go, too, for her nerves had been bothering her. Initially planned for six months, the trip soon seemed too short. "We *must* stay abroad a year," he pleaded. Phillips Brooks had another tempting suggestion—why didn't Wister accompany him on a winter tour of India? "There are so many things I am getting to want to do that I feel lost & hopeless," Wister said. Europe took priority, however.[42]

The proposed jaunt gave Dr. Wister an idea of his own. While he realized all too well that his son's musical talents had won raves from Professor Paine and others, these opinions were unsophisticated American ones. Mere talent, Dr. Wister was convinced, was no guarantee for a successful career in the uncertain world of music. Before his son undertook to be a composer it seemed to Dr. Wister that a more detached, capable judgment was needed, a European judgment. Thus, he suggested that the European tour should include a test for his son. If Wister could convince the finest judges in Europe that he had original talent as a composer, then Dr. Wister would pay for musical training on the continent, where the very best could be had. Wister readily agreed to this condition.

Meanwhile, the final weeks of school remained. For his musical thesis Wister wrote a paper, "An Inquiry into the Future of the Opera." In it he analyzed the works of Italian composers with the unbounded self-confidence of an undergraduate who could declare them to be products of "uncultivated and unintellectual minds."[43]

As commencement approached, Wister, who always before had sought his parents' attendance at school festivities, now discouraged it. "Don't let anyone come to Commencement. It's horribly stupid, even for the graduating class." Yet Wister shone at commencement, for he graduated *summa cum laude* with a double major in music and philosophy.

44

He was a Phi Beta Kappa as well, and his achievements as a music student were so superlative that a history of Harvard written nearly fifty years later recognized Wister as one of a handful of "well-known musicians" graduated by the Department of Music.[44]

On the day after commencement exercises Wister and some of his friends celebrated with a wild bacchanalia that took them to New London to see the Harvard rowing team compete with Yale. When Harvard won, Wister and his twenty-odd friends were jubilant. They pummeled the excited crew and shouted with joy, then continued the celebration in New London. ("Harvard owned the town," Wister recorded.) Finally, time came for Wister to say a fond goodbye to George Waring, his business partner in the Pudding theatricals, as well as to the crew and other friends before boarding the train himself for the return trip to Harvard. As the train jostled northward Wister took out his notebook and pen to write: "It's all over, & well over. I'm a graduate & Harvard College will soon see me no more. As Endicott, H. Cabot, H. Sears sleep around me, I reflect that tomorrow the 'Baltic' will be taking Sears & me away from all those things. . . . Wharton says he didn't mean to get drunk. Amen."[45]

The *Baltic* was to carry Wister, accompanied by his ill-tempered mother, as well as by friends Harry Sears, Evert J. Wendell, and Frederick M. (Rocks) Stone, across the Atlantic. There awaited the European judgment.

Chapter III

THE EUROPEAN JUDGMENT
(1882–1883)

THE YOUNG HARVARD GRADUATES FROLICKED LIKE COLTS as the *Baltic* sailed across the Atlantic. Foot racing and greased pole climbing were part of the shipboard activities, and even a cockfight was staged. The passengers celebrated the voyage's final day with a special musical program in which Wister sang a tune called "Griggs." When the audience demanded an encore he obliged with a melodramatic burlesque song. Evert Wendell, terribly seasick, lifted himself from bed to sing a song to Wister's piano accompaniment, then hurried back to his room to resume his illness in private. Sarah Wister watched such goings-on with quiet detachment. For her, an extended stay in Europe was therapy for her growing nervousness and depression.[1]

No definite itinerary awaited the group in Europe. They would be together when it suited them and apart when it did not. On making port at Liverpool, Wister went with Wendell straight to London, separating for a while from his mother and the others. The city abounded with divertisements. He attended the opera and theater, saw cricket matches, dined with family friends and new acquaintances, and mixed thoroughly in London society at its several levels.

One early evening as he walked in broad daylight along a busy street, Wister got the shock of his life when a prostitute grabbed him. "[This] lady in the street suddenly took hold of my balls—I was surprised for the moment, but passed on, intrepidly," he recorded in his notebook. "Surprised" could hardly have been an adequate word for the shock the young gentleman felt, and the use even in his private notebook of such an indelicate word as "balls" was a rarity. Less unseemly aspects of London were revealed when an actor named Key took Wister "all over town" in a hansom and introduced him to actors and actresses as "an amateur of note from America." Wister did not feel confident making conversation in these surroundings, and he confessed to imitating a behavior which had never failed to impress him: he acknowledged introductions simply by bowing and saying nothing.[2]

On the day after this evening of introductions, he had dinner at Aunt Fanny's house. Wister sat next to William Gladstone's private secretary. Following his evening with the entertainers, this dinner gave him "both sides of the question" on the London social scene. He declared that many eligible young women who were omnipresent at this and other occasions disgusted him. They were "giggling ladies" and "vapid man hunters," inspired and assisted by their mothers, who were "on the man hunt from May till August" in London before moving to the country to resume their search. Wister, as an American, was not considered eligible, and the ladies paid him no attention.[3]

English manners and customs both attracted and repelled him. The nation's stuffiness often seemed illogical and unbearable. When he observed proceedings at the House of Commons for an hour, a "dreadful person in livery & badges" interrupted him as he made journal entries to say that he could not take notes. In the final analysis, though, the pomp and respect for tradition in England won his heart. At the season's last performance of Gioacchino A. Rossini's *Il Barbiere di Siviglia*, Wister shivered with emotion when the company sang "God Save the Queen." American society, in contrast, seemed shallow and crass. In his notebook he recorded an observation he never would forget, "I noticed a reverence for what English people deem is to be revered, & a certain traditional propriety, or observance of customs which is in pleasing contrast to our practical, level headed American respect, which is so entirely on a cash-basis."[4]

During his two weeks in England, Wister also called on Henry James ("Saw Hen Jim too—But Hen Jim is very nice after all, & was particularly nice to me") and various Kemble cousins, and he traveled to Canterbury and Dover. James thought the grown-up Wister was "attractive and amiable," but also "light and slight, both in character and in talent."[5]

After England Wister headed for Paris. He managed in three days not only to go to the theater every evening, but also to visit friends, to tour the Louvre, to play tennis, and to walk along the Seine at moonlight. He enjoyed French cuisine, too, affecting a fine cigar after his meals. His mother had rejoined him now, and at Amiens she embarrassed him by getting involved in an imbroglio with a cabdriver. As a result, she barely escaped being arrested.[6]

En route by train to Lucerne, where they would visit his grand-mother, Wister and his mother stopped at Bâle, Switzerland, to spend the night in the Hotel des Trois Rois on the banks of the Rhine River. The romantic setting flooded Wister's mind with the realization that the happy days of college were truly over; a new and unknown life lay before him. "The noise of the Rhine flowing under my window is lonely & sad," he recorded in a sentimental rush that Sunday evening in his notebook. "It makes me feel homesick, & reminds me of that last night at Cambridge. . . . Ah! Cambridge—Cambridge—How happy I have been there."[7]

For the past half-dozen years Fanny Kemble had alternated between living in London and in Switzerland. At the age of seventy-four she had finished publishing the seemingly interminable flow of letters that had poured effortlessly from her pen over the years. When Wister arrived in Lucerne in mid-afternoon on the last day of July, he found his grand-mother youthful-looking and alert. If Fanny Kemble's sprightliness surprised him, Fanny found in her grandson a surprise, too, which erased her lingering doubts about his capabilities. His original musical compositions particularly pleased her. She challenged him by supplying him with poetry to set to music, and he did so in a single hour. During the five-day visit Wister also took time to ride horseback, fish, and attend a performance of *La Perichole*.[8]

"I found your mother-in-law very pleasant indeed," Wister happily wrote to his father. However, he confessed to growing weary after a few days of "doing the son & grandson," and he was eager to proceed alone with his tour. "Crabbed age & youth can not live together," Wister quoted Shakespeare. "Still, your wife & your mother-in-law are both very remarkable women in their respective ways, & I congratulate you on them heartily."[9]

Berne, his next stop, revived his memories as a student at nearby Hofwyl. The memories commanded a visit, and he decided to walk there. He found the forests, the lake, the school buildings, and the town exactly as remembered, but the school was closed. Dr. Müller had retired to Berne; the school had withered away to mediocrity under his replacement; then it had closed completely. Dr. Müller's brother, who remained at Hofwyl, offered the visitor a key to the buildings. But Wister chose merely to stroll over the grounds and to meditate over his year there. Sitting at the edge of the woods, he pulled out his notebook and recorded his thoughts. The woods, he observed, were far more pleasant now than they had been years before when Italian and French youths had bullied him. "It was awful—I was only ten—had never been away from home before, & could speak nothing but English. I was very miserable here, homesick & sick too [,] for continental regimen didn't agree with my vitals." Still, he believed, the Müller family had been very kind to him, and he did not blame them for his unhappiness. It was "the fault of the system they believed in." That time seemed "very strange & far off," and he now could see it as "the end of a very slow childhood." Back in Berne he located Dr. Müller, who greeted him cordially. They chatted, and Wister could laugh now as he listened to his former schoolmaster reminisce about old Hofwyl days.[10]

On the days when their European paths crossed, Wister, Wendell, Sears, and Stone did not suppress their holiday spirits. Singing, drinking, hiking, and admiring the young women of Europe brought many happy hours. At the Hotel National in Fribourg a barmaid, "flirtatious—& very pretty," caught Wister's attention. "Should have liked to have taken steps toward increasing the population with that young bar-maid. She was passing pleasing—but I had only 24 hours & that is not enough," he wrote in his notebook.[11]

In the Swiss Alps they took exhilarating hikes, savored the beauty, and breathed deeply of the crisp mountain air. "Switzerland is the Coney Island of Europe," Wister exclaimed. From the mountain heights, glimmering, distant glacier fields shone. At Furka Pass the youths scrambled over the Rhone glacier. Intoxicated by the view and perched on an ice hill, they sang a selection from *Dido and Aeneas* to the accompaniment of a banjo which went with them everywhere.[12]

A few days later they were in Bayreuth, the letter of introduction for Liszt from Wister's grandmother ready to be sprung upon the maestro at the *Parsifal* intermission. Wister's abilities, subsequently winning Liszt's praise in the home of none other than Wagner, appeared confirmed by the European judgment. Wister tentatively planned to spend the fall and winter in Berlin, where he could dedicate himself to musical study.

Despite the natural beauty and artistic marvels of Europe which seemed to be at Wister's disposal, he could not help but look back to Harvard with longing as the time arrived for the fall semester. His friend Stone departed for America to enroll at Harvard as a graduate student, and Wister was filled with nostalgia. "Alas for the days that are gone & for the good things that came & went with them," he wrote.[13]

In late September he was again in Vienna, dreading an approaching reunion in Paris with his always difficult mother. His plans to study in Germany had gone awry. For some reason he had decided to stay in Paris in October and November at least, and he had made the mistake of telling his mother. She subsequently made definite housing arrangements for the two of them there, and he could find no graceful way of backing out.[14]

Paris, of course, did hold an attraction since it was the home of opera-comique, a form especially appreciated by Wister. To attend the musical theater in Paris was more than to be present for a musical event —it was to be a part of a grand social affair at which visiting and gossiping were at least as important as the performance. The music itself, though, was truly outstanding. Offenbach's *The Tales of Hoffman* had opened posthumously the year before in 1881; Gounod's *Redemption* was performed there this same year; and Saint-Saëns's *Henry VIII* was to be introduced the following season. Other active composers whose works were being performed in Paris music halls included Massenet, Debussy, Chabrier, Franck, Lalo, and Fauré.[15]

The city was the intellectual and artistic capital of Europe, a testing ground for ideas and arts. Already the Eiffel Tower, being constructed for the International Exposition of 1889, soared above the city. All the arts prospered. The Impressionist painters—Boudin, Pissarro, Monet, Renoir, Degas, and Cézanne—had held their first special exhibit less than ten years before; now the exhibits were becoming annual events. Mallarmé was composing poems of genius; Maupassant was writing short stories destined to become classics; and Zola had published *Nana* in 1880, *L'Assommoir* three years before. The famous philosopher Henri Bergson lectured at the Collège de France.

The Wisters' rooms were at the Hotel de Rivoli. Owen immediately began a series of musical lessons with Antoine-François Marmontel, a famed composer at the Conservatoire whose former students included Georges Bizet.[16] When Wister first played his compositions for Marmontel, the sixty-six-year-old professor made discouraging sounds. Wister felt optimistically that perhaps his poor piano playing had caused the lack of enthusiasm rather than the quality of his compositions. Then he went away with his mother for a few days to Tours, where he composed a very short piece. Upon returning he played it for Marmontel, who declared this new composition extraordinary. He insisted that Wister play

51

it again, and then he called in his son to hear it. Both Marmontels exclaimed that the composition was not at all ordinary or "*de tout le monde*," and they congratulated the young American for being "highly gifted." In the days to follow Marmontel repeated his compliments, adding that Wister was fortunate in possessing "*original talent*," supplemented with a "capacity & inclination to work."[17]

Meanwhile, Wister had waited more than a month before telling his father of his successful audience with Liszt. He had been reluctant, knowing the news would not be welcome. Wister had reason to be wary, for the exchange of letters now revealed that Dr. Wister insisted not merely on evidence of talent but on evidence of musical genius. Sarah Wister indignantly chastised her husband. She had been indulgent and amused, she said, when he—untrained in music—had undertaken single-handedly to doubt Professor Paine's capacity for forming an opinion about their son's musical talents. Now, not only the great Liszt, but also the highly respected Marmontel had approved of their son's capacities. Sarah had asked Marmontel if he thought her son had "*original talent*," and he had answered affirmatively. She had not realized that her husband required a "certificate of genius," and she knew of nobody on the continent save Liszt capable of such a judgment. Yet, for some unknown reason, Dr. Wister had discounted even Liszt's opinion. Sarah Wister said that her husband's rationale was on "unusual grounds." Why must Owen be acclaimed a genius? Furthermore, she simply did not have the "effrontery to go about asking people if they thought her son was a genius." If Owen were to study law, she declared, neither would her husband be willing to ask George W. Biddle or any other leading lawyer if he considered the young Wister certain to become a Story or a Trent.[18]

"I suppose I know what you will reply to this, but mediocrity in all professions seems to me about the same thing, & to be obscure in a career in wh[ich] you have no heart is certainly worse than obscurity & contentment," she continued. "The test of genius is a new idea to me. I don't *think* Dan has musical genius; I am *sure* he hasn't any other." With that, she said, she now was finished with the subject.[19]

Wister, learning of his father's moods, told Marmontel, "My father thinks I ought to have genius to follow music." "You must tell your Father," Marmontel replied, "that no one can tell you that until hard study has brought it to light in a developed form." Wister responded, "I don't think I have any such thing, but do *you* think I have enough talent to warrant my becoming a musician?" "Most decidedly, yes," Marmontel answered, adding that Wister had "original ideas" and a "serious grasp of harmony."[20]

Reinforced, Wister wrote at length to inform his father that he had decided "fully, & finally" to make music his profession. Perhaps, he acknowledged, Professor Paine's opinion had not counted for much; even for him it had done no more than cause him to solicit other opinions. Perhaps Liszt's judgment could be tempered, as his father suggested, "because of the man." But now Marmontel's conclusions could not be disregarded; his opinion had been carefully measured.[21]

"Now I have fulfilled the program," Wister told his father. "I have come abroad & seen two authorities—& one of them has had a chance to see all my defects & all my strong points, & the opinion they have given me coincides precisely with what Paine & Korbay said, which seems to me sufficient." He might never rise above mediocrity as a composer, but if he became a lawyer or a railroad man as his father preferred, he was "quite likely to be mediocre," for his talents in these fields certainly were not evident. "Mediocrity being assumed then in any case, I think I have the best, in fact the only right, to make my choice as to which it shall be, as *my* career, *my* life, and *my* happiness are the question & not anybody else's." The disaster of this choice, should it be a disaster, would rest on his head and not on his father's. But if he were forced to enter law or business, any calamity there would be laid at his father's feet. He hoped that his father would not think his letter "too self-asserting or too rash." He meant it to be neither, and he concluded by writing: "Good bye. You understand me perfectly well & you know . . . I am not a fool."[22]

Stated in such terms, the decision seemed irrevocable; never had Wister argued his case so positively. He acknowledged that he would need an indefinite subsidy from his father in order to follow an artistic career, and he did not wholeheartedly approve of that. But Wister saw nothing wrong in a person taking advantage of being part of an affluent family. He was, as he put it, "the only son of a gentleman who is comfortably off," and so long as that son occupied himself in serious and legitimate work he saw no harm in subsidization.[23]

Dr. Wister, however, was not swayed. In fact, he had been discreetly inquiring for a suitable position in business for his son, and he had found one. Family friend Henry Lee and his partner, Henry Lee Higginson, agreed to hire Owen in their Boston brokerage firm, Lee, Higginson and

Company. Dr. Wister, upon telling his son in November of this possibility, did not order him to accept the job, but he informed him that he would finance his musical studies in Europe only through the spring and no further.[24]

This shattering news brought no reply from Wister. He merely let the matter rest, evidently determined to make his own way. Meanwhile, he now began studying under Professor Ernest Guiraud, a New Orleans-born musician in his mid-forties who had composed his first opera at fifteen.* A charming, benevolent man, Guiraud often spoke to his new student of his close friendships with Louis Hector Berlioz, Offenbach, and Bizet, and he frequently had Wister come to his room at rue Pigalle to work. Among Guiraud's other students at this time were Claude Debussy, already acclaimed, and Paul Dukas, who later would compose *The Sorcerer's Apprentice*. Both Marmontel and Guiraud were professors at the famous Conservatoire de Musique, but Wister evidently studied with Guiraud on a private basis, for admission to the Conservatoire was highly limited, and there is no mention of it in Wister's letters.[25]

Wister's most ambitious musical project at this time was composing an opera entitled *Montezuma* which centered on the Aztec ruler's court in the time of Cortez. A less ambitious effort was a one-act comic opera entitled *La Sérénade*. His lyricist was a Frenchman, Le Comte Solohub. Details are sketchy, but the latter opera actually was performed in Paris at a place called Munroe's on April 30, 1883, sharing billing with a one-act comedy, *Love and Rain*. Wister wore a white flower in his lapel to the premiere, carefully pressing it afterwards and placing it in an envelope as a keepsake. The comic opera was performed at least once again that spring, the second time on a bill with a one-act comedy entitled *Second Thoughts*. These, it is easy to imagine, were heady experiences for Wister, especially when Guiraud told him, "*Vous avez parfaitement le sentiment de l'orchestre.*"[26]

Sarah Wister also was being creative, analyzing the musical scene of Paris in articles. In an unsigned piece for *Atlantic Monthly*, she declared in typically negative fashion that Paris opera already was "in its decline." Undoubtedly it had been Wister, who still worshiped Wagner and sought to make his mother appreciate the composer, who had insisted that she attend in February the Société Artistique's first Wagner me-

* Guiraud's light operas include *Piccolino* and *Galant aventure*; his more familiar works are his composition of the farandole in Bizet's *L'Arlésienne* and his orchestration of Offenbach's *The Tales of Hoffman*.

morial concert. The occasion caused a near riot between Wagner devotees and haters. When the "wild gallop" of *The Valkyrie* began, a storm of hissing, hooting, stamping, shrill whistling, calling, crying, and counter-crying erupted: "That's not music!" "Superb! Magnificent!" "Stop it!" "Turn out the blackbirds [the men with the whistles]!" "Down with the circus-riders!" Finally, though, the pro-Wagnerians prevailed, and the conductor, M. Colonne, bowed while "every hair of his well-brushed brown curls stood on end." It was, Sarah Wister confessed, the "most tremendous musical impression" of her life.[27]

Wister, with good entree into Paris salons, could not resist the exciting social opportunities about him. "Dan has been out every night but one!" reported his mother in the spring to Dr. Wister. Moreover, he took lessons to augment his social graces—singing, fencing, and French. He also acted in amateur theatricals, playing the character of "Henry Spreadbow" in a two-act play, *Sweethearts*, by W. S. Gilbert.[28]

He spent the Christmas holidays, at his mother's insistence, in England, staying first in the Burlington Hotel at London and then in Lady Jersey's "great house" at Middleton Park, Bicester. He sought right away to visit Henry James, but the first three times he called James was out. When they finally got together James escorted him on a round of social visits. Wister reciprocated by asking James to visit him and his mother in Paris. This upset Sarah Wister, who felt that their rooms were not adequate and that James might be offended by the accommodations. "You must find some way of explaining the matter to Mr. James, or what will he think of us?" She urged Wister to explain to James that her son had misunderstood her in extending the invitation. "Add however that there is a spare room in the apartment & that it wd. be a great pleasure to me if he wd. take it anytime in the next three months."[29]

The visit to England boosted Wister's spirits immensely. A flattering professional offer even came to him. He was asked to assume the management of an operetta at Hains beginning January 1, but he declined the honor. London itself was "fearfully dirty," and the fog was a perpetual bother, but nothing detracted from his pleasure at being there. "I like it as a city forty times better than Paris."[30]

For a youth whose lifelong ambition was being realized in the glamorous mecca of Paris, this preference may seem strange. In truth, however, Wister already had become disenchanted with Paris. It was a side effect of a depression such as he had never before experienced. "It is a wretched, wretched life," he exclaimed. The cause was not dissatisfaction with his musical studies, nor really with Paris; it was, he was convinced, a mental toll exacted from his demanding, impetuous, and overly sensitive mother.[31]

Sarah Wister had become miserable in recent years with life in general. She complained of poor health and of being overly fatigued; she argued with shopkeepers and continued her usual complaints with servants; she could find nothing to satisfy her meticulous requirements. One of the purposes for accompanying her son to Europe had been to improve her mental outlook. It now was obvious that the "treatment" had not worked. On one occasion she entered into a nearly violent argument with a dressmaker that caused a confrontation with the law. She had ordered a dress, and when it arrived late she refused to accept it. One morning when she was away, however, the dressmaker placed the garment in her antechamber. Sarah determinedly sought to return the unwanted dress, but the dressmaker just as adamantly refused to accept it. One morning before breakfast, four officers arrived to seize the Wisters' effects because of the unpaid bill. To avoid this unpleasant development, Owen and his mother had to pay not only for the dress but also for the sheriff's expenses. Sarah decided to carry the dispute to court, but her lawyer persuaded her that such action would be ill-advised.[32]

She turned even the supposedly simple task of writing letters into an all-consuming job. She strained for hours to write just three letters one day, and Wister remonstrated without results. "She is acting as though she was incapable of reason, & this nearly every day," he wrote to his father in mid-October. Yet he was reluctant to express to her his opinion because it merely irritated her further.[33]

"I thought a few days ago of begging you to come over here," Wister wrote to his father,

> but I hardly think it would do any real good whatever; all you could do would be peremptorily to forbid her doing anything you thought imprudent, & that would lead to more trouble, probably. . . . The trouble is all in her own self. She has made up her mind she will never be better & has told me so—& to insure the truth of her opinion she seems to be taking the worst steps possible the whole time.[34]

It was during this unhappy time that Sarah Wister, along with Fanny Kemble and Owen, met Henry James for a week of sightseeing at Tours and nearby areas. James, once so enamored of her, described her now as being of such "a tragic nature, so much worn, physically, that I am sorry for her."[35]

Sarah Wister, always high-strung, had no discernible physical ailments, but twice a week an oculist treated her with a "water cure." When Dr. Wister mildly admonished her about her "Bohemian" nature, she replied: "I don't know how you can call me Bohemian; I, who must have all things done decently & in order, & who have so strong a conventional fibre amidst my eccentricities."[36]

Wister, frustrated on one hand by his father's pressure on him to forsake music and on the other by his unnerving mother, found an outlet for relieving his own tension: he attacked his father. In a long letter of reproof he claimed that Dr. Wister had failed to provide his wife with the varied and active social life her temperament required. His father had been the obstacle to the very cure that Dr. Wister himself had proposed—social activity. "You do not, & have never lived like other people," Wister reprimanded him. "How many times a year do you dine out with her? How many times do you take her involuntarily to the theatre, or indeed anywhere?"[37] Wister warned his father that if he did not conquer his aversion to society he would never succeed in curing his wife's nervous tension. He added that his mother herself often lamented that her European visit could have no lasting effect because she would return to the same circumstances that had made her ill.[38]

All these comments were simple enough for Wister to make; his relationship with Sarah Wister was one of son to mother. Dr. Wister took his son's stern directive with equanimity. He had some things of his own to say about life with Fanny Kemble's daughter, being a greater expert on the subject than his son. He acknowledged in his return letter that his wife had neither variety nor society enough, yet she had far more than she would admit when compared with other people who lived in the country on "moderate means." Even if money were not a problem, he thought Sarah's inability to get along with the servants would cause even further problems if added demands were made. On more than one occasion, Dr. Wister said, he had been in "momentary apprehension of the appearance of a Police Officer with a summons for your mother in the midst of a reception going on in the house." She had known nothing of this, nor had she been aware that he had lain awake all night worrying over such dismal possibilities for the next day. "She is incapable of believing herself wrong, regards advice of moderation as a manifestation of timidity, and has again & again involved me in very great trouble, of which she is entirely ignorant, to protect her from the results of her own unreasonableness."[39] The years he had devoted to building an estate to provide for her and for Owen had taken a toll on his health, Dr. Wister added.

> I had nothing when I married; was morbidly anxious to provide for your mother's comfort in case of my death; knew that she would get very little in the way of income from her Father, even if I outlived him; and that my share of my Father's estate must be small. One does one's best in one's circumstance & with one's lights, makes many mistakes & is often less really selfish than outside eyes can discern.

Owen's position, he acknowledged, now was difficult and trying, but he must accept it as "part of a calamity which involves us all."[40]

In closing the letter, Dr. Wister related startling news. He supposed that by now Sarah had read to his son the letter in which he had acquiesced to Wister's desire for a musical career. Yet Wister responded on the day after he read his father's letter: "I have not only merely accepted what you wish, but I *wish it myself.* . . . I want you please to write to Mr. Lee that I am most grateful for his offer & that I accept it as a rare privilege. I shall write to him myself & tell him that I will do my best to be a good office boy." The apprenticeship was to last for one year at a minimum. If business proved by then to be a "shut door," or if talent and usefulness were found wanting, then Wister would return to music. After all, he had no reason to *assume* failure in a subject about which he knew nothing, he acknowledged, and if business "liked" him and if he received encouragement in it, he would continue.[41]

Wister knew that his father would be puzzled by this sudden reversal, and he stressed that the "generous revocation" had nothing to do with his change in heart. Nevertheless, he could not resist pointing out that his father's "repeated objections" were the fundamental reason for his decision. Secondary was his own hesitation, expressed now for the first time, in committing himself to such an unconventional life. "It occurred to me that business ought to have the first chance because you wished it, because it was the usual & not the unusual thing to do, (& I have a horror of doing the extraordinary) & lastly because it took me among my own people & in my own country—a reason by no means to be despised." His yearning to return to America and particularly to New England, he said, grew stronger every day.[42]

The decision, despite this falsely optimistic front, brought much personal anguish. For years he had resisted his father's wishes; now he had yielded. He could not refrain from scoring still more points in his letter. "Long ago at college I said to myself, 'I wish to Heaven I had never cared for music, & then every thing would be simple enough.' This, I said to myself, & now I say it to you in order that we may cry together over a little spilt milk." As for Dr. Wister's misguided notion that he understood his son and could correctly assess that son's capacity for music, this was impossible in Wister's eyes since he himself did not know these things fully. Neither could Wister resist complaining that his father had refused to accept the judgments of the very experts he had sent his son to get. "Of course they didn't judge *me*; they said here is a man X: X has a talent for music sufficient to make a career of. They didn't say unless X has Southern property; unless X has a position to maintain in an un-musical country. They saw a man X who had a talent Y. However this is nothing to the point, & does not change my strong desire to get that year's chance at Lee & Higginson's."[43]

As for his mother, Owen told Dr. Wister that their relationship was at its absolute nadir. "I would rather after I return to America never see her except by short visits again," he declared. Sarah Wister had worried her son by making a statement in all sincerity that henceforth her life must consist only of odds and ends. "My mother's calm statements about herself are annihilating. It will be a relief to herself, & ought to be to all who love her, when Death closes her story. I hope there are not many like it in the world—So utterly out of reach of outside help."[44] To make such a statement about his own mother, he told his father, naturally was upsetting. But he supposed that neither his father nor his mother would be deriving much pleasure from their lives in the future. "I will try to remember that it must come out of mine, & shape my ways accordingly."[45]

Thus, Wister's decision to relinquish his musical career seems many-faceted. In the years to come, however, Wister would remember the career change with a certain simplicity: his father had demanded that he return home for a business career. While his father's resistance certainly was an overriding factor, this explanation overlooks the fact that at the last minute Dr. Wister had yielded to his son's wishes. Neither would Wister's later explanations acknowledge the problems caused for him in Paris by his mother. Still, it was not a happy decision, and the effect of it would plague Wister forever.

Before his return to the United States in the summer, Wister made a final pilgrimage to Bayreuth. Wagner was now dead, but Liszt was at Weimar, and Wister called on him. He accepted Liszt's offer to return the next day and observe him at work with his students.

The next day he found gathered in Liszt's music room a number of "teutonic maidens" with their hair hanging in plaits and with their worship for Liszt shining in their eyes. One by one the pupils, who paid nothing for their instructions, took turns at the piano with "uninspired mediocrity." When a young German with obvious talent played, however, Liszt hovered over him closely, stopping here, suggesting there, and occasionally playing a few measures to illustrate what should be done. It was clear how Liszt operated: pupils of little or no talent could come and go and be welcome, but when a genuine talent emerged that person received the great man's most careful attention.

After the pupils departed, Liszt asked Wister to remain for supper and a game of whist. "It was Russian whist (if I remember the name)," Wister recalled years later, "but something of which I was totally ignorant." Nevertheless, Liszt made his guest his partner in the game after supper. Wister was rescued by a kind English lady who sat next to him and instructed him as to which cards to play. At about 9:30 P.M. Liszt announced that he must retire for the evening, and the guests left.[46]

Afterwards at the hotel, Wister joined two of Liszt's male students who were playing the piano and drinking wine. They stayed up very late, each performing on the piano in turn. The next morning, suffering from a dreadful hangover, Wister went to the train depot to return to Paris. Liszt was there, accompanying a departing friend. Wister, not wishing to force his presence again, kept a respectful distance, venturing only to touch his hat in greeting. Liszt, however, approached him and spoke. As Wister would later translate the conversation, Liszt had said: "I am growing old. I shall not be here very much longer. Whenever you find yourself where I am, come to me without ceremony."[47]

Soon the train boarded its passengers, and as it pulled away from the station Wister leaned out the window to look back on Liszt, standing alone on the platform, his hair flowing from hat to collar. This, Wister knew, would be his last glimpse of the renowned artist.[48]

Back in Paris, Wister resumed his final days of study with Guiraud. On his last evening in the city he took his professor to dinner. Afterwards, the two of them rode round and round the streets of Paris in a downpour of rain. Wister years later remembered that the gentle Guiraud repeated time and time again: "N'abandonnez pas la musique! Oh, n'abandonnez pas la musique!"[49] But Wister had abandoned music. A business career in the esteemed brokerage firm of Lee, Higginson and Company lay before this twenty-three-year-old man.

Chapter IV

A BOSTON STOPOVER
(1883–1885)

IN A CITY WHERE THE RIGHT CONNECTIONS probably counted more than they did anywhere else in America, Wister could have no better connection than to start a business career with the firm of Lee, Higginson and Company. Owing in part to the rarified social status of the Lee and Higginson families, after its founding in 1848 the firm established itself as one of Boston's most respected businesses. And while the family names brought immediate honor, the firm's wise investments for its clients in the westward railroad boom and in gold, copper, and manufacturing brought what counted even more in many eyes—profits.

Having already socialized with the firm's two principal partners as a Harvard undergraduate, Wister was on personal terms with both of them. Henry Lee Higginson carried his Civil War title of "Major," and Henry Lee also was known by his former military rank of "Colonel." Of the two, it was Higginson whom Wister came to know best because of unusual similarities in their backgrounds. Higginson, too, had studied music in Europe as a young man, and he too had forsaken music with great reluctance for business. This he had done in 1868 upon reaching his mid-thirties and concluding that the musical accomplishments he dreamed of never would be realized. He had prospered in the firm that bore his family's name, and when he acquired a fortune he paid homage to his first love by singlehandedly founding the Boston Symphony Orchestra. Even now, as he would do for many years, he directed its affairs and underwrote its expenses. Higginson, married to the daughter of famed Harvard Professor Louis Agassiz, also preceded Wister in another direction. This sophisticated Easterner had developed a keen interest in the raw American West, especially because of its investment opportunities but no less because of its Indians, its cowboys, and its badmen. He traveled to the West on many occasions, examining railroad properties and maintaining a sharp eye for other investment opportunities. Henry Lee, whose own family prominence was not at all diminished when he married a Cabot, already had been friends with two previous generations of the Wister family. Owen Wister later would describe him as "one of those fine Americans with colonial traditions who knew how to be rich."[1]

The initial offer had been for Wister to join the firm as a broker rather than as—in Wister's deprecatory description—an "office boy." But by the time he arrived in December business had slumped; instead of working at 44 State Street he was sent next door to the company's sister firm, the Union Safe Deposit Vaults, where as it turned out he was not much more than an office boy. The vaults themselves were exemplary, the first of their kind for Boston, and a model for future savings strongholds throughout the nation. Their construction in 1868 had been Colonel Lee's inspiration. An unusual test indicated the care taken to insure their strength and safety: a huge safe had been lifted five floors above the vaults and dropped. Having survived this awful blow without undue harm, the vaults were deemed sturdy enough. The doors then were opened to the public, and almost overnight the Union Safe Deposit Vaults became the principal depository for Boston securities.[2]

Wister's duties were not difficult. He had three chores. First, he acted as a receiving teller. "When people come in to make a deposit I record it in their books to their credit. If their deposit is cash I count it, if checks, I see that they are properly endorsed, & if I'm not sure I ask some one." His second duty was to go to the bank next door to make deposits and withdrawals. His third and most onerous task was to calculate interest at two and a half percent, which he did while perched on a high stool. Occasionally, when another clerk had the interest book, he sat on his stool with nothing to do but ponder his situation. It did not take him long to realize that the job bored him.[3]

Still, after a month on the job, he maintained an optimistic front for his concerned mother, whose behavior in Paris he now had forgiven in her absence. "As far as I can tell, [I] am considered a promising clerk. So waste no sympathies on me." If his mother thought his circumstances less than stimulating, which she did, he assured her that his father must have had "10 times as bad a time" when he started his career. In short, Wister resigned himself to make the best of an existence that never had been his real choice.[4]

His social life in the beginning was limited. His presence in the city was not widely known, nor did he seek to advertise it. He did not feel like mingling just now anyway, and he knew that he soon would have more of society than he desired. When Dr. Wister hinted that he wanted to give his son two items for Christmas that would be helpful in his social life—a traveling bag and a cutaway coat—Owen rebuffed him by saying that he had no use for either one. He declined likewise the gift of a membership in the Social Art Club. Even the rooms he lived in were simple—fitting, he declared, for a mere apprentice such as himself. Social amenities, he maintained, must not distract him; he had vowed to concentrate on succeeding in business.[5]

He could not resist society for long. Before two months had passed he was visiting not only the homes of the Lees and Higginsons, but also those of such families as the Brimmers, the Warrens,* the Forbeses, the Russells, the Curtises, the Jameses, the Winsors, as well as those of Mrs. Sarah Whitman and Mrs. Louis Agassiz. He resumed as well his friendship and lunches with the Reverend Phillips Brooks, and he played the piano at the golden wedding celebration of Mr. and Mrs. John Murray Forbes.[6]

Boston's social life was rich and—for an American city—deep in the tradition that Wister had come to admire in Europe. Conversations in salons such as Mrs. Sarah Whitman's and Mrs. Jack Gardner's carefully avoided low and common topics. A fascination for Europe seemed to dominate discussions; American topics were avoided as uncouth. William Dean Howells summed up the situation that very year in his novel, *A Woman's Reason*:

> They talk about London, and about Paris, and about Rome: there seems to be quite a passion for Italy; but they don't seem interested in their own country. I can't make it out. It isn't as if they were saying so —they try to give it. They always seem to have been reading the *Fortnightly* and the *Saturday Review*, and the *Spectator*, and the *Revue des Deux Mondes*, and the last French and English books. It's very odd![7]

Having just returned from Europe, Wister made a perfect dinner guest in such circles. Yet the fact that there was much that was artificial in such evenings did not escape his attention. When he dined at the home of Mrs. Sarah Whitman, a leading Boston socialite of ultra-refined tastes, he sat between Mrs. Helen Choate Bell (the daughter of Rufus Choate) and Miss Maud Howe, who droned on interminably. Across the

---

* Six years later Samuel Warren would become so perturbed with newspaper reports of such social gatherings that he would coauthor with Oliver Wendell Holmes, Jr., an article in the *Harvard Law Review* urging a new "right to privacy." The article is credited with originating legal recognition of such a right.

63

table his friend Minna Timmins, soon to become Mrs. John Jay Chapman, made faces at him through a vase of flowers, nearly causing him to lose his dignified mien. He shared, at this time in his life at any rate, John Jay Chapman's and Minna's feelings of contempt for such scenes. His hostess, Mrs. Whitman, he privately declared a "fraud" and "precieuse." He daringly amused himself by conversing with her in exactly the same haughty tones she used with him, although he professed that he occasionally made his own talk even more ridiculous by giving it a "slight burlesque twist." The result was that Mrs. Whitman thought the attentive young Wister "perfectly charming." For all appearances, the two got along perfectly.[8]

As the year passed, Wister's misgivings about society intensified. While the Puritans had been cold in principle, he privately theorized, they had been "hot blooded & healthy" in spirit. Unfortunately, their cold principles—not their healthy, hot blood—had survived in their modern-day descendants. This could be seen, he declared, in a family like the Cabots, which in spite of "unusual gifts both of brain & conscience," lacked "achieving power."[9]

Neither did Wister have a high opinion of Boston's young women. He declared them "always ill-bred & often ignorant of all things in Heaven & Earth except what their first cousins are doing and saying." They were either unbearably stuffy or overly familiar. As a result, Wister, despite evidence to the contrary, insisted that he attended few parties, and on those occasions he talked to only a few young women. Exaggerating, he said he chose not to see anybody in a "society way" because it "ain't worth making the effort."[10]

To relieve this proclaimed—if exaggerated—boredom, Wister began visiting old Harvard friends, particularly two undergraduates named Winthrop Chanler and Amos French. The trio began meeting regularly after Wister's work hours, taking buggy rides or dining. "No friends of my youth surpassed, and very few others ever equaled, the wit and humor of that pair of gay seniors," Wister later remembered. He renewed his friendship, too, with Oliver Wendell Holmes, Jr., now a state judge. The friendship was cemented when Holmes, seeing Wister across the room at a Porcellian Club gathering, moved his plate and glass to sit by him. For some reason, the conversational sparks flew, and despite their age difference of two decades they were to become fast and lifelong friends.[11]

Boston society occasionally was punctuated by titillating episodes, and one of them involved Wister's good friend and former partner in Harvard musical presentations, George Waring. Waring, despite the determined opposition of his parents, precipitously married his stepmother's sister, Helen Clark Greene. At the age of thirty-six, Mrs. Green was more than a decade older than her new husband. Moreover, she brought a ready-made family of three: her own children and a fifteen-year-old adopted son. Waring, like Wister, was little more than a year out of college. "If what I hear is true, his step is literally maniacal," Wister wrote home. His own parents, he reminded them, should "never cease" to thank their lucky stars that their only son, alone in a house with attractive and kind landladies, had not married one or all of them. Waring confirmed the news to Wister in a letter, along with the information that because of intense family opposition he must "seek my fortune elsewhere." "Elsewhere" was the distant Territory of Washington, where he was to remain for many years as a pioneer settler.[12]

Music, no longer a part of Wister's daily existence, nevertheless maintained a strong grip on Wister's soul. He filled his letters with detailed descriptions and criticisms of Boston's wide offerings of musical events. His friendship with Higginson extended far beyond working hours; together they paid careful attention to the affairs of the Boston Symphony, which was destined to be a model for other city orchestras. When Higginson obtained the services of a new conductor from Vienna named Wilhelm Gericke, who did not speak English, Wister engaged Gericke in a three-and-a-half-hour conversation in German. It was the first of many such conversations between the two.[13]

When the symphony performed, for the first time, selections from Wagner's *Tristram and Isolde*, no one was more elated than Wister. "Wagner certainly supplies a need felt by *this* time," Wister wrote to his mother. "Whether for *all* time I don't think anyone can say." The continuing debate between Wister and his mother over Wagner showed no signs of abating. Sarah Wister argued that certain established canons simply should not be violated in music; Wister rejoined that great composers set their own canons, and there was no profit in one generation telling another generation what to like.[14]

At the age of twenty-four, Wister remained close to his parents. A steady flow of letters continued to emanate from Boston to Butler Place. In them Wister listed in detail his activities and his thoughts. In return, the letters from Butler Place subjected him to a close and critical scrutiny. Alternating spells of cordiality and anger marked the exchanges with his father. A residue of resentment remained because of the dominant role Dr. Wister had played in ordering his only son's life. Distance, however, had eliminated virtually every trace of Wister's hostility toward his mother. The correspondence between parents and son remained prolific if for no other reason than that Wister depended upon them for subsidy. His own salary could not accommodate his standard of living.

No sooner had Wister settled in Boston than the first argument via mail arose. Dr. and Mrs. Wister were disturbed because the trunk Owen had left behind for them to forward seemed exceptionally heavy. Dr. Wister opened the top to see why. He found that it was, in his words, "stuffed with worthlessness, bad habits, and elements of failure." To make matters worse, he had just received from Owen a request for a check of $650, a fact he bluntly pointed out.[15]

The sharp reprimand caught Wister off guard. He testily replied that in the interests of economizing he had rented "extremely small & rather inconvenient rooms" because they were the cheapest to be found. Furthermore, as a further economy he had declined to subscribe to the Assemblies (Boston's series of balls). He begged his father to recognize his new and less than satisfactory circumstances. "I did not expect to be very happy in the course of life which I have chosen though I tried to think I expected to—Perhaps as I get used to it things will not seem so bad."[16]

Dr. Wister, upon seeing his son's understandable reaction to his harsh criticism about "worthlessness, bad habits, and elements of failure," reversed his tone. "Cheer up my hearty, all fellows find the learning of a business rather a bore," he wrote. The allusions to the too-heavy trunk, he maintained, were "poetical," and he was genuinely sorry to hear that they had depressed him. Nevertheless, he could not resist the opportunity to elaborate on the matter. "I find you extravagant in a dangerous way, capable of denying yourself comfort, and indulgences of a costly sort, but inclined to be indifferent about small sums, a fatal neglect, & sure to grow." Up to now, he said, Owen's existence had been a pleasant one without worry about supporting himself. His life in Europe had not provided the best basis for an appreciation of economic necessities. "Now good night my dear Dan, and don't be unhappy because you find yourself in School after so fine a holiday," Dr. Wister concluded.[17]

This checkered pattern of correspondence continued through the spring and into summer, when Wister blamed his father for always alternating between satisfaction at his ability and irritation at his green-ness. It amused him, he observed, for he realized that his father could no more refrain from such behavior than he himself could change his own qualities or his youthfulness. Something less genial, though, had been gnawing at him for some time. He had heard from relatives and friends that Dr. Wister entertained them by mocking his son's actions and thoughts. As a result, Owen declared, he now cared less and less for home and family, and he never looked forward to visits. "There are several houses I would rather stay at, several people I would rather talk to than either of you," Wister proclaimed. Dr. Wister admitted that he had made fun of his son on one occasion, but he said that he had re-gretted it ever since because of its obvious bad taste. Aside from that single transgression, however, he pleaded innocence.[18]

To his mother, Wister expressed pride in her accomplishments and reputation. "I think your immortality is insured more by a thing you once said than by all your writing put together," he wrote to her. On the day before, but not for the first time, he had been asked to confirm whether it had been she who had originated the biting witticism: "Gen-tlemen, we understand your language, although we do not speak it." Wister said he had swelled with pride upon acknowledging that his mother was indeed responsible for that comment.[19]

Bored with his job, disillusioned for the moment with society, and at a standoff with his parents, Wister had reached a lull in his life. He turned introspective. He began reading history, savoring its meaning, and for the first time questioning his formal education which had de-viated little from traditional approaches. As a result of that education, he felt that he had been driven away from the study of history because it had been taught not as the story of human development, but as a series of sterile facts—accounts of individual Greeks, Romans, Frenchmen, and Englishmen instead of "a study of how they came to be the sort of people they were." Since the progress of human thought and civilization had been omitted, Wister believed that he had not received a "liberal" edu-cation. Now he was reading that a "*science*" of history had been dis-covered—too late it seemed for his own generation to profit, but in time for him at least to see how interesting history truly was. He charted for himself a vigorous path of reading to "remedy" the defects of his formal education.[20] In addition, he readily relayed these attitudes to his parents, who were offended that their son failed to appreciate the St. Paul's and

Harvard education which they so conscientiously had provided. Moreover, they disagreed with his opinions.

St. Paul's in particular exemplified the educational approach that Wister criticized. The school's merits or demerits were widely debated in a dispute traveling through the mail. Dr. Wister, proud and protective of the classical learning approach which continued to reign in American education, believed that Owen should be thankful that he had learned the history of the world at St. Paul's. "That is just what I should have liked to learn, and what was never taught me," countered Owen, adding that his academic honors at St. Paul's proved that he certainly had learned the required material. But what he had actually learned, according to Owen, were largely worthless facts about kings and generals, which he avowed represented about as important a contribution to knowledge as would a mere listing of his father's patients and their illnesses over the last ten years.[21]

Despite these critical feelings about his St. Paul's education, Wister's sentimental ties to the school remained undiminished. One of his particular pleasures at being in Boston was the town's proximity to St. Paul's. He visited the school often on weekends and on special occasions during this period and throughout his life. Dr. Coit and others on the school staff prized Wister as well. When it became known that he was not pleased with his job on State Street, Wister was flattered to receive another offer to join the school as a master—the ultimate compliment for any graduate.[22]

Even with his fondness for St. Paul's, Wister had no qualms in declining the invitation. As the debate with his parents had shown, his misgivings about the classical curriculum were too profound for him to teach in such a system. More instrumental than that, perhaps, was a more substantive change: the radical shift in his religious beliefs. He no longer accepted the literal scriptural interpretations that were so thoroughly a part of Dr. Coit's instruction and of St. Paul's. In the summer of 1884 Wister felt compelled to proclaim his rejection of literalness, and he boldly described his new beliefs to Dr. Coit in a conversation. He reaffirmed his position by letter.[23]

Wister's boldness made Dr. Coit so angry that he at first declined to answer his former pupil's letter. As far as Dr. Coit was concerned, Wister's beliefs qualified as a rejection of Christianity. His answer to the young "heretic" eventually came, however: "I have been very much grieved and shocked about you. While I cannot cease to care for you, and to pray that God would so deepen your moral nature that you may be led to the knowledge of Himself and of His Blessed Son." Dr. Coit admitted that because of this he no longer could hold Wister in the same relation to himself, or to the school, as before. "No one can be really loyal to this place who regards the starting point and basis of its life & teaching a delusion, or even a matter of uncertainty." Only Wister could suffer from such beliefs, Dr. Coit pointed out, for God's faith was none the worse for this defection.[24]

Wister, not having fully realized the impact his message would cause, appeared truly contrite for having brought so much pain. He apologized sincerely to Dr. Coit, imploring him to excuse any comments that might have seemed unsuitable coming from one so young as himself. If he had been guilty of presumptuous behavior it was only because he had wished to be "absolutely candid." Dr. Coit repeated that he had not been offended, only shocked and grieved, and that to answer Wister in proper detail would be immensely time-consuming. "You might not quite understand if I told you how your letter strikes me, and you might only be stimulated to look up arguments instead of really caring for & reaching after God's truth."[25]

The breach obviously distressed Wister. Four months afterwards he was still expressing his concern to Dr. Coit's brother, vice-rector at St. Paul's, who sought, as he had done before, to reassure Wister. Dr. Coit, Wister was told, still felt "kindly and affectionately" toward him, but at the same time he was "greatly pained & shocked." Wister was reminded that he would feel the same way if he held Dr. Coit's views.[26]

This "heretical" shift in the thought of a favored alumnus could not remain a secret. Sherman Evarts, a former St. Paul's classmate, wrote to Wister to say that he was "so sorry to hear that you too have entirely cut loose from all the belief to which you were brought up." Such a thing, he said, was not uncommon in this age of Darwinism, for "all" of his best friends had adopted scientific notions which would not permit them to accept any part of the Christian faith.[27]

This painful episode taught Wister a lifelong lesson. Never again would he acknowledge anything that smacked of unorthodoxy in his religious views. In all his later religious utterances, he held, in every respect, the fundamentalist notions he had been taught as a child.

Boston was a city of clubs. As in London, the best men in the area had a tradition of meeting for conversation, food, and drink in organizations like the Radical Club and the Saturday Club. One group which sprang up in 1884 was destined to carry this mantle of intellectual companionship far into the twentieth century and served as a lifelong retreat for Wister. "We are getting up a little club," artist Benjamin Porter told Wister and other employees of the Union Safe Deposit Vault. Wister agreed to join the Tavern Club as a charter member along with a group of writers, artists, doctors, lawyers, and businessmen who formed its core. They prevailed upon William Dean Howells to be their president, obtained meeting rooms at One Park Square, and set a membership limit of one hundred.[28]

"Last night I had a most delightful evening," Wister wrote after his first session. After dinner the members had enjoyed music and singing, then they had retired upstairs to a studio belonging to a member, Frederick P. Vinton, for more talk. "Altogether it was extremely wholly & unlike America," Wister observed. The club was "just what was wanted." Dinner could be had for sixty cents, yearly assessments were just twenty-five dollars, and all the men of the "nicest" connections and backgrounds had become members. For Wister, one especially noteworthy meeting occurred that first night, when he sat just one chair removed from William Dean Howells. Just as Wister earlier had developed friendships with older men of distinct achievement—Phillips Brooks and Oliver Wendell Holmes, Jr., for instance—he now struck up a conversation that prompted Howells to ask Wister to call on him soon. This Wister would do.[29]

The Tavern Club proved at once to be a very bright light in Wister's life. His letters brimmed with references to pleasant evenings spent alongside the liveliest men in Boston. The members made up a "rare, harmonious motley" who jested and romped and drank Chianti. One person even brought in a bear to be the club mascot, but that experiment failed. A guest from England one evening told a joke about Henry James which Wister repeated to his mother. " 'Oh, in London most of us don't have time to go out much,' " the visitor said. " 'But we can generally tell when the season is over—for when the Duchesses have gone out of town Mr. Henry James is very apt to look us up.' "[30]

One of the most satisfying relationships for Wister was his new friendship with Howells, the sturdily framed, kindly, and graying literary hero. He began to visit Howells often that summer and autumn, sounding out his opinions on various matters. It soon dawned on Wister that Howells was much further to the left in politics than he had imagined.

Wister recalled an afternoon in which he found Howells in his library overlooking the Charles River, where the writer earlier had been watching the Harvard Class races.

"I had a sort of religious experience this afternoon," Howells told his visitor. "People down there in the alley along the water climbed on my back fence to watch the rowing; and a policeman was busy making them get off. I sent for him and thanked him. Then it came over me, what better right than those in the alley had I to be sitting comfortably in this room?"

Wister protested, assuring Howells that he had earned his luxury through his literary gift and hard work.

"Yes, yes; but it oughtn't be," Howells responded.

On another occasion the pair were discussing Weir Mitchell's novels. Howells regarded them highly, and he exclaimed sadly, "But I fear he's on the side of the nobles."[31]

Although Wister could not fully realize it at the time, the friendship had begun during an important year in Howells's life. For one thing, this was the period when he began his thorough questioning of the existing social system. In addition, Howells had begun writing that summer one of his greatest novels, *The Rise of Silas Lapham*. While his approaching deadline for the first installment in *Century* magazine caused him to limit his activities, he did not close his doors to the young clerk from State Street. Years later Wister would feel justified in calling Howells his mentor in these days.[32]

Meanwhile, amidst such stimulating experiences, the drudgery of office routine paled even further by comparison. No doubt inspired in part by Howells, Wister returned to an old enthusiasm: writing. At first he only nibbled at its edges by urging others to write. He suggested that his grandmother write a novel; she declined. Then his mother spurned the same recommendation.[33]

A friend named Tom Wharton already was writing fiction, and Wister criticized the manuscript of his second novel, *Cradge,* with uncommon confidence. Wharton's style, he told him, was "not dignified"; his heroine was common. Overall, however, the book impressed him, for he told his mother—if not Wharton—that it was "surprisingly good."[34]

Wister surely thought that he could do better, and in the fall of 1884 he decided to try. During work hours he outlined the plot of a novel from the same high stool on which he computed interest at two and a half percent. He entitled it "A Wise Man's Son"; the plot was entirely

71

predictable. It described the youthful adventures of a boy at "High Church School" who was born to be an artist but whose father forced him into business. Not quite so familiar was the romantic subplot: after experiencing an unsuccessful love affair, the hero wound up in the arms of a wife who was wrong for him. The plot was easy enough, but writing the story was not. Wister soon determined that he needed assistance. He persuaded his friend and distant cousin, Langdon Mitchell, to assist him. Mitchell, a Harvard student, was S. Weir Mitchell's son. The two youths worked diligently on the manuscript past the New Year and into the spring of 1885, with the bulk of the work falling on Wister.[35]

Despite his busy and not altogether unsatisfactory life in Boston, an old nemesis—ill health—had been bothering Wister off and on since the spring of 1884. A strange malady, probably one known today as Bell's Palsy, struck in April; an entire side of his face was semiparalyzed for more than a month. Blinking on that side was difficult, and the slowness of his reflexes caused some concern for the eye's condition. Dr. Wister came to Boston to check on his son, but there was little to be done, and he agreed with a specialist that Owen might as well continue to work as long as it involved no special pain or damage to his eye.[36]

"I wish I were a stronger person," Wister lamented in September. "It will prevent my ever doing very much." He believed that his capacity for enduring prolonged hard work was "certainly limited," and while he hoped his constitution would strengthen, he was not confident of it. "This is the sort of thing one must reconcile oneself to once for all—and I think that I have done so. But the possibility that I am mistaken is not to be taken into account as a working principle." He declared that he had made every effort to get fresh air and exercise, but this had not been enough. He continued to express concern over his health in January 1885. He declined to attend a reception and ball merely because he felt "seedy," and the next day he stayed home from work. He warned his father not to be alarmed. "I am becoming more particular about the state of my body than about anything else in the world." He feared a renewed siege of paralysis of his face. A year earlier, under the same circumstances, he would have worked. The problem now, he believed, was his recent failure to get proper exercise.[37]

Adding to Wister's problems was the fact that the promised position as a broker with Lee, Higginson and Company still had not materialized. The fault, evidently, did not lie in his performance at the Union Safe Deposit Vault. His friendship with the Lees and Higginsons continued as close as ever. When his face was paralyzed he had spent a week in the Higginson home. He and Colonel Higginson were often together at the Tavern Club or at symphonies. Nevertheless, it was becoming more and more apparent that he could not remain a clerk indefinitely; he must think of his future. By August of 1884 he and his father had agreed upon a new career. He would become a lawyer. There was no mention of returning to music. Wister could not leave his job until the January work rush was over, though, and that meant enrollment at the Harvard law school had to be delayed until fall 1885.

The earlier plan—to resume his musical studies if business failed—obviously would not have received his father's endorsement, and Wister did not seek it. Yet he lacked enthusiasm about becoming a lawyer. "I would go to the Harvard Law School, since American respectability accepted lawyers, no matter how bad, which I was likely to be, and re-jected composers, even if they were good, which I might possibly be," Wister wrote years later. On a weekend at Manchester he showed Henry Lee Higginson a letter to Dr. Wister concerning his willingness to study law. Higginson replied that the plan "probably" was the best course, and he advised Wister not to be too critical of his father, for parents' roles were difficult.[38]

Wister thus returned home to work temporarily in Francis Rawle's law firm while awaiting the start of law school. Rawle was an influential attorney who specialized in corporation, railroad, and patent law. Wister's heart, predictably, was not in his new job, and he spent much of his time working on the novel with Langdon Mitchell.

By April 1 they had finished a first draft of some 200,000 words. "There's a good deal to be rewritten—wasn't direct enough—too pale," Wister wrote to Chapman, who received frequent reports on the book's progress. The work was "full of faults," but Wister thought rewriting already had improved the passages by as much as fifty percent, and thus he was optimistic.[39]

They based their characters on people they knew or knew of, and few if any of those people would have appreciated their characterizations. In the manuscript's pages, one could find Dr. Coit, Budd Appleton, George Abbott James, August M. Swift, Matthew Arnold, Oscar Wilde, a "half dozen Maison Dorce strumpets," and some clerks at Lee, Higginson and Company. No one would be fooled by the thin disguises, Wister realized, and if the book ever were published he would be forced to "retire to Tasmania." Their great hope for publication was an anticipated recommendation by William Dean Howells. In January Howells had read thirty of Wister's pages, and he had complimented the work—or so Wister and Mitchell thought—by saying that even he could not have written it with so much energy. Now, six months later, Wister thought he was improving those pages through rewriting. His optimism knew few boundaries. "If he [Howells] thought that about some 30 pages that did not satisfy me at all—he'll think so doubly now, for I've made 'em 20% better at least—and so with several other short portions." The plan was to offer the manuscript, accompanied by a flattering note from Howells, to the publishing firm of Osgood & Co. Meanwhile, Wister made sure to send Howells occasional notes outlining his progress.[40]

On May 21, the revision complete, Wister mailed the manuscript to Mitchell in Cambridge to give to Howells. At the same time, Wister wrote Howells a flattering letter, citing the many instances in which he had followed his earlier suggestions and thanking him for his past encouragement. "I am more grateful to you than I can say. Your remarks have had more influence on my really doubting estimation of what I've done than anyone's would have had that I can think of. Perhaps this is because they took me by surprise with their favourableness. If you had been severer & less encouraging, I suppose I might have not believed you so easily!!" Meanwhile, he complimented Howells on *The Rise of Silas Lapham* which now was being serialized in *Century*. "If you like to hear lay readers give vent to their enthusiasm I wish you could hear my father & mother & all of us."[41]

Wister's high expectations soon were shattered. Howells promptly returned the manuscript with his candid opinion: Wister should never show the manuscript in its present form to any publisher. It wasn't so much that it did not reveal talent, for it did, but someone might print it, and years later a mature Wister would regret that fact. It was a "rebellious" work, and such a book from such a young American would shock the public gravely, Howells warned, for its pages contained hard swearing, hard drinking, and too much knowledge of good and evil. "So much young man never seems to have gotten into a book before," he told the aspiring author. He suggested, too, that Wister's plan to publish the work anonymously was inappropriate. It indicated that he was not willing to stand behind his own book. There was no doubt, he added, but that inside Wister there resided whatever mysterious element was required to be a writer. But the present manuscript should undergo major revision or else simply be put away. If put away, Wister might yet benefit, for in time it would furnish him a "mine of material."[42]

The effort surely was difficult, but Wister managed in his response to conceal what must have been acute disappointment. "You are right— perfectly right," he wrote back to Howells. He professed that now he himself could see that the novel just "won't do." At present he could not alter the book, for that would be "hypocritical." Thus, he told Howells, he was consigning the manuscript to "a high dusty shelf to possess whatever soul it may have in patience." Meanwhile, he hoped to begin calling on Howells once more in the fall when he was back in Cambridge.[43]

But before fall arrived, an event occurred that Wister himself would hail as a major turning point in his life. He suffered—or at least he thought he suffered—a collapse in health. Its specific origin and nature are unclear, and the precise time it occurred is unknown.* Certainly the date was after his June 1 letter to Howells in which he responded to his criticisms, and before June 30. Perhaps the breakdown was precipitated by the rejected novel, perhaps by his disappointment in business, perhaps because he was going to law school rather than returning to music. It is impossible to do more than speculate. It seems certain that the collapse was more a case of shattered nerves than of physical decline. Langdon Mitchell's father, Weir Mitchell, was a renowned specialist in treating nervous disorders, and Wister went to this physician-novelist for consultation. Dr. Mitchell, tall and distinguished-looking, had devised in the 1870s a unique treatment for the nervous and mental ills that so frequently seemed to afflict the upper classes in this age. It was a treatment that had gained widespread acceptance. Known as the "Weir Mitchell treatment" or the "rest cure," it was based on Mitchell's emphasis that a person's mental and physical conditions were closely related. Typically, the treatment was based on rest, massage, diet, and exercise, and the cure often consisted of prolonged visits to Europe for relaxation. Dr. Wister had taken such a "rest cure" a dozen years earlier when the family went to Europe; Sarah Wister had done so only a year earlier,

* One writer, Ben Merchant Vorpahl, has claimed without documentation that Wister experienced a "severe breakdown in health" in January 1885, suffering from intense headaches, vertigo, terrifying dreams, and optical and auditory hallucinations. Yet if a breakdown of this precise nature occurred, the recovery was remarkably rapid, for the major portion of Wister's novel was written in the spring of that year, and Wister did not mention these problems in the available letters of that period. (Vorpahl, *My Dear Wister: The Frederic Remington-Owen Wister Letters* [Palo Alto: American West Publishing Co., 1972], p. 17.)

when she stayed in Paris with her son. Both likely had done so on Mitchell's recommendation.[44]

Mitchell prescribed for Owen a different geographical setting for recovery, a prescription that ultimately would affect the popular culture of an entire nation. He advised this young sophisticate, this eastern dandy, to go where he had never had the slightest inclination to go—to the great American West. There he should live out of doors and get a healthy dose of plain surroundings. "And make acquaintances, my friend," Dr. Mitchell said. "See more new people. Learn to sympathize with your fellow man a little more than you're inclined to." It was not the kind of advice one expected from the fastidious Dr. Mitchell, a man who habitually wore a velvet office coat and carried handkerchiefs redolent with cologne, but the eminent physician had unusual insight. He knew his patient well; he had delivered him into the world as an infant, and he had watched him ever since. "You don't feel kindly to your race, you know," he advised the distraught young man, who was in a mood to listen. "There are lots of humble folks in the fields you'd be the better for knowing." Be certain, he said, to carry riding clothes and half a dozen light novels—but not French ones.[45]

There had been disappointment in music, in business, and in novel writing. Now came the moment that would change Wister's life forever.

Chapter V

DISCOVERY
(1885)

IF HE WERE NOT ACTUALLY BROKEN IN HEALTH, certainly Wister was disillusioned and dispirited when on June 30, 1885, he stepped aboard the Limited Express at the Philadelphia train station to carry out Dr. Mitchell's prescription for recovery. It had been arranged for him to go to Wyoming to regain vigor at a cattle ranch north of the Laramie Mountains. With him were two of his mother's spinster friends, the energetic Maisie Irwin, who with her sister Agnes operated a Philadelphia girls' school, and a Miss Sophy, who assisted the Irwins. The women, both in their forties, were to watch over their young companion, as well as to refresh themselves through the invigorating atmosphere of the raw West.

Less than an hour after leaving the train station Wister dutifully wrote a message to his mother on a postal card. On it he recorded a singularly striking fact: in thirty short minutes the train had carried him—a seasoned traveler who had crossed the Atlantic several times—farther west into America than he had been in his entire life!

In Chicago the trio changed trains and then sped westward in earnest via the Union Pacific's great Overland Route. By the third day out of Philadelphia, the tracks had crossed the Missouri River between Council Bluffs and Omaha, and Wister observed from his Pullman car that the West was "a very much bigger place than the East." With nothing more than the view from his window as a basis, he decided that here was the future America, "bubbling and seething in bare legs and pinafores." It was a state of mind that for many years would provide his framework for viewing the West. And considering his own eastern heritage and values, it was a judgment that easily could have assumed an altogether opposite nature. As the tracks stretched pleasantly over rolling plains, he sensed an absence of the kinds of eastern pressures that had harmed his spirit and health. "I don't wonder a man never comes back after he has once been here for a few years," he wrote. He had not yet alighted, but already he seemed fully aware that the West offered to him challenge and opportunity of a new kind. Never mind that his stay was to be only for a summer. His family connections would be of far less assistance here than in the parlors and counting rooms of Philadelphia and Boston. Perhaps it was this realization that prompted him to forego his customary reserve and chat amiably with the "nice nigger" who served him breakfast. Upon finishing the meal he tipped the black man fifty cents and entreated him to pray for him. The waiter readily consented, but he pointed out that the traveler also "must do a little praying" for himself.[1]

Life, it seemed, was beginning anew. Past frustrations and old dreams could be left behind. Rather than the failed novel, it was the abandoned musical career that haunted his thoughts. Somewhere along the way, amidst hours of idleness on the train, he composed a soul-searching poem. Was he a failure? Should he have persisted with music? The answer to the latter question, it seemed, was yes. Music had been a challenge which stood clearly before him. "I had heard it close beside the pillow, whispering in my ear." Then came morning and doubts which caused him to lose "sight of that I had to do . . . And then the sun set, with my task not done."* (Not until ten years had passed did he publish the poem, and then he noted on the margins of the original that he had written it when he was on "bad terms" with himself and the world and "sick" as well.) On another scrap of paper he wrote a more plainspoken "confession," subtitling it with his age, "Aet 24 and 11 mo." "Were I surer of my powers,—or rather were my powers surer—I think I should not now be in America, but wandering with musicians and other disreputable people—having kicked over all traces." He had not done so, he realized, because of the existence of "a fortunate grain of common sense self knowledge which says 'You're too nearly like other people to do more than appreciate & sympathize with revolution'—thus I remain conventional & am saved from fiasco." The problem for Wister—and surely one source of his inner turmoil—was his conviction that his deep in-stinct for music was true. Yet his conventional sense of what was proper did not permit him to pursue his talent. Unable to reconcile the two, he opted for convention and safety.[2]

As the train moved into Wyoming, the scenery brought romantic visions. The landscape reminded him of northern Spain and Wagnerian opera sets. "We passed this morning [July 3] the most ominous and forbidding chasm of rocks I ever saw in any country. Deep down below

* He entitled the poem "The Pale Cast of Thought."

a camp fire is burning. It all looked like Die Walkure—this which is much more than my romantic dreams could have hoped." That evening, after four days on the train, Wister and his two lady companions disembarked at Rock Creek, some forty miles north of Laramie, and gazed about with unrestrained wonder at the primitive surroundings and plainspoken Westerners. They spent the night there in a hotel owned by the former territorial governor of Wyoming, John M. Thayer, and the next morning they arose at 6 A.M. to climb aboard a stagecoach pulled by a four-horse team for a fifty-five mile ride through the Laramie Range to Fort Fetterman.[3]

The scenery was breathtaking, and so were the smelly characters who regaled endlessly at rude stagecoach stops, perhaps exaggerating their words and actions for the open-eyed, conspicuous eastern dudes. Wister began filling his journal with examples of this metaphorically rich language. One man complained that he did not know what time it was because "his watch was bucking." At a "road ranch" where Wister slept on the rough wooden floor between blankets, he overheard another colorful description: "Now I want you to understand that Little Jim was afeerd of just nothing at all. Why he'd pile into an elephant or a Zodiac or any of those almanac critters just as lief he would pile into a skeeter—and him the size of the latter animal." As for the valleys and mountains, Wister said he could not possibly relate their beauty—but he tried anyway. Their desolateness reminded him of what the moon must be like, but then the stagecoach would round a bend and descend toward a green valley filled with horsemen, wagons, and hundreds of cattle. It was so elemental, so dominated by nature, it was "like Genesis."[4]

Compared to the East, Wyoming Territory certainly may have been "like Genesis." Although it was not to become a state until five years later, the area already had experienced several distinct stages in its development. Its mountainous terrain and sparkling streams and rivers, rich in fur-bearing animals, first had attracted adventurous trappers who made money from this natural resource. One of those fur traders, Manuel Lisa, built the first fort in that part of the country in 1807. The Choteau brothers, working with Lisa, formed the Missouri Fur Company in 1808 and operated in the area, too, as did William H. Ashley, who created with John Jacob Astor the North American Fur Company. Other early explorers, adventurers, and entrepreneurs who crisscrossed the land that would become Wyoming were Wilson Price Hunt, Jedediah Smith,

William L. and Milton Sublette, Captain Benjamin L. E. Bonneville, and Jim Bridger. General John Charles Frémont, accompanied by mountain man Kit Carson, led his first expedition to South Pass in 1842, and Army outposts of more or less permanent nature ultimately followed. The Oregon Trail, gateway to the Pacific coast for thousands of restless and ambitious Americans, cut a path directly through Wyoming to cross the Rockies at the remarkably accessible South Pass.

A more substantial avenue to the West across Wyoming came later. The steel tracks of the Union Pacific Railway tied the territory inextricably with the rest of the nation in 1869, and in the following decade the scent of gold attracted a new kind of visitor intent on economic gain: the prospector. Beginning at about the same time, still another venture proved to be longer lived: the cattle industry. The 1870s and 1880s were marked by the wide utilization of open ranges for fattening cattle, many of which came up trails from Texas. By the time Wister arrived, Wyoming was a cattle country first and last. No other interests were nearly so powerful as the stock raisers. The human population of the entire territory numbered less than 65,000, a puny figure compared to the 1.1 million cattle roaming over the unfenced and nutritious grasslands. The attention of investors from the entire world focused on this latest El Dorado; Europeans owned many of the ranches in absentia. One cowboy reminisced that the territory was the "last frontier" and that "all cowboys were bent on reaching Wyoming, the haven of adventure and romance." Wister thus received his initial impression of the cowboy empire while it was in its heyday, a period he would later popularize. The timing was important, for just a year away loomed the hard and devastating winter of 1886–87, a winter that signaled the beginning of far less prosperous times for the cattle industry.[5]

The bumpy, cramped stagecoach ride took the travelers through mountainous terrain that had seen Indians, explorers, trappers, prospectors, and now cowmen. The inevitable contact with coarse characters of uncertain background would have disgusted many of Wister's friends. Those eastern tourists who had begun going West in the 1870s usually managed to carry with them many of the appurtenances of their customary lives; they largely avoided unpleasant encounters. Pullman cars, their usual mode of travel, were lavishly furnished. Grand hotels and resorts such as the Manitou at Colorado Springs had the clear aim of reproducing eastern comforts and habits in a rural setting. Wister, though, had no intention of duplicating the setting he had fled: he sought a change in both health and soul. His college friend Theodore Roosevelt already had set a pattern for embracing the strenuous life of the West at its own level. Roosevelt had found the West so stimulating that he purchased a Dakota ranch in 1883 and at this very moment was seriously engaged in life as a cattleman. Roosevelt was not the only Harvard man to go West. Already in the Wyoming ranching business were three other Harvard classmates of Wister's: Hubert Teschemacher and Frederic deBillier, owners of a cattle company bearing their names, and Richard Trimble, who served as their co-manager. Trimble, in fact, met Wister on a brief stopover at Cheyenne's train depot, welcoming him to Wyoming over a round of drinks at the Cheyenne Club.[6]

Late in the day on the Fourth of July, the stagecoach delivered its passengers to a stop some twenty-five miles southwest of Fort Fetterman called "Point of Rocks." The stop amounted to no more than a crude log cabin, its cracks stuffed with mud and its walls lined with old newspapers for warmth. While Wister huddled with the two ladies next to a tiny hot stove to ward off the evening mountain chill, he scribbled at length to his mother for the first time since leaving home, using the only instrument available at the moment, a blunt violet pencil.[7]

His mother, he knew, would have despised the entire experience, and it was fun for him to tell her how much he, on the contrary, welcomed it. "When I've been most enjoying myself I've laughed and likewise shuddered to think how you would have probably hated every minute." Everything she most abhorred had happened at least twice, including such activities as "going to bed with your brothers and sisters, visiting with them, talking with them, eating & drinking with them." At the current humble stage stop, a Mr. and Mrs. Morgan from Virginia were the proprietors. She lay ill in bed, but her husband cheerfully fulfilled his wife's duties, including making the beds for the guests. Wister noticed especially the extreme gentleness with which Morgan cared for his ailing wife, and he never forgot it.* The simple meal, punctuated by the cowboys' and stagecoach hands' lively and homespun conversation, was an absolute delight.[8]

The elevation at Point of Rocks was 8,200 feet, and Wister proclaimed the air to be better than any. "Each breath you take tells you no one else has ever used it before you." The scenery was "wild and

---

* Wister later said that this man from Virginia served as the original inspiration for his fictitious cowboy hero, the "Virginian." (Owen Wister, "Preface—a Best Seller," *The Writings of Owen Wister: The Virginian* [New York: Macmillan Co., 1928], p. xiii.)

desolate"; he and the ladies already had seen from their stagecoach antelope, wolves, and all sorts of wild animals. "Altogether everything is all & more than could be expected."[9]

In such an exhilarated state, Wister and his companions reached their final destination shortly after noon on the next day, a Sunday, just in time for lunch. The VR Ranch, their home for the remainder of the summer, was in what soon would become Converse County. The Oregon Trail and Pony Express both had crossed on VR Ranch property. The ranch house in this picturesque mountainous setting was a "marvelous" one-storied stone structure, cool and clean. Persian rugs covered the inside hall floor; a giant fireplace encircled by comfortable chairs offered cheer; a piano, in better condition than the one at the Wister house, stood waiting; and a delightful dining room was tended graciously by a Chinese waiter and complemented nicely by an abundance of white linen.* Fifty yards above the house was a tributary of the North Platte River, a pretty, clear stream called Deer Creek which spilled over rounded rocks through an undulating green valley. Rolling hills beyond the valley introduced mountains which stood up "long, regular & blue." They were not unlike the Jura, Wister thought, although more severe. Behind the creek and the main house, stretching for a quarter of a mile until interrupted by a bluff, were other structures—various log cabins for the ranch hands, stables, and corrals. The ranch, an old Mormon station, had been placed at an elevation of 6,640 feet, at the spot where the Little Deer Creek joined the main tributary as it flowed down from the Laramie Range to the North Platte. About a mile to the north the creek passed through the walls of Lower Deer Creek Canyon. One could easily imagine that a tenderfoot such as Wister would be overcome by such a lovely scene, but even longtime Wyoming residents agreed that the VR Ranch was exceptionally situated. One such resident who visited it in this same summer of 1885 described its setting as one of "supreme beauty" enhanced by a "pleasant garden, little rills of water, bubbling, singing, spreading themselves about the plots of vegetables, and over the lawn."[10]

The man who owned the ranch was a plainspoken gentleman named Frank Wolcott, a Kentuckian of Scottish descent who had acquired the title of "Major" by serving on the Union side in the Civil War. Wolcott

* An 1889 visitor to the ranch stated that all the servants were Chinese. (Lucia G. Putnam, "The Romance of Old Trails," *Annals of Wyoming* 6 [July-October 1929], p. 197.)

had been United States marshal for Wyoming Territory in 1871–72. Before that, he was the territorial receiver of public monies. In 1878 he founded the VR Ranch (the initials honoring Queen Victoria Regina and also standing as the appellation "Valley Ranch") and served simultaneously as the area's justice of the peace. A hearty, stocky, mustachioed man whose brother was a senator in Colorado, Wolcott possessed soldierly virtues, but, as the history of the Wyoming Stock Growers Association relates, he was handicapped by the shortcomings of a military martinet. A few years afterwards Wolcott was to gain national headlines when, as the commander of a vigilante group, he was arrested by the United States Army for insurrection. "He was a fire-eater, honest, clean, a rabid Republican with a complete absence of tact, very well educated and when you know him a most delightful companion. . . . Most people hated him, many feared him, a few loved him," an acquaintance said of him. Wolcott, his wife, and their young daughter were kind and generous, however, to their guests from the East. How the family happened to play host to Wister and the two ladies in this instance is uncertain. They may have been friends of Wister's parents or of Dr. Weir Mitchell's; there also was a possibility that the Irwin family had a small financial interest in the ranch.[11]

The tonic for Wister's restoration was a robust, spartan existence in this unspoiled land. On the first night he bedded down on the floor of a room normally used as an office, but on the next day he set up a tent for sleeping outside which would ensure an abundance of fresh mountain air. After his first night in the tent he began what would become his daily habit: a soul-stirring dip in the "very cold swift crystal" water of Deer Creek. After the first of these morning baths, while dressing, he suddenly heard a commotion on the bridge above. Looking up, he saw a herd of steers curiously eyeing him. Presently a cowboy came along who observed that if the pale tenderfoot would hide himself, the steers might move on across the bridge. Wister readily obliged, frightening in the process eight wild ducks who flew away. After breakfast he joined Wolcott for a horseback ride over the nearby countryside, dodging in and out of the undergrowth and hearing the Major point out and describe the various breeds of cattle. In the afternoon Miss Maisie and Miss Sophy joined them for a rough carriage ride to the beautiful wild canyon that Deer Creek penetrated not far away. Pennsylvania did not seem to be in the same hemisphere as this remarkable place.[12]

The summer was filled with long horseback rides, hunting and fishing expeditions, roundups, and other special occasions. On his first hunting trip, Wister surprised himself by killing two grouse in four shots and bagging a deer on a first shot that hit it "plumb" in the shoulder and "broke its heart." He also hunted and shot ducks, curlews, snipe, prairie chickens, sage hens, and rattlesnakes. He caught a live gopher, intending to game it until it escaped the box. A week later he acquired for taming two fierce young hawks. The familiar "hare" he knew in the East became something altogether different here—the jackrabbit. "Every time one of them gets up from under a sage clump and goes lolloping over the prairie I am sent into fits of laughter," Wister said. "He doesn't look as if the Lord made him—but exactly as if he had been wound up & taken out of Schwarze's [sic] window."[13]

Wister was not altogether a typical eastern dude, for he was a skilled horseback rider. However, when he first mounted one of the ranch horses it lay down in protest. Wister, unruffled, remained calm and persistent; the horse finally climbed to its feet and the ride began, continuing without further incident. The same horse, "Stockings," some days later opened the corral gates and released the other horses into the "wide, wide world." Wister, upon seeing what had happened, mounted another horse and singlehandedly rounded up the loose animals. Despite such episodes, Stockings became his favorite mount. The horse was about fourteen hands high with a very thick mane and top knot, the "most knowing-looking animal" Wister had ever seen. "I am convinced he could speak French if he tried." Wister soon began spending hours every day on horseback. "I find riding these bronchos the easiest long-distance riding I've ever experienced," he recorded in his journal. If horses represented no difficulty, some of the terminology did. Wister, a careful speller, spelled "corral" first as "Koral" and then as "Coraal." He confessed in a letter to John Jay Chapman's mother, with whom he corresponded frequently, that he spelled it differently every time he wrote it.[14]

The impact of the Wyoming environment and routine was immediate and personal.

> To ride 20 miles and see no chance of seeing human traces; to get up on a mountain & overlook any number of square miles of strange volcanic looking convolutions—& never a column of smoke or a sound except the immediate grasshoppers. . . . You begin to wonder if there is such a place as Philadelphia anywhere—& if so—*where?*[15]

Wister's deep sense of antithesis between the civilized East and the untamed West was constant. Now and in the next few years, as he traveled on the frontier, the contrast was paramount in his mind. Because he had been so steeped in the genteel society of the East, and indeed of Europe, the differences made an especially vivid impression. The unique condition of the West, where the ties of tradition did not bind, held significant import, Wister believed, for the nation's future. Whatever the "American" might become in the future, he was still in the process of creation here in the "utilitarian civilization" of the West. Wister became convinced that the true American would be shaped not in the East with its artificial restraints, but in this primitive land, where the natural processes of evolution were weeding out the inferior man. Easterners, Wister wrote to John Jay Chapman, would not be the pattern because they were "too clogged with Europe to have any real national marrow." It did not matter that nearly every man, woman, and cowboy he met came from the East and usually from New England, for once in the West, eastern traces soon disappeared. "No matter how completely the East may be the headwaters from which the West has flown and is flowing," he said, "it won't be a century before the West is simply the true American, with thought, type, and life of its own kind." The western-produced man could not possibly be mistaken for anything else; he would be "an entirely original American gentleman." He would be just as independent as the man Wister and Wolcott saw one day walking along with a pack strapped on his shoulders. "Left off?" shouted Wolcott. "Yes," the dusty walker replied. "Got enough of the work up there?" Wolcott asked. The man responded readily, "Yes, my system's full of it."[16]

Wister feared, however, that unless the West took special precautions, undesirable attitudes of the East might infiltrate and "damn this western expanse of virgin soil." Already he saw people who wanted Wyoming to have a town as "good as New York." If better sense than that did not prevail, he knew he could forget his idea that a superior American civilization would develop here. "It will slowly New Yorkify and rot. We'll have horses better bred than the women who ride them, and dogs with pedigrees longer than their masters."[17]

One thing, and one thing only, did Wister dislike—the wind. He would be sitting quietly in his tent on a cloudless day or on a moonlit night when suddenly with no warning a gush of wind would sweep through, blowing things off the table and ripping out tent pegs. Once the entire tent collapsed. Such gales usually would last about fifteen minutes.[18]

Methodically he set out to master the details of the embryonic civilization about him, recording carefully in his journal every pertinent event and observation. He indicated no desire to be the chronicler himself of this nascent society, but the idea occurred that *someone* should be describing it before history passed it by. He wrote to Mrs. Chapman of his conviction that a book must be written about the cowboy. Since Wister himself was making copious observations in his notebook and in letters, it is certain that he did not exclude himself from one day fulfilling that role. But he did not admit to such a goal.[19]

Two days after his twenty-fifth birthday he saw firsthand the potential violence that loomed just beneath the surface in a land where the power of the law—other than that wielded by Wolcott himself—often was miles away. The occasion was a confrontation, punctuated with profanity and cocked rifles, between Wolcott and a squatter named Branam who once had been a gardener at the ranch. The dispute had been simmering for a year, after Branam had settled on land claimed and improved by Wolcott. What brought it to a head was a chance discovery by one of Wolcott's hands that Branam now was digging a ditch on the property. Wolcott, accompanied by Wister, went to investigate. When Wolcott found the squatter working with a loaded rifle at his side, the rancher retreated in order to get his own rifle. Then he went back to confront Branam on equal footing. Nothing more violent than profanities were exchanged, Wolcott cursing the man with a wide vocabulary of swear words gained from the military. He considered the possibility of a "little court on the premises," but the affair ended two days later when Branam quietly picked up his belongings and disappeared.[20]

Wister himself deliberately refrained from carrying arms unless he was hunting, as did "any sensible person," he wrote to Chapman. "A revolver in your belt is a mere invitation for a row. I concluded before I came I would bring none, and I find I anticipated the education a tenderfoot receives on coming here with concealed deadly weapons." To be armed was a tip-off that you were either a knave or a fool, and he had escaped both fates.[21]

His relations with the cowboys were mostly amiable, and certainly revealing. One night a group of them just in from the range brought him unwelcome guests. "Oh heaven," he declared, "last night—bed bugs. Cowboys brought 'em when they paid our tent their visit." The only way to escape the pests was to move the tent, which Wister did, "far away from the horrid site."[22]

In mid-June Wister and Wolcott made a 180-mile round trip to the

frontier settlement of Medicine Bow to pick up trout and bass fingerlings to stock Deer Creek. The journey was full of misadventure. Wister
found Medicine Bow itself a "fearful place" consisting of little more than
a train station and a number of "wooden horrors for various purposes."
Having nothing else to do, he determined to record the precise details
of this mean town while waiting for the train to arrive with the load of
fingerlings. As he walked over the settlement he carefully listed in his
notebook each structure: one store, two eating houses, one billiard hall,
six "shanties," one feed stable, and enough additional miscellaneous
buildings to total twenty-nine.* At supper a waitress whose stomach
protruded awkwardly served corned beef which tasted like a "hammock."
The train was not due until after midnight, and the owner of the one
store in town permitted Wister and Wolcott to bed down on the counter
top, making mattresses of coats and comforts from the sale racks. When
the train arrived with the one thousand bass and the two thousand trout,
the containers were transferred to the wagon, and at 2 A.M. Wister and
Wolcott headed their team across the moonlit plains for Deer Creek.
Before dawn they briefly lost their way, and the next day the hot sun
killed all the trout. Wister shot at eight mountain sheep on the seven-
teen-hour return ride, missing them all because of the distance. The ride
through one spectacular canyon made the trip worth all the trouble,
though, in his opinion.

> Rocks were thrown together in such architectural heaps that I could
> have imagined a druid sitting beneath them, and where the lifeless trees
> stood up on the plain like monsters on their hind legs or lay sprawling
> like the skeletons of fearful spiders, we saw a sunset more remarkable
> than any yet.[23]

After only three weeks of ranch life, Wister thought that his health
had virtually recovered. "But I must have been very thoroughly wrong
somewhere—nerves, I fear." By August he was spending as many as six
hours a day in the saddle without undue fatigue, and he expressed in his
notebook great pride at this feat. Moreover, on the frequent hunting
expeditions away from the ranch he learned that to eat, one must kill
game, and he held up his share of such killing with a gusto that carried
over into hearty, story-filled evenings around the campfire.[24]

Occasionally, of course, he thought about the society to which he
soon would return. He had his mother send some Wagnerian opera music

---

* In *The Virginian*, Wister's narrator gave a very similar description of Medicine Bow, including even the twenty-nine buildings.

(selections from *Die Meistersinger* and *Die Walküre*) for playing on the Wolcotts' piano. His mother and Mrs. Chapman kept him informed about social activities up and down the East Coast (Mrs. Chapman wrote him one twenty-two page letter giving an account of a party at Bedford, Massachusetts), and of course he talked about such things every day with Miss Sophy and Miss Maisie. John Jay Chapman sent him an up-roarious letter about a visit to the Cabot family, whom Chapman mis-takenly had presumed he knew quite well. The cool reception he received convinced him of his error: the Cabots were so ultra-formal with him that Mrs. Elliot Cabot referred to her niece—Chapman's friend Ruth, who was about eighteen—as "Miss Cabot." The Cabots, as Wister quoted Chapman's letter, lived "buttoned up in prejudices and did not think it good manners to be at ease themselves or to permit their guests to be at ease."[25]

In this time of introspection Wister grew a beard, and he thought hard about Mrs. Chapman's candid observation that he lacked a sense of humor about himself. She was right, he confessed. "When anything con-cerning myself of a humorous nature comes along I'm lamentably de-ficient. It's a weakness which I recognize but can't correct."[26]

Such thoughts, however, often got lost in the busy round of daily activities. One of those incidental activities was the killing of all rattle-snakes that happened to signal their presence. Wister plunged eagerly into their massacre. He described one such encounter for Mrs. Chapman:

> I walked after this fellow until I got near enough to put my boot suddenly on his head, & hold it down while he coiled and twisted to get out. Then I crushed it down tight until it was sufficiently mashed to make it pretty safe to take out my knife & decapitate the reptile. . . . Then I put the bleeding stump behind the saddle & tied it on—During this it struck blindly at my arm several times, covering the sleeve with its own blood.

Upon arriving at the ranch he skinned the snake. He noted on killing another rattlesnake that the "eye of Satan when plotting the destruction of the human race could not have been more malignant than the stare which this decapitated head gave me with its two clouded agate eyes." He omitted entirely such vivid details in his letters home, telling Mrs. Chapman that if he so much as mentioned the word "rattlesnake" to his mother, Sarah would depart at once for Wyoming with an antidote for her endangered only son.[27]

"Had a roundup yesterday," Wister recorded in mid-July, declaring it to be a "wonderful thing." He had mounted a horse and joined the cowboys in "cutting out" the black cattle from the herd. In August he participated in a more elaborate roundup. He joined a party from the ranch, camping out at a big plain nearly twenty miles away where two herds of hundreds of cattle were located. Cattle bearing the "VR" brand were separated by about twelve cowboys who darted in and out of the mass of animals and then herded them westward over the high plains. He told John Jay Chapman that he also helped the ranch hands "brand calves, castrate bulls [and] deliver mares of their offspring." The precise details of these events, now so familiar through the vast literature of the cowboy but then largely a mystery, Wister meticulously recorded.[28]

Miss Sophy, who observed the roundup with Miss Maisie from a safe distance, asked ranch foreman Tom King, a native Easterner, whether he would not grow tired of the cowboy's life and return East upon reaching old age. Never, replied King, adding that cowboys never lived long enough to grow old anyway.* "They don't, I believe," agreed Wister. The cowboys to him were a "queer episode" in the nation's history—a unique part of a cycle through which Wister, following the historian Theodor Mommsen's lead, believed all nations passed. "Purely nomadic, and leaving no posterity, for they [the cowboys] don't marry. I'm told they're without any moral sense whatever. Perhaps they are—but I wonder how much less they have than the poor classes in New York."[29]

In the midst of the August roundup Wister's friend and distant cousin, Dr. John K. Mitchell, arrived at the ranch for a two-week stay. Mitchell, whose father had recommended the West as therapy for Wister and whose brother had been Wister's partner in the failed novel, surely was surprised at the picture of health he saw in his lately distressed Philadelphia friend. Now tanned and thoroughly at home in the ranch routine, Wister took Mitchell on a hunting expedition with a large party from the ranch that included even Miss Maisie and Miss Sophy. The men slept on the ground between buffalo robes while the two ladies shared the tent. One night when it rained, propriety gave way to necessity: the men moved inside the tent with the women. Miss Sophy and Miss Maisie hung up a blanket "that served for convention in the abstract, but for no other purpose." Appearances in a more literal sense also suffered. The only "mirror" available was a "miserable little superannuated watercourse," and even its water was too murky to reflect the

---

* It was a remark Wister never forgot. Years later *The Virginian*'s hero made the same comment.

grimy faces that peered into it. "Don't know exactly what I look like. . . . But shall take a strong stimulant before approaching the first looking glass I encounter," Wister wrote.[30]

When the hunting trip ended, Mitchell and the Philadelphia ladies returned East. Wister was left behind to savor this uncluttered society which had so unpredictably captivated him. Had he known what lay ahead for the ranch he might have considered himself even more fortunate, for he was staying at the VR during its grandest days. Emboldened by recent successes, Wolcott borrowed $50,000 that summer, secured by cattle and real estate, to buy additional property adjoining the ranch. The following summer of 1886 he was to borrow $30,000 more for further expansion and improvements. The hard winter of 1886–87, however, nearly ruined him, as it did so many ranchers. The VR herd was decimated by a third of its total number, and Wolcott was forced to turn ownership over to his creditor. Wolcott was permitted to remain as manager of the spread under the direction of its new owner, the Tolland Company, a Scottish firm.[31]

By fall Wister was back in Cambridge, ready for the opening of law school in 1885. As much as he adored the West he had no thought of staying and missing school. But the summer adventure served as the pivotal point in his life. It convinced him of several things: real life, the life that mattered, was being lived in the West. He had encountered the challenge of such an existence and had passed all its tests. He had found a spiritual home, very different from Boston or Europe, which now could nourish and sustain him for many years to come.

Part Two

THE WESTERN STORYTELLER

Chapter VI

AN UNCERTAIN SCHOLAR
(1885–1888)

HARVARD'S LAW SCHOOL STOOD PREEMINENT IN THE NATION. Christopher Columbus Langdell, upon assuming the deanship in 1870, had introduced, to a storm of criticism, an innovative plan called the "case study" method. That furor now was over, and this system of learning was a distinct success. Langdell's case study method, his establishment of a sequential three-year curriculum, and other refinements had revolutionized the training of lawyers and signaled the demise of the age-old practice of learning law by "reading" in an office. The school's 180 students enjoyed a new facility as well, the Austin Building, designed by noted architect H. H. Richardson. No better place for studying law existed in America.[1]

Law school was important to Wister for none of these reasons. True, law promised a proper and acceptable profession, but more to the immediate point, the school's setting offered a chance to rejoin old friends. Certainly Wister had no passion for the law.

"Everything is completely chaotic," he wrote as the semester began. "I'm not eating at any particular place and I wander about among the Law Books trying to find myself. They say it always begins like this." One special friend was his roommate, John Jay Chapman, as impetuous as ever. Chapman, himself a first-year student, also had elected to study law despite an inclination for more creative endeavors. Eager to surround themselves with convivial companions, the two soon arranged for old friends such as Joe Lee, Ted Cabot, Harry Cabot, Arthur Legman, and others to share meals with them at seven dollars a week per person at the small frame house that Wister, Chapman, and several others occupied. This humble dwelling they soon anointed as "The Palace," and it evolved quickly into a popular center for studying and socializing, a place where "Trusts, Wills, Contracts, and Equity Pleading, argument about the Civil War, toasts to the Supreme Bench of Massachusetts, and games of poker" were equally at home. The houseful of students began asking to dinner undergraduates from the Porcellian and A. D. clubs, and they also had as guests prominent older friends such as Oliver Wendell Holmes, Jr., who had left a law school faculty position two years earlier for his appointment to the Supreme Judicial Court of Massachusetts; William James, a wonderful dining companion who now was teaching philosophy rather than psychology at Harvard; Charles Eliot Norton, Harvard's renowned historian of the fine arts and friend of John Ruskin; and John Ropes, a historian from Boston. "A more familiar and delightful mingling of young and old over good food, good talk, and good wine can seldom have flourished in the bleak, prim, and dessicated climate of Cambridge," Wister later recalled.[2]

So good was the fellowship that he resolved not to study at all in the evenings, provided he could get along respectably in class. But by December he felt compelled to add one hour of study each evening to his daylight study time. He could feel a "stress of work," but no recurrence of headaches or other symptoms of illness, and he declared himself to be "in a highly contented and cheerful condition." By spring he had worked out a relaxed schedule consisting of classes and study from 9 A.M. to 1 P.M., lunch with "agreeable companions," tennis until 4 P.M., a group study session until dinner at 6:30 P.M., and study again until 10:30 P.M.[3]

One of his greatest pleasures lay in his continuing friendship with Oliver Wendell Holmes, Jr. By now Holmes was not only a judge, but also the author of the classic work *The Common Law*, and a formidable figure about town. When Holmes lectured one evening on law as a profession so many students jammed into the room that Wister and others were unable to squeeze in. It hardly could have mattered, for afterwards Wister dined privately with Holmes. Soon it became customary on Saturday and Sunday evenings for Wister to have dinner with Holmes and his wife at their house at 9 Chestnut Street in Boston. The two men became a common sight in Boston, going together to the Saturday Club, to concerts, and to many other events of mutual interest. They bantered together jovially about Boston society and life in America, and Wister lent French plays and novels to Holmes. On one occasion Holmes, with some reticence, asked Wister if he thought his mother would care to read one of his recent speeches. Wister forwarded it to her for her comments; Holmes would continue this practice for many years. The close and lively rapport between Wister and Holmes was destined to last a lifetime. A biographer of Holmes believed that Holmes, then forty-five, was attracted to the youthful Wister because of his "quick and witty" talk and his "sense of gusto."[4]

Wister renewed another Boston friendship—with William Dean Howells—at the law students' dinners. This association, however, did not flourish; Wister did not resume his calls of the previous year. It is likely that he was becoming disenchanted with Howells's political attitudes, and surely he had been sorely disappointed at Howells's reaction to his novel. In Wyoming, Wister had read *A Modern Instance*, and while he declared it superior to anything he had yet read of Howells's, the book's implied criticism of Boston irritated Wister, and he lamented that Howells always yielded to temptations to slap the city. Wister claimed not to look forward to Howells's dinner with the students, predicting that Howells would not "crawl out of his shell." What he did anticipate with excitement was the forthcoming dinner at which both William James and Judge Holmes would be present—"that will be a romantic-philosophic repast, and undoubtedly delightful."[5]

The brilliant but difficult Chapman constantly enlivened all gatherings with a stream of ideas and observations that inevitably ran contrary to conventional wisdom. The study of law did not agree with him: he became hypochondriac about supposed damage to his eyesight, and he hired students to read his lessons aloud to him each day. When Chapman was midway through the second year of law school, his short temper brought tragedy. In love with the woman who was to become his first wife, Minna Timmins, he got the notion that Percival Lowell, then an engaging man of thirty-two, was his rival for Minna's hand and that Lowell had taken advantage of her unfairly in some way. In such a state of mind Chapman attended a party at Mrs. Walter C. Cabot's house in Brookline. There he encountered Lowell and without warning beat him severely with a heavy cane. Back in his Cambridge room Chapman received a note from Minna asking him to apologize to Lowell. Despondent over this communication, Chapman wrapped a pair of suspenders tightly around his left forearm to make it numb, plunged his hand deep into the glowing red coals of the furnace, and held it there, counting the seconds. When he finally withdrew his hand, great hunks of flesh had been burned away. Doctors had to amputate.[6]

Chapman concocted a false story about the incident, claiming that a horse car had run over and severed his hand. Wister, knowing the truth, agreed to repeat the falsehood to his parents in Philadelphia. Inevitably, however, the true nature of the mutilation became known, and Wister had to apologize to his parents for having lied to them. He said he had related "exactly" what Chapman had insisted and that he never should have agreed to do it. He concluded that Chapman's nature had become "utterly and irretrievably warped." If he were not actually unsound in mind, there was little difference. "I think his future very hopeless, unless this disaster he has brought on himself takes the scales from his eyes." Wister, however, constantly visited Chapman in the hospital, so much so that he was able to read aloud to him the entirety of Robert Louis Stevenson's *Treasure Island*. Chapman, upon being released, left Harvard and took up the study of law in New York. Ultimately, after a tempestuous two-year separation from Minna Timmins, he married her.[7]

Even with the energetic presence of Chapman only a memory, the most spirited gatherings of the law students still occurred not when they talked of torts but when they debated literature and the arts. But when artist John Singer Sargent, responding to their invitation, arrived for dinner, the students became stumped because Sargent, a shy man, knew only Wister and Grafton Cushing, and he directed all his conversation to them alone. A disaster loomed, and Sargent, in Wister's opinion, was beginning to look "a good deal like a cultivated fool." Soon after dinner, however, a student named Robert Simes reached deep into his intellectual reservoir and saved the evening by referring astutely to Russian novels and thereby bringing Sargent to life. "The result was that for the remainder of the occasion—two to three hours—we smoked[,] drank rum-and-ginger-ale, and got into a string of heated discussions," Wister later said. Sargent revealed himself to be clever and interesting, and the evening was miraculously converted into a delight for all.[8]

Wister's own literary interests did not wither in such an atmosphere: he found time to write again, and he read as much as ever. He debated the notion of developing a distinct literary style of his own. In the midst of reading *A Tale of Two Cities* he commented to his mother: "As for style—what on earth is style? The only thing I know about it is that it's something I haven't got myself." Certainly he wanted a "style," but how to achieve it? He had just finished writing a piece which seemed to lack style entirely; it was "a perfectly simple and direct telling of what I have to tell." Neither did Howells appear to have any "style," and as for Henry James, who obviously had a style, Wister vowed not to write that way even if he could.[9]

In the summer of 1886 Wister wrote upon request a short story, "The Palace of the Closed Window," for inclusion in a collection of tales, *A Week Away From Time*, published by Roberts Brothers in Boston. The various stories were linked by a scheme whereby six visitors in a seaside home took turns telling ghost stories. Neither the editor, Mrs. James Lodge, nor the authors were identified. Only the initial "W" provided a clue to Wister's authorship. He believed his own story so superior to the others that he was "disgusted" with the book.[10]

In another literary effort, he wrote an article describing a Greek play performed at Harvard, submitting it to Thomas Bailey Aldrich at the *Atlantic Monthly*. Bailey praised the effort, but rejected it. He told Wister that he had just accepted a similar piece; otherwise he would have published it. Wister promptly sent it to the *Harvard Monthly*, where it was printed.[11]

He demonstrated his continuing attention to music, and to opera in particular, by writing a four-page article, "Republican Opera," which Aldrich accepted and published in the Contributors' Club section of the *Atlantic*. In this unsigned article Wister compared American opera to European opera, sought to analyze the problems of "republican opera" which he claimed could not exist without subsidies, and declared that "no art so much as opera is at the mercy of the humor of the times." While his poem on Beethoven had been published earlier in the *Atlantic*, this was Wister's first article to appear there. One might assume that it would signal a grand celebration, but it did not. In fact, Wister deprecated his article as a "pleasant but shallow discourse" containing only a "few commonplaces" and "nothing at all [done] scientifically." But the ease with which he had produced it indicated to him something more important: given the opportunity he knew that he could write much better. He had composed the article at a time busy not only because of his studies but also because Chapman was in the hospital. Under these circumstances, he was "proud to be able to get it into a magazine at all."[12]

Wister's parents evidently were pleased with their son's progress in law school, but Dr. Wister worried about having to support a son who now was in his mid-twenties. In March of 1886 Dr. Wister's savings were reduced by $30,000 because of bad investments and rice planting costs on the Georgia farm. A sum of $100,000 was earning five percent when eight percent seemed more appropriate, and that meant the annual interest was $3,000 less than it should have been. Another $90,000 to $100,000 was idle because he could not find safe investments that would yield better than three or four percent annually. His medical practice earned no more than $12,000 a year. Such assets would have been the envy of practically any family in America, yet Dr. Wister despaired. Normal family living expenses cost $14,000 annually; Sarah Wister never curtailed her travels or other expenditures; and Dr. Wister fought desperately not to draw from his capital. His son added not a little to his concerns with messages such as this: "Please send me some money quick. I'm paying wash & breakfast bills with Miss Fox's birthday money —a bad arrangement."[13]*

In the spring of Wister's second year at law school, some of his old symptoms of illness reemerged. He vaguely described the problem as "neuralgia or gout." Studying seven days a week by now, he complained of "being awfully hard worked and very tired." This concern over his health made him decide to travel again during the summer. His preference was to take a steamer for the south of France and there go on a walking tour of some twenty miles a day. An alternate scheme was to return to the West for a tour. He estimated the costs for the European trip at $400; the western tour would be less expensive. He could furnish $150 of the amount, but he needed the remainder from his father. As far as Dr. Wister was concerned, his son's ideas proved that he still knew almost nothing about financial matters. Neither trip could be done on $400, Dr. Wister insisted.[14]

"I had rather your mother had a voice in this matter, if only that it might be drowned," he told his son. But since she would not return to Butler Place from her wanderings for more than a week and since Owen wanted a quick decision, Dr. Wister responded on his own, thankful that he could do so "without the din of discord." If Owen would go West instead of to Europe, Dr. Wister would bear all the costs.[15]

Thus, on the first day of July, two weeks short of his twenty-seventh birthday, Wister was on a train going West with a friend from Boston, George Norman. They went to Niagara Falls and into Canada where another friend, Copley Amory, joined them at Qu'Appelle. The travelers were not to reenter the United States until after they reached Vancouver, British Columbia. Along the way Wister wrote in his second western journal, making detailed entries again about the people, customs, and land.

Alongside the wild and winding Fraser River he clung for hours to the cowcatcher, his spirits soaring as the train "slid downhill without steam, through snow sheds and tunnels (once under a shower bath in

* Miss Mary Fox was Wister's generous godmother.

the dark, drenching and cold), round turns into a new vista of cataracts or avenues between the pines." Perched there in front, the air whistling in his ears, he felt that he had severed all earthly ties. The only people seen in these beautiful woods were occasional gangs of Chinamen working with picks and shovels on the track.[16]

When the three adventurers returned to the United States and reached Portland, Oregon, Wister was conscious of a distinct change in the people. In Canada they had been "colorless and inert"; now, suddenly, as if to confirm his belief in the vigor of the American West, "extraordinary looking folks" filled the hotels and trains. Thick blue upper lips and eyebrows as wide as hat ribbons marked the energetic men. Women redolent with perfume evoked flirtations from train employees. "French-looking," well-dressed little boys ate food in everybody else's seats, and their mammas were "deuced fine" with big black eyes and lots of lace around their necks.[17]

"I keep thinking how you would hate nearly all of it," Wister wrote to his mother. "The only way you could ever come West and enjoy yourself would be inside a large party of friends who would form a hollow square whenever a public place was to be entered." That recurring idea— the realization that his mother would abhor the West—somehow pleased him. The fact that he could revel in this unvarnished society represented a triumph which was his alone; it was a feat beyond his mother's reach or comprehension.[18]

California, in the midst of a boom that would see its population more than double between 1880 and 1890, was the first prolonged stop. In San Francisco, where they stayed for a week, the trio visited the Golden Gate and Chinatown, and they saw the seals flopping on the rocks in the Pacific at Cliff House. Wister sampled a Chinese opera which astounded him. He described its music to his mother. "Sit at the piano and strike A & E together for an hour with your left hand and play anything you like with your right—high up—& never touch a black note. If Sally Cadwallader will then talk continually through the process, you'll have a perfect Chinese opera."[19]

From California they turned eastward to the high point of the summer outing—an extended hunting trip in Wyoming. Before July ended, the trio was north of South Pass at Fort Washakie, a pleasant collection of military buildings named after a popular and very much alive Shoshone chief. Wister presented to the commanding officer a letter from General Philip Sheridan urging all courtesies for these eastern visitors.

The officer in charge, Colonel Homer W. Wheeler, did not need such a reminder. He had been a friend of Amory's father since their service together in the Civil War. He showered the guests with meals, cigars, whiskey, and conversation. Wister, meanwhile, arranged a four-week-long hunting expedition, engaging an Indian guide named Tighee and two white men, Jules Mason and George West, as packer and cook.[20]

When finally they had accumulated the necessary provisions, the group rode off by horseback, following the Wind River east of the Continental Divide. Four years earlier General Sheridan had accompanied President Chester A. Arthur along the route, and it now was known as the Sheridan Trail. To the left, the men could see snow-crested peaks; to their right, a vast brown landscape interrupted by buttes, brush, and the narrow green valley of the frigid Wind River. To the north, not yet visible, stood the inspiring Grand Tetons and beyond them Yellowstone Park. By the third day out, having consumed their provisions, the men began to subsist on animals or birds they shot and fish they caught.[21]

For almost a week they camped nightly alongside the Wind River. The stream possessed "every magic a river has had allotted to it." The water was "clear green to the bottom—rushing and tumbling—cool to go into, cast over, and full of trout that live behind the jutting rocks under wild rose bushes." When they left the river Wister declared that he would be forced to "go into mourning."[22]

One night as they lay around the campfire, hearing nothing but the popping of burning logs and the tinkling of a bell around a horse's neck, a solitary cowboy came upon them. Learning that he was en route to Fort Washakie, now ninety miles behind, Wister hurriedly scribbled a letter to his mother for the man to mail. "I am very well—very thin— hungry at all meals and find this sort of thing even more utterly enchanting than two years ago," he told her.[23]

For Wister the high point of the trip occurred when he killed a giant grizzly at Jackson Hole under the shadows of the Tetons. The men had planted bait not far from camp, and one frigid morning just after breakfast Tighee shouted that a bear was near. Wister grabbed his rifle and jumped behind the Indian on the horse's bare rump for a wild ride to a good vantage point. "My horror," he later wrote, "was that I should slide off somewhere with a crash and ruin the whole thing." As Wister and Tighee hid in a sparse grove of trees they saw the huge bear leisurely sauntering along. Wister observed that the grizzly "looked brown and gray, his gestures . . . those of a good-natured old gentleman taking a little morning air for health's sake." Still concealed but now running parallel to the bear's path, Wister, at an approving nod from Tighee, finally dashed into the open meadow behind a solitary tree as the creature passed on the other side. Standing up to his full height, Wister took careful aim at the surprised animal, fired once, and the stricken bear plunged headfirst to the ground. Twice the grizzly attempted to rise, but both times it toppled down in a heap. The normally stolid Tighee was alive with animation, gesturing and shouting furiously at Wister to keep shooting. Wister did so reluctantly. "I felt like a murderer as I pumped the bullets into the poor old gentleman who swayed about on the grass, utterly gone." Back in camp he learned that the betting had been three-to-one that he had hit nothing.[24]

The friendships between the eastern hunters, the two hired white men, and the Indian guide flourished amid such intimacy. Wister was attracted especially to the confident and proficient West, whom he described as "much better looking than any of us." There was much to admire about a man who at Wister's own age, twenty-seven, so gracefully exhibited all the outdoor prowess that Wister so envied. Even more impressive was the fact that West had learned his skills fairly recently. He was a native New Englander who had come to Wyoming just seven years earlier as a tenderfoot, having quit his job in Boston as a telegraph operator. Yet intimacy bred irritations as well. Less than two weeks out, Mason lost his temper and struck his horse so fiercely that he shattered the limb he had used. One chunk struck Wister's own mount, causing Wister to retort, "Don't trouble my horse, Mason, and I think a milder treatment of your own would be better." West quickly pulled Wister aside, quietly warned him to avoid even such a mild criticism as this, and told him that he was lucky his comment had not caused considerable trouble. "All right," Wister recorded in his journal, "but I should do the same again and take the consequences." Some hard feelings did result. Not until four days later when the group reached the head of Jackson Lake, mirroring the needlelike Tetons, was harmony restored.[25]

A photograph of the group at their Jackson Hole campsite shows them lounging languidly by their tiny white tent, looking much like a band of bandits. Wister, an ammunition belt slung around his hips and a broad-brimmed hat covering his head, stands in the background pouring a drink from a flask into Tighee's huge cup. The others—West, Mason, Norman, and Amory—are semireclined in jaunty postures.[26]

A few days later they reached Yellowstone National Park—eighty years after its wonders had bedazzled John Colter, the first white man to set foot in the area. For the past fifteen years Yellowstone had been a national park, the nation's first, but in this preautomobile age it was not yet accessible to many Americans.[27]

For those few present on this day, though, Wister's party—five dusty men and one solemn-faced Indian—created an attraction every bit as provocative as the geysers. They rode into the park single file on horseback, leading six packhorses laden with pelts, trophies, and supplies. Tourists in stagecoaches craned their necks and grabbed their cameras at this vision of men who seemed as wild as the landscape. "Had we been bears or bandits (I am sure some of them took us for the latter) they couldn't have broken into more excitement," Wister recalled some fifty years later. Since rifles were forbidden, the men checked their weapons with an Army sergeant who, with other cavalry troops, supervised the area. Rather than sleep in the hotel, on their first night the visitors camped out in a grove of trees in the Upper Geyser Basin. But they could not resist the luxury of a hot bath ingeniously rigged into a cabin by the cavalry, and when they ate at the hotel in Mammoth Hot Springs, Wister's spurs clattered so noisily on the wooden floors that he removed them in embarrassment.[28] At the Lower Falls of the Yellowstone they saw initials carved everywhere. Wister was disgusted. "A curse on people who carve their names at these places."[29]

The Lower Falls was to Wister "the most beautiful thing I have ever seen." Wister, West, and Norman attempted to climb down the river's nearly vertical canyon walls to the bottom, a perilous adventure. Only Wister and West succeeded. Wister thought it may have been the first time anyone had made the climb.[30]

The geysers, by contrast, repulsed him. Neither Old Faithful, the Castle, the Giant, the Beehive, nor any of the others were attractive to him. The problem was their sulphuric stench. They did prove useful, though, for Wister and the others washed their soiled clothing in the hot water. But at the puddles around Old Faithful, Wister shuddered again to see tourists' names carved on the hard ground and rocks.[31]

As August ended so did the western adventure. Good-byes were said and the accumulation of the hunting expedition, mostly hides and left-over ammunition, was packed in a huge trunk and shipped home. On September 1 the Easterners themselves boarded a train for the return.[32] Not until he was outside of Chicago did Wister slip into a freight house and out of his rough western clothing, donning what he called the "garments of civilization." A group of rough freighters viewed his transition from outdoorsman to gentleman with fascination, and Wister, always ready for repartee, advised them that California was the place to live and that they had better go there and drive out the Chinese.[33]

Even though he dressed—as far as his own standards were concerned —in a relatively casual manner on this western train ride as well as on others, passengers frequently mistook Wister for a sightseeing Englishman. Even the English people he encountered frequently thought him to be a fellow countryman, for Wister's cultivated diction resembled theirs more closely than it did that of western Americans, and much of his clothing came from England. To avoid such mistaken notions he professed frequently to add western idioms to his conversation.[34]

Much as he regretted leaving the West, Wister was happy at least to be returning to Boston and Cambridge rather than to Philadelphia. As he told his father on one occasion, his "blueness" at leaving Butler Place was driven away in Boston by walking the streets and "meeting in every square so many who nod & smile to me." Such recognition seldom happened in Philadelphia, and it certainly was a comfort in Boston "to feel you're known about."[35]

Years later Wister's daughter, in editing her father's journals, would note that "nothing of note occurred" during his third and final year at law school. Such seems to be the case. He wrote regularly to his mother with details about various parties he attended, books he read, music he heard, and the dramatic performances he saw by the renowned Joseph Jefferson in *Rip Van Winkle*. He appears to have moved into a private dormitory, Beck Hall, a fancy accommodation with high ceilings, handsome chandeliers, ash trim, and steam heat. He participated in moot court competition by arguing an uninspiring case concerning a receivership for a Bradford Electric Light Company.[36]

One thing seems certain: the lack of details in his letters about law school confirms that he found no magic in the law. It was a profession that might be profitable and that certainly would be respectable—no more than that. What seemed more personally rewarding at this time was the continued development of his writing talent. If only he had the time, he told his father, he could "probably do some modest writing that would bring me in a few modest sums." Ideas were dancing in his head for that day's arrival.[37]

Shortly after Wister's return to Cambridge, his new Wyoming friend

George West surprised him with a detailed letter which undoubtedly stirred his literary imagination. West was leaving to hunt horse thieves who had stolen thirteen head from him, forty-six from a neighbor named J. K. Moore, and eight from Jules Mason. "Shall not be back until the 1st of Nov.[,] possibly later and possibly not at all," he said in his succinct fashion. Through quiet work among Indian friends he had located the stolen horses, and with a posse of two white men and three Indians he had intended to travel in the dark of the night to the Fish Lake area and steal them back. However, one of the aggrieved parties had convinced him of the need for stronger measures, and West now was determined to capture the thieves and return them for vigilante execution by hanging or shooting. He feared the rustlers might not even live through the return trip, though, for West himself was "too much agrevated [sic] at the idea of having lost my own horses and 7 days hard work hunting alone." The loss represented a severe setback to his goal of establishing a horse ranch. Unless he recovered the stolen horses he could not have forty-six colts by spring. The result of this vigilante expedition is not known, but an idea was planted in Wister's head. Years later just such an episode would mark one of the high points of *The Virginian*.[38]

If Wister had been captivated by West's mastery of the outdoors, so had West obviously been captivated by the charm of this cultured Easterner. Wister had not been reluctant to ply West with endless questions about western life. Now, however, it was West's turn to be obeisant.

"I don't know why it was," he wrote to Wister, "but it always struck me that you would some day be one of the leading men of the country, and I shall hope to see it that way." Meanwhile, he deeply appreciated the quilt Wister had presented him, and he hoped the report untrue that Mason was to receive an even greater gift of a six-shooter. It irritated West that Mason already was claiming full credit for the success of their hunting expedition.[39]

In Boston, Wister continued his close friendship with Judge Holmes, and he surely applauded and perhaps influenced the Holmeses' decision to depart in May on "a great big jaunt all over the West in a director's car." When they left, Wister told his mother that he missed them "awfully" on Saturday and Sunday nights.[40]

Probably one of Wister's most satisfying moments of the school year came when he communicated with Robert Louis Stevenson, the famous author of *Treasure Island* and *Dr. Jekyll and Mr. Hyde*. In Boston briefly on a stopover from Saranac Lake, New York, where he had been in a sanitarium in an attempt to gain strength, the gaunt-faced Stevenson invited Wister to call on him. Evidently the note responded to a request from Wister in which he had invoked Henry James's name. "Anybody who comes in the name of our dear Henry James will be welcome to my door. . . . Let us see you soon." Whether Wister went is unknown, but such a visit seemed distinctly more inviting than the prospect of beginning the law career that suddenly was upon him.[41]

It already was settled that upon graduation Wister would join the Philadelphia firm of Francis Rawle. But that was to be delayed, for it seemed more important to refresh himself once again in Wyoming before beginning this supposed lifelong commitment. There was no request this time for funds from his father; probably he could afford the expedition himself, for with his father's assistance he now was investing money of his own in stocks.[42]

Once aboard the train for Wyoming in mid-July, Wister resumed a familiar routine—the keeping of a journal. "Here begins Western trip the third—may I someday write the thirtieth with as much zest!" With Wister were two friends, George Norman and Robert Simes, the man who had enthralled the artist Sargent with his knowledge of Russian novels. Already making arrangements in Wyoming for another hunting expedition were George West and Jules Mason.[43]

The wide range of characters encountered continued to fascinate Wister. Their stories of how they happened to come to the West could never be predicted. In Rawlins, where Wister and his pals swapped their train for a stagecoach, Wister fell into an absorbing conversation with the bootblack who labored over his boots. The man told Wister that he had come only recently from the East, headed for San Francisco, but he had been stalled in Wyoming because his partner was bedridden with the ague. The hard-luck story touched Wister, and he immediately hired the bootblack to perform several extra errands as an excuse to give him money. He also purchased quinine and sent it to the ailing partner. On the stagecoach for Fort Washakie another curious figure emerged, a cocky young man who boasted of his prowess as a cardshark and all-round adventurer. Once, he bragged, he had won $12,000 at stud poker. When the stagecoach stopped for the noon meal Wister observed that the young gambler loafed outside rather than coming inside to the table. The same thing happened at the stop for the evening meal. Finally, when the passengers shouted at him to come to the table and eat, he replied loudly that *he* was not hungry. By now aware that he obviously had no money to pay for his meal, they yelled at him not to be a fool and to come join them, which he did. Thereafter, Wister and the others took turns buying his meals as a matter of course. At the town of Lander they got their thanks when "that lighthearted and vicious spirit left us without any sign or word of formality."[44]

West and Mason, "both not changed a whit," met the party at Fort Washakie. Two additional guides were hired—Richard Washakie, the Shoshone son of Chief Washakie himself, and a grumpy half-breed named Paul LeRose. The post's new commanding officer, a Captain Smith, and his wife entertained the visitors with whiskey and dinner before the hunters departed for the Tetons in search of mountain sheep.[45]

This expedition proved to be many things: vexatious, dangerous, and at the same time rewarding. En route to two lakes just south of Jackson Lake, the hunters got lost. Tempers frayed—especially that of the half-breed LeRose, whose irritability angered the entire party. Finally, Wister took the lead himself despite LeRose's scoffs and won a victory when he led the party to the two lakes, the lower one turning out to be a superb site for a base camp because of its abundant trout.

Days later, while riding in high mountains to find the elusive mountain sheep, the group was surprised by a freak summer storm. When the men had left camp at the middle fork of Owl Creek in the Washakie Needles, the day had been warm and sunny. After having grown weary with climbing and with ludicrously chasing mountain sheep to no avail, the hunters watched as the sky suddenly darkened, the wind began whistling, and the air turned frigid. Their alarm intensified as black streamers of precipitation appeared beneath giant thunderclouds. Across the valley the sky turned white, and an anxious moment passed before they realized that a fierce hailstorm such as they never before had seen was approaching. The timberline was far below, and their only protection was to huddle beneath their frightened horses. Once the storm hit, nothing could be seen but a "shooting slant of white." Lightning and thunder flashed and boomed. The only raised objects in the area were the men, their horses, and their guns, and Mason suddenly realized that all were dangerous attractions for the lightning bolts. Above the storm's noise he shouted to the others to crawl away from the horses and guns, which they all did. Wister later described the scene:

> I turned around and saw Richard's bent head and Paul wearing a
> most miserable expression, and the shrinking horses with their tails

tucked in and their heads stuck down and all four feet converging into a point under their middles. Turning again, I saw George, gingerly slinking a little farther away from electric annihilation. This gave me a notion of my own appearance—and I roared enough to have made me warm in any other weather.[46]

As the storm eased, the group noticed that the ground had turned solid white with hail except in places too steep for the hail to lodge. Then, as Wister wandered about the whitened mountain noting the storm's effects, something near his head strangely began hissing or spitting—it was a noise resembling the sound of a cork slowly being withdrawn from a bottle. The sound was so close, yet so mysterious, that it was utterly bewildering. Wister stood very still and listened as carefully as possible with "very fine and gentle" hail still falling. Suddenly he became aware that a stinging sensation just behind his ear was hurting him worse than had all the hail during the most violent moment of the storm. Removing his hat, Wister found that the pain immediately ceased. Examining the leather binding and stitches, he realized that the buzzing had come from the hat's brim! The same phenomenon was occurring simultaneously to the panicky Mason, who shouted that the pain was becoming unbearable. Wister told him to take off his hat; when Mason did so, the stinging stopped. Trying to understand what had happened, the men concluded that their damp hats had become charged with electricity that had saturated the atmosphere. When their hats had become heavily laden with the electricity, it discharged itself through the men into the earth. This sudden and total conversion of a late August day into a harsh winter afternoon was one of the strangest spectacles Wister had ever seen, and the electrical charges made it all the more bizarre. The next morning, viewing the same location, Wister found it difficult to imagine that such turbulence could have occurred there on such a day.[47]

The laborious efforts to locate mountain sheep at high altitudes and the resulting poor marksmanship caused the hunting expedition to be noted more by failure than by success. Finally, after great effort, the men killed a few sheep. The difficulties experienced by the hunters made Wister conclude that mountain sheep should be placed "among the front ranks of intelligent mammals."[48]

Just before returning to civilization, the hunting party received a visit from three Indians who talked privately to Washakie. One of them was Tighee, the guide from the previous summer. Tighee knew who Wister was, their earlier association had been too close not to, but he made no nod of recognition. Wister understood that Tighee had not intended to be unfriendly. "Having nothing to say to us except good day, he followed the Indian fashion and did not say that."[49]

Chapter VII

WESTERN STORYTELLER
(1889–1892)

WISTER SHOULD HAVE BEEN EXTREMELY PLEASED to join a firm such as Francis Rawle's. Members of the Rawle family had been distinguished Philadelphia lawyers since 1725.* Wister was the third member of the firm. Each day he walked the city streets to the office at 402 Walnut Street from his rooms at the Hotel Hamilton. (He had resolved not to stay at Butler Place except on the weekends or on the days he wanted to keep his father company while his mother was away.)[1]

Yet Wister showed absolutely no enthusiasm for his new profession. He believed that as a beginner, none of his cases would be demanding, and he was right. His first client was a "penniless widow" whom he routinely assisted in acquiring a few assets left by her deceased husband. He declared his second case, a suit filed to recover an unpaid bill of two hundred dollars, no more than a "crumb" that Rawle had tossed him.[2]

Tied unhappily to his desk, Wister fought a nearly "irresistible influence" to flee and dissolve from view into the West. He complained privately to friends of his despondency. Judge Holmes, whom he still managed to see despite the miles between them, professed an inability to see the "melancholy" that Wister claimed to suffer. Holmes tried to ease his friend's distress, relating his own pessimistic conclusion he had drawn over the years: "Life is a process of getting used to being skinned. Even to a man who has been as fortunate as I have been." In April of 1889 Judge Holmes suggested, as a form of relief, a trip by just the two of them to Europe. They could travel together or alone over the continent as they liked so as not to impair each other's freedom and yet still gain "much happiness." But the West, not Europe, was now Wister's source for relief and inspiration. He told Judge Holmes that he planned to return in the summer to his "beloved mountains."[3]

---

* Francis Rawle was forty-two years old when Wister joined him. He was a graduate of Harvard, treasurer of the American Bar Association (a position he held from 1878 to 1902 when he became president for one term), and editor of *Bouvier's Law Dictionary.*

Just as in Boston, when he grew despondent over his work at the Union Safe Deposit Vault, Wister now undertook in his spare hours a number of creative endeavors. These undertakings continued to involve his twin loves—which the West could never replace, although certainly it might alter—music and literature. Dr. Wister squirmed uneasily as he saw what was happening. Wister, aware of his father's displeasure, wrote to his grandmother, "If my father did not wish to run the risk of begetting a progeny in whom a stripe of art &c could be visible—why did he marry into your family?"[4]

In one of these projects, Wister and his Philadelphia friend Thomas Wharton, a lawyer turned newspaperman-novelist, had begun composing a comic opera with a feudalistic setting called *Charlemagne*.* To Wharton, the lyricist, the project held the promise of financial windfall; to Wister it was "a matter of comparative indifference & diversion." Neither he nor Wharton, he believed, had the "popular vein" necessary to attract the masses and their money. The problem, he observed stuffily, was that to be successful, *Charlemagne* required excellent producing, acting, and singing, and not a musical company in America filled those requirements.[5]

Wister also persisted in his literary efforts. He was inspired, perhaps, by his recent inclusion into a select Philadelphia literary group which revolved around the colorful personage of Weir Mitchell. The weekly meetings at Dr. Mitchell's house were called simply "Saturday evenings after nine." Wister's literary project was a Christmas story for young people, "The Dragon of Wantley." John Stewardson, a Philadelphia artist and lifelong friend, was the illustrator. "I think it is going to turn out highly diverting," Wister told his mother. He planned afterwards to add a libretto so that this, too, could be performed as a comic opera. In addition, he decided to retrieve the dusty manuscript of his completed novel and to carry it to the offices of the *Atlantic Monthly* to show editor Thomas Bailey Aldrich. This was the novel that William Dean Howells had told him to forget. Aldrich was in Europe, and Wister returned the pages to his shelves, not to dislodge them again.[6]

A prominent, eligible young man who, for all appearances, had settled into a respected legal career would seem to be ready for the next logical step: marriage. Such was not the case with Wister, however. His only reference to courtship at this time was in a letter to his grandmother in

---

* Some of the lyrics for *Charlemagne* are reproduced in Thomas Wharton, *"Bobo" and Other Fancies* (New York: Harper & Brothers, 1897).

which he said he was "going to the theatre with young women (several)." Many of his friends were marrying, though, including John Jay Chapman, who finally had triumphed in his courtship of Minna Timmins. Wister held a dinner party for Chapman, and after the wedding ceremony he inspired the others to join him in grabbing the decorative roses and showering them upon the bride and groom as they departed.[7]

Because of Chapman's wedding, Wister had to decline another invitation. Theodore Roosevelt had sought to renew their neglected friendship by inviting Wister to his Oyster Bay home for the Fourth of July holidays, promising "music and Walter Damrosch." But that reunion would have to wait. Just as Wister and Roosevelt earlier had pleasantly discovered in the Porcellian Club that their ideas on literature and world affairs coincided, they now would have been pleased to find agreement in their notions that the West was the wellspring of manly virtues and the hope for the nation's future. Independently, too, each had concluded that annual western hunting trips helped combat the effects of the artificial society of the East. They soon would be comparing notes on these ideas.[8]

By the spring of 1889 Wister had discarded *Charlemagne* to resume work on the comic opera he had started in Paris, *Montezuma*. Wister was certain that the music for *Montezuma* was the *"best thing I've done yet."* The setting was Mexico City at the time of the Spanish conquest, 1519 A.D., and the plot concerned the Aztec Indians' belief in the prophecy that a light-skinned god would appear to rule over them. Montezuma and Cortez, naturally, were central characters. Wharton, once again, was Wister's collaborator and lyricist. Wister felt it likely that some theatrical manager would stage the production in the fall season, thus he needed to finish it by early summer. Because of this alluring prospect he abandoned his summer plans to go West. Music, suddenly, had reemerged in his life.[9]

He wrote to his mother, now in Europe, that he was eager to study the French school of instrumentation. Would she send him some of the music? He needed works by Offenbach, Bizet, and any one of several pieces by Léo Délibes or Lecocq.[10] Sarah Wister, delighted to help, was not optimistic about the collaboration with Wharton, whom she believed incapable of writing an adequate script. In midsummer her fears seemed confirmed. The first theatrical manager to examine the two completed acts of *Montezuma* said that the story was so complicated and the dialogue so dull that it would never work. He refused even to listen to Wister's score.[11]

Wister was disappointed, naturally, but he did not lose all hope, for the opera's subject seemed right to him. "I internally know that for color, contrast & spectacle, & an American subject, Montezuma is a good starting point—and then, if my music has enough of the popular element in it, backed by clever verse (already commended) what is needed is amusing dialogue & the action cleared up and brightened." This could be done, he felt, but now he agreed with his mother that his long collaboration with Wharton should end. He determined not to finish the third act of *Montezuma* until Wharton rewrote the first two acts to the point where some manager would accept them on their own merits. "The fact is," he told his mother, "(Oh! how angry you must be) Tom will never be able to write the dialogue & action of a play—because 1, he isn't funny (humorous) & 2, he isn't dramatic." If the ultimate verdict of all prospective producers was that the music was unsatisfactory, then Wister would believe it himself—but not until then. Meanwhile, as soon as *Montezuma* was off his mind he would resume work on "The Dragon of Wantley," where he would be his own master and have nobody but himself to blame for failure. His mother regretted her son's having spent years of energy and talent in collaboration with Wharton with no tangible result. Still, all was not lost. "Real work is never wasted, & it remains to hear the verdict on the music," she assured him.[12]

Another matter about her son concerned her more: he seemed preoccupied with his health. He was not reluctant, now or ever before, to discuss his infirmities with anyone, and his current complaint was simply that he could not regain the healthy glow he had enjoyed in the West. This young man—from every visible indication as fit as anyone could be —forever was taking his temperature and feeling his pulse. Sarah Wister urged her son to stop dwelling on these matters. "Of course you do not feel in the condition now that you did in the Rocky Mountains, but you shd'nt expect to be always, or even often, at the acme of physical well being." She advised him to go to bed earlier, to rise earlier, and to take frequent horseback rides—as many as six a week rather than the half dozen times he had done it all summer. "I who know both health & ill health, have come to the conclusion that while health is a great blessing, it is like wealth merely means to an end, & not an object in itself." The modern emphasis on health for health's sake alone was not a balanced viewpoint, she felt.[13]

Less than a month after his mother had cautioned him, Wister was on the train for Wyoming. His ostensible purpose was to reestablish his health. As he wrote to his mother:

> The constant lameness of both right & left arms means either gout or rickety nerves; also I don't want to continue to re-arrange my whole manner of playing the piano on account of the numbness of my wrists that has been with me since early in August. I consider health a means, as you say; but also as a sine qua, non—and that, more than half, is why I came here this year instead of paying the round of visits to Mr. Coit, Ned Tibbits, Boston, Cambridge, Hempstead, Tuxedo & New York.[14]

His father, he knew, still stirred restlessly. "Assure him my plan is not to become a pioneer, or a settler, or even to winter here—but to return and complete the index of the law book on which Bob Ralston & I are at work—and continue to walk down Walnut Street in the A.M. & up Walnut Street in the P.M." Yet he could not say precisely when he would return, for he would not be back until his conscience bid him, and that he knew would "not be particularly soon."[15]

Traveling alone, he filled his idle hours with thoughts about the nation he was crossing. In his mind he divided the country into three social strips. From the Atlantic to the Appalachians the people were "civilized and decent"; from the Appalachians to the Continental Divide they were "half civilized filth"; and from the Continental Divide to the Pacific they were "wild but decent." This low-spirited assessment of the American midcontinent was prompted by the drummers he disdainfully watched in the smoking compartment as they talked obsessedly of their "two cent commissions and their five dollar bonanzas." The commercialism that he and his parents believed had been defiling the best values of the East since the Civil War now seemed to be overwhelming the Midwest. And here the problem seemed worse, for citizens lacked cultural props to support them in the battle against the almighty dollar. Would this "defilement" of the Midwest extend to the West? Wister began to wonder.[16]

On the following day the drummers moved out, replaced by two sheriffs and their prisoner. Wister found the lawmen to be exceptionally companionable, as he did the prisoner, who had been indicted as one of a six-man mob that had hanged a man and woman without benefit of judge or jury. The vigilante killing of "Cattle Kate" Ella Watson and James Averell had received national attention, and the press had portrayed the pair as fully deserving their fate. Cattle Kate's alleged crime was rustling and prostitution, and the man with whom she was linked as lover was accused of cattle theft. Wister, accepting their lynching as justified, thought the sheriff's prisoner was "a good solid citizen." He hoped that he would be freed, for as one of the sheriffs told him, "All the good folks say it [the lynching] was a good job; it's only the wayward classes that complain." Eventually, as Wister wished, the prisoner and other suspects indeed were freed, but only after three persons who had witnessed the doomed pair's abduction, and a fourth man who actually had seen the hanging, mysteriously disappeared. This approval by Wister of vigilante justice under certain circumstances, as well as his disdainful attitude toward the drummers he saw on the train, would both find expression in his stories and in *The Virginian.*[17]

When Wister transferred from train to stagecoach at Rawlins, the stage driver grumbled at having to handle his bulky trunk. Wister noted that two years earlier he would have "tried to be winsome and whisked him up." But now, feeling very confident in this environment, he merely ignored him. At the end of the long ride to Fort Washakie, Wister found George West waiting. West, elated at the reunion, dogged Wister's every step as he made arrangements for the hunting trip. Fort Washakie's new commanding officer, in contrast, eyed the ebullient Easterner caustically and said, "You know, sir, I don't sympathize with you men from the East who come here and shoot our game." Wister replied, "Well, sir, did you but know how little of it I shot, you would sympathize with me very deeply."[18]

His riposte proved accurate, for Wister had poor luck on this trip in the mountains. The Indians had hunted so thoroughly that the game had moved away. In mid-November, after a month's stay, Wister regretfully decided to return to Philadelphia and his law practice. He vowed to "count the months" until his return. In his journal he composed a poem to celebrate these "most enchanting mountains," writing in the first stanza:

> Would I might prison in my words
> And so hold by me all the year
> Some portion of the Wilderness
> Of freedom that I walk in here.[19]

Not until two years later, however, would Wister return to the West. He now determined to concentrate on law, to give it an honest chance. His most important case, one that he would be forever proud of, concerned a suit brought by the Putnam Nail Company of Massachusetts for infringement of its trademark. Putnam had created a distinct image over the years by painting its nails bronze, and when a competitor began duplicating the practice Putnam sued. The case was lost in trial, but Wister persuaded Rawle and the reluctant client to let him appeal it. Wister won the appeal at circuit court, but lost before the Pennsylvania Supreme Court. He was proud of his performance, though, for he appeared to have won a victory of sorts. "My brief led Judge Mitchell to write a dissenting opinion, based upon the line I had taken, and that opinion changed the law as to equitable trade mark in our state," Wister later wrote.[20]

The young barrister, now thirty years of age, began an involvement in civic activities, including appointment to the board of the Pennsylvania Institution for the Instruction of the Blind. This and other such activities enhanced his standing in the law firm as well as in the community, and Francis Rawle began to see "symptoms of a lawyer" in his associate. But Wister still could not get Wyoming out of his system.[21]

His friend George West's regular letters reminded him of that land. In them, West described his hunting exploits, his hopes for his own horse ranch, and other details of his life on the range. Wister lent West five hundred dollars to establish a ranch, later named Horse Creek Ranch. (The attractive log house West built adjacent to a stream on the ranch was to be shown in a photograph several years later in *Lin McLean*.) It soon became evident, however, that West had overextended himself. Month after month he skirted financial calamity. He hired one man to break horses and another to work on his log fences, then after paying them, realized he was short one hundred dollars for other pressing obligations. "If you can advance this am't at the same rate as the $500.00 I shall be obliged & it will help me out wonderfully and I shall settle my account with you when I get into Nebraska & sell some horses," West wrote. Then, as an afterthought, he added, "If this is going to discourage you—*don't do it*." Wister evidently issued the advance; he found vicarious pleasure in helping West. West constantly sought and relied on Wister's advice for handling his affairs. Should he work hard and long hours to improve his ranch, or should he take the sudden offer of a job as a railroad dispatcher? The question had two edges, for if Wister recommended keeping the ranch there would exist the implied obligation to help West financially. Wister responded by asking West if he did not still want that wife and home in the mountains he had dreamed of so often, rather than a desk job. The more practical West responded, "Yes, I want a house Wister and a loving little wife—but how on earth can

I have such if I stay here all my days." Nevertheless, buoyed by Wister, he spurned the railroad job. To assist West through these difficult days, Wister forwarded to him his own discarded clothes and other practical gifts such as a skinning knife. West, in return, presented Wister with two elks' teeth. Wister lamented his own existence as a desk-bound lawyer, but West called his bluff, "Am sorry you are so unhappy or discontented but judging from what I know of you, think you must be enjoying life or you wouldn't stay in Phil. all winter." Indeed, if Wister were so miserable, then why did he not accept West's standing offer to come to Wyoming as his partner? And if that were impossible, then perhaps Wister might persuade some of his friends to join him in investing a few thousand dollars to buy horses that would yield a substantial profit when sold in Nebraska. Wister declined, pleading that his own financial condition was "hard up." Still, there was another summer hunting trip to anticipate. "Well it won't be long before we will be out in *our mountains* again," West wrote to Wister.[22]

Wister had his own choice to make in the spring of 1890: whether or not he himself should attempt to be the historian of the West. Wister did not use the term *historian* in its literal fact-recalling sense, however; rather, he intended to draw a portrait of the emotional aspects, a portrait such as only fiction could relate. He had been convinced since his first visit to the West that someone should capture for posterity the robust life of this unique society—the cowboys, Indians, and badmen. He saw no reason why he should not be that person. A personal fact reinforced that idea: throughout both his European musical adventures and law school he had never been able to discipline himself to keep a proper diary. Yet in the West he filled his journals effortlessly and delightfully with detail after detail about packhorses, campsites, nights in town, cardgames with cavalry officers, meals with cowpunchers, roundups, scenic landscapes, fishing trips, hunting outings with Indians, and shooting attempts for all sorts of wild game. He had not really known why he had written so thoroughly about this routine, but the truth dawned on him now that Wyoming had saturated his blood and marrow. To test himself, he began composing a western tale. By the time he finished he had written some fifty pages.[23]*

* Wister later wrote conflicting versions about his decision to write about the West. In 1930 he said he had decided to write western stories on a whim one evening *after* his 1891 trip while sitting in the Philadelphia Club with a friend. (See Wister, *Roosevelt: The Story of a Friendship, 1880–1919* [New York: MacMillan Co., 1930], p. 29.) In 1928 he said the "sketches" had been done "on the side" as

When he returned West in the summer of 1891 it was with the avowed purpose of soaking up "literary impressions" for more stories. Eventually, there would be "a great fat book" entitled "Chalkeye," the name of an actual cowboy he had encountered on a previous trip. This 1891 journey, his most prolonged to date, thus was pivotal in Wister's development as a writer, for he traveled with no other purpose than to find literary material. His timing was propitious, for this western journey was to be marked by an event he could never forget, providing the basis for one of the most unforgettable episodes in all his writings.[24]

The trip began much like his last one. Again he found on the train the traveling drummers he so detested, those "fetid commercial bores" who represented the creeping commercialism he felt endangered the nation's spirit. Drummers and all middlemen, he was convinced, produced nothing, improved nothing, and helped nothing. The conductor who took tickets and the brakemen who swung lamps seemed immeasurably superior. Such feelings help explain what often appears to be an inconsistency in Wister's personality: his easy movement from the genteel society of the East into the rough environment of the West. The similarity between the two was that neither bowed before the almighty dollar.[25]

When at last the train reached open country, the sight of two bunches of cattle encircled by cowpunchers made Wister almost cheer out loud. "This glorious, this supernatural atmosphere meets me again better, clearer, more magical, even than I remembered it," he wrote. His plan was to visit a cowman named Cheston Morris on the TTT Ranch in the Powder River valley between Casper and Buffalo, then go to Cheyenne to rendezvous with Lawrence Brooks of Boston, Dr. Charles B. Penrose of Philadelphia, and law associate Robert Ralston for a hunting trip in the Wind River country. When Wister reached the ranch he found his would-be host away on a roundup. The ranch's owner, David Robert Tisdale,* known as Rob or Bob, became Wister's host. Tisdale, whose

---

a "sort of outburst of the cumulative excitement which my Wyoming ranch and hunting experiences had awakened." (See Wister, "Preface—Thirty Years After," *The Writings of Owen Wister: Lin McLean* [New York: Macmillan Co., 1928], pp. viii-ix.) Yet as his own journal clearly affirms, the deliberate decision to write about the West was made *prior* to the 1891 journey.

* In his journal Wister identified Tisdale only by his last name, but the description of the ranch he visited fits that of the TTT—owned by Tisdale and his brother —on Willow Creek, a branch of the South Fork of Powder River. The TTT continues operations today from its headquarters south of Kaycee, Wyoming.

brother was a state senator and partner in the ranch, had moved to Wyoming from Canada. Wister had not previously met Tisdale, yet the two got along amiably for several days.[26] They traveled together on horseback for the various errands necessary in running a ranch and shared a wooden floor for a bed when they went to the community of Riverside to await the mail. Wister recorded in his journal the anecdotes and stories that naturally arose from conversations with Tisdale and other ranchers and cowboys: how one boastful broncobuster's wild horse had rolled over him and crushed his insides so severely that his body was almost too swollen to be squeezed into the coffin; how the remains of the murdered old-timer had been left to rot alongside the trail so that his bones were still visible; and how a cowhand named Hank had found a plain-looking wife, and another named Gregg had imported a wife from England.

These anecdotes were richly suggestive. In fact, soon Wister would combine the stories of the marriages into his first published short story. But the incident Wister would use to best advantage was an event he witnessed himself, an occurrence that repulsed him and immediately altered his relationship with Tisdale. The two men had been driving two horses in front of their own when the animals ran away and led them on a tiresome and frustrating chase over rough terrain. Eventually, when Tisdale's weary mount became exhausted, it stopped and gasped painfully. Tisdale, losing control of himself, dismounted and began to punish the animal for its failure. The horse patiently suffered kicking and pummelling to its ribs, legs, and jaw. Soon bloody foam oozed from its mouth. "I'll have to ask you to swap horses for a time," Tisdale told Wister. "This — brute's given out on me. They'd [the runaway horses] never got away if he hadn't given out. Just refused to go, for no reason whatever. No call to give out." Wister, fond of all animals, quickly offered his horse to Tisdale so the brutal beating would stop. But instead of taking it, Tisdale resumed punishing his horse, kicking it and wildly jerking its head about. Wister, speechless and reluctant to intervene, simply watched as Tisdale, swearing mightily, made several vicious grabs at the horse's eye. Then he climbed once more into the saddle and slowly rode forward some twenty yards, continuing to beat and kick. Finally the animal stopped altogether, and Wister, "dazed with disgust and horror," saw Tisdale lean forward with his hand over the horse's forehead. Suddenly the horse fell to the ground, pinning its tormentor. Wister ran forward to help. Tisdale assured him that he was not hurt and added that he had "got one eye out all right." The horse, still on the ground, pitifully turned its head—where its left eye was supposed to be Wister could see "only a sinkhole of blood." Stunned and sickened, he walked back to his own horse, sat down numbly, and watched the maimed animal struggle to its feet under the weight of Tisdale, who had mounted it again. Tisdale asked to borrow a spur, and Wister immediately obliged, hoping again to save further brutality, for as he recorded "the spurs were not severe and all horses answered to them from training." Incredibly, the ride then resumed. Tisdale had to dismount at several gulches where the horse was too weak to carry him. Once it fell to the ground going up a steep bank. For the remainder of this torturous ride to the ranch, Wister responded to his host's conversation only with monosyllables— his only thoughts being hatred for such a man and regret that he himself had lacked the courage to halt him. He determined to leave as soon as possible.[27]

Leaving was not immediately practical for Wister, though, for someone would have to take him sixty-five miles to Casper. So for three days he remained, brooding over his failure to prevent the torture. "But," he rationalized,

> the situation was a hard one. Here was I, the guest, and the very welcome guest of a stranger, who had done all he could to make me at home because I had come to see his friend. He could have told me the horse was his horse, not mine, and I was riding another of his. And I should have done no good, and reduced the relation between us two solitary people to something pretty bad, with nothing to do but sit together, eat together, and sleep together.

There was nothing to do but wait for Morris. Meanwhile, Wister remained coolly civil to Tisdale, nothing more. "Hand him the things at the table and then it stops." He did not know what Tisdale thought about his demeanor, and they did not discuss the episode.[28]

Finally Morris arrived and the tension eased. Wister, though, could not refrain from dwelling over the incident. Nothing had ever sickened him so much. He wondered if he were exaggerating in his mind the incident's significance. Had he been a coward, a "moral craven who did not lift a finger or speak a word"? As Wister chatted one day with the ranch cook, the man called Wister's attention to Tisdale down near the creek beating another horse over the head with a stake. Nobody in Wyoming had such a reputation for cruelty as Tisdale, the cook told him, and he added that sometimes the man even gouged out an animal's eye! Wister

began now to reassess his image of the western man. "I begin to conclude from five seasons of observation," Wister wrote, "that life in this
negligent irresponsible wilderness tends to turn people shiftless, cruel,
and incompetent." He had seen the trait in Major Wolcott in that first
summer, and he began to notice now among other Westerners a "sloth
in doing anything." Such a people, such a land, could not be chronicled
easily. Yet he was more certain than ever that this must be done. If he
believed in the efficacy of prayer, he wrote in his journal, he would
petition the Almighty to make his the hand that "once and for all
chronicled and laid bare the virtues and the vices of this extraordinary
phase of American social progress."[29]

After a few days Wister and Morris left Tisdale's ranch by horseback
for a forty-four-mile ride to Buffalo and nearby Fort McKinney. There,
Wister renewed an acquaintance with the only "unabridged bad man"
he had known—"Black Henry" Smith, a Texan who had been "run out"
of every country in which he had lived. He had been in Wyoming for
some six years working for big outfits. He was extremely tall and dark,
smiled sardonically, spoke with an unpleasant and raspy voice, and his
eyes burned with the color of mottled yellow.

> They are the very worst eyes I have ever looked at. Perfectly fearless
> and shrewd, and treacherous. . . . And all the while he talked I watched
> him as intently as I have ever studied the day before an examination,
> noting every turn in his speech and every lift of his head. He is not
> a half-way man. Not the Bret Harte villain with the heart of a woman.
> Not the mixed dish or Cambric tea so dear to modern novelists. He is
> just bad through and through, without a scruple and without an affection.
> His face is entirely cruel, and you hear cruelty in his voice.

He was a brilliant talker, too, and Smith found in Wister exactly what
Wister intended for him to find—an eager listener. Wister vowed to
his journal that when he came to his "castle in Spain" he would "strain
his muscles to catch Smith." Smith, a member of the notorious "Red
Sash gang" (members wore red sashes around their waists), would be
arrested twice within the next year for separate crimes: trying to burn
down the Fort McKinney barracks with kerosene, and murdering from
ambush a special United States marshal. In both cases he was freed for
lack of evidence.[30]

In Cheyenne Wister greeted Robert Ralston, Dr. Charles B. Penrose
(whose brother, the future United States Senator Boies Penrose, was
coming later), and Lawrence Brooks. He led them to Fort Washakie to

meet George West, their guide. The men rode and hunted, as Wister and West had done before, along the Wind River toward Yellowstone National Park. Wister marveled anew with the Easterners over the natural wonders they saw, especially two natural bridges in Warm Springs Canyon which he photographed, predicting that one day the spot would be a tourist attraction echoing with the howls of the summer mob.[31]

All the while Wister's mind churned with ideas for the stories he would write. Resting one evening on the shores of a beautiful lake near Meadow Creek, the pale blue snowcapped Tetons glimmering above the pines, he thought of an opening line for a tale called "The Adventures of a Bad Shot." The opening would be: "No man tells the truth about himself and his gun." In the autumn he planned to begin "Chalkeye" (now reduced to a short story) and something called "Raymond and His Three Lives." But the one major book he would write, his "castle in the air" which would tie together the full sweep of the land, now would be called "The Tenderfoot." He was not yet ready to write it, but he was confident that some day he would be.[32]

Yellowstone National Park was bursting this time with wagons, people, and screaming children. Still, the area's natural majesty reigned. The lower falls and canyon of the Yellowstone River inspired Wister no less than they had four years earlier. The view reminded him of the most beautiful passages of Wagner's trilogy: "those moments when the whole orchestra seems to break into silver fragments of magic— sounds of harps and violins all away up somewhere sustaining some theme you have heard before, but which now returns twice as magnificent." He tried to describe the power of the setting in a letter to his mother by relating a conversation he had once had with a Mrs. Lawrence about her visit to the lower falls. "She said to me, opening her eyes staring wide, 'When that sight came over me I—I was so *emotioneé* I had to be helped to a log.'" The tourists who scuttled like mice to the site and then turned away after only a brief glimpse disgusted Wister.[33]

After Yellowstone the hunting party broke up, and all but Wister returned East. Wister stayed behind for more hunting and fishing. His health was at a peak. He could endure horseback rides of fifty miles on one day and spring back the next without evidence of fatigue. He could sleep on the ground or on wooden floors with equal ease, and he could subsist on greasy bacon and coffee made of gravel and game. Not until September did he return to Philadelphia, to the place he said he would not choose for himself or for his friends if he could help it.[34]

Once more he resumed—half-heartedly perhaps—his career in law. He kept himself busy with the inevitable social activities. His resolve to write the stories circulating through his head faded. There was no time. He could not, for instance, turn down his friend Major Higginson who wrote to him with a special request: Would Wister tell his friends about the forthcoming Philadelphia concert of the Polish pianist Ignace Jan Paderewski, known the world over except in Philadelphia? A slim crowd was unthinkable. Wister energetically complied with the request, and when the gifted artist arrived at the Philadelphia train station Wister was there to meet him, chat with him in French, and escort him to his hotel. As the hour for the evening concert arrived, however, countless rows of empty seats could not be concealed. Spectators filled only the first ten or so rows, the remainder of the three thousand seat Academy of Music Hall was embarrassingly empty. Wister clapped hard to try to compensate for the empty chairs, and afterwards he went backstage to take Paderewski to dinner as they had previously agreed. The pianist, however, was so enraged about the sparse turnout that he refused to go.[35]

One evening, some weeks after his return from Wyoming and while chafing over his failure to write his stories, Wister dined in the refined atmosphere of the Philadelphia Club with his friend Walter Furness. The two, as Wister much later would recall, began talking fervently about the West and bemoaning its lack of a "Kipling" to tell its story. They agreed that Roosevelt had observed the region's magic firsthand and had written good facts, and that Frederic Remington had illustrated the land admirably with his art, but that no one had probed the West through fiction. Wister remembered that he exclaimed, "Walter, I'm going to try it myself!" And he immediately went upstairs to the library to begin. By midnight, as he later related the incident, he had composed a substantial portion of his first western story, "Hank's Woman." Wister's recollection of his start, written down some forty years after the fact, has led to a long-held belief that he determined on sudden impulse to write about the West. As we have seen, this was not true. He had delayed interminably the plans made prior to his last visit to write about the land, and the conversation with Furness evidently served to remind him that he must waste no more time. At any rate, when he had completed "Hank's Woman" he wrote a second story entitled "How Lin McLean Went East." Both stories won praise from the several friends who read them, but soon this surge of creative energy dissipated. He permitted the manuscripts to languish in his desk until Weir Mitchell promised an accompanying letter of introduction if he would send them to Henry Mills Alden at Harper & Brothers. Wister, of course, agreed to do so, and Alden soon sent back good news: he would publish both stories.[36]

"Hank's Woman," a somber tale-within-a-tale, was narrated by an overall-clad cowboy named Lin McLean to an eager eastern tenderfoot as they fished at a stream in the Teton basin. Wister borrowed this device —in which the narrator tells the story to a participant—from Prosper Mérimée, whose *Carmen* and *Mateo Falcone* he had recently read. (In fact, Wister once declared Mérimée to be his primary inspiration in seeking to put Wyoming into prose fiction.) Hank was a mean-spirited shrimp of a frontiersman who precipitously married a bulky, plain-looking European named Willomene after she was fired as a maid and stranded by her European mistress at Yellowstone National Park. Hank brought his bride on horseback over mountain trails to his job at a mining camp where McLean and others were working. From the beginning the newlyweds were mismatched; they argued constantly. The unfortunate Willomene, totally out of her element, retreated more and more to prayer and to her crucifix. This only infuriated Hank more. Eventually, McLean and the other miners had to bring in a fresh supply of meat, leaving the quarreling pair alone in the mining camp. Upon returning after three days they found the camp desolate. On searching, they spotted a bloody ax and Willomene's bullet-pierced crucifix. At the edge of nearby Little Death Canyon the tragedy that had occurred in their absence was revealed. Hank, his skull smashed, was "stiff and stark" at the canyon's edge, held up from a long fall to the bottom only by the roots of a dead tree. Far below at the bottom was Willomene, "tumbled all in a heap." It took only a moment's calculation for McLean and the other miners to reconstruct the sequence of events. Willomene, having killed Hank after he shot her crucifix, had attempted to toss his body from the precipice to make his death look like an accident. In the process, however, she slipped and fell to the canyon's depths.[37]

"Hank's Woman" exemplified the reportorial approach that soon would win Wister a reputation as the "Kipling of the West" or as the new Bret Harte. He based the story on the two anecdotes related to him by "Black Henry" Smith: one concerning a real cowboy named Hank who had married a plain-looking woman after only a week's courtship, and the other about a cowboy who had gone to England for a bride and "fetched one along aback." "Lin McLean," identified by the eastern tenderfoot as "the man whom among all cowpunchers I love most," was his good friend and guide, George West. For dialogue, Wister employed an extreme vernacular which he had sought to capture in his notebooks. The geographical setting he knew intimately from firsthand experiences. Moreover, the hopeless conflict between Hank's western and Willomene's European cultures represented a theme that Wister himself felt intensely and that would mark everything he would write concerning the West.

"How Lin McLean Went East" also was based on an actual incident, this one concerning George West. Even less dramatic license was required for this story. McLean is seen here as a footloose, gambling, woman-chasing cowboy who has long since forgotten his eastern roots in favor of his carefree and happy existence in the West. He decides, however, to return to Boston and visit his brother, a respectable bank teller and club man. It soon becomes apparent that Lin's cowboy clothes are embarrassing his brother, who suggests that Lin not wear "that style of hat" while with his crowd. McLean, angered, returns immediately to Wyoming where he knows he belongs, realizing that his visit to his brother and to Boston's artificial life was a mistake.* The tale was Wister's clear affirmation of the superiority of the spontaneous, open western society over the false eastern values.[38]

"This second story is harmless & you can read it," Wister told his mother, who did not approve of the sort of violence depicted in "Hank's Woman." Wister felt certain, too, that "Lin McLean" exhibited superior writing. " 'Hank's Woman' makes its effect by means of loud orchestration, cymbals, kettle drums, & c; but this one is andante sostenuto, generally p, never ff, and with not a single brass instrument."[39]

The stories earned Wister a check for $175 from Henry Mills Alden and congratulations from his employer, Francis Rawle. Secretly, Wister felt that the check signified much more than money—it meant a release from the "detested occupation" of law. This soon proved to be true. But it would not mean a total severance, because for the next twenty-five years Wister maintained an office in the firm, not as a law practice but as a headquarters for his writing.[40]

---

* West's brother in Boston was North M. West. West's son, George M. West of Seattle, Washington, repeated the story, as told to him by his father, in an interview on August 16, 1978. West quoted North from his father's account of the incident, "Take that darn hat off; I don't want to walk down the street with you."

Chapter VIII

IN SEARCH OF MATERIAL
(1892–1895)

WHILE WISTER ANXIOUSLY AWAITED PUBLICATION of his two stories, the land and people depicted in them had become embroiled in a controversy. Splashy headlines in newspapers all over the nation told the story: Major Frank Wolcott, Wister's host that first summer in Wyoming, and nearly fifty armed men under his command, many of them Wister's friends, had been arrested for insurrection! Behind that startling fact lay a tangled set of circumstances. In the six years since Wister first had gone to Wolcott's ranch, a series of hard winters, incursions by farmers, and a declining cattle market had greatly reduced the profit margins of the big ranchers. Some, including Wolcott, even lost control of their property to creditors. Their frustrations prompted them to take decisive action against one tangible menace: rustlers.

Inspired and organized by Wolcott, the ranchers determined to drive out or even to lynch a group of rustlers operating out of nearby Johnson County. Wolcott and certain members of the powerful Wyoming Stock Growers Association, accustomed to wielding influence, had few qualms about taking the law into their own hands. Accordingly, they compiled a list of suspected rustlers (including the Red Sash gang of which Wister's "bad man," Black Henry Smith, was a dominant figure) and set out en masse.

Wolcott's force included twenty-five Wyoming ranchers and twenty-one imported Texas gunmen, the latter smuggled into the state aboard a special train. The Texans, distinguished only by their prowess with arms, contrasted sharply with the ranchers, who were among Wyoming's most prominent citizens. Besides Wolcott, Wister's friends among the ranchers included: Fred G. S. Hesse, William C. Irvine, Hubert E. Teschemacher, Frederic O. deBillier, Frank Canton, and—if not exactly a friend, a man he knew only too well—David Robert Tisdale. An entirely unexpected member of the vigilante force was Dr. Charles B. Penrose of Philadelphia, whom Wister himself had introduced to the area. Penrose served

the force as physician. The expedition, accompanied by a "war" correspondent brought in from the *Chicago Herald*, came together at Casper.
To cloak their activities, the ranchers cut the telegraph wires north of
the city and rode boldly into Johnson County. En route they camped at
Tisdale's TTT Ranch, then continued northward until they located two
suspected rustlers in a tiny ranch house near Buffalo. The vigilantes surprised the pair, fatally shot one of them, then flushed out the second
suspect by rolling a wagon filled with burning hay against the frame
house. As the second suspect fled the burning structure he, too, was
mortally wounded. On the next day the invading force found their situation suddenly reversed; a huge mob of armed Johnson County residents,
angered by this excursion into their backyards, surrounded the ranchers
and prepared to attack. Many were angered by a belief that the invasion
had an ulterior motive—not merely to curb rustlers but to stamp out the
small, honest ranchers who were legitimate competitors. The besieged
invaders were saved before an armed conflict broke out, only after Acting
Governor Amos W. Barber (another of Wister's friends) requested and
gained intervention by federal troops stationed at nearby Fort Mc-
Kinney.[1]*

Meanwhile, Wister and George West were making plans to meet in
Wyoming that summer for another prolonged hunting trip. West was
especially eager to see this man who he unabashedly proclaimed to be
the best friend he had ever had. He wanted advice on how to handle the
affairs of the small ranch he had bought at DuBois, especially its debts;
he wanted to apologize for some cross words exchanged on their last
hunting trip which he feared had offended Wister; he wanted encouragement about the bid he had submitted for the mail contract at Fort
Washakie; and he wanted quick advice on what to do about his deteriorating teeth. Not the least of his worries concerned Wister himself. "Now
Wister listen to me," he had written. "You are not overly strong—you
need a long rest and one away from city & fast life." He intended to
persuade Wister to spend six months or a year with him at his ranch.[2]

All the while, Wister was watching events in Wyoming carefully,
compiling an extensive collection of clippings. There was no denying

---

* These dramatic events might not have been surprising to Wister. George West
had alerted him in February 1892 to "quite an excitement" in the area about horse
thieves. The same group of cowpunchers he and Wister had observed camped below
them on the Snake River the preceding year had been identified as horse thieves.
"They are being watched from all sides & will be taken in the spring," West had
informed Wister. (West to Wister, February 14, 1892, Box 37, Owen Wister Papers.)

whose side he was on in the cattle "war." He publicly blamed the trouble on rustlers whose depredations had become bolder and bolder until "what seemed to be a regular organization resulted." In his mind the ranchers had had little alternative but to act forthrightly to prevent "wholesale robbery."[3]

The arrested ranchers expected Wister to act as their own literary spokesman and historian. Teschemacher, sitting in court watching preliminary proceedings against the group, took notes to hand over to Wister. "Come and see us as we can furnish a great deal of material for your magnum opus," he wrote. Dr. Penrose also wrote a long letter explaining the vigilantes' side of the affair, and Acting Governor Barber informed Wister that he had "considerable data" for him to use in preparing an article on the "rustling troubles." (Barber was accused of siding with the big ranchers, critics alleging that his request for federal troops was plainly motivated by his desire to save the invading vigilantes from annihilation by Johnson County citizens.)[4]

Talk of retribution against the vigilante ranchers and their property was widespread.* President Benjamin Harrison issued a proclamation ordering all unlawful assemblages in Wyoming to disperse. The time certainly did not seem to be propitious for an outspoken eastern friend of the imprisoned vigilantes, namely Wister, to make a prolonged visit to Wyoming. Certainly Wister knew that he could not easily resume his relationships with common cowboys and noted badmen like Black Henry Smith. Perhaps it was this consideration that caused Wister to cancel his planned hunting trip with West.[5]

Curiously, however, instead of writing a letter, he made a round trip of some five thousand miles to tell West in person. His friends were puzzled that he would take such a journey only to turn around and come back, and indeed a hint of mystery exists as to why he did. That his decision related to the Johnson County troubles was indicated by a journal entry stating that Dr. Penrose's son accompanied him to the train station for his departure and that even if the trip were a mystery to others, young Penrose "appreciated the reason." (Dr. Penrose's release from custody already had been obtained.)[6]

On July 11 Wister's train rolled into Cinnabar, Montana, and there on the platform stood an expectant George West. Wister was reluctant

* In fact, while the ranchers awaited trial, Black Henry Smith and other accused rustlers were riding free over the Wyoming countryside, thus giving good cause for fears of retribution.

to admit that he was cancelling the hunting trip and returning East that very afternoon. But, as they walked up and down the platform, he at last managed to tell West. They drank beer and talked for the rest of the afternoon, and at 6:15 P.M. Wister boarded the East-bound train for the return trip.[7]

In his journal Wister stated that the only reason he hated giving up his trip to Wyoming was because a man named Keller (evidently a Philadelphia acquaintance) would think it was out of "personal fear for my carcase." At least one historian has suggested that the seemingly pointless journey was sheer bravado by Wister to prove that he was not afraid to go West. Another possible explanation was Wister's insistence that he pay George West the full fee of seventy-five dollars which they had agreed upon for his services for the hunting trip, and he may have wanted to do so in person. West already had arranged to take time off for the hunting expedition, and he was as usual in financial difficulty.[8]

The return trip to Philadelphia was not without incident. Wister had organized a game of whist with other passengers when east of Billings, Montana, a prolonged cry, apparently from outside, interrupted them. Investigating at the rear platform, the passengers could not determine the source, even as the desperate wailing grew louder. At last, when the conductor stopped the train, they discovered that the cries came from a tramp who, while adjusting himself beneath the train, had had his foot run over by a wheel. While others attended to the injury, Wister offered the victim his flask of whiskey to ease the pain. When the train resumed its journey Wister walked the length of the passenger cars and collected donations. When he returned with the money the frightened tramp clutched Wister's leg tightly and begged for help. Wister comforted him as best he could, silently noting that an amputation surely must be performed, and at the next town the crying man was taken from the train for treatment. That experience had been unsettling, but on the whole, the nine-day round trip became for Wister one of "almost unalloyed pleasure and content."[9]

Wister always loved Wyoming above all other western states, but it perhaps is no coincidence that after the Johnson County war his next trips were to Washington, Texas, New Mexico, and Arizona. Moreover, his belief that the West would create an improved breed of Americans suffered a setback when he saw the popular reaction against the measures taken by Wolcott and his vigilantes. In the years ahead, frontier support for movements that he detested—such as populism and labor—brought further doubts.

Only a few months after his abbreviated trip, Wister departed Philadelphia once more, this time for the distant state of Washington to visit his pal from Harvard, George Waring. Having left the East for the Northwest after the surprising marriage which alienated his family, Waring now was operating a small general store on the Methow River in a primitive, central area of the state. Here, certainly, new literary material as well as an old friend awaited Wister.

He was not to be disappointed in either expectation. In Coulee City, where he transferred from his long train ride to a stagecoach for the final leg of the journey, Wister checked into the available hotel in hopes of a restful night before the next day's arduous ride. Upstairs in his tiny room he turned down the bed sheets and found "several thousand" cockroaches scrambling frantically over one another. He shuddered to see that the walls, ceiling, and floor quivered with the insects. The landlord could only apologize, observing that the cockroaches had fled from the downstairs kitchen because he had dusted it for insects that day. Wister chose to bed down on the office table, dozing as best he could between the shouts of an all-night poker game in the adjoining room.[10]*

The next day he saw that the practical joke, so much a part of Wyoming life, was equally a custom in Washington. A fellow passenger on the stagecoach, a salesman, offered a drink to the stage driver going the opposite direction. "Well I never *do* refuse," the thirsty teamster responded. Then, as the knowing passengers watched expectantly, he accepted the bottle, uncorked it with a pop, looked amiably at Wister and the others, and said, "My regards, gentlemen!" Tilting his head far backward, he drank deeply before the truth dawned. "I'll be son of a bitched!" he exclaimed. The bottle held only water, and Wister joined the other passengers in loud guffaws. "That's one on me," the driver said, recapping the bottle, "but I'll fix somebody before sundown."[11]

When Wister finally reached Waring's humble store and house in the Methow Valley, things were not so funny. For as exhilarating as it was to see his former theatrical partner, Waring's circumstances were too severe to generate mirth. Despite his novel welcome for Wister—

* Wister later made his experience with the cockroaches a pivotal incident in a short story he would claim as one of his three favorites. (See Wister, "The Right Honorable the Strawberries," *When West Was West* [New York: Macmillan Co., 1928], pp. 146-211.)

flying an improvised Porcellian Club flag—Waring appeared to live a "very, very awful" existence. Wister was further saddened to learn that Waring thought his situation to be as bad as Wister did. Having departed his comfortable circumstances in the East after marrying his stepmother's sister, Waring now was reduced to a subsistence level, not only for himself and his wife but also for three stepchildren.[12]*

One of Wister's purposes in visiting was to hunt wild goat, the only American game he had never seen. Waring did not have time to accompany him, but Wister vowed not to return East until he had shot a goat. Two weeks after arriving he accomplished the feat, and he recorded the deed in his appointment book while skinning the animal, staining the page with blood in the process.[13]

Meanwhile, word of Wister's new writing career had preceded him to Washington. The Warings had heard of "Hank's Woman" through a man who had read it in Spokane and was surprised to learn that they knew the author. Then, to Wister's amazement, when a *Harper's Monthly* solicitation for a subscription arrived at the Waring house it featured "How Lin McLean Went East" as a forthcoming attraction. Nearly a year had passed since Alden had paid for the story, but he had liked it so well that he purposely delayed publication for the special 1982 Christmas issue.[14]

Not until Wister was on the Northern Pacific railroad en route home did he see the issue. His first glimpse of it came in the Dakotas over the shoulder of a fellow passenger, an Army officer, who was looking through the magazine. When Wister got the magazine himself he feigned a casual air and began leafing through the pages, commenting to the officer beside him, "This looks like a good number." The officer said he preferred *Scribner's*. Finally—fatefully—the officer added that he had read one story in the issue—"Mac, MacKay, or something." Wister, his spirits rising, concealed his interest and subtly inquired as to the story's subject. "Oh, it's a cowboy," the officer replied, thumbing through the pages to find it. "There, Lin McLean. That's it. He went East." Wister then enjoyed the rare luxury of having his own story related to him, and he beamed happily but anonymously when his seatmate

* Waring had settled in the Methow Valley in 1891 after several years of wandering in search of a suitable location. In 1893, a year after Wister's visit, he was to leave the area for Michigan, only to return to Washington in 1896. He did not relinquish control over the business he had founded, the Methow Trading Company, until 1924. Meanwhile, he gained a regional reputation as the pioneer settler and businessman in the Methow Valley.

concluded, "Oh, it's a good cowboy story." Wister said he would be certain to read it.[15]

At home in Philadelphia he basked in the awaiting praise. One friend said "Hank's Woman" was "very strong—quite like Bret Harte." The wife of a colonel who once had entertained Wister said that "Lin McLean" took her happily back to Fort Washakie. Theodore Roosevelt surprised Wister by quoting from memory his favorite passage from "McLean" about a Westerner being "only slightly stabbed" as he walked to a dance hall. Basing his opinion on these first two stories, Roosevelt saw hope in his friend's future as a recorder of the western scene. "And —I—don't—*think*—you'll—peter—out," he said, measuring Wister carefully.[16]

An entirely different kind of writing venture earned him further praise in 1892. J. B. Lippincott Company published his earlier short effort, *The Dragon of Wantley*, in an edition handsomely illustrated by John Stewardson. The book reminded the *Literary World*'s reviewer of Mark Twain's parody of the legend of King Arthur except that it seemed "in much better taste."* To Wister, though, the book was "intentionally & confessedly bric à brac." It had been three years since he had written it.[17]

He was working already on other western tales. The most important one was "Balaam and Pedro," the story of Tisdale's gouging of the horse's eye. In it, Wister introduced an enigmatic character known only as "the Virginian." Wister sent the finished story to the *Atlantic Monthly*, where it was promptly rejected. Then he mailed it to William Dean Howells, recently named editor of *Cosmopolitan*. Howells accepted "Balaam and Pedro," but soon he resigned, and the editor-owner, John B. Walker, kept the story without notifying Wister of any plans for it. Finally in December, responding to Wister's frantic queries, Walker notified him that he would not use the story. Disgusted, Wister placed the story in limbo until he could decide what to do with it.[18]

Writing was now a daily morning preoccupation for Wister. He seldom wrote more than a few hundred words, composing these in an unusually tiny, neat hand. He spent much of his other time with luncheon or dinner engagements, evenings at the Philadelphia Club,

---

* Three years later Samuel L. Clemens would congratulate Wister on the book: "I have taken the Dragon of Wantley away from my wife & daughter—by violence— I am reading it with a delicate & tingling enjoyment which goes searching & soothing & tickling & caressing all through me everywhere like balm of Gilead with a whet of apollinaries in it. I owe you thanks, and thanks, & still thanks and more thanks, for writing it!" (Clemens to Wister, August 4, 1895, Box 45, Owen Wister Papers).

letter writing, playing or writing music, and other social affairs. The practice of law was but a minor part of his life, and it was this year, 1892, that he later identified as the time he abandoned the profession.[19]

Music remained close to his heart. In 1892 he had begun to perform publicly in a piano quartet with John Ingham, Molly Moss, and Mary Channing Wister, the latter an energetic distant cousin who intrigued him. Miss Wister, or "Molly" as she was called, did not like "Hank's Woman," but she approved of "How Lin McLean Went East." In a complimentary note she added, however, that if she had her way, Wister would write on paper filled with musical staffs. In fact, the quartet already was playing some of Wister's own compositions, and other musical groups in the city also were performing the numbers in public.[20]

A friend in San Francisco, Francis Michael, sought to have *Montezuma*, at last completed, presented for its premiere performance at a theater there, but Wister's attention by now was turned to another work which he had again written in collaboration with Tom Wharton. Entitled *Villon*, it was a "romantic opera" in four acts with François Villon and Louis XI as its central characters in a 1463–64 Parisian setting. The first producer to whom Wister and Wharton offered the opera rejected it. The next one, Reginald De Koven, according to a notation made on a copy of the libretto, agreed to stage it, then promptly lost the score. He never found it, and *Villon* never was performed. A successful performance might have caused Wister to return full time to music and to abandon his literary career.[21]

As it was, he now was growing impatient during a long hiatus that had developed since the acceptance of his first two western stories. Discouraged, Wister proposed a series of musical articles to Horace E. Scudder of the *Atlantic Monthly*. Scudder was not enthusiastic; a "series of articles" had an alarming air to it. He preferred a specific article Wister had mentioned on "catholicity in musical taste"; this had "an attractive sound." Wister agreed, and the article appeared in the November 1893 issue. In it, he lamented the narrowness in taste that seemed to be the hallmark of musical debates such as those he had had with his own mother. Wister earned thirty-five dollars for the article, far less than he had received from *Harper's* for his western stories, and it was easy for him to see that the best money did not lie in writing about music.[22]

In the spring of 1892, feeling the need for fresh western air, Wister went to Texas with a Philadelphia friend, Harry Groome, to stay at the ranch of still another Philadelphian, Fitzhugh Savage. Savage trained polo ponies at his ranch at Seven Springs near Brownwood before shipping them to the East Coast. There was an unusual concentration of Easterners in this west central Texas area, for two other men whom Wister had known at St. Paul's, Frank and Dick Conover, owned nearby ranches. The men all were bachelors, and during Wister's month-long stay they practiced polo in the afternoon, playing cards and drinking whiskey in the evenings. While his old friends naturally were fine fellows, Wister found the typical Texan to be far less congenial than his counterpart in Wyoming; Texans were in his opinion hypocritically "moralistic," murderous, and of the "poor white trash" caliber despised by the southern Negro for meanness. The stay was not unpleasant, however, nor was it without special interest. A tune sung by a Brady, Texas, cowboy at Savage's ranch so struck Wister that he carefully wrote down all five verses. When Wister's western journals were published nearly sixty years later his rendition became the earliest documented proof of the use of the classic cowboy tune, "Git Along Little Dogies."* He also heard a neighboring Texan named Jim Neil tell of a practical joke involving the wholesale swapping of babies at a frontier party while the parents danced. The tale seemed so pat that Wister accused Neil of having stolen it from an almanac. Neil admitted that he did not know of the incident firsthand, but had heard it in San Saba, Texas.* Still another anecdote Wister heard concerned a mixed-up hen; he put this tale in a story called "Em'ly." Upon finishing "Em'ly" he sent it to Alden at *Harper's*, along with "Balaam and Pedro."[23]

Back in Wyoming, George West was distressed. His part of the country seemed less and less important to Wister. If his friend no longer were to spend his summers there, West was not certain he cared to stay himself. He had come to depend upon Wister's summer payment, and he had remained in Wyoming largely because of his patron's advice, encouragement, and loans. Now, four hundred dollars in debt, he felt trapped. He asked Wister for more money, even though he still had not repaid earlier loans. He reminded Wister that at one time they had discussed the possibility of becoming partners, and West still welcomed

---

* In his journal Wister noted the uniqueness of the song. The American public became generally familiar with the tune when John Avery Lomax published his 1910 pioneer collection, *Cowboy Songs and Other Frontier Ballads.* In 1932 Wister presented Lomax with his own rendition of the song's musical notations, and Lomax included this, along with Wister's comments, in *American Ballads and Songs,* published in 1934 by Macmillan.

* The story would gain lasting fame when Wister included it in *The Virginian.*

such an opportunity. The constant requests for money had begun to annoy Wister, however, and he asked West to explain what had happened to the other money. West complied, adding that except for Wister's advice, he would have left cowboy life two years earlier to work on the railroad. Wister was so swayed that he cancelled all West's debts. West was overwhelmed at the kindness: the letter "sent a chill" over him. "You are good, Wister and a Christian if there are any on earth. . . . Yes, you are a friend to me & the best I have ever had or will ever have I know. I never thought one man could love another as I have grown to love you." To show his gratitude further, West announced that he was breaking a horse for his friend's personal use. Three months later West again asked for a loan. Wister refused to give it.[24]

In June Wister was in Chicago to help arrange the Boone and Crockett Club's exhibit for the 1893 World's Columbian Exposition. He, Theodore Roosevelt, Winthrop Chanler, and other friends on the club's executive committee devised a rustic exhibit—a hunter's cabin situated on a wooded island. Club members met there for a meal of fish and beefsteaks, and Theodore wanted to have whiskey and beer in keeping with the simple nature of the cabin. But Wister and two others insisted on champagne, and they won. The champagne was in keeping with the Exposition's grandiose architecture, described since as the "climax" of the genteel tradition. Wister, in fact, was rebelling against this very tradition with his western stories, straying only slightly from real incidents and refusing to inject extraneous material designed to uplift the reader. Yet the Exposition's white columns, magnificent facades, statues, lagoons, and fountains set his head swimming with their "beauty and brilliance and stateliness." He met the American sculptor, Augustus Saint-Gaudens, who had advised the planning of the Exposition's art and architecture. Saint-Gaudens escorted Wister about the grounds, commenting knowledgeably and with great pride over the spectacle.[25]

At home in Philadelphia two letters from Henry Mills Alden awaited, confirming without question the "wreck" of Wister's dwindling legal career. *Harper's* would be proud to publish both "Balaam and Pedro" and "Em'ly" and would pay three hundred dollars for that privilege. The magazine's prize western artist, Frederic Remington, would illustrate "Balaam and Pedro." Wister proudly noted that this was an encouraging forty-eight percent increase in pay compared to the $175 he had earned for his first two western stories. In the second letter Alden expressed his hope that Wister would not desert *Harper's* with his writing. Alden said he could hardly believe the news that Wister had been to distant Texas. Had he "really" gone there? If so, Alden was interested in any material with a Texas setting.[26]

A few days later, Wister received the first of what eventually would become a deluge: a New York man whom Wister did not know wanted his autograph! This came as a surprising and somewhat senseless request, and Wister penciled a notation on the fan letter for his own enjoyment, "It takes all sorts of people to make a world." In the years to come, the growing number of requests by "autograph friends" whose only interest was in the signature itself caused Wister much consternation. He grew to resent them deeply.[27]

The two new stories demonstrated once more Wister's combined use of firsthand information with literary imagination. "Balaam and Pedro" was to be one of the most significant stories of his career, and he sensed that fact. By the time the tale appeared in *Harper's Monthly*, Wister had written several other stories, but still declared of "Balaam and Pedro," "I know that I have never done anything so good, or that contains so big a swallow of Wyoming."[28]

In the story, Wister not only worked out his personal frustrations at his failure to prevent Tisdale from mistreating the horse, but also introduced the never-to-be-forgotten cowboy known only as "the Virginian." Wister's plot centered on the maiming: Pedro was the favorite horse of a carefree cowboy named Shorty, who had sold the horse to Balaam in a weak moment, fully intending to buy Pedro back as soon as he got the money. The Virginian was a strong, quiet cowboy assigned by his employer, Judge Henny (renamed Henry in *The Virginian*), to retrieve two other horses that Balaam had borrowed but neglected to return.

In Wister's mind it was only a character such as the Virginian who could handle forcefully and properly the incidence of extreme cruelty. The Virginian acted as Wister wished he had been able to act himself. When Tisdale had told Wister he would have to use his horse, Wister had eagerly offered it as a lame means to halt the abuse. With the Virginian in the same situation, however, the Virginian told Balaam (the name substituted for Tisdale), "You ain' goin' to touch my hawse." Wister, recoiling in shock upon seeing what Tisdale had done to the horse's eye, could only walk back to his own horse in numb silence. The Virginian, in contrast, acted immediately. He threw Balaam to the ground, and when Balaam drew a pistol the Virginian stomped on his hand and roughed him up again.* Then, instead of merely watching the villain ride away on the maimed animal, the Virginian unsaddled the horse ("Pedro") and led him tenderly to the ranch.

Attempting to date the first appearance of this cowboy—who was to become an inspiration and model for future generations of literary and film western heroes—leads to confusion. This is understandable for several reasons, but the confusion is easily cleared. When Wister rewrote "Hank's Woman" some years later, he replaced Lin McLean with the Virginian. Readers who encountered the rewritten version of "Hank's Woman," rather than the original, erroneously assumed that the Virginian appeared in the first short story Wister ever published about the West. The matter is complicated further by the fact that *Harper's* published "Em'ly" before "Balaam and Pedro." As a result, it seemed that the Virginian first appeared in "Em'ly." But the order in which Wister actually wrote the two stories is clear: he had completed "Balaam and Pedro" by June of 1892, and he finished "Em'ly" nearly a year later between April 10 and July 12, 1893. This clarifies the fact: this most famous cowboy hero originated in "Balaam and Pedro," stemming from Wister's own frustrations over an unfortunate personal experience.[29]

Wister was particularly eager to learn of readers' reactions concerning "Balaam and Pedro," for he feared they might reject it because of its cruelty. He soon received a firsthand report, again on a train, this time between Harrisburg and Philadelphia. A young man with whom he had been playing whist picked up the issue of *Harper's*, thumbed through the pages, and stopped to study Frederic Remington's illustration for the story. He read a few sentences of Wister's text opposite the drawing, resumed his thumbing through the remainder of the magazine, and then returned once more to read the story. Three pages later he observed to Wister, "Don't it make you hot to read about cruelty and horses being abused?" Wister answered coyly, "Yes, is that story about such things?" Affirming that it was, the young man continued reading, skipping hurriedly through the last half of the story. "My author's pride was chastened by his not reading every word I had written, of course," Wister later wrote. But it helped to realize that the man had read nothing else in the magazine. "If such as this will read me, I am secure. But I think I owe it to Remington's picture; otherwise he might not have been arrested."[30]

---

* When Wister later rewrote the story for *The Virginian*, he made the retribution even more severe. The Virginian "beat his face and struck his jaw," causing Balaam to commence a "hideous screaming of hate and pain" to which the cowboy responded, "If you are dead, I am glad of it."

When Wister encountered Theodore Roosevelt at a Boone and Crockett Club dinner in New York, he heard this advocate of the strenuous life, of all people, vigorously protest against including an exact description of the maiming. He informed Wister that his own cousin, West Roosevelt, had thrown the magazine down in disgust, declaring that he never would read another word Wister wrote. Informed that the horse incident was based on truth, Theodore nevertheless refused to change his mind, despite Wister's reminder that neither of them ever had liked "tea-cup" tales. Theodore admonished Wister, "I think that *conscientious descriptions of the unspeakable* do not constitute an interpretation of life, but merely disgust all readers not afflicted with the hysteria of bad taste." The desired effect would have been greatly strengthened, he contended, if the reader had been left to imagine what horrible deed Balaam committed on Pedro. Wister disagreed.[31]

His first inkling that the Virginian might be a character with unusually broad appeal came from a law office clerk named Henry Esling who had been reading Wister's manuscripts before their publication. The fate of the Virginian had been left uncertain in "Balaam and Pedro," and when Esling asked the author directly if the cowboy were dead, Wister could only reply that he himself did not know. "If you kill that man, I'll never speak to you again," Esling threatened. Not until that moment, Wister later recalled, had he contemplated bringing the Virginian out from the woods into which he had disappeared.[32]

A month after having heard that Alden would publish both "Balaam and Pedro" and "Em'ly," Wister was in New York City discussing with Alden his future writing and hearing praise for his latest story, "The Bear Creek Barbecue." Alden listened approvingly to Wister's idea for a "novelette" about the cowboy named Chalkeye. This would be appropriate, Alden thought, for *Harper's Weekly* more so than for the monthly. A longer book, a projected historical narrative of Wyoming which Wister called "The Course of Empire," would fit the monthly better. Alden urged his author not to give the *Atlantic Monthly* any of the Texas stories, telling Wister about an important proposal being developed which Alden could not yet divulge. Wister was not ready to commit himself wholly to the Harper firm, however. Before leaving town, he stopped by *Scribner's* to inquire about an article he had submitted to them about the practice of law entitled "The Twenty-fifth Hour." The editors greeted him cordially, said they knew of his work, and promised an early answer. A month later they rejected the article.[33]

By then the rejection hardly mattered, for Alden's proposal had materialized to Wister's immense delight. *Harper's Monthly* desired to publish a series of articles on the West, and their first choice to write it, Rudyard Kipling, had declined. Alden enthusiastically had recommended Wister as the ideal substitute, and J. Henry Harper had agreed. The ensuing telegram reached Wister just before he departed to take his mother to the Columbian Exposition in Chicago. It read, "I have an important proposition to make which if accepted by you [will] modify your whole summer campaign and so ought to see you before you go west." Wister doubted that at this date he could change his plans. His head, hands, and throat had been suffering lately from the gout, and he felt a desperate need for exercise and outdoor life. But if the proposition were important enough he could make adjustments.[34]

On the next morning he was in Alden's office in New York's Franklin Square. The first two western stories, Alden said, had attracted much attention, and he now wanted Wister to write a series of eight western sketches to be published in consecutive issues of *Harper's Monthly*. If Wister wished, Alden would send along Frederic Remington as the illustrator. Wister did not know Remington personally, but the artist's reputation was such that already Wister secretly had been hoping for a collaboration. Wister would be paid thirty-five dollars for each one thousand words, substantially more than the twenty-dollar rate he had received for his last two stories and far above the twelve-dollar rate for his first stories. Equally exciting was the promise that the stories would be compiled in a book for which Wister would receive royalty payments of ten percent. Alden stipulated:

> Each must be a thrilling story, having its ground in a real incident, though you are left free scope for imaginative treatment. Where possible . . . you will confine yourself to actuality. . . . We wish in this series to portray certain features of Western life which are now rapidly disappearing with the progress of civilization. Not the least striking of these is that of the appeal to lynch law, which ought to give capital subject for one of your stories.

He was to go to those regions in the western country that would yield the best material. Furthermore, he was to devote himself "steadily and exclusively" to the project until its conclusion. To make certain that Wister understood Harper & Brothers completely, Alden stressed in a follow-up letter that the firm attached more importance to this series than to "any of our undertakings for 1894, and shall make a great point of it in

our Prospectus . . . beside the widest announcement of it in other ways."
Meanwhile, a check was included for the latest Wister story, "The
Winning of the Biscuit Shooter." In this story the Virginian met a young
and attractive schoolteacher named Molly Wood.[35]

"Events in my literary life have crowded so thick of late that I am
a little bewildered," Wister confided to his journal. The alluring offer
could not be declined, and Wister pledged himself to "hunt material of
adventure voraciously."[36]

His first story was not due until October 1, and he still had time to
take his mother to Chicago to show her the Exposition. In late June,
Wister, his mother, and Miss Molly Moss, a member of Wister's musical
quartet, boarded the train for Chicago. So eager was he to take his
mother that earlier he had dreamed she had consented to go as far as
Yellowstone with him. "You see, you are enjoying the West after all,"
he had told her in his dreams. But as close in spirit as Sarah Wister could
get to Wyoming was when she bravely hoisted Wister's hunting rifle to
her shoulder as he handed her two valises while they were changing
trains.[37]

Sarah Wister was not feeling any better these days. Despite her
nearly constant traveling, her disposition and nerves remained a problem.
"She cannot help feeding on her self," Dr. Wister wrote to his son.
"Everywhere she at first seems to make a step forward, but as soon as
the novelty wears off, she slips back to the old place. Now she is sleeping badly again." But she continued to be her son's most faithful critic.
Having seen him gain some acclaim for his western stories, she feared
he was succumbing to the temptation to revel in his success. She cautioned him to hide his genius.[38]

They spent two busy weeks in Chicago. At the same time, also in
Chicago, a young historian named Frederick Jackson Turner was pro-
claiming to the American Historical Association that the frontier had
been the most important influence on American history and that the
improvisations required in the West for daily living were creating a
unique national character. Had he heard Turner, Wister would have
been fascinated and pleased, especially noting the similarity of their
ideas. Yet Wister did not hear Turner, sharing his time instead with his
mother and Molly Moss, hearing musical programs, dining at various
places, touring the exhibits, and seeing many friends who had come to
the Exposition. After attending a performance of Wagner music, Wister
approached the German-born conductor, Theodore Thomas, and asked

him to dine. Although Thomas did not know Wister, he accepted the invitation and even had Wister accompany him to his room while he changed clothes. The two found that they had much to discuss—music, America, and politics. Thomas offered "bitter criticisms" of the nation, and Wister forcefully defended the United States, contending that a hundred years was hardly sufficient time for the development of the high culture that he too desired. Thomas finally agreed with Wister's pet belief that the nation was great "in spite of politics." When the singers in the cafe recognized Thomas as the conductor of the symphony, they serenaded him and Wister. "We rioted amid smoke, beer, and light music," said Wister in summing up the evening.[39]

Mary Channing Wister also was at the Exposition. Wister hoped to see her, but somehow he failed. Other friends were there, though, including Joe Lee, several Cabots, and many old St. Paul's friends who had come for a reunion. This latter group prevailed upon Wister to write a special poem for the event. Wister felt that he did not have time for a first-rate effort, but he could not decline.[40]

After two weeks in Chicago, Sarah Wister and Molly Moss returned to Philadelphia. Wister, meeting his artist friend John Stewardson who would accompany him, continued westward for his first visit to Wyoming since the Johnson County war. It was a hunting trip unrelated to his *Harper's* assignment, but in his own mind Wister saw no reason not to gather materials. En route to Fort Washakie a genial stagedriver informed Wister and the other passengers that four men who had been involved in the Johnson County trouble deserved to be killed. The driver did not know that three of the four he named—Wolcott, Canton, and Irvine—were friends of his passenger. At Fort Washakie, George West greeted Wister and Stewardson, and while they gathered supplies and equipment for the expedition up Wind River, Army officers entertained and regaled them with stories, including some particularly vivid and unflattering accounts of General Custer's character. Tighee, now a sergeant in Company K of the 8th Cavalry, was "one of the best soldiers." Chief Washakie still lived, "tall, spendid, [and] a wonderful figure of a man" despite his ninety-odd years. Wister posed him for his camera by standing him "stark straight with one hand uplifted" in a typical Indian pose. The degree to which Washakie and other Indian chiefs had been domesticated was evident, for many of them gave Wister gold-edged calling cards: "North Axe, Chief of Pregan-Blackfeet," "Red Crow, Chief of Blood-Blackfeet," and "Bull Head, Chief of Sarcis-Blackfeet."[41]

140

Invigorating though it was to be back in Wind River country, writing, rather than hunting, dominated Wister's thoughts. While encamped for ten days at Fish Lake, he used a tale given him by the new commander at Fort Washakie for a story entitled "The Kinsman of Red Cloud." Soon after, on September 8, exhausted after more than a month in the mountains, the group awakened at the Grand Canyon of the Yellowstone River to find three inches of snow on the ground. Shivering, they rode to Norris Basin for the warmth of North's Inn and a hot meal. To Wister's surprise and delight, already warming up at the inn was none other than Frederic Remington. Wister introduced himself at once. The artist, having illustrated Wister's "Balaam and Pedro," was himself very much aware of the western author, and the two fell into a lively, long-overdue conversation. While Alden had offered to send Remington across the West with Wister if needed, Wister had not acted on the proposal. Now, though, he was nearly overcome with excitement at this chance meeting with the man who for half a dozen years had been sketching the soldiers, cowboys, and Indians of the West for *Harper's Weekly*. An Easterner who had studied at Yale, Remington was a "huge rollicking animal," a plain and pungent speaker on any topic, a man who reveled in manly companionship and the camaraderie of the trail.[42]

The meeting of the two men was, in retrospect, a momentous occasion, for here were two of the three men destined to provide for this era the popular image of the West: Wister in fiction and Remington in art. The third man—Roosevelt—was a friend of both. His nonfiction and larger-than-life persona added yet another powerful dimension to the supposed virtues of the strenuous life. Remington already had collaborated with Roosevelt, too, having illustrated his *Ranch Life and the Hunting Trail* in 1888 at Roosevelt's request.[43]

"Remington is an excellent American," declared Wister. "That means he thinks as I do about the disgrace of our politics and the present asphyxiation of all real love of country. He uses almost the same words that have of late been in my head, that this continent does not hold a nation any longer but is merely a strip of land on which a crowd is struggling for riches." Remington's attitude, so near to his own skepticism, surprised and pleased Wister. They dined together that evening at Mammoth Springs and later, still talking, rode the train together to St. Paul, Minnesota, en route to the East Coast. Wister pulled out his latest story, "The Promised Land," solicited Remington's suggestions, and incorporated them into the tale.[44]

Back in New York, Wister showed Alden "The Promised Land" and the other story he had written in Wyoming, "A Kinsman of Red Cloud." They were not suitable for the projected series, Alden said, because they were not the result of a "special journey" for the magazine. Moreover, the stories were too bloody for Alden's taste. Wister reminded him that *Harper's Monthly* was "not going to get much American Western adventure without blood." Indeed, both stories were closely based on fact. The story of the capture of the Indian Toussaint in "A Kinsman of Red Cloud" had been told to Wister by an officer who had helped in the capture, and only "a couple of drops of invention" could be found in "A Promised Land." Only the last hours of Wild Goose Jake's life and the character of Leander, the feebleminded boy, had been imagined. Wild Goose Jake was identified correctly by many readers in Washington as Samuel Wilbur Condon, who still lived there and whose middle name was used for the town of Wilbur. If unsuitable for the projected series, these stories were suitable for publication on their own merits. Alden bought them and assigned Remington as illustrator.[45]

Concerned now because he would miss his first series deadline, Wister was introduced to J. Henry Harper himself, who amiably assured him that there was no need for concern. Wister could wait as late as December 20, and the series could extend into 1895. If the stories proved successful, a second volume seemed likely. While he was in the office, Wister corrected proofs for "Em'ly" and then had lunch with Alden and Charles Dudley Warner, Mark Twain's collaborator for *The Gilded Age.* The day was so successful in every way that Wister broke into a verse of celebration in his journal:

> Well, my gracious Master Alden,
> Gracious in that me you called on
>   To procure
>   Literature
> For the potent Harper Brothers
> When you might have called on others.[46]

In early October, Wister was ready for his first official trip in behalf of Harper & Brothers. His itinerary included Arizona, New Mexico, and the West Coast. He chose the Southwest largely because of a friendship made in September 1891 at Yellowstone with an Army officer named Frank A. Edwards of the 1st Cavalry. The acquaintance had been renewed at the Chicago Exposition when, as fellow members of the Boone and Crockett Club, they dined together in the hunters' cabin. Edwards, born in 1851, had been an officer in the West since 1873, and he now commanded the post at San Carlos, Arizona Territory. Wister found him articulate and knowledgeable, and "with all the egotism of a new fledged writer" he had invited himself to call on Edwards. Edwards, eager to help, suggested that en route Wister stop at Fort Bowie and Fort Grant, Arizona, for more color. (The possibility of using the military in the West as guide and host had been suggested, perhaps, by Remington, who had found Army officers unusually helpful in his career in the West. It was—for the military and for its officers—an effective means of self-promotion.)[47]

At Fort Bowie, where Wister stayed a week, his search for provocative material was especially successful. The officers there eagerly reminisced about their experiences, and the area's place names were all good—Apache Pass, Dos Cabezas, the Dragoon Mountains. Most important, though, Wister encountered a remarkable twenty-seven-year-old corporal named Charles D. Skirdin. Skirdin eventually would be identified widely though erroneously as the prototype for the character of the Virginian. (Wister, as we have seen, already had introduced that character.) Assigned to accompany Wister on hunting and exploring forays, Skirdin was a happy contradiction—he was "absolutely fearless, but exceptionally quiet and peace-loving." He was uncouth, ugly, and virtually illiterate, knowing little more than what he had taught himself. But to Wister his conversation was as "simple and strong as nature," and he had a "most beautiful eye." Skirdin's life held material for a book, his story as absorbing as Robinson Crusoe's. As Wister understood it, Skirdin's parents had abandoned him in Arizona when he was just six years old. Two years later he pulled a gun on a man who had beaten him, then he fled on horseback to Apache country. Soon he obtained a mule or burro team and began earning his living by taking supplies between the mines and a distant town. He was the kind of honest, self-reliant man Wister hoped that the West would spawn.[48]

Arizona Territory was nothing like Wyoming—the sun blazed down "like a curse," the Indians were different, the culture was Mexican, and the civilization seemed more primitive than at Fort Washakie. An individual as fascinating as Skirdin emerged from the enlisted ranks at San Carlos: Merijildo Grijaloa, chief of scouts. At the age of eleven, Grijaloa had been stolen by Cochise's band of Apaches. At eighteen he escaped to join government service as a scout and interpreter. Wister rode with this remarkable individual nearly every day, visiting the Gila Indians, buying

Apache baskets, seeing an Indian woman whose nose had been cut off by the other squaws for being a "chiricua" or whore, and asking questions everywhere he went. In the evenings the congenial, loquacious Edwards and other officers entertained Wister with liquor and tales of adventure. Edwards patiently endured his guest's endless questions. As Wister recorded, "Several times I sat down and made him dictate to me for two hours together, and half a dozen times a day I came to him with a new bushel of questions." Armed with this rich new material, Wister tried to begin a story but failed. He was so intent on absorbing material that he had difficulty making the transition from listener to narrator. By the time he left San Carlos for California, however, he had more than a hundred pages of notes which were sufficient not only for his first story in the projected series but also for a mine of material in the years to come. And his friendship with Edwards had been cemented so that it too would last for many years.[49]

So rich were the anecdotes and details gained that it was nearly impossible for Wister to maintain a cohesive image about these "irrepressible" United States. He illustrated the problem for his mother: "Take for instance meeting a Mormon bishop who has been hiding for polygamy . . . on account of nine wives; he has forty-seven children and can't read or write but signs contracts and letters with an X. He is seventy-four and the other day had twins. Now don't you see that it's quite impossible to preserve any proportion?"[50]

His December deadline for the first story loomed, and when Wister reached the sumptuous Palace Hotel in San Francisco for a month's stay he forced a rigid schedule upon himself. Fun-loving friends such as Francis Michael tempted his resolve, and in the evenings he joined them for entertainment at the University Club. Each day, however, he shut himself into his hotel room to write a story called "Little Big Horn Medicine."* It was based on an incident Edwards had experienced firsthand in Montana concerning a chief's rebellious son who provoked the Crow Indians into a confrontation with the 1st Cavalry. Edwards appeared in the story as a man named Stirling, and Wister's version precisely repeated his actual role. Two weeks before deadline, the story was in the mail to Alden. When friends who read it in advance praised it warmly, Wister alerted Edwards to "beware" because their chance meeting in Yellowstone during target practice "may turn out a controlling

* It was published in the June 1894 issue of *Harper's Monthly* and reprinted as the opening chapter in *Red Men and White* (New York: Harper & Bros., 1895).

incident in the destiny of a poor beggar of an Eastern dude." Edwards, in fact, also had directed Wister to his next location, Oregon, where one of Edwards's friends would provide details about the Modoc War.[51]

By the time Wister returned to Butler Place he found that his reputation suddenly had mushroomed. A *Harper's Monthly* advertisement described his forthcoming series illustrating "striking features of Western life now rapidly disappearing under the pressure of civilization." Wister was, the prospectus elaborated, already known as the author of the "brilliant sketches" which had previously appeared. Other praise came from reviews in the nation's press, which in those days felt obliged to review magazine stories. The *Pittsburgh Bulletin* said Wister was "a grandson of Fanny Kemble, and evidently inherits genius."[52]

More praise came from Frederic Remington, who had just read "A Kinsman of Red Cloud" prior to illustrating it. He declared it a "bully story—it's so subtle—dead true and so well thought out." Remington said he had been looking "through all the ages" for a proper collaborator to portray the West, and now he had found him. He had assumed that such a man would turn out to be an army officer, a cowboy, or perhaps a mining engineer.

> But then hell, I might have known that the man who would do the West, & did know he would have been born and have lived and will die in sight of the Atlantic Ocean. To tell a thing is one thing—it takes brains, cultivation and an ativism [*sic*]—thousands of men have lived it and died it and don't know any more about it than the chickens we kill for dinner but you have an air tight cinche [*sic*]—Work it and when they write {Here lies it will mean something of O. Wister.
> {O Wist

Remington urged Wister to let "oceans of blood" flow as he drove his quill and commanded the author to come see him at his home in New Rochelle as soon as possible.[53]

Theodore Roosevelt, now with the United States Civil Service Commission, echoed Remington's praise with flattering comparisons which soon would become common. "I greedily read all your western articles, and . . . I can quite sincerely say that they rank with Bret Harte's and Kipling's pieces." He had "long been praying" for someone to write such stories, and he was delighted that it should be "a friend of mine who has risen." If the stories were collected in a volume, he declared that he would ask permission of the *Atlantic Monthly* to review them.[54]

Such flattering tidings further bolstered Wister's already high spirits, and as he passed the last minutes of 1893 at Butler Place he recorded his thoughts in his journal: "Good night 1893! I shall not see you again. You brought me the beginnings of a success that I pray the power be granted to make me more worthy."[55]

His mood sharply contrasted with the general pessimism enveloping Butler Place. Dr. Wister did not think it possible for 1894 to be a happy year. Perhaps he referred to his own perennial worries, perhaps to the light case of typhoid fever that had struck his wife, or perhaps to the continuing problems confronting the nation politically and economically.[56] If it were the latter, his son shared that concern. For Wister, as he matured, was relinquishing his rebellious youthful notions. Instead, he was absorbing the views of his parents and other members of traditional genteel society who were becoming increasingly disturbed at their displacement as guardians of the nation's social, cultural, economic, and political standards by brash newcomers who were achieving status merely through money. The good manners that once had been the unique province of their own aristocratic class now were believed to be within the grasp of all classes. In short, class distinctions that had helped the gentry reside on an elevated platform were disappearing, and with that loss of uniqueness the influence of the gentry class was also dissipating. The growing assertiveness of labor and the influx of immigrants seemed to debase even further the traditional Anglo-oriented values which Wister cherished. The panic of 1893 and the rise of populism heightened his concern. No escape seemed possible from the saturnalia into which politics was hurrying. "The American people have been looking on lying and stealing for so long that we have lost the power of being shocked. Our country and its government are now two separate things, not greatly unlike a carcass and vulture." The only solution Wister could foresee was the ultimate collapse of business credit which would shake the nation into sensibility. "I hope this earthquake will come as soon as possible . . . for this is our only hope."[57]

When he heard of the Burlington Railroad's proposal to extend a railroad track into Yellowstone National Park he exploded with fury. "Damn this stinking money dredging prostituted country. Civilized! We're not so civilized as we were fifty years ago. Not nearly." He declared in a letter to Captain Edwards that the "stench of politics & public standards of decency" was permeating the East. President Grover Cleveland and his "sound & enlightened" refusal to annex Havana struck

(left) Fanny Kemble, Wister's grandmother and the noted Shakespearean actress, who thought it unlikely that her grandson would be a "book man." *Portrait by Thomas Sulley. Courtesy Mrs. Walter Stokes. (right)* Sarah B. Wister, a regal mother. *Courtesy Mrs. Walter Stokes. (below)* Dr. Owen J. Wister in the 1860s, at about the time his son was born. *Courtesy Mrs. Walter Stokes.*

Young Owen, or "Dan," enjoyed all the privileges of the only son of a well-to-do family. *Courtesy American Heritage Center, University of Wyoming.*

Butler Place, home of many generations of the Wister family, in 1912. *Illustration by Herbert Pollinger. Courtesy Mrs. Walter Stokes.*

Mary Channing Wister at graduation from the Irwin School, 1878. *Courtesy Mrs. Walter Stokes.*

Owen Wister in Harvard theatricals as a freshman. *Courtesy American Heritage Center, University of Wyoming.*

On a walking tour of the Berkshires, Wister and his friend Henry Chapman—John Jay's brother—take time for a studio portrait, with their knapsacks. *Courtesy Library of Congress.*

Owen Wister, on his return from the West, about 1890. *Courtesy American Heritage Center, University of Wyoming.*

Owen Wister as a young Philadelphia lawyer. *Courtesy Arizona Historical Society Library.*

Wister and his hunting party at Jackson, Wyoming, 1887. Wister, standing at right, pours a drink for the Indian guide, Tighee. Seated from left to right are George Norman, Copley Armory, George West, and Jules Mason. *Courtesy American Heritage Center, University of Wyoming.*

George West's cabin at Horse Creek Ranch, which Wister helped to finance. Wister took the photograph, dated 1891. *Courtesy American Heritage Center, University of Wyoming.*

Wister with his camera in 1891 at Yellowstone. *Courtesy American Heritage Center, University of Wyoming.*

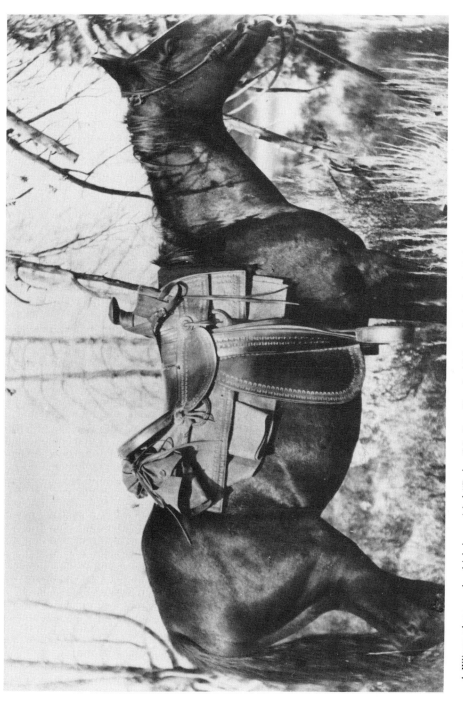

A Wister photograph which he entitled "Pedro (My Pony)" and which no doubt inspired the story, "Balaam and Pedro." *Courtesy American Heritage Center, University of Wyoming.*

Wister labeled this photograph "West and Smith packing." It apparently was taken in 1891, and it is likely that Smith, on the left, is "Black Henry" Smith, whom Wister described as the only "unabridged bad man" he had known. Smith may have served as an inspiration for the villain Trampas in *The Virginian. Courtesy American Heritage Center, University of Wyoming.*

George West poses in front of the post trader's store, in 1893, at Fort Washakie, Wyoming, the departure point for so many of Wister's outings. *Courtesy American Heritage Center, University of Wyoming.*

"Soldiers eating" was Wister's brief description of this photograph, taken probably in 1893 at Fort Bowie or Fort Grant, Arizona Territory. *Courtesy Arizona Historical Society Library.*

Wister poses casually, probably in the early 1890s. *Courtesy American Heritage Center, University of Wyoming.*

Frank Campeau as Trampas in the stage version of *The Virginian*. *Courtesy American Heritage Center, University of Wyoming.*

Henry James, who as a young man was influenced by Sarah B. Wister and who in turn influenced Owen as a writer. *Painting by Emile Blanche, in Carnegie Institute of Fine Arts, Pittsburgh, PA. Courtesy The Bettmann Archive.*

William Dean Howells, who urged Wister never to publish his first youthful novel. *Courtesy The Bettmann Archive.*

(*above*) Oliver Wendell Holmes, Jr., with whom Wister spent so many enjoyable hours in Boston. *Courtesy The Bettmann Archive.*

(*below*) Rudyard Kipling, who met Wister at a party arranged for that purpose by Theodore Roosevelt and later exclaimed to Wister, "I *approve* of you thoroughly!" *Courtesy The Bettmann Archive.*

President Theodore Roosevelt in 1903, the year after Wister dedicated *The Virginian* to him. *Courtesy The Bettmann Archive.*

Wister as fine, but in general both Democrats and Republicans were "rotting together in ignorance."[58]

A four-line poem, "To Our Senators," for which he earned five dollars from *Harper's Weekly*, summed up his beliefs about the lack of honesty among politicians.

> Young Politics, lest knaves should him beset,
> Began to memorize each knave he met;
> But reeling in the task he changed his plan,
> And soon could say by heart each honest man.[59]

When Chicago's mayor was assassinated in 1893 Wister expressed to his mother a dark wish that several more assassinations might be performed against "silver men" and politicians who promised without delivery. The "dastardly" pardoning of the surviving Haymarket anarchists by Illinois Governor John Peter Altgeld was another indication to Wister of the low morality of politicians. He tied the rise of these labor agitators to the influx of European immigrants with socialist backgrounds. Such immigrants did not fit the distinctive American type that Wister hoped was emerging and that Theodore Roosevelt now celebrated in an essay entitled "What Americanism Means." Roosevelt urged in this patriotic paean that immigrants be "Americanized" in speech and in thought. "We have no room for any people who do not act and vote simply as Americans, and as nothing else." Wister, agreeing totally, sent Roosevelt his hearty congratulations.[60]

Soon after New Year's Day, that "excellent American" Remington again began urging Wister to visit him at New Rochelle. "We must *make a talk*," he wrote. "Come up here—come for a day or two—got bed-board-horses-grub-am working hard and want to talk—bad. . . . You heap sabe 'make a talk' all same injun. . . . Honest—if you are honest—when will you come up (Kim up as the Sargent said to the Corporal) and we will know whether the great Owen W. is to collaborate with the Puke of the Plains." On the letter Remington sketched a drawing of Wister and himself deep in conversation.[61]

Importunities from such a man were not to be resisted, and in mid-January Wister visited Remington and happily discovered that the artist even then was busy illustrating another of his stories. Remington proposed that they unite now on a project that would "bring meat" to their tables. The idea was simple: "[To] tell the story of the cow puncher, his rise and decline." Such a suggestion coincided precisely with a historical work Wister already had envisioned but postponed at Alden's request.

There was no time for a collaboration now, but the two men agreed to work on the project as soon as their schedules permitted. With Remington's prompting, the time soon arrived, and Remington began feeding ideas to Wister by mail. The completed work, "The Evolution of the Cow-Puncher," appeared in the September 1895 issue of *Harper's Monthly.** The article gave the definitive statement to Wister's notion that the cowboy was an atavism, a throwback to the lordly knight of the Middle Ages, a concept that Remington did not favor.[62]

Meanwhile, producing a story a month for *Harper's* was a constant concern. Yet Wister did manage to write, also finding the time to make social calls up and down the East Coast. In Boston he visited among others Judge Holmes, who did not seem happy. Holmes said he was "growing more and more a recluse." The society women he knew were "empty humbugs." In Tuxedo, New York, where Wister stayed two weeks in late January, he wrote a story he thought better than "Balaam and Pedro." Entitled "Specimen Jones," this tale about a western soldier prompted reviewers generally to agree on its superiority. A *New York Tribune* reviewer was not the only one who contended that the story went far toward establishing the author as "an American Kipling."[63]

Back in Philadelphia, Wister had become entangled in estate problems upon his grandmother's death. Fanny Kemble had died in London on January 15, 1893, too soon for her to know that the grandson she had predicted would never be a "book man" was becoming an acclaimed author.

In the spring the West beckoned again. Wister's destination was Arizona and California, where solicitous friends and more material awaited. This time Wister was brimming with confidence instead of doubting his own ability as he had the previous fall. *Harper's* already had accepted five of the eight stipulated stories, and Wister expected the remaining three to be achieved just as easily. Still, the fact that he had so quickly won an audience suggested that he could lose it with equal speed. But the only people who, as a class, had found fault with his stories, he noted, were his Philadelphia acquaintances. He accepted this as an unavoidable fact of life.[64]

---

* In "Preface—Thirty-Three Years After," *The Writings of Owen Wister: Red Men and White* (New York: Macmillan Co., 1928), p. vii, Wister declared that he had written the article in December 1893 in San Francisco. His memory was faulty, for the story he had worked on so hard that month in San Francisco was "Little Big Horn Medicine."

At Fort Bowie, Arizona, the quartermaster greeted him with the news that whenever *Harper's* arrived they "all tore the cover off" to look for his stories. Wister was eager to cement his friendship with the redoubtable Corporal Skirdin, believing that he had much in common with this semiliterate man. "We grew very intimate," Wister wrote, "riding about the hot hills, and our views of life were precisely similar." The corporal continually intrigued Wister with stories of his colorful past, including the time when as a footloose child he interrupted a couple's lovemaking beneath his cabin loft by pouring water over their panting bodies. Skirdin's uneducated tongue surprised Wister time after time by tripping off phrases that "many a celebrity" would have been happy to claim. At the end of the stay, Wister attempted to express his gratitude to Skirdin by pressing a gold piece into his hand. The corporal, however, resisted it. He did promise to visit Wister in Philadelphia, for he had a younger sister living there whom he had not seen for many years. This was not the only friendship renewed at Fort Bowie. In addition, Wister reacquainted himself with Major Thomas McGregor, Wister's host on his previous visit. Major McGregor punctually prepared toddies each day before lunch and dinner, and he especially pleased Wister by occasionally addressing him as "Old Man."[65]

At Fort Grant, Edwards and the other officers continued to display similar hospitality. "To speak of our army except with kindness will forever be impossible," Wister concluded in his journal. Edwards offered only one correction for Wister's rendering of the story he had related to him, "Little Big Horn Medicine." Wister had described the Indians as being on the "war trail," although the usual expression, Edwards explained, was "war path." The post's bandmaster, Erastus Walker, was not unaware of Wister's musical background. On the day of his arrival Walker presented a special evening of music, going so far as to have a special program printed with Wister's name on it. The music was so ambitious, including Beethoven's Sonata Pathetique and Fugue in D Minor from the *Well Tempered Clavichord*, that Wister feared it was "a trifle taxing" to the average soldier. A month later still another musical program, billed as "Souvenir for Mr. Owen Wister," included music only by composers whose last names began with B—Bach, Beethoven, Brahms, Berlioz, Bizet, Benedict, and Boccherini.[66]

Wister was flattered further at Fort Grant by a forwarded letter from the editor of the *Writer* asking him to suggest a friend who might write a biographical sketch of him for that publication. "What a vulgar absurdity!" Wister exclaimed in his journal. "My life, set at 34; work done, a handful of brief sketches! No, I'll not be one of the Americans who thinks publicity is the same thing as reputation. The public part of me shall be what I'm able to write, and if that is destined to be good enough to give me a reputation, tant mieux. But no advertising!" Nevertheless, a flattering biographical sketch by Sidney G. Fisher appeared in the magazine's September issue.[67]

Tombstone, Arizona, Wister's next stop, held a reputation as having once been the most lawless mining camp in the West. Wister's primary purpose there was to learn about the Earp-Clanton feud that had erupted in 1881 in a bloody gunbattle fought at the O.K. Corral. In the early 1880s, the surrounding silver mines, now silent with rusted machinery, had attracted some eight thousand residents; by the time Wister arrived in June 1894 he found only six hundred people there. Their life was difficult. Water had to be imported from thirty miles away. Entire blocks of buildings stood deserted with doors nailed shut and windowpanes broken. The vacant houses, saloons, hotels, and shops sometimes were two and three stories high. To Wister it was "the most depressing town" he had ever seen.[68]

But amidst such forlorn surroundings came a ribald evening in the Parlor Saloon, where one of the town's leading lawyers, George W. Swaim, had taken him. There, during the course of a long evening, Swaim introduced Wister to the bartender, the mayor, the probate judge, a deputy sheriff, the county clerk, the agent of the express company, and about thirty other private citizens. This motley assortment took turns treating one another to rounds of drinks. At one point, the probate judge used a powerful firecracker to blow up the unsuspecting sheriff's chair. At 2 A.M. Wister found himself playing whist in the back room with a visiting Englishman, the express agent, and a freight-wagon driver. After a few hours' sleep back in his room, Wister arose to meet the town's German-born district attorney, who talked hungrily of Europe, music, and high culture. An impromptu musicale sprang up. Wister accompanied the district attorney, the express agent, and the freight-wagon driver to the doctor's house (where the English visitor was a guest), and there they all performed their specialties. The district attorney produced a violin on which he played Robert Schumann's "Traumerei" by memory and with great feeling; the doctor sang to the accompaniment of a guitar; Wister played Wagner and Offenbach on the doctor's piano, while the others again joined in song; they concluded with feverish dancing. Wister's presence had sparked a rare moment of bliss for these citizens of Tombstone. When he left they implored him to return. "But I shall never do that," Wister wrote to his mother.[69] As for his purpose in visiting, Wister managed to hear and record so many details of the Earp-Clanton feud that he despaired of telling it all in a single story. Unfortunately, not until his last day in town did he get to see Wyatt Earp, the only one of the five Earp brothers surviving. There was no time for a lengthy conversation, and Wister expressed his regrets about that to Earp, who "grinned heavily." Wister was satisfied, though, that at least he had seen this fabled gunman, and he believed that he understood the type of men the Earp brothers must have been. Despite his voluminous notes, Wister never wrote of the famous feud.[70]

The labor upheavals of the 1890s which so irritated Wister affected him directly for the first time en route to San Francisco. The strike of 1894 boycotting all Pullman cars halted Wister's train at Los Angeles. Having little other alternative, he boarded a ship on which he had to sleep on the floor with fifty-five other cabinless "wretches" as it sailed along the California coast. After two nights of twisting to avoid carelessly placed feet, he arrived "greatly disgusted" in San Francisco and repaired to the familiar Palace Hotel, suffering from a bad cold.[71] The presence of this promising young writer was noted by the *San Francisco Examiner*. One of its reporters called on him. In the resulting feature story the reporter described the subject as "tall and athletic in appearance with regular features and very dark hair, eyes and mustache." Thomas Bailey Aldrich was quoted as having said that Wister was one of "two or three" young American authors with exceptional talent. Wister freely discussed his own work habits in the interview.

> If you want to know how I write, I must tell you it is done very slowly, and often the stories are written over two or three times. I write first in pencil, and then change, cut out and turn about in such a way that the original draft would scarcely be recognized. As a general thing it takes from two to five weeks for me to write a story of 6,000 to 8,000 words.

He said he always wrote early in the day, usually from 9 o'clock until noon. In the afternoons he rode, played billiards, attended the theater, or did anything else that rested him. "I find my brain is clear in the morning, and usually otherwise, at least not exactly what I would wish, later," he was quoted as saying. He consented to show the reporter a thin "morocco memorandum book," which was described as being full of "all kinds of curious notes made in a very small hand." Wister was, the reporter wrote, a "good deal of a club man," yet also "a very pleasant conversationalist" who was easy to approach.[72]

In his hotel room Wister not only wrote, but also read—to his "great, very great delight"—works by Kipling and Henry James. His intention in San Francisco, to write a piece about western stagecoach robberies, was dashed by a Wells Fargo official's comment that such matters were too familiar to interest readers in the West. This would not do for Wister, for he relied heavily on support from admiring western readers.[73]

He did not lack for subject material, though, for as one reader indirectly reminded him, he had created one character who above all demanded elaboration. The reader lamented the absence of the Virginian, who had disappeared so ominously in "Balaam and Pedro." "Cannot you find 'the Virginian'? . . . It seems such a pity that one like him should perish," the reader wrote. "He has qualities like my boy Charlie who is a cow-boy in the far West, and night after night I have dreamed of him."[74]

For the moment, however, Wister had other concerns. On the way home he passed through Wyoming to enjoy the hospitality of former governor Amos W. Barber in Cheyenne. It is probable that he also paused at the civilian settlement that had sprung up around Fort Fetterman, for he made what would become in retrospect an unusually significant entry in his 1894 journal. He wrote:

> *Card Game* going on. Big money. Several desperadoes playing—one John Lawrence among others. A player calls him a son of a b———. John Lawrence does not look as if he had heard it. Merely passes his fingers strokingly up and down his pile of chips. When hand is done, he looks across the man and says: "You *smile* when you call me that." The man smiled, and all was well.

An uncertainty exists as to the precise date that Wister overheard this comment, for while he recorded it in 1894, he placed it under a section entitled "Fetterman Events, 1885–86." Perhaps he had first witnessed the scene in September 1885 when he visited the Quadrangle at Fort Fetterman and saw card games being played. His return to Fetterman nearly a decade later may have refreshed his memory, prompting him to make a belated 1894 notation. In any case, several years later Wister altered the quotation slightly, creating for the Virginian probably the most famous line ever spoken in the literature of the cowboy: "When you call me that, smile."[75]

Back home in Philadelphia, Wister had hardly unpacked when Albert Bigelow Paine, editor of *Harper's Weekly*, asked him to go to the Pennsylvania National Guard's encampment to collaborate on an article with Remington. Wister initially declined, but Remington persuaded him to change his mind. The resulting article contrasted the Americanism of the militia with the un-Americanism of labor, whose destructive strikes occasionally had to be contained by troops. It also gave Wister an opportunity to demonstrate his growing conservatism by lashing out at two Army generals who seemed to him overly soft in their attitudes. Of a general who had condemned a certain punishment as "unchristian," Wister wrote, "but one knows Gen'l Howard. Of all the insults to which the dictionary submits, his chronic abuse of the word 'christian' is the most offensive." Of General John M. Schofield, commanding general of the United States Army who recently had reversed his opinion that the Army was large enough, Wister wrote, "I am glad the General has changed his mind; it shows that he has one." The western tales had not permitted such scathing remarks on contemporary affairs. But such opinions by an author whose reputation lay in western storytelling did not please *Harper's Weekly*. Paine deleted the harsh remarks.[76]

Theodore Roosevelt, one of several who had labeled Wister an "American Kipling," arranged in the spring of 1895 for Kipling and Wister to meet at his home in Washington.* Other guests were there, including John Hay, Nelson Page, Austin Wadsworth, and three others— too many for an intimate conversation. But on the following day Wister and Kipling rode together on the train to Philadelphia for three "extremely pleasant hours." As Roosevelt had anticipated, the two writers were exceptionally compatible. Wister found Kipling, five years younger but already famous throughout the English-speaking world for *The Light That Failed* and other works, to be "impulsive, boyish, enthusiastic [and] perfectly simple." In the midst of their animated conversation, Kipling,

---

* Roosevelt also had invited Frederic Remington, knowing of the close relationship that appeared to be developing between the two men. Remington, though, declined to come, pleading illness. In fact, he had been upset to learn that despite the intimate friendship he thought he had with Wister, Remington had not even been privy to Wister's nickname, "Dan," a fact that seemed to indicate Wister did not wish to be so familiar after all. (See Peggy and Harold Samuels, *Frederic Remington: A Biography* [Garden City: Doubleday and Company, 1982], pp. 230-31.)

judged to be snobbish by his American neighbors in Vermont, suddenly burst forth: "I like you! I'm awfully glad to have seen you. I *approve* of you thoroughly!" Wister, as he later described the meeting, responded: "I needn't say how glad I am to hear it, I approve of you. The fact is, you've been agreeing with what I say, & I've been agreeing with what you say, and each thinks the other a remarkably intelligent person." Kipling did disapprove of Wister's projected title for his short story collection—"Tales from the Sage-Brush"—and suggested instead "Various Citizens." Wister did not like that title, though, and he afterwards implored Roosevelt to give him *"the* name for the book."[77]

About this same time, Wister had occasion to visit for one captivating hour another famous writer, Mark Twain, who in the midst of struggling to repay his creditors had taken time to send Wister belated compliments for *The Dragon of Wantley.* Wister thought Twain resembled a parrot with a "great strong beak of a nose, strong blue eyes, a strong chin, and a mound of strong hair that tumbled all over his head." They talked of the more liberal outlook toward literature in France, of Wister's present story in progress ("Sharon's Choice"), and of Bret Harte, whom Twain professed no longer to admire. Wister believed that Harte had fallen out of Twain's favor because of "sentimentalism" evident in his work. ("Sentimentalism is the mildew of American intellect," declared Wister, the author whose critics eventually would declare him to be oversentimental.) Twain, sixty years old at the time of the meeting, surprised Wister with his severity. He had expected to see the humorist of "The Jumping Frog of Calaveras County," but by now bankruptcy and disillusionment had taken their toll.[78]

In January 1895 Wister played host in Philadelphia to a very special visitor—Corporal Charles D. Skirdin. Unfortunately, few details of the occasion exist, but it is not difficult to imagine that the outdoorsman Skirdin felt ill at ease, for now Wister was lord of his very polite surroundings, and Skirdin was the rough outsider. As the visit ended Skirdin had to borrow five dollars from Wister to return to his new assignment at Fort Logan, California. Five months later he repaid the loan by money order. "I remain yours respectfully," he wrote in concluding the brief note of thanks.[79]

The magazine editors who now clamored for Wister's work did not forget his knowledge of music. When Antonin Dvorak began composing an opera based on Hiawatha, *Atlantic Monthly's* Horace Scudder was asked to recommend a librettist as a partner. "Your name is the first to suggest itself to me," Scudder informed Wister, "and I write to ask if I may name you to the publishers, the family, the composer." Wister's precise response is lost, but he did not agree to the tempting project. At Harper & Brothers, Henry Harper himself urged Wister to begin writing a regular musical column for the weekly publication. Another editor at the same firm asked him to do regular columns on affairs of general interest to Philadelphia and Baltimore citizens. The musical column was especially inviting, and Wister stalled his decision for six months before finally declining. He reasoned that his busy schedule would not permit the essential frequent visits to New York City, and it seemed unwise to divide his literary interests at this point. He did consent to compose original music for a play, *The Dolls*, and it was published in the Christmas 1894 issue of *Harper's Young People*. He earned only twenty-five dollars for the effort. This contrasted markedly with the five hundred dollars he received a month later from Harper & Brothers for a western story, "La Tinaja Bonita." As for the original music, the *Louisville Courier-Journal* commented that "Mr. Wister was interested in music long before he thought of writing. In fact, some of his friends have for years been urging him to devote himself entirely to music, for which he has great natural talent."[80]

But music, despite the continued pleasure it afforded him, now played a distinct second fiddle in Wister's choice of desired professions, for in May he again was in the West to collect material. For the first time, however, he was not especially eager to go. But on the train between New Orleans and El Paso his spirits revived when he had the miraculous fortune to encounter a Russian expatriate from Los Angeles named Demens, with whom he had been corresponding about translating his short stories for publication in Russia. They talked about Wister's literary creations all the way across Texas.[81]

Then, at El Paso, the appearance of a jovial young ranch foreman who was to be Wister's first host in New Mexico further enlivened the ride. The cowboy's name was Dean Duke, a man to whom Wister had been directed by a wealthy San Francisco rancher named William Kellogg. Wister spent half his time in New Mexico with this cowboy host and the other half with the United States cavalry. By the time he departed for San Francisco he and Duke had become steadfast friends. Duke, twenty-seven and of "superlative humor," had survived more desperate chances, it seemed, than any person of similar age Wister ever had encountered. Duke's cowboy crew proved to be equally delightful.

"They are of the manly, simple, humorous, American type which I hold to be the best and bravest we possess and our hope for the future. They work hard, they play hard, and they don't go on strikes." Duke was to become, Wister later would claim in *ex post facto* fashion, yet another model for the Virginian.[82]

Captain Edwards was not to be seen on this trip; he was on leave in the East, "very gravely ill," Wister feared. Wister implored his parents to show Edwards "every possible kindness" if he should come to Philadelphia. Besides the debt of hospitality that he owed him, Wister said he had obtained from Edwards either directly or indirectly most of the information for his stories. Wister assured his parents that they would find Edwards clever and interesting. But "as you like nobody," he said to his mother, "I can't say you'd like him." He felt certain, however, that his father would.[83]

While in San Francisco, Wister one day stepped happily onto an elevator and so impressed a stranger with his cheerful countenance that the man said: "Well, sure I'd like to live as you do, sir, and look so smiling and happy every morning. It's a pleasure to see your face." At Fort Logan, Colorado, where he visited Skirdin, an officer pulled Wister aside and told him that he had totally won the corporal's loyalty. "Well! What is better than the regard of a good man?" Wister observed in his journal. "Woman's? Ah—I've never won that; yet I believe one who does not know both is partially starved." The winning of a woman's heart surely was occupying some of Wister's thoughts, but where was the time to do it?[84]

Throughout the West, Wister encountered people who knew him through his writing. When former Wyoming governor Amos W. Barber, Wister's "intimate friend" whose name was disguised as Amory W. Barker in his stories, introduced him in Cheyenne to his successor, the governor knowledgeably inquired if Wister were in search of another rainmaking story.* A schoolteacher who sat net to him at lunch expressed a hope that Wister's next story would not be as sad as "La Tinaja Bonita." A youth on a train near Denver recognized him and apologetically asked if indeed he were Owen Wister. "And as for the Army people, that is continual," Wister wrote to his mother.[85]

When he returned to the East he entered into a new round of social calls with old friends and awaited publication in book form of his now

---

* The governor, presumably Democrat John E. Osborne who served from 1893 to 1895, referred to "Little Big Horn Medicine."

completed eight stories. He had selected as a title *Red Men and White.*
On November 8, 1895, this first western book by Wister went on sale in
bookstores across the nation. He sent an early copy to his friend Kipling
with an inscription:

Here to the chief do I present
    Red Man, White Man, Dago;
Powder and smoke, Tramps dead broke—
    And a piece of my hard-boiled ego.[86]

Chapter IX

FAME AND MARRIAGE
(1895–1898)

IT HAD BEEN TEN YEARS SINCE WISTER FIRST HAD GONE TO WYOMING
to regain his health and to forget his disillusionment with business and
his abandonment of music. Since then still another profession—the law
—had been tried and given up. Now, at the age of thirty-five, he had
found a highly satisfying success. Mindful of this happy turnabout in his
personal fortunes, he appended a postscript to the "confession" he had
written en route to Wyoming ten years earlier: "[I] have ceased to drift
unhappily in search of something that I can do. I believe that I have
found it, and am deeply thankful to Providence. I can not hope it will
be great; but it shall not be unworthy."[1]

His western stories had created for him a national reputation; *Red
Men and White* enlarged that reputation. His verisimilitude was obvious,
and reviewers commonly remarked that Wister was preserving for all
time the flavor of a primitive society destined soon to vanish. This, of
course, had been his intention. He had reason to feel happy.[2]

Even William Dean Howells joined in the praise for him. "Despera-
does, good and bad, have been done before," Howells wrote in *Harper's
Weekly*, "red savages and white semi-savages, gamblers, traders, miners,
ranchmen, and the whole wicked world of the border have been done
before, though never, I think so well as Mr. Wister has done them."
Yet Howells noted in Wister's realism a tendency for melodrama. These
special effects belonged, Howells thought, with muted music and other
mawkish theatrical devices; they did not fit the "robust honesty" of most
of the author's work. A month later Theodore Roosevelt offered his
opinions in the same publication: "He has . . . the power to arouse and
sustain interest, the power of the born story-teller. His tales are clean
and fresh and strong, and healthy with an out-of-doors healthiness; they
quicken our pulses, and our hearts beat faster for having read them."[3]

Some unpleasant reactions surfaced too, one of them potentially
serious. The last story in the book, "A Pilgrim on the Gila," which had

159

appeared in *Harper's Monthly* in November, contained remarks critical of Arizona Territory law enforcement. A flurry of angry responses (including a protest from the Department of Justice in Arizona Territory) resulted in talk of a libel suit. The resentment was enough to cause the *Cincinnati Tribune* to observe that Wister was "about as cordially hated a man as this country fosters."[4]

Hated or not, Wister at least could feel important. He sensed a new perspective emerging. "I think I am changing—& that it is not a mood," he privately recorded. A hint of the change had been his recent reluctance, for the first time, to go West. What he finally had realized and accepted was that he could not escape the fact that he was an Easterner. He and all men, he felt, were governed by the same historical forces that inevitably doomed western society as it then existed; an individual might help or accelerate or retard basic forces, but only temporarily. This moment of personal insight had come during an afternoon spent with the Cabots in Brookline when Mr. Cabot had remarked that mankind was but "sap in God's tree." As such, he said, the shape of man's life already had been defined in at least rough outline, and it was folly to deny or resist "indestructible realities."[5]

In the years ahead, this new mood was to place Wister securely in the orthodox stance expected of his social standing. The widespread labor strife and the emergence of populism, both of which were especially visible in the West, already had shaken Wister's faith in the region's future. The populists' leader, William Jennings Bryan, especially disgusted Wister, but everywhere he went in the West he encountered obstreperous Bryan supporters and free silver advocates. If such was the caliber of the new man developing in the West, Wister had nothing in common with him.

In such a state of mind Wister undertook a new project while awaiting publication of *Red Men and White*. He determined to write an "Eastern chronicle" as a "postscript" to his western journals. Not since his days at Harvard had he kept a record of his life in the East. The idea had occurred to him just before a three-week visit to New England which he made "for the sake of seeing those I love there & with whom I want to keep my memory green." These included blue-blooded families such as the Cabots, Higginsons, Lees, Holmeses, Brimmers, and Forbeses.[6]

Had his parents realized their son's changed outlook they likely would have rejoiced over his visit to New England. Instead, they protested against even a short trip. "They grow to hate my going anywhere, more & more," Wister observed. But he had to go. Just as his western trips had been important for learning and replenishing, his eastern visit now was necessary to renew roots.[7]

He did not turn out to be like the prodigal Lin McLean—New England welcomed him warmly. At Beverly Farms, where Mrs. Sarah Whitman entertained, John Jay and Minna Chapman rode up to greet him on their "safety" bicycles—a new rage of the day which, with two wheels of equal size, was replacing the high-wheeler. Wister borrowed Mrs. Whitman's bicycle and pedaled with the Chapmans to Pride's Crossing to meet a former law school classmate, William Ropes Trask, for a "beautiful ride together." Wister determined to get himself a "safety" bicycle. At various social functions over the weekend he visited with Henry Higginson, William James ("not in his best form"), Harry Sears, Ollie Ames, George Peabody, Harry McKean, and others. Many old friends greeted him enthusiastically at a dance at the McKean's, including "the tolerant Minna" for whom no one existed, Wister wrote, except her husband. As for Chapman, "no one quite exists except himself." Wister, having learned this years before, enjoyed Chapman's company for what it was.[8]

At the Cabots in Brookline he joined Charles Cabot in a rendition of Mendelssohn, Wister at the piano and Cabot on the cello. Next day at John Murray Forbes's island home off Cape Cod, Wister marveled at the ancient Forbes's sagacity and wit. Forbes, whose fortune came from shipping, railroads, and the telephone, regaled Wister with memories of Fanny Kemble. Forbes's penchant for reminiscing made the venerable New Englander think of the last time he had seen Oliver Wendell Holmes, Sr. Holmes, eighty-three, had fallen silent amidst a spirited conversation at Mrs. Jack Garner's house. "But my world is different," Holmes had suddenly exclaimed. "I live mostly with ghosts."[9]

Wister's most unusual evening occurred when he and Ned Martin dined at the palatial "Marble House" of Oliver H. P. Belmont in Newport. The pair's first shock came when the door was opened by the butler impeccably attired in eighteenth-century formal dress. He had a powdered head, livery, and fat white calves. The butler, without a word of explanation about his odd apparel, turned them over to a second man with powder, livery, and calves. This second herald delivered them to yet a third—a gentleman scrupulously plain in butler's attire. When Wister and Martin finally reached their host, they found him "surrounded by stained glass and armor, with banners hanging above him." Here and there could be seen a breastplate or an equestrian steel leg, and in the loft of this room stood an organ. The ostentatious display was partly amusing and partly disgusting. It reminded Wister of an Offenbach opera, entirely out of place in a democracy. "Why doesn't he [Belmont] have humor and imagination enough to do something with his money and his home that shall be just as expensive as you please, but inspired by our native soil?"[10]

More in line with Wister's notion of pleasure was a birthday dinner in Newport for Winthrop Chanler, who had married the niece of Julia Ward Howe. On this occasion the formidable Miss Howe arrived on Belmont's arm, and Wister, Chanler, and Royal Carroll entertained the guests by singing Porcellian tunes. Afterwards, in Wister's room, Chanler joked about Wister's protruding stomach. What he needed, Chanler told him in all seriousness, was some "boudoir gymnastics" to regain his trimness. It was past time, he said, for Wister to take a bride. A few days later Elizabeth Chanler raised the subject again, and Wister discussed it with enthusiasm, confiding with her "more than I've ever told to any one." Up to this point he had purposefully decided against marriage. Now, however, he had concluded that he should marry. How tragic it would be, he told Elizabeth, if now that he had determined to marry, he could find no mate.[11]

After a week in the Boston area, Wister's next visit was with Theodore Roosevelt, who had less time than Wister these days for maintaining ties with the parlor society of the East. Roosevelt had assumed a position demanding the sort of masculine virtues he championed, that of president of the Board of Police Commissioners in New York City. At the 300 Mulberry Street police headquarters, Wister found Roosevelt "humming with business" and brimming with as much vitality as ever. Over lunch, Roosevelt assured Wister that his political future was dead; he was working along lines that would result in his being booted from the Republican Party. In four years, he said woefully, their friends would be describing him as a man of promise who had failed to move ahead. "I hope this is not true," Wister wrote afterwards in his journal. How could either man realize that during the next six years Roosevelt would hold the offices of the governorship of New York, the nation's vice-presidency, and the presidency itself?[12]

Another visit made by Wister was to Rudyard Kipling in Brattleboro, Vermont. The English writer and his wife had settled here in 1892, constructing, in view of Mount Monadnock, a unique home they called

"Naulakha." Kipling, the object of wide public interest, told Wister that when he and Mrs. Kipling recently had taken a walk through nearby woods, they had returned home to find an overly aggressive woman reporter in their upstairs bedroom! The two men shook their heads together, deploring the growing vulgarity of the American nation. Strolling about in the woods, Kipling and Wister talked of "most things that there are," discovering anew that they agreed on every topic they discussed. When Kipling heard how Walker of the *Cosmopolitan* had kept "Balaam and Pedro" without a word for six months before finally rejecting it, he added his own complaint—Walker had changed the title of one of his stories without permission. Kipling had steamed for a while over that, but now he got mad again over Wister's treatment, and to avenge the wrong he vowed to stop publishing stories in *Cosmopolitan.* After dinner, Kipling entertained by reading his poem, "The Banjo Song," and his newest story, "The Brushwood Boy," which Wister thought "fantastic & charming—with the touch of genius." Long after the others had retired, the two writers continued to exchange ideas and opinions. Kipling shared Wister's "disappointment and distrust" over America's hero, Richard Harding Davis, who only a few months earlier had praised Wister heartily. Like Wister, Kipling had a contempt for Richard Le Gallienne and for the "neurotic & erotic of the day." On a positive note Kipling joined Wister in his reverence for Sir Walter Scott. "I'm delighted to find your tenets so wholesome," Kipling told his guest. "And I'm equally gratified at your orthodoxy," replied Wister. Then the two contented men drank a whiskey and went to bed. What particularly pleased Wister once more about Kipling was his total lack of posing, his naturalness. "Again I noticed . . . that the real man of success doesn't talk methods or go puffing about," Wister recorded in his notebook. "Kipling might be a young lawyer or doctor or football player without practice or glories." Especially flattering was Kipling's appreciation for Wister's work and his eagerness to say so. Kipling now suggested playwriting as a possible new direction. Before Wister departed for a visit to the Cabot family in Brookline, Kipling proposed an exchange of *The Second Jungle Book* for *Red Men and White.*[13]

One of the men Kipling and Wister both held in contempt was Hamlin Garland. Garland, with the success of his *Main-Travelled Roads* two years behind him, attempted to befriend Wister shortly after Wister had visited Kipling. Garland wrote in January 1896 to say that although he had not met Wister, he admired Wister's work and was eager to visit him. *Red Men and White*, Garland wrote, "has confirmed me in my original impression of your power and definiteness of statement." A second letter followed within three weeks in which he urged Wister to come and see him, for he had been over some of Wister's western territory himself. "Of course I can't afford to take in any airs of chief adviser but I would like to see you get in a little near the heart of things," Garland wrote. Wister, offended at the hint that Garland might advise him about such matters, wrote a cold note of acknowledgement for the book Garland had sent him, *Prairie Songs*. Kipling, on being told of the correspondence, gave Wister immediate reinforcement by declaring Garland to be a "plain common ASS" for whom there was no hope because God had deprived him of all humor. Years later Wister privately expressed regret for the terseness of his own reply, but he still thought Garland had been guilty of "ignorance and bad taste" because of his "didactic intrusions."[14]

Wister continued to be pleased by his relationship with Harper & Brothers and rightfully so since the firm sought to accommodate him as a prize author. When he requested a rate increase to thirty-five dollars for every thousand words, the firm readily assented for stories of less than ten thousand words. The magazine did not wish to publish longer works. A test of this intent soon arose when *Harper's Weekly* flattered Wister by requesting that he write the Christmas story for the December 1895 issue. He accepted the offer, but the completed story, "A Journey in Search of Christmas," was fourteen thousand words long. Never had the *Weekly* published anything of such length. Since the story was longer than the ten-thousand-word agreement, proper payment was a matter of debate. Wister finally agreed to accept whatever the editors thought the piece was worth, and to his surprise they agreed to pay the original asking price of thirty-five dollars for each thousand words. In "A Journey in Search of Christmas," Wister returned to the irresponsible cowboy named Lin McLean, who, on the verge of a prolonged drinking spree, straightens up to assume responsibility for a runaway boy. Wister now began to concentrate on McLean in his other writing. Since he already had published several tales about the carefree cowboy, he was pointing toward a second book that in a single volume would combine the McLean stories with those of the Virginian.[15]

J. Henry Harper was so proud of Wister that the publisher arranged a special dinner in January 1896 to honor him at the Union League Club. A distinguished group of literary notables came to acknowledge

Wister's emergence as one of their own. Among them were William Dean Howells, Paul Dana, Howard Pyle, Carl Schurz, Edward Martin, Brander Matthews, J. K. Bangs, Richard Harding Davis, Charles Dudley Warner, and Theodore Roosevelt. The fancy menu for the ten-course meal, dedicated "To Owen Wister, Esq.," was written entirely in French. Such a gala occasion did not seem at all inappropriate for the man described in a newspaper article as "Philadelphia's gifted musician-poet-novelist."[16]

Henry Harper surely knew that some cultivation of his author was in order, for other publishers were soliciting Wister to write for them. One pursuer, Appleton & Company's Ripley Hitchcock, asked Wister to produce a book for his firm along the outlines of "The Evolution of a Cowboy." But he would be just as willing to follow Wister's own stated preference for a railroad history. Since Harper & Brothers had not particularly liked Wister's idea for a book on Wells Fargo, Hitchcock's enthusiasm was especially appealing. Wister left Hitchcock's office without a commitment, but he promised himself to think the notion over carefully. Another editor, George P. Brett of Macmillan, also made serious overtures early in 1896, urging Wister in several letters to meet him at lunch to discuss the possibility of doing a book. Wister, however, was not ready to throw over Harper & Brothers, and for the moment he rejected all offers.[17]

In February 1896, following a brief illness, Wister's father died at the age of sixty-seven. "There was nothing untimely or miserable or bitter," Wister recorded of the death. To the last, his father had viewed with mild disapproval his son's predilection for creative rather than legal endeavors. Langdon Mitchell had written Wister not long before his father's death with a description of an evening at Butler Place. "Your father was exquisitely funny. Good Lord he was really fine. . . . Of course he attacked you bitterly. You were a 'whelp' a 'hound' and 'mongrel miserable mountebank' and so on—and so was I, and so were all the young men of the present day. We had no brains—but (by God) we were original for all that." Mitchell's female companion had collapsed into convulsions of laughter at this tirade, and despite Sarah Wister's icy, disapproving silence she could not regain her composure. With his father's death, Wister had to attend to many business matters. A more important function, however, would be assuming his father's place as the anchor in Sarah Wister's life.[18]

Wister had not been too well himself since late November, prompting Kipling to offer this pungent formula for good health: "Keep your bowels open and your feet warm." (He also had a bit of literary advice: write slowly.) Dr. Mitchell urged Wister to go to Europe to recuperate. This was a pleasant recommendation, and soon after his father's death Wister sailed the Atlantic with Sarah Whitman and two other ladies. For some reason, he announced plans to avoid Henry James, fearing no doubt an unwelcome analysis of his western stories, but the ladies protested so much that he assented. James turned out to be "delightful" company, "full of talk" and very anxious about Sarah's health. He also sat down with Wister before a copy of *Red Men and White*, no doubt just as Wister had feared, and gave a page-by-page critique. His principal advice was that Wister should put more landscape into future stories. Wister, however, feared that additional description would interfere with the action and repel his readers, but he recorded in his journal his determination to follow this suggestion and all—"save one or two"— of the others.[19]*

Hardly had he returned to Philadelphia than he departed once more in July for Wyoming. Accompanying him were Grant La Farge, an architect, and Jack Mitchell. La Farge, son of the stained-glass artist John La Farge, had peppered Wister with questions about hunting and camping, and his interest had won him the invitation. He rapidly was becoming a close friend despite Sarah Wister's belief that he was "plain and provincial." Mitchell, of course, had been West with Wister before. In Cheyenne the state's governor, William A. Richards, greeted the trio cordially, and on the opposite side of the state, at Dubois, they visited with George West at his Horse Creek Ranch. West accompanied them on a hunting expedition along Wister's favorite Wind River.[20]

West had been struggling relentlessly to succeed as a rancher. His letters to Wister revealed daily problems, and he beseeched him to join him as a full partner. Otherwise, he warned in a not-so-subtle form of blackmail, financial difficulties might force him to leave the area. The implication was clear: if Wister did not give greater assistance, his faithful guide no longer would be available during summers.[21]

Wister, by now having accepted his eastern ties as the primary part of his life, had little interest these days in a partnership, nor did he accept West's alternate suggestion that they open a hunting lodge. What

---

* Less than eighteen months later he told Sarah Orne Jewett: "Alas for landscape in fiction! One dares not indulge oneself." (Wister to Jewett, December 2, 1897, Houghton Library, Harvard University.)

occupied him now was his progress toward a second collection of stories, these concerning Lin McLean. He had abandoned his resolve to include stories dealing with both the Virginian and McLean, realizing that such a book would be too long. Having reduced his rate of writing in the first half of 1896, Wister now resumed his earlier, more hectic pace.

One significant hindrance was the time required to untangle the affairs of his father's estate. Many of Dr. Wister's investments had shrunk considerably in the years since he had made them, and he had allowed, as Wister said, "too many eggs to get into one basket." Now it appeared that half the family income was threatened. When the Delaware Hudson Company lowered its dividend from seven to five percent, for example, the family income was diminished by six hundred dollars a year. Such matters were serious because interest, dividends, and royalties were the only income Wister and his mother had. For a while they thought they would have to sell Butler Place, which cost between $110 and $175 a month to maintain. It was an idea that would recur in the years ahead. There was also the Georgia farm which earned no money. "We are what is called 'land poor,' " Wister declared.[22]

One of the principal problems was Sarah Wister's irresponsibility concerning money. She knew nothing of economizing. When it finally became clear that her husband's estate would yield an annual income of $4545, Wister cautioned her that in recent months she had been spending at a rate equal to twice that amount. The contrast in attitudes showed in the gift that Sarah wanted to give Wister for his thirty-seventh birthday: a country club membership. He declined, pointing out that he was even on the verge of quitting the Tavern Club because he seldom went there. What he really needed, he told her, was "a good pocket knife."[23]

Despite these burdens, Philadelphia now held a very special attraction for Wister. His determination to find a wife seemed on the verge of success. He had begun to court one of the members of his musical quartet, Mary Channing Wister of Germantown. She was the daughter of his second cousin, William Rotch Wister. Molly, as she was called, was no flighty socialite. She was a determined, handsome, dark-eyed woman who already had shown remarkable ability in organizing worthwhile projects. This was not surprising, for she was the great-granddaughter of the prominent Unitarian minister and Transcendentalist, William Ellery Channing. She had taught Sunday school since the age of seventeen at Germantown's Unitarian Church; she was president of

167

the 1889 graduating class of Miss Irwin's school,* and she was almost as skilled a pianist as Wister. The deepening attraction Wister felt for Molly, ten years younger than he, began to be evident in 1897 when he started noting her whereabouts in his appointment book.[24]

Even apart from Molly, Philadelphia no longer was just a place to be tolerated. Wister found genuine pleasures there in the musical evenings, literary club, and fellowship with other men at the Philadelphia and Rittenhouse clubs. Musical opportunities other than his own quartet existed too, such as joining another pianist to perform one of his own compositions for four hands, "A Frontier Symphony," for the Manuscript Music Society of Philadelphia. The quartet itself performed works by composers such as Wagner, Brahms, Beethoven, Dvorak, and Mozart. (A tragic event had ended his musical collaboration and friendship with Thomas Wharton, who, six weeks before his wedding, drowned at the age of 37.*) Wister's poetry, too, had a ready outlet—he became president of a select group of Philadelphians organized in 1887 and known as the Pegasus Club. Among the club's twenty-one active members were Weir and Jack Mitchell. Once a month, members met in a sand-floored German eating house to vigorously criticize one another's poems.[25]

One evening at the Philadelphia Club, long past midnight, Wister heard his western stories severely criticized for their failure to adhere to the conventional standards of the age's genteel tradition; the stories did nothing to elevate the human race. His tales, said Harry Mercer (who at Wister's request often responded to his manuscripts before publication), were merely photographs. Two other members, Inman Horner and a Dr. Brinton (probably John H. Brinton, M.D.), echoed Mercer's criticism. The comments were almost too much for Wister to endure. "I left them at 1:30 A.M., and to-day I am very ill. My one hope is that they are dead." Wister soon forgave Mercer at least, for when he published *Lin McLean* he dedicated it to him for having "helped and affec-

---

* This school was operated by the sisters Maisie and Agnes Irwin. Maisie Irwin was Wister's companion on his 1885 trip to Wyoming.

* At Wister's suggestion, Harper & Brothers collected some of Wharton's short stories and verses posthumously (including some from *Montezuma* and *Villon*) and published them under the title *"Bobo" and Other Fancies*. Wister wrote a laudatory introduction for the volume. Wharton's career had paralleled Wister's in many respects. Despite a pronounced literary bent, he had become a member of the bar and worked for a trust company, writing in his odd hours. A lonely figure, he had turned to journalism in 1888 and was Sunday editor of the *Philadelphia Times* when he died. Tragically, just before his death, his story "Bobo" brought him the recognition he had long sought.

tionately disciplined" Lin McLean when he was only a "hero in manuscript."[26]

Despite Mercer's sharp comments to the contrary, Wister's stories were beginning to be more than "photographs," for he now was inserting in them his own political ideas. In "Sharon's Choice," appearing in the August 1897 *Harper's Monthly*, he ridiculed the leveling tendencies of the populist movement. In this story, a western town awarded a small boy the elocution prize, not because of his talents but because of his misfortunes. "We cannot help suspecting," wrote the *Nation*, "that he [Wister] is a victim of the pseudo-patriotic virus which is doing so much to poison letters." Wister also used his art to slap the populist leader William Jennings Bryan for appealing to ignorance in offering "quack remedies" instead of reason. In "Pilgrim of the Gila" he referred sarcastically to Bryan as the "boy orator of the Prairies."[27]

Wister's health—or perhaps more appropriately his nerves—became in the middle of 1897 a subject of genuine concern to his friends. Dr. Weir Mitchell wrote to Alden at *Harper's* to notify him that it was imperative his patient take a rest and not be pushed for manuscripts. Alden, alarmed, told Wister not to force himself to write until he could do so with "perfect safety." This meant, as Alden understood, a delay in the publication of *Lin McLean*. That book's contents basically had been completed with "Destiny at Drybone," finished in July, but rewriting and editing remained to be done. When Dr. Mitchell advised Wister to recuperate at a spa for two weeks, Wister seized the opportunity and took with him to Bedford, Pennsylvania, a party of half a dozen friends, including Molly Wister. There, they all enjoyed daily horseback rides, among other festivities. Few "recoveries" could have been more enjoyable.[28]

Afterwards, though, still feeling "a horror of the pen," Wister went to New England to visit the Holmeses, Higginsons, Lees, and others. There, he found Judge Holmes uncharacteristically silent. "It's hard to tell what's the matter. Something is," Wister told his mother. Two weeks later he thought he had learned the answer—Bostonians had grown tired of Holmes. They were disenchanted with his rulings, as well as with his personality. Wister wrote to his mother that the legal profession thought Holmes had an ego problem. Besides that, the Judge had "remained a flirt too far into the middle years and maybe his wife, but certainly other folks's wives, got tired of this."[29]

From New England, Wister went to visit Remington at New Rochelle in early September. They had plenty to talk about—the still-pending publication of *Lin McLean* as well as the upcoming publication of Remington's picture book, *Drawings*, for which the tardy Wister was writing the preface. Wister had declined Remington's initial cover sketch for *Lin McLean*, evidently because it made the cowboy more youthful and innocent than Wister intended. Remington's second interpretation, executed after Wister's visit, showed a more hardened, yet jaunty cowboy with arms akimbo. This cowboy appeared on the book's cover.[30]

Two weeks before the publication of *Lin McLean*, the *Boston Herald* wrote: "There seems to have come quietly into American literature in the last few years one of the most original and effective story writers that it has yet produced. He is Owen Wistor [*sic*]." The rival *Boston Globe*, neglecting an obvious jibe at the misspelled name, found the *Herald*'s "discovery" of such a well-known writer to be hilarious—perhaps the newspaper next would be "discovering" Mr. Howells and Mr. Richard Harding Davis. The *Rochester Post Express* proclaimed at about the same time that of the critics who now were attempting to predict Kipling's successor, "many of them agree that Owen Wister is the man."[31]

The collection of stories constituting *Lin McLean*, published on December 7, 1897, did much to solidify such judgments. The *Lexington* (Ky.) *Morning Herald* declared that although Bret Harte had been the first writer to portray the West with clarity, Wister now ranked first among the region's interpreters. The *Manchester Guardian* in England called *Lin McLean* "perhaps the truest presentment of an actual cowboy that American fiction has given us." Wister's sharpest criticism came from the *Bookman*, where the realism that had won praise elsewhere was not appreciated. He was scorned as a "so-called realist" who failed to inject nobility and idealism into his characters. Another less than laudatory appraisal came—again—from William Dean Howells when he was interviewed by the *New York Sun*. Howells wished that his Philadelphia friend would "get out of the purely local vein. . . . He ought to. He was born here in the East among the fine linen . . . and he has written of that Western life just because he went out there and understood it and felt that he wanted to put it into his stories." Howells encouraged Wister to write about a "more broad and comprehensive subject."[32]

Agreeing with Howells was John Jay Chapman, who believed Wister was doing nothing more than writing genre that, by its very nature, was "falsetto." He urged Wister to let his imagination run free. Yet if these two enlightened critics tugged one way, Wister's western contacts pulled him in another direction. Dean Duke, the New Mexico ranch foreman, wrote: "My dear old Smiley. . . . You're a pretty good sort of Injun for an Eastern dude. The only piano playing chap I ever saw that was worth a cuss. You've got the making of a cowman in you if you'd stay by an outfit and study their moves."[33]

As far as his literary career was concerned for now, Wister was destined to please his western friends instead of Howells and Chapman. Plans already had been made for his next volume to be dedicated solely to the Virginian. Stories scheduled for it included "Em'ly," "Where Fancy Was Bred," "Balaam and Pedro," and "Grandmother Stark." Only two more stories would be needed to complete the book, and Harper & Brothers urged that this be done at "an early date."[34]

As he began examining the existing Virginian stories with the book in mind, Wister queried Roosevelt to see if he had changed his opinion about the eye-gouging incident in "Balaam and Pedro." Roosevelt had praised *Lin McLean*, after all, for its depiction of "men of strong and simple nature" and their "strenuous endeavor." But, no, he still was convinced that this particular episode of cruelty should not be described specifically. Wister bowed to his admired friend's judgment and began considering how best to delete specifics without diminishing the emotional impact of the incident.[35]

Yet in this December of 1897 something besides a book occupied Wister's foremost thoughts. He had decided to ask Mary Channing Wister to become his wife. On New Year's Day he proposed to her. Six days later Wister called upon her father, William Rotch Wister, to ask his consent. The answer would not be long in coming, Molly's father replied, but it could not be given immediately. That afternoon, having discussed the matter with his daughter, he sent his distant cousin a note. "We only wish the happiness of our daughter, and you may feel quite at liberty to make such advances as you desire."[36]

The news brought scores of congratulatory notes, but one message innocently revealed potential conflict. "Molly is such a stirrer up, and reformer of all things wrong, that I am sure she will lead you through pleasant paths, onward & upward toward the light we all hope for." In fact, Molly's many activities already were causing Wister concern. She recently had been appointed to the Philadelphia Board of Education, being at twenty-seven by far the youngest member. Wister could not bring himself to tell his fiancée of his misgivings, but he revealed them to his mother. "I am in a to-do about the Board of Education. I hate to have Molly give it up. I also hate to have her keep it." It did not seem proper for his wife to hold such a position of responsibility. "I have at times a rush of blind feudal hatred at seeing my girl on her feet in public, talking to men—& such men!" He knew that these feelings, so much a part of his own background, were illogical. He hoped for the strength to overcome them. As for Molly's involvement in the socially conscious Civic Club, which she had cofounded, he was absolutely opposed "because I don't believe in it." For the moment, these matters remained unresolved.[37]

The long hiatus from writing caused by his health now was replaced by a hiatus caused by his excitement over the forthcoming wedding. "Are you writing nothing?" his mother wanted to know. He was like the artist, she said, who could not paint because he was too unhappy; then, upon falling in love he could not paint because he was too happy. He consequently lost the affections of the lady who had been captured by his genius. Wister responded, "I am totally unable to think about them [the stories] at all, & they must wait—& I don't care!"[38]

The engagement was only four months long, and Wister declared to Winthrop Chanler that if he had had "more sand" he would have eloped. At 4 P.M. on April 21, 1898, on the same day that the United States declared war on Spain, the couple were married at Molly's home in Germantown. Only twenty-five immediate relatives and close friends attended. There were no bridesmaids, and Jack Mitchell served as best man. The *Philadelphia Item* reported that "although the wedding was a quiet one . . . it was one of the most important social events of the season, owing to the prominence of the contracting parties." Newspaper stories focused more on the groom than on the bride. One said that Wister, "like his wife, cares more for literary and educational work than for the pleasures of the fashionable circles in which they move." Another described the Wister family as a distinguished one in which "every generation for the last century or more has seen at least one of its members a leading figure in the social, political, or business world."[39]

The newlyweds departed on an ambitious six-month honeymoon that would carry them from Charleston, South Carolina, to the state of Washington. Charleston, their first destination, provided an opportunity for renewing roots. Wister's great-great-grandfather, Pierce Butler, had signed the Constitution for the state, and distant relatives were buried in

Charleston, but Wister never had been there. Until now he had spurned his mother's suggestion that he go there and write about that unique culture as he was doing for the West. Upon hearing of this choice for a honeymoon setting Sarah Wister presented the couple with five hundred dollars to spend on the trip.[40]

Charleston struck Wister's senses immediately and favorably in a manner entirely opposite that of Wyoming. "Charleston is simply delicious," he wrote to his mother. "It's precisely what we hoped, only a great deal more so. Of all the American towns I've ever come into as a stranger, it's incomparably the most charming." The couple immediately found themselves welcomed by "very distant cousins and *their* cousins" into the city's finest houses. On their first morning they were greeted in their rooms with a bowl of fresh garden flowers sent by a friend of the family's whom Wister did not yet know. On the first Sunday at the Unitarian church services a member told them that although small in numbers, the church members were determined to "keep the tradition of Dr. Channing." Molly beamed silently, and Wister proudly informed the man that he had the privilege at that moment of speaking to Dr. Channing's great-granddaughter. The minister was summoned right away, and a lengthy conversation ensued with the promise of future meetings.[41]

As Wister later wrote, he found Charleston to be "all of a piece"; an oasis in "our great American desert of mongrel din and waste." The traditional gentility whose disappearance Wister lamented had survived in Charleston, where events occurring fifty years earlier were discussed as if they had happened yesterday. Wister's "discovery" of Charleston meant that the West, for which his fascination as a unique social setting was fading, was to be replaced as a source of inspiration by Charleston. The newlyweds had planned to stay there just two weeks, but the many rounds of social calls, the walks in beautiful Magnolia Gardens, the visits to St. Michael's Church, the meals at the Woman's Exchange, the Confederate veterans' parade at The Citadel, and other activities so pleased them that they extended their visit to a month. At the well-known Pringle House, the couple was honored with a bottle of madeira and a hundred-year-old tablecloth. At a tea in Dr. Manigault's fine old home they sat around a small table in a beautiful room with a painting by John Singleton Copley hanging on the wall, and they examined a collection of ancient mementoes and miniatures of distant ancestors.* "Nothing of the kind has ever happened to me," Wister observed after-

* Both of these houses are preserved today.

wards. The city and its dignified citizens equally captivated Molly. "Charleston seems very close to Paradise," she wrote to her new mother-in-law. On their last day in the city on May 18 Wister wrote to his mother that nothing could force them to leave except the knowledge that they both needed mountain air for their health.[42]

Their destination was only as far away as the North Carolina highlands, where they rented for a month a three-room cottage with a fireplace at the pleasant resort town of Sapphire. They rode horses, boated, hiked, and tried in more tranquil moments to finish the thank-you notes Molly was sending to some two hundred well-wishers. Among the things to decide in their conversations was where they would establish their home. John Jay Chapman implored them to settle in New York City; he wanted Wister's help in editing a periodical he had begun entitled *The Political Nursery*. This was no temptation for Wister, too much aware of Chapman's idiosyncracies, but New York City itself did seem appealing. He even had in mind a set of rooms at the Berkley on Fifth Avenue which he could "perfectly afford" at sixty-five dollars a week. Beneath his changing moods on the subject he believed at this moment that it was "wisdom to go." One important reason was that he could reconsider the offer by *Harper's Weekly* to write a regular column on music.[43]

An unspoken reason was that the move would solve Wister's personal dilemma over Molly's civic endeavors in Philadelphia. His continuing uncertainty about the matter surfaced in a letter he wrote to George Waring in Washington. He and Molly would arrive there in midsummer, he announced, for a stay of several months or several years —he did not know which.[44]

In late June, having gone into Tennessee to be entranced by phrases such as "we uns," "you all," and "h'it," they returned briefly to Philadelphia to change wardrobes before heading for Washington via Chicago by train. The journey was filled with adventure. When they reached the Columbia River at Wenatchee, they boarded the "awfullest boat" Wister had seen, which would take them seventy difficult miles upstream. Wister found another superlative for the river, "the most dreadful thing" he had ever seen, "something to have nightmares about for 20 years." The churning waters lay in a deep canyon, "away below the world." Sometimes the boat could scarcely move against the water's terrific force. At one point the Wisters elected to disembark and walk upstream for nearly a mile rather than experience the boat's agonizing battle against the rapids, a battle that required an intensive buildup of steam. They had plenty of time to walk the mile, as they could see the boat laboring against the rapids, three times failing and slipping back into calm waters to renew its energies for another assault. Afterwards, as the Wisters reboarded the ship, they encountered good-natured jeers from the stewardess and her assistant. Wister cheerfully informed them that indeed he had been "frightened to death" and would walk again if the opportunity arose. The seventy-mile voyage required twenty-eight hours to complete, as compared to four and a half hours to cover the same stretch downstream. "I would sooner climb along outside the Brooklyn Bridge than take that trip again," Wister concluded.[45]

When they finally reached their destination, forty-seven miles away from the river by stage, they found that the Warings had provided them with a simple one-room cabin on a foothill overlooking the Methow River. Winthrop's business establishments consisted now of a hotel, store, and saloon. Waring operated the store, and his stepson ran the tiny, half-log, half-plank structure that served as a hotel. "If our acquaintances were to see us, Molly making the bed & sweeping, & me hauling water up the 50 foot bluff from the well below, it would be a novel sight to them all, I rather fancy," Wister wrote. Mosquitoes were so abundant that their bites caused Molly's feet, legs, hands, arms, and lips to swell.[46]

Their days, "so quiet and uneventful," merged one into another. They spent much of their time reading, especially Anthony Trollope. Molly was asked to speak to the parents and students at the schoolhouse; Wister shuddered involuntarily at the prospect. When finally she did, though, and he saw the happy effect on her audience, his depression changed to elation. It was a conversion for Wister that seemed critical if Molly were to continue her involvement on the Philadelphia school board. It may not have been coincidental that they now decided to settle in Philadelphia rather than in New York.

During these peaceful days the news from the East often centered on developments in the Spanish-American War. "What is very conspicuous," Wister observed, "is the number of Porcellian men engaged in it & of those the number winning attention and distinction." Theodore Roosevelt, William and Winthrop Chanler, the three Norman brothers, Woodbury Kane, Morton Henry, and Randolf Appleton all had won laurels. "It's a very honorable showing," Wister said.[47]

He had declined an opportunity to accompany Remington to troubled Cuba before the outbreak of war. Remington had pleaded with him to join in a two-man expedition, treating Cuba in words and pictures as they had treated the West. "We are getting old and one cannot *get* old without having seen a war," he had implored. Remington went, but he was disappointed. When he protested to William Randolph Hearst that there was no action in Cuba, the publisher reputedly told him, "You supply the pictures, and I'll supply the war." Remington evidently now was convinced, for he predicted to Wister a "lovely scrap around Havana —a big murdering—sure." He sent his regards to Wister's bride: "Tell her I think she got a pretty good fellow but she wants to keep a rope on you—you have been *broncho* so long. . . . Put this in her kind of English. We hope to see you some time after we lick the Dagoes."[48]

Wister's own martial adventure was to take Molly on a hunting and camping expedition. In the midst of the outing he became ill, and he made the mistake of writing to his mother about it. Already nervous and angry over the indignities and crude conditions to which her son had subjected his delicate new wife, Sarah Wister fairly exploded over this final straw.

> I have been completely horrified by the account of yr. life at Winthrop; you are not yet fit to have charge of a woman; if I had had the slightest idea of the sorts of thing you were going to do I wd. have opposed it to the utmost. . . . If Will Rotch & May [Molly's parents] ever know the details they will be justified in being very angry, though I shall not let them speak of it to me.

Sarah thought that a recent graphic letter from her daughter-in-law revealed that even Molly's own sensibilities were being numbed by the rough life. Molly had written of her shock at seeing the wild Columbia River, "the most unlovely wilderness, almost desolation" at Winthrop, and the "stern & unforgiving" nature of the landscape. Molly added that after a few days, however, she had gained a sense of freedom of repose, inspiring new thoughts and converting the setting to one she loved and could enjoy for a long time—except for the times when the mosquitoes were "beyond endurance."[49]

Wister accepted this rebuke with equanimity. His mother knew and enjoyed only one kind of life; his own particular experience encompassed an entirely different one as well. At any rate, Molly's parents had not protested the western journey, and Molly herself seemed healthier than she had in several years. "Now if the woman you are trying to take care of not only enjoys what you offer her but improves in health under it, I think that is sufficient defence of your treatment." He earlier had boasted that "she has gained flesh, & says her dresses are tight."[50]

The debate was not ended, however. Sarah accused her son of having "daubed out delicacy" and of "pigging it." "We aint, & I didn't," he protested. Furthermore, he would be happy for any of their friends to see their little cabin. The fresh air, clean-swept floor, bearskin rug, shelf of books, photographs on the wall, and chintz screens made the dwelling charming and appropriate. As for the indelicacy of man and woman (even if married) living in a single room, "a little tact on both sides" had upheld proprieties. These accusations did not bother him, he said, but they reflected on Molly, and he wanted it understood that "whatever she is, she is a puritan damsel."[51]

What if, Sarah continued, it had been Molly rather than he who had fallen ill while camping, with no doctor near? Reversing Wister's own arguments that the West promoted good health, Sarah contended that he had fallen ill at some point during every visit except the first one, spent in relative comfort at the Wolcott ranch. That fact alone confirmed her belief—one that had been shared by Dr. Wister, she contended—that his health would be benefitted better by "less distant journies & less rough modes of life." She knew her chances of convincing him of this were remote, but she was absolutely disgusted over his poor judgment at placing his bride of less than three months into a crude, one-room cabin.[52]

As they returned that fall Wister could not help sending a final rejoinder by mail from a Yellowstone stopover. He would not be returning from his western travels in the peak physical condition that he had enjoyed in years past, nor had he expected it. But he had been very well during the early stages of the Washington visit, and the only thing that now hampered him was "the approaching strain of return."[53]

Chapter X

OVERNIGHT CELEBRITY
(1899–1902)

TAKING MOLLY TO THE WEST HAD BEEN OBLIGATORY. She could not know all of Dan Wister until she had seen him far from Philadelphia's cool parlors and clubs—making camp, starting a fire, aiming at a fleeing pronghorn, exchanging quips with stagecoach drivers, and perspiring freely under the hot sun. Having introduced her to this aspect of his life, Wister now felt it was time to establish a normal life. He was thirty-eight years of age.

One of the couple's first major expenditures was a new ebony Steinway grand piano bought for $1350. Yet there was no place to put it until they found a house. Their determination to buy a home redoubled in the spring when Molly's physician confirmed important news: Molly was pregnant. Wister, using handsome Rittenhouse Club stationery, gave the news to his mother in a quaintly formal statement: "I wish to say that sometime in September Molly and I expect to be parents."[1]

After the long hiatus from serious writing—one and a half years—Wister had cause for concern. His lack of productivity had begun to attract attention. There was no lack of story ideas, for they arose one after the other, more than he could hope to use. He reported daily to his office at 328 Chestnut Street, and although his stationery still identified him as "attorney at law," he was that in name only. The law office served only as a place for writing. In January he dictated to a secretary the details of the unusual electrical storm that had struck his hunting party in the Washakie Needles in late summer 1888. By April he had completed a long story, "Padre Ignazio,"* in which a cultured padre in California struggles with his yearning to forsake his poor Indian mission after twenty years of service, to return to Europe for the opera he loves so much. Wister felt the story to be a special accomplishment because he had created tension through dialogue and thought, rather

---

* Wister changed the spelling to "Padre Ignacio" when Harper & Brothers published the story in book form in 1911.

179

than through action. Remington, asked by *Harper's Weekly* to illustrate the story for the Christmas issue, gave up in despair because he could find nothing that lent itself to vivid portrayal. Thus, instead of appearing in the *Weekly* in "gaudy colors," "Padre Ignazio" was given to the *Monthly* for a subdued appearance in April.[2]

That same spring Wister was delighted at an invitation from Harvard to compose and read the annual Phi Beta Kappa poem. He saw the occasion as an opportunity to make a personal statement about the depths to which he believed the nation had sunk. He chose "My Country: 1899" as his ambitious title, and he wrote it as a dialogue between "Uncle Sam" and "Columbia" over national priorities. "Columbia," representing the nation's conscience, chastised materialistic "Uncle Sam" because of the "gnawing, scheming, screeching vermin band" of criminals and politicians who threatened the nation's welfare. The epic poem concluded with a vow by Uncle Sam to heed Columbia's wisdom so that the nation's future could be protected. Columbia was clearly Wister, who in the midst of composing the poem told his mother that he was denouncing "through Columbia's mouth" President McKinley's takeover of the Philippines. After he read the poem at Harvard, *Harper's Weekly* observed that Wister had "poked the standard of the Harvard Phi Beta Kappa's annual poetry up so unwarrantedly high that . . . a Pegasus with real wings will be needed to reach it."[3]

The poem had been written at a pleasant Rhode Island coastal village, Saunderstown, where the Wisters had gone for the summer and fall. They liked Saunderstown so well that it became their principal summer home for the rest of their lives. Saunderstown was "very friendly, very simple, very informal, very quiet, very unvarying, and entirely peaceful." One of its attractions was the fact that their friends Grant and Florence La Farge lived there.* Another summer resident was the conductor Walter Damrosch, who had "the head of a genius—and . . . enthusiasm in his talk that's like genius."[4]

Saunderstown offered uninterrupted time for reading as well as for visiting and writing. The book that stirred Wister most deeply was Frank Norris's novel, *McTeague*, the naturalistic tale of a crude San Francisco dentist, a work totally unlike Wister's own. "If you want to

---

* The La Farge's son, John, destined to win a Pulitzer Prize for his novel, *Laughing Boy*, frequently visited "for music," and Wister thought he united "the charm of an innocent well-mannered boy with the mental maturity of the Serpent of the Nile." (Wister to Sarah B. Wister, August 4, 1899, Box 10, Owen Wister Papers.)

see a really new American talent, read the book of a boy who graduated from Harvard in *1895*," Wister wrote to his mother. "It is one of the most brutal, repulsive, and painful novels I've read for a long while. . . . Yet . . . one feels a quite extraordinary and original power. . . . It's in pages crude & inexperienced, as one might expect; but in other pages done so astonishingly well that one's breath is taken away." Sarah Wister attempted the novel, but as Wister suspected, *McTeague*'s crudity so repulsed her that she soon abandoned the book.[5]

As enjoyable as life was in Saunderstown, problems nevertheless arose. As the head of a household, a new experience for Wister, he began to sympathize with his mother's problems in managing servants. In years to come Molly would assume these duties, but as an expectant mother she now was excused. Wister's summer problems involved his establishment as an authority figure. He first had trouble with the cook, "an awesome creature," who sorely challenged the new master. Wister sent for her, and when she appeared she impatiently sat down without invitation. When he ordered her to stand in his presence, he had no idea what he would do or say if she refused, but she complied. A week later came "oh! melodrama" when a servant named Alphonso directly challenged his authority. "We had no physical encounter (in which I should have been licked, and of which I stood in frank terror for I thought it might be necessary) but we had a moral battle in which I established complete ascendancy, said everything I had to say with corrosive clearness, & had him take back various threats & insolences and ask leave to shake hands!" The episode ended when Alphonso acknowledged Wister as master and "begged forgiveness."[6]

The Wisters remained in Saunderstown for the birth, and on September 20, 1899, Wister announced the infant's arrival to his mother by telegram: "Your granddaughter is here. All well." They named her Mary Channing Wister, but just as Wister had been called "Dan" rather than Owen, Mary was to be "Marina." Wister assumed with the birth the mammoth job of notifying their many friends and relatives. Less than a week after Marina's birth he had written more than fifty letters; a month later he still was composing as many as sixteen letters a day. They did not yet claim beauty for the baby, but they announced proudly and honestly that she had "successful eyes, good hands, a tendency to smile often, and a liking for her bath."[7]

From Saunderstown Wister made a weekend trip to Boston, attended services at Trinity Church, saw Harvard president Charles W. Eliot, as well as Robert Simes and Henry Cabot, and decided all over again that Boston had "so many more people worthwhile" than his hometown of Philadelphia. He also paid a call to the offices of the *Atlantic Monthly* to see the new editor, Bliss Perry, and ostensibly to offer him an essay. Wister confessed to his mother that he actually had wanted merely to see what Perry looked like.[8]

As soon as Molly could travel, they returned to their home city and to a newly purchased house at 913 Pine Street. The house had a side yard, thus "good light & air," and its downtown location made Wister believe it would increase in value. He had considered renting, but the cost would have been no less than one thousand dollars a year as opposed to the seven- or eight-hundred-dollar annual expense for the Pine Street house, which was twice as big. Friends were near: across the street lived Agnes Repplier, a clever, sharp-tongued Philadelphian who regularly matched wits with a group of women whose numbers included Maisie and Agnes Irwin and Sarah Butler Wister. Wister, jubilant over owning his first home, exclaimed, "You can't imagine how it feels."[9]

A few months earlier, Wister had completed "The Game and the Nation," in which the Virginian narrates an elaborate story about frogs in order to humiliate the villain Trampas. Harper & Brothers now reminded Wister that just one more story was needed to publish the volume about the Virginian. The firm was eager. For some reason—probably because he felt overextended on western stories and was feeling content to be an Easterner—Wister replied that at present he could not finish the series. The publishing house accepted the news gracefully. "We shall await your pleasure in the matter, for what the gods give we accept with thankful hearts." Wister's decision did not mean that he had no time to write, for soon he accepted an opportunity offered by M. A. De Wolfe Howe to broaden his literary scope. Howe, editor of the Beacon Biographies series, suggested that Wister write a brief biography on "some notable man of action" such as Ulysses S. Grant or William T. Sherman or a frontiersman. Pleased at the idea, Wister responded right away that his own preference would be the hero of Gettysburg, General George G. Meade. When Howe insisted on Grant, Wister agreed to write it "with zest" even though the terms offered were far less favorable than those he got from Harper & Brothers for his western writing.[10]

By now, the acute financial difficulties facing the publishing house of Harper had become common conversation. In early December the worst rumors were confirmed when the company went into receivership under the control of J. Pierpont Morgan. One result was that Harper authors such as Wister found themselves being courted by other publishers. Wister's reaction was one of disgust: if there ware anything on which he prided himself it was loyalty to friends, and Harper & Brothers was a friend. While he had balked at completing the book on the Virginian, he determined, upon hearing of Harper's problems, to collect some of his other western stories to be published as a personal expression of allegiance to the firm. Meanwhile, he sent warm letters of sympathy to J. Henry Harper and Henry Mills Alden.[11]

The title of the new book was *The Jimmyjohn Boss and Other Stories.* It would include all the tales written between "Hank's Woman" in 1891 and "Padre Ignacio" in 1899 that had not gone into his two previous books or that were not intended for the Virginian's book. Several revisions were made, the most interesting occurring in "Hank's Woman." This was when Wister replaced Lin McLean with the Virginian, believing that the story needed a "Greek chorus of an intelligence more subtle than Lin's." With this substitution, the Virginian could make a comment that would not have been characteristic of McLean. Wister inserted it as a slap against the vulgar New York society which he and his mother frowned upon as "nouveau riche." A comment by his mother, who was at Magnolia Inn in Aiken, South Carolina, seemed to inspire the remark. She had supposed that the society at Magnolia Inn was similar to that of Newport, but she declared she "never before saw wealth assert itself so unconditionally as the only reason for everything, including social intercourse." Wister replied that he had "just vented a drop of my own spleen in that direction" by revising "Hank's Woman." The Virginian remarks of the lady who dismissed her German maid: "She was rich an' stinkin' lookin', an' she'd discovered where all our Philadelphia servants have gone to. They've all joined New York society." For his own use, Wister prepared a line that he hoped to say in New York when next asked if he knew a certain person: "No—It's been ten years since I saw New York society, & they were not in it at that time." Sarah Wister advised her son to "find something better to say to the New York snobs than that." The New York "richissimes" knew they had not been in society ten years ago, and many of them did not pretend otherwise, she advised. As for the Virginian's comment, she did not think such a man would say of any woman that she was "stinkin' lookin'." Wister disagreed, for his own "internal sense" told him the woman was not a lady, and his "democratic sense" resented her pretensions. "Of course, *I* should never *really* say any of the things I wrote you," Wister added, preferring to reveal his personal attitudes about society through his characters.[12]

The Jimmyjohn Boss included not only the title piece but also "A Kinsman of Red Cloud," "Sharon's Choice," "Padre Ignacio," "The Promised Land," and "Twenty Minutes for Refreshments." They all were stories in which Wister had taken "hardly any liberties with the actual facts." As was the case in his other western stories, Wister's imagination took hold chiefly in his characters. Publication came on May 3, 1900, and Wister's dedication of the book to the "Messrs. Harper & Brothers and Henry Mills Alden" was a pleasant surprise which he had managed to conceal. The accompanying note to the dedication read, "Whose friendliness and fair dealing I am glad of this chance to record." The book contained some of his best stories, and it gained widespread and favorable notice as a realistic portrait of the West of yesteryear. "If the title of 'The American Kipling' appertains to any one of our country's present writers," wrote a *Minneapolis Tribune* reviewer, "we are inclined to believe that the cultivated Philadelphian, who belongs to the Brahmin class exploited by Oliver Wendell Holmes, can most justly lay claim to the title. Owen Wister has humor and pathos in equal parts. . . . Wister knows the human heart, too." Despite such favorable notices, Wister correctly prophesied in his scrapbook that the volume would not sell many copies. Years later he would observe that about as many people bought it as could "comfortably enter a hotel elevator." Because of the limited sales, the act of friendship that had inspired the collection was destined to end in disappointment. The Harper firm had been genuinely flattered at the dedication, but Wister became disappointed at what he felt was their indifferent promotion of the book. He began complaining to J. Henry Harper and to Henry Mills Alden. They were unable to satisfy him, perhaps because their own independence now was compromised by the presence of a Morgan man. Thus, the relationship between publisher and author began to deteriorate at the very moment Wister had hoped to cement it.[13]

In the course of such events, Wister missed his April 1 deadline for the biography of Grant. He did not like what he had written. "It is no better than what any man with the knack of bookmaking could turn out." While that might satisfy Howe, he acknowledged, it did not satisfy his own standards. He offered to yield the assignment to another writer, but Howe declined. Wister pleaded a need for a prolonged period free of daily interruptions. This came in midsummer at Avon on the Sea, New Jersey, where he took Molly and Marina. As he completed the Grant biography, two other writing propositions were offered him. Without much deliberation Wister rejected the first—William Dean Howells's proposal that he write a book for a series that would include such authors as Mark Twain and Hamlin Garland. Howells's increasing radicalism, his growing emphasis on realism, and even his rejection of Boston for New York had given Wister reason to question the sagacity of the genial literary arbiter. Wister took no pains to soften the rejection. "If I am to win any fame," he told Howells, "I want to do it in the same way that you won yours, and not through these devices." The other offer, from Henry Lee Higginson, he accepted. Thanks to Higginson's underwriting, the Boston Symphony Orchestra was to have a magnificent new concert hall on Hunting Arms, and Higginson asked Wister to compose and read a special poem for the music hall's opening in October. There would be nothing on the program but music and Wister, Higginson told him. Wister agreed to the flattering proposal. He would be able to demonstrate the range of his abilities, for he was chafing at being known only as a writer of western stories.[14]

Earlier in the year Wister had astonished certain critics by writing for the *Philadelphia Press* a two-part series on Wagner to commemorate special performances of his tetralogy in Philadelphia. In the articles, he had discussed with great self-assurance the merits and shortcomings of the composer's work. The *New York Times* chuckled aloud at the spectacle of this western storyteller so brashly attempting to assay Wagner. "Most of Mr. Wister's comments show that he has not made himself acquainted with the Wagner literature of the last dozen years. . . . Mr. Wister will perhaps live to discover Brahms and Tschaikowsky." No record exists of Wister's reaction to this harsh appraisal, although surely he was infuriated at the suggestion that he knew little of the music of the great masters. Someone notified the *Times* of his connections with music, however, and less than two weeks later the newspaper apologized: "A peculiar blunder was made. . . . Information has since reached the editor of this department to the effect that Mr. Wister is first of all things a musician. He knew all about Wagner many years ago, when others were still groping in the dark, and he has an intimate acquaintance with the music of Brahms and Tschaikowsky ever since it was first known to any one in America." The newspaper could have pleased Wister by stopping there; instead it then declared that given such a background Wister's assessments were all the more peculiar.[15]

Despite the urge to broaden his literary range, Wister continued with other western stories. A new subject circulated in his head, even though the volume on the Virginian remained unfinished. Captain Frank Edwards earlier had intrigued Wister with tales of the Bannock campaign in the Northwest and of the Bannock Indian tribe's chief, E-egante (simplified commonly to Egan), whose friendship Edwards had lost when he refused to let the chief spend a night with him in his quarters on a stormy night. Wister had written of E-egante in *Red Men and White*. Now he determined to examine this Indian and the campaign against his tribe. Leaving Molly and Marina in Philadelphia, Wister departed in August for a leisurely trip to the West Coast. Passing once more across the flat lands of Nebraska and eastern Colorado, he began to fear that his romance with the West was over; old feelings were not emerging. Then the Rockies came into view, and his breath was "taken away with pleasure" just as it had been on his first trip. "So I am safe. *Can't* become blasé," he wrote in his journal. He stopped in Denver to visit Edwards at nearby Fort Logan, but learned, to his disappointment, that the captain had been sent recently to China. Three Denver newspaper reporters tried to interview Wister in his hotel room, but Wister assumed what he described as an "urbane and reticent" posture and engaged only in brief conversation.[16]

His next destination was the San Joaquin Valley in California. There he met Dean Duke and found adventure, for Duke was in the process of fulfilling a contract with the United States government to deliver 1,100 wild horses and 500 mules. In San Francisco Wister visited briefly and more sedately with Francis Michael, and then he moved northward to Heppner, Oregon.[17]

There he visited at length with J. W. Redington, a veteran of the Bannock campaign who had been inspired to write Wister by the appearance of E-egante in *Red Men and White*. Redington's letters about the Bannock campaign were so fresh, so laden with intriguing detail, that a firsthand meeting seemed imperative. Wister's presence in Heppner's Palace Hotel caused the hotel clerks to debate among themselves as to what this dignified man's business was. "He was a fine looking gentleman . . . [who] came down late for breakfast and to the chagrin of the waitress took a long time to eat it. In fact, he ate all his meals slowly," one of the clerks later remembered. Finally, the mystery was solved when Wister told the manager he was preparing a book.[18]

Actually, he was also attempting to complete his poem for the Boston Symphony Orchestra's new hall. His progress did not please him. He was reminded of the fact that in front of him would sit "several hundred of the most intelligent people in Boston." The poem had to suit the occasion perfectly, and he plotted it carefully. Another writing assignment was more lighthearted: an essay for the *Boston Transcript* on the impact of the motorcar on the horse. The automobile, Wister concluded, was helping the horse by liberating it from drudgery, but the automobile would never completely replace the animal that had so faithfully served the human race. The bicycle had flourished briefly before assuming its proper role, and so would the automobile. The essay came easily, and Wister was pleased with his work. Still another literary job during this western trip was the correction of proofs for the Grant biography. Howe, his editor, pronounced the short biography a "corker." Wister relayed this praise to his mother, telling her to ask someone for the meaning of the word.[19]

By early October he was back in Philadelphia, the completed poem ready for delivery. He grandly entitled it, "The Bird of Passage: An Ode to Instrumental Music." He already had sent a copy of it to Professor Charles Eliot Norton at Harvard for a preliminary assessment of this effort to reach a "higher flight." If Norton could tell him he had succeeded, it would "matter very little" what others might think. Norton, unfortunately, could not tell him that. His primary suggestion was to use a child as a metaphor for music instead of a bird. Wister declined, "This would too seriously change my whole idea." In Greek and Hebrew culture, the figure of music persisted as a wild bird, and Wister simply could not substitute an undeveloped child.[20]

In fact, the substitutions would have mattered little. The poem was beyond redemption. Wister had attempted to soar too high. His flowery words filling 244 lines evoked images of forests and gardens, gods and goddesses, and all things beautiful.

> Yea, sweep thy harp which hath a thousand strings!
> The joy that sometimes lives in darkest night,
> And the strange sadness which the sun-shine brings,
> The splendors and the shadows of our inward sight,—
> All these within thy weaving harmonies unite.

For a man to stand before 2,569 people—in competition with Beethoven and with a hall designed by McKim, Meade & White—and to read such lines as these—in iambic pentameter acatalectic—simply would not work. Wister's own performance on this gala occasion for the city, for the orchestra, and for Higginson was an acknowledged failure.[21]

The "bard from Philadelphia," as one of the Boston reviewers called him, indeed made a striking appearance with his dark hair, mustache, and sturdy frame. He introduced the poem laboriously and to little purpose. "Poor Mr. Owen Wister," commented the *Boston Journal*. "Why did he find it necessary to tell the audience . . . what he had thought of doing, what he might have done, and what he did not do?" The *Boston Courier* reported that he read his poem with an "unmelodious voice and in an inexpert manner. . . . It was confused and drawn in delivery, and one could not help sympathizing with Mr. Higginson, who stood courteously near the poet until he had ended." The *Boston Daily Advertiser* regretted that the long poem had not been delivered in "weekly installments." A spectator wrote to the *Boston Journal* wondering why a poet had been imported for the occasion. "Nor did Mr. Wister look as though he relished the honor that had been thrust upon him; indeed, to me, he appeared singularly depressed, a melancholy man with soulful eyes." Shocked by such a hostile reception, the first he had encountered, Wister privately acknowledged that the poem was too long and his reading of it indifferent. He pasted the newspaper notices in his scrapbook and added a notation: "I don't know why they were all so angry at me. . . . It may be because I was not a native, and it may be because I withheld the manuscript from them. But they are truly amusing."[22]

Before the year ended, Wister had regained some of his lost luster. His short biography, *Ulysses S. Grant*, was published. Few profits resulted, but reviews were so favorable as to lead one to believe, Wister commented, that "wealth beyond the dreams of avarice had rolled in." The work had required eight months' effort, and the financial rewards, as he pointed out, were hardly enough to keep him in cigarettes—and he was not a cigarette smoker.[23]

The book renewed a flurry of communications from his readers, a fact that was not without its problems. Genuine responses to his work were pleasing, but "autograph fiends" always angered him. He used every ruse he could imagine to thwart their best efforts. One Kentucky woman wrote that she liked his writing so well that she would consider it an honor if he would delegate some minor chore to her. "This is the most remarkable communication I have ever received," he jotted on her letter. It was, he was certain, only a subterfuge to get a signed letter from him. To thwart her ambition, Wister had office assistant Henry Esling respond in his behalf.[24]

With more writing projects facing him these days than he could handle, Wister was working as many as ten hours a day. This he declared was "too much." As the year 1900 approached an end, he returned to a more deliberate pace of two thousand words a day, composed largely in the law office. Such a schedule left him time for other important activities such as taking care of his health and fulfilling his social obligations.[25]

He had been concerned since his marriage about extra pounds which had sent his weight to nearly two hundred pounds. He began visiting a "trainer" twice a week who prescribed exercises and told Wister that he bathed too often. How much is too often? Wister asked. Every two days was too often, the trainer replied. Wister, who bathed daily, was informed that this was one reason his health had always been poor. Excessive bathing had damaged his skin, and his health would have been even worse if he had not been endowed—in spite of his nerves—with a rugged constitution. So said the trainer, at least.[26]

Wister's social activities were more varied than ever. In December 1900 he went to New York City to join twenty-three literary figures at the head table for the Aldine Association's Mark Twain Dinner. (Some of the other guests included William Dean Howells, Winston Churchill, Richard Watson Gilder, Joseph Jefferson, Brander Matthews, and Twain.) In 1900, Wister was elected secretary of the Library Company of Philadelphia and a life member of the Historical Society of Philadelphia. When St. Paul's School opened its new library in mid-1901 Wister delivered a short, reminiscent speech, and when the *Harvard Lampoon* observed its twenty-fifth anniversary, past and present editors heard Wister read a poem he had composed for the occasion, "The Genesis of the Lampoon; a Legend of John Harvard." This visit to Massachusetts was enlivened by a luncheon given in Wister's honor by Mrs. Henry S. Whitman with guests such as Mrs. James T. Fields, Miss Sarah Orne Jewett, and Josiah Royce. Mrs. Whitman revealed a letter sent to her by William James from Rome in which he lavished high praise on Wister's biography of Grant, calling it "really colossal" and saying that he had not known Wister was "so great a man!" Wister did not repay the compliment in kind—three months later he wrote to his mother that she should be reading Josiah Royce instead of James because Royce was a "very much more efficient thinker."[27]

On this visit to New England he stopped at Oyster Bay on Long Island to see Theodore Roosevelt. Despite Roosevelt's earlier prediction that his role as police commissioner would finish his career in public life, Roosevelt now was vice-president of the United States, having achieved that office in 1901 after becoming the hero of San Juan Hill and the governor of New York. (Roosevelt had called Wister's *Grant* "the very best biography which has ever been written of any prominent American.") Now, the "delightful visit" reaffirmed in Wister his conviction that Roosevelt was "one of the best influences in our country."[28]

Later that summer, when Roosevelt was in the Adirondacks on an outing, President McKinley was assassinated in Buffalo by a solitary gunman. That "damned cowboy," as Roosevelt was called, suddenly was president of the United States. Wister, on learning of the assassination, sent a telegram to Roosevelt, and on the following day, the day he took the oath of office, Roosevelt found time to respond in his own hand: "There is very little for me to say now. All that in me lies to do shall be done to prove that I have the power, as I certainly have the will, to perform aright the task that has been set me." The office of the presidency would seem to bring about an even closer relationship between these two men. Wister was to be a frequent guest in the White House, where Roosevelt could momentarily forget the burden of the presidency by swapping tales about Harvard and the West, and by letting Wister entertain the family at the piano with his wide repertoire of songs and music.[29]

With Roosevelt's accession, Wister immediately wrote several glowing articles about the new president and the significance of his assumption to the office, going so far as to proclaim that by virtue of his gentleman birth he had overcome more obstacles in his rise to power than would have an underprivileged man. Thus, in Wister's mind, one of Roosevelt's great services would be to certify that "there is no reason in the nature of things that an educated gentleman should not be President of the United States." For *Outing* he wrote a sketch of the president directed not to the politically sophisticated but to the "out-of-door plain uneducated, shrewdminded men of sport, who hunt & fish & own dogs and fancy pigeons . . . & do not give much thought to politics." What was so important about Roosevelt, Wister contended, was that his presidency demonstrated that the present low state of public morality in politics was not inevitable—a gentleman *could* rise to the top.[30]

To Richard Watson Gilder, of the Century Publishing Company, the time seemed propitious for a biography of the vigorous new president, and Wister seemed to be the logical choice as author. Gilder wrote to Roosevelt to see if he agreed. Had Wister known of Roosevelt's reaction he would have been dismayed, for Roosevelt did not want Wister as his biographer. He urged Gilder not even to mention the possibility to him. "I have a kind of feeling that the man who is to write about me ought if possible to be a man who has lived near the rough side of things, and knows what it is actually to accomplish something—not just to talk about accomplishing it," Roosevelt wrote. He preferred the Kansas editor William Allen White as his biographer. Roosevelt's feelings about the several articles Wister did write about him are not known, although he requested that Wister avoid mentioning his family since he was doing what he could to prevent them from being "self-conscious through being talked about." Wister never indicated that he ever heard about Roosevelt's harsh assessment of him as a man who was protected from "the rough side of things" and as one who talked of accomplishments rather than achieving them.[31]

Roosevelt's sudden arrival to the seat of power was fascinating to Wister, who yearned for a forum to express his own deep-seated opinions about the nation's condition. A minor anecdote indicates the degree of his desire for recognition in more serious affairs. The *New York Times* borrowed for an editorial one of the Virginian's comments from the story "The Game and the Nation" and applied it to international politics. The editorial assessed as a bluff a German threat to kill Chinese citizens unless negotiations accelerated, and it quoted the Virginian's quiet comment in a poker game, "Cyards are only one of the manifestations of poker in this hyah world." Wister's delight was suggested by his penciled note: "This indirect praise has pleased me more than any printed complimentary I have so far received. It's worth 40 'notices.' "[32]

In this same year, another man who was destined to become vitally interested in public affairs—taking a radically different viewpoint—entered Wister's life. He was Upton Sinclair, a struggling, twenty-three-year-old writer one year away from a conversion to socialism. Sinclair sent Wister a copy of his novel, *Springtime and Harvest*, which he had privately published with money borrowed from a relative. After an exchange of several perfunctory and amicable letters, Wister obliged Sinclair's request by sending him a detailed analysis of the book. The grateful Sinclair declared it to be the "very best" analysis he had received "though by no means the most favorable." Moreover, Wister's letter was "beautifully kind." Sinclair implied that he thought he may have found the inspirational figure in Wister that he needed, and he offered to come to Philadelphia so that Wister could personally show him how to correct his faults. "I write to you as to a kind of oracle," said Sinclair, "for I have passed a deadly dull winter of despair in which a wonderful thing called Specimen Jones stands out like a lightning feast. It was cymbals and trumpets, and I tell you I was stunned as I am not often. It was so brilliant and so dazzling that I'd have been quite in despair about my own work if I'd thought of it." Wister did not send an invitation, and the exchange of letters halted temporarily.[33]

Wister's own literary interests were too pressing to devote time to an unknown writer. For one thing, he was negotiating with two young Harvard graduates in New York City about the possibility of having them dramatize *Lin McLean.* The two playwrights were constructing a scenario, and Wister was to do most of the dialogue himself. After one hard five-hour session he "seemed to feel a drama" in his hands. By December just one act was "fit to see" but "quite a prominent actor" had heard of the dramatization and was eager to have a role in it. "I have not spoken of this to any one," Wister wrote to his mother on a postal card. "I don't like . . . people talking about an unachieved thing. So understand, it's for your ear only." Sarah, delighted at the news, was alarmed that he had put such "secrets" on a postal card. "Some servants always read them, & even servants are in the pay of newspapers for private information of all sorts." Wister read the completed act to her, and she was unsparing in her praise. "I know of nobody but Cable & Mark Twain who cd. write with as much power." Yet the play never materialized—Wister was busy with still other projects, and he became dissatisfied with the two dramatists.[34]

One of the projects concerning him most was his long negligence in completing the stories about the Virginian. Aside from the dramatization of *Lin McLean,* one of the distractions which delayed him was the writing of a humorous story about Harvard students entitled "Philosophy 4." The story revolved around a true incident in which two lazy students earned a higher grade than the one who tutored them. "Philosophy 4" caused discussion in the Boston newspapers as to whether Harvard students could be guilty of using the language depicted, and Wister was amused when some outraged correspondents revealed him "as a corrupter of youth." Another writing project in 1901 deterred him further: the preface for Remington's new book, *A Bunch of Buckskins.* Still another project was dropped when Wells, Fargo & Co. officials informed Wister that they had promised another man the right to do the firm's history. This ended Wister's longtime goal to relate the dramatic story of that pioneer company.[35]

Now, at last, there seemed to be no choice but to finish the volume on the Virginian. Before leaving for Saunderstown for the summer he notified Alden that he now would begin work toward the book's completion. The episode on which he worked, "In a State of Sin," had been in his mind so long that writing it became "merely a question of adequate execution." The Saunderstown summer was noteworthy in another way: on September 21, 1901, Molly gave birth to twins. They were named Owen Jones II and Fanny.[36]

Before 1901 ended, Wister had made an important decision about the Virginian's book—he would meld its various independent episodes into a continuous whole and avoid the disjointedness of *Lin McLean.* The working title, "The Virginian: A Tale of Sundry Adventures," had indicated a loose structure. It would be changed. The new plan meant that some entirely new chapters and some extended transitional sections would have to be written. But to Wister, who at last had become excited over the book's prospects, it was "very pleasant" labor. He struggled with one technical difficulty—some of the stories had been written in the first person, others in the third person, and still others from an omniscient point of view. Achieving a book-long uniformity turned out to be virtually impossible, and after adding interpolations to ease the jolts, Wister decided to let the conflicting points of view remain.[37]

Another problem confronted him. Should he give the anonymous Virginian a name? Wister had not deliberately created him as a nameless character, but the story of "Balaam and Pedro" had been about a horse, and a name for the Virginian had not seemed so important. He finally decided to leave the character nameless because the determined cowboy had by now come to represent a larger-than-life figure who embodied all the traits and character that Wister hoped for the nation.[38]

Meanwhile, on this eve of the most significant publishing adventure of Wister's career, his relations with Harper & Brothers were deteriorating further. Having been disappointed over the firm's treatment of *The Jimmyjohn Boss and Other Stories,* he now concerned himself with their advertising and promotional plans for *The Virginian.* While all of his Harper & Brothers books had been critical successes, he had not earned from any of them as much as he had been paid for one short story, "A Pilgrim on the Gila." In Wister's opinion, the firm had failed to advertise his books sufficiently. He warned the officials early in the summer that unless they guaranteed a much better promotional effort for this book, he would publish it elsewhere. Harper & Brothers' responses failed to satisfy him. "They have neglected answering my questions for months, they have published my books in a cheap way, and they have spent insufficient money in advertising them," he complained. "In the present huge world a book *must* be advertised or no one knows of its existence."[39]

Harper & Brothers did not seem to realize the depths of Wister's disillusionment until early December when J. Henry Harper hurriedly launched a campaign to keep their author. But it was too late. Not until four or five urgent telegrams arrived did Wister agree to dine with Harper, and then only if Harper promised not to mention the book at all. The publisher sent his author a letter saying the news of Wister's dissatisfaction "greatly disturbed" him and came as a distinct surprise. *Jimmyjohn* had been published, he said, during uncertain times for the firm and at a moment when it "possibly may not have had the personal attention which it deserved." He implored Wister to reconsider. "If I seem to be too insistent you will please pardon me, for my personal regard and friendship for you will not allow me to look with indifference to the possibility of a break in our exceedingly pleasant business relations which have continued through so many years." Such attention pleased Wister, but he refused to yield. "It looks as if they were really anxious to keep me. But it's too late. . . . Their 11th hour manifestations have been a surprise. I suppose the fact is they took me for granted and never thought much about it." In fact, Harper's last appeal came after Wister already had signed a contract with the Macmillan Company to publish the Virginian's stories the following spring. George P. Brett of Macmillan was elated. "I trust the time will soon come when we shall reckon ourselves the fortunate publishers of all your books."[40]

Wister realized his debt to Harper & Brothers, and he acknowledged that neither Alden nor Harper was responsible for his switch. He blamed it on economy measures instituted by the Morgan forces. Thus, while he maintained the good wishes of Alden and Harper, the breach would have a decided impact not only upon the firm's book publishing arm, which lost one of the best-selling novels of years, but also on *Harper's Monthly*. Between 1893 and 1902 Wister had contributed nearly half of the western items published in the monthly's pages. Wister's last two episodes of the Virginian, "Superstition Trail" and "With Malice Aforethought," went to the *Saturday Evening Post*, where they each appeared in two segments. The partnership which had been so fruitful for both author and publisher was over.[41]

Despite their fine new house on Pine Street, the Wisters could not seem to stay there. Having spent the summer in Saunderstown, they now took their three children to the site of their honeymoon, Charleston, South Carolina, for a three-month visit. The immediate reason for the stay was Molly's appointment to represent the state of Pennsylvania at the Charleston Exposition. Wister had work of his own to do with his Virginian stories, but that he could do anywhere.[42]

No sooner had the family arrived than Wister began an unusually rigid writing schedule. Molly, a good organizer, insured that none of the routine of caring for infants or directing servants fell to him. He was able to work nine hours a day, and by February 9, his fourteenth day of writing, he had composed twenty thousand new words constituting four entirely new chapters as well as the revising, simplifying, elaborating, and "general licking into shape" of "Em'ly" and "Where Fancy Was Bred." He was determined, in this novel, to give readers the transitory links that he had omitted in *Lin McLean,* and before he was through more than half of the book was new material.[43]

Historic Charleston's romantic spell did not loosen the grip it had fixed upon Wister during his previous visit. Rarely, if ever, had he been in a better mood. As he "pegged away" at the book he "wandered and meditated and looked across the dreamy, empty rivers to their dreamy, empty shores and the grey-veiled live-oaks that were all of a piece with the wistful silence." Nearly thirty years later he speculated that "it may well be that this portrait" colored his writing. There was, indeed, a striking contrast between the stories published prior to his arrival in Charleston and the material written there. It was in this new material that the Virginian became thoroughly involved in his tender love affair with the young schoolteacher Molly, acquiring in the process a deeper dimension for his character.

Earlier fictitious treatments of cowboys had portrayed them as coarse men with no time for romance; Wister's addition of a gentle, romantic nature to the Virginian set him apart from the established genre. In so doing, Wister created a hero who was capable of capturing the nation's imagination, who appealed to both men and women, to both Easterners and Westerners.[44] "My book is like going up a mountain," Wister wrote to his mother.

Each time I think I have reached the last rise another unfolds. . . . What I have written seems satisfactory; and some I think is good—some of the dialogue ahead of any, I think, in the way of lightness and immediacy. Wholly new work I don't mind, and at times greatly enjoy. It is the revision and interpolation that I do certainly hate. If you look at this sheet of paper you'll see cuts—knife cuts. Those are where I have sliced my short stories, and pasted them in pieces with the interpolations between. Sometimes a page needs a change for consistency; sometimes it needs an addition for clearness & emphasis; sometimes it needs more elision; sometimes the style offends me and I re-write it according to my present standard.

He was surprised that so much of the earlier writing displeased him, but whenever he encountered offensive passages he removed or rewrote them.[45]

In the midst of this work President Theodore Roosevelt arrived for an official three-day visit to the Charleston Exposition. Wister last had seen him in the fall at the White House when he had asked the president to intercede with Secretary of the Interior Ethan Allen Hitchcock to designate the country at the head of the Wind River as a national forest reserve. The visit had been disrupted several times by Roosevelt's energetic daughter, Alice. Finally, in exasperation, Roosevelt had told Alice that if she interrupted their conversation one more time he would throw her out the window. This time, in Charleston, they had the opportunity to talk without Alice. Wister once more brought up the subject of "Balaam and Pedro." Did Roosevelt still think the hideous detail which had shocked him nine years earlier should be suppressed? "Speak now or forever after hold your peace," Wister said. Roosevelt replied: "I shall never change my mind about that. I beg you won't keep that passage. It will deform the book." Upon returning to his desk Wister eliminated from his pages the description of what Balaam did to Pedro.[46]

Two other friends, even closer than Roosevelt to the character of the Virginian, continued to be on Wister's mind as he worked. Charles D. Skirdin, who had suffered crippling wounds to his arm and hand in the Philippines, had left the Army. Having come to Wister for advice about his future, he got a job as a streetcar conductor in Philadelphia. "I am well satisfied with what I have goten [sic] if I only have success," Skirdin wrote in early 1902.[47]

George West, still corresponding faithfully, had experienced good and bad times in the past few years as a rancher. In 1898 he had written, "When I clearly see what you have done for me I must acknowledge you as my God, for I know that *you* have saved me." In 1900, with West continuing to experience lean times, Wister had asked Roosevelt to use his influence as governor of New York to obtain an appointment for West as a forest ranger. Roosevelt had declined, pointing out that he had absolutely no influence in Wyoming. Soon thereafter West took a position as tax collector for Fremont County, a job that permitted him to continue his ranching activities. His letters to Wister indicated that the two of them still talked of establishing a hunting lodge. But in April 1900 he sent shocking news: "I was arrested for cattle stealing, and gave bond." Perhaps the allegation had slim foundation; nothing ever came of it.[48]

That same year West realized his longtime dream of marriage. His bride was a refined Massachusetts woman whom he had pursued diligently from afar for a number of years. She was Mable Roberts, an accomplished singer and graduate of the Boston Conservatory of Music. Wister served his friend as best man at the wedding, and before the Wests departed the East Coast for their log cabin home on Horse Creek Ranch they visited the Wisters in Philadelphia. Back in Wyoming, West wrote to Wister:

> I do wish you could see me in my new house. . . . When evening comes and Mrs. West [is] at the piano singing some sweet soft air while I am lying on an easy couch dressed in some of the nice clothes that you have sent me[,] I cannot help thinking that life is sweeter to me than to any other man.

The combination of roughhewn cowboy appreciating and even reveling in refinements brought by a feminine wife was very much a part of the character of the Virginian, and it was an ingredient that Wister was adding to the book at the time he received West's letter. West's own good fortune, West declared, was due largely to Wister. "I love you for it," he wrote. He now had managed to attract local investors and to form a corporation to finance his cattle operations. It was named the West, Lovering Land & Livestock Co., and West served as president.[49]

By March the story of the Virginian was drawing near its end. Wister declared the last chapter, in which the Virginian and his eastern bride camped on a river island for their wedding night, to be "the best pages I have ever written." Their depiction of the Virginian's concern for Molly in a beautiful natural setting also made them the most romantic he had ever written.

On the last day of the month he wrote a preface in which he described the book as a "historical novel." The Wyoming that it portrayed was a "vanished world," and the cowpuncher who worked there was "the last romantic figure" upon the American soil. As for the enigmatic hero of the book, he wrote: "Sometimes readers inquire, Did I know the Virginian? As well, I hope, as a father should know his son." He offered no further clues.[50]

With the preface completed and the Exposition over, the Wister family returned to Philadelphia. There Sarah Wister, who already had read the manuscript, was waiting with the first of her many criticisms. Yet these could not shake Wister's faith in the merit of his creation. In fact, he was immensely pleased with the work. Less than two weeks before publication he wrote to Judge Holmes that the book was his "best so far." What he had set out to do, he said, was to "draw a man of something like genius—the American genius." The judge could decide for himself if he had succeeded, for an advance copy was being sent to him.[51]

On May 30, 1902, the book at last appeared. Its full title was *The Virginian: A Horseman of the Plains.* The author dedicated it to the president of the United States. A personal note to Roosevelt pertained to the Balaam and Pedro chapter. "Some of these pages you have seen, some you have praised, one stands new-written because you blamed it; and all, my dear critic, beg leave to remind you of their author's changeless admiration."

The Virginian had as its setting the Wyoming cattle frontier between 1874 and 1890. The book told of the persistent courtship by the Virginian of the plucky new schoolmarm, Molly Stark Wood, who had come to Wyoming from Bennington, Vermont, to see the world and also to escape the boredom of her sedate eastern environment. Between his duties as a trusted hand at Major Henry's ranch, the Virginian persistently seeks the hand of the attractive schoolteacher, who at first is concerned about her suitor's rough western ways, but who ultimately sees beyond to his innate goodness and worthiness. In this courtship there is compromise on both sides, for as Molly grows to accept the Virginian, he pleases her by reading books she recommends. Besides his involvement with Molly, the Virginian must handle his cowboy adversary, Trampas, and deal with rustlers, Indians, and the vicious rancher Balaam. In the end, having gained Molly's approval for marriage, the Virginian is issued an ultimatum by Trampas the day before the wedding: he must leave town before sundown. Faced with Molly's demand that he either avoid bloodshed by doing as Trampas orders or else cancel the wedding forever, the Virginian regretfully but without hesitation follows the unwritten code and stays in town to confront his adversary. In the inevitable duel, the Virginian shoots and kills Trampas. Molly, though, reneges on her ultimatum, and the wedding takes place as scheduled. The concluding chapter tells of the couple's romantic honeymoon in the lovely Tetons and ends with a brief projection in which the Virginian becomes an important man in the West with a strong grip on various enterprises.

"Owen Wister has come pretty near to writing the American novel," said the *New York Times Saturday Review of Books.* "Easily the best book of the year," wrote the reviewer for *Current Literature.* According to the *Dial's* critic, the central character was "one of the most distinct personalities" ever to appear in American fiction. The *Bookman's* assessment that Wister had "driven into the soil of Wyoming a stake which seems likely to remain for a long time to come" turned out to be an understatement. What *The Virginian* ultimately did was create a nearly insatiable appetite in the American public for cowboy heroes whose hearts were purer than gold, whose intentions for their women were beyond reproach, and whose quiet courage made them men to be feared by all. Only a few reviewers cast negative votes; the most penetrating of these appeared in the *Sewanee Review.* That publication called the book an "impossible love story" with a sentimentality that was "psychologically unconvincing, and artistically untrue."[52]

Even after the unusual demand for the book became obvious, Wister, now in Saunderstown with his family, remained cautious. He reminded all who would listen that two factors still could mitigate against a "really big sale." These were the possibility of a "poor book year" and the fact that his topic was, after all, "unfashionable."[53]

As startling reports about *The Virginian's* enthusiastic reception continued to mount, however, it was difficult to reduce them into realistic terms. A few weeks after publication, its impact was becoming clearer. A Boston dentist refused to accept Wister's payment for his work because he insisted it was his privilege to serve such a distinguished guest. Determined to return the favor, Wister went to a nearby bookstore and asked for a copy of *The Virginian.* "That's a great book," exclaimed the clerk, not realizing who his customer was. Then he became silent as he watched Wister inscribe his name in it. "I hope you understand that I did not recognize whom I was speaking to," the clerk said. He asked Wister to sign another copy to replace the one he already had at home. Presently, the store's proprietor walked up to greet Wister and to tell him of his great admiration for the book. "But is it a *practical* success?" Wister asked him. "It is one of the best books I have had for years," the owner replied. "All right," said Wister, "but being good has nothing to do with *practical* success. Does it sell?" Wister surely already knew the answer, but the owner assured him that it led every book in the store. "I prayed it might have similar fate elsewhere & many wheres, [and] I departed," Wister noted. After the purchase he returned to the dentist's office with a copy of *The Virginian* to give the dentist.[54]

The author's initial skepticism about the sales was understandable. As he later commented about the profits from his previous books, "the sum total . . . might possibly have bought hay enough to keep one horse alive, but certainly not a pair." Only one month after publication it began at last to dawn on him that this book was to be different from the others. The $485 he received in English royalties alone was added on July 2 to the $500 advance he had been given. That was the beginning, for by now the book already was nearing twenty thousand copies in sales, with no end in sight. For every $1.25 copy sold, Wister's share was twenty-two cents.[55]

Armed with knowledge of his success, Wister made a triumphal visit to Harvard's graduation exercises to represent his class of '82 as a marshal. Roosevelt received an honorary degree, addressed the audience, and retreated to a tree with his own graduating class for an informal meeting. Then Wister and several Porcellians escorted Roosevelt to the Club and through the new Porcellian gate, permitting the president to be the first man to pass through it. That evening at his class dinner Wister made a short speech and won loud applause.[56]

He was happy to learn that the president already had read *The Virginian*. In fact, Roosevelt had read it within eight days of its publication. The dedication to him, he said, came as a "total surprise" and "immensely pleased" him. He had not believed that the melding of diverse short stories into a novel could be achieved without loss of "charm and power." Yet he felt that both charm and power had been enhanced in the process. "It is a remarkable novel. If I were not President, and therefore unable to be quoted, I should like nothing better than to write a review of it," he said. The chapter Roosevelt named as his favorite, "Superstition Trail," was also Wister's favorite.[57]

Back in Saunderstown, where the Wister's were enjoying "many, many visitors," parties, and congratulations, Wister learned that after two months, *The Virginian* had sold more than fifty thousand copies. It was leading all best seller lists. Orders were arriving at Macmillan at the daily rate of one thousand, and on one unusual day four thousand orders were received. With such an immense popular success assured, Wister began to think of posterity. The only critic remaining whose opinion concerned him, he said, was the one he would not be able to hear—"Time."[58]

There was one mortal whose opinion he did treasure, and that was Henry James. That opinion soon came in the form of an eight-page letter. First, James wanted it understood that he was hurt that Wister had failed to send him a copy. Nevertheless, he had taken the trouble to obtain it himself, and he found the entire book "a rare & remarkable feat." What he liked best, surprisingly, was the subject itself,

> so clearly & finely felt by you, I think, & so firmly carried out in the exhibition, to the last intimacy of the man's character, the personal & moral complexion & evolution, in short, of your hero. On this I very heartily congratulate you; you have made him live with a high, but lucid complexity, from head to foot & from beginning to end; you have not only intensely seen & conceived him, but you have reached with him an admirable objectivity.

James wished he could be with Wister to discuss "elements of the art we practice & adore," for despite his overall praise, there remained a few elements about the book with which he differed. His primary reservation ("perverse perhaps") was the happy ending. "Nothing would have induced me to unite him to the little Vermont person [Molly]. . . . I wouldn't have let him live & be happy; I should have made him perish in his flower & in some splendid way." But his reservations did not "touch the essence" of the achievement, and, moreover, he acknowledged that he had not been asked for his comments. Still, he had an "impertinent apprehension" that Wister would be tempted to return to the Virginian in a later work. "*Don't* revive him again," he cautioned. "Write me something equally American on this scale or with this seriousness— for it's a great pleasure to see you bringing off so the large & the sustained."[59]

Sarah Wister, like her friend James, was a critic too, and even if her son had achieved a success of immense dimensions, she still was not satisfied that the work was artistically true. In fact, a popular success of such proportions was reason itself for her to be suspicious. The common crowd, as her son agreed, never had been discriminating in its taste. Wister's mother found little to admire in the book from its title to its ending, and she did not attempt to disguise this fact. She judged the construction to be piecemeal, the last chapter superfluous, the heroine a failure, and the lynching illogical and improper. Wister took vigorous exception to these criticisms. While the construction admittedly was not orthodox, the developing character of the Virginian unified it "quite fundamentally, rendering the ordinary construction unnecessary." Proof of the book's fundamental unity, he contended, lay in the fact that every critic who spoke of it said that the interest held from the first page to the last. "That," he contended, "is the proof of a very deep kind of unity." While he agreed that the last chapter might be "superfluous," it also was "very wise," and, given the opportunity, he would write it the same way again. "After the harsh drama preceding, it was desirable to have some serene closing cadences. . . . And it was desirable his unromantic future should be indicated in a book of this kind, and no chance left for the reader to ask what did they do?" The heroine Molly was "a failure," Wister agreed, "without personality." As for the lynching, he claimed his mother's facts to be so wrong and her theory so fallacious that he could not attempt to enter on a discussion. She contended that the lynching of the cattle thieves had achieved nothing, but Wister replied that "in real life the lynching was perfectly successful in Montana and ended the reign of thieves there!" She could not know this from the book, he knew, but she should realize the fallacy of arguing against principles from a single result. Wister's mother also thought the title was wrong. The subtitle, "A Horseman of the Plains," would have been better standing alone, in her opinion. To Wister that title did not seem "short & sharp enough."[60]

"Well—never mind," he wrote finally. "I wish the book was 20 times better than it is. I'd already like to have it back to make certain things better." He was absolutely certain, though, that it was "very much of an advance" over his previous books. "And *next* time I shall write a very big book indeed if I can do it as I feel it in my bones. But never again can I light on a character so engaging. That only happens once, even to the great ones of the earth."[61]

In this judgment he was right. In August the *Atlantic Monthly*'s H. W. Boynton declared the Virginian to be the "final apotheosis of the cowboy," a judgment duplicated more than fifty years later by two scholars who again proclaimed the character to be the "final apotheosis of the range rider." He was a composite figure representing Wister's dream of the kind of superior individual the American West should have produced. The Virginian was ruggedly masculine, honest, and tender. He was not perfect; he recognized in himself a need for culture and learning. Such a character contained in one piece two notions conflicting in Wister's own mind: his early belief that the West would spawn individuals free of the suffocating culture and commercialism of the East, and his ultimate acceptance of the values of eastern culture.[62]

Years later Wister acknowledged some individuals who had inspired his famous cowboy. His first glimmering, he said, had come in 1885 on his initial journey to Wyoming. At a rude stopover he had seen the proprietor, a man from Virginia, treat his ailing wife with unembarrassed gentleness. Corporal Skirdin, whom he actually met after he had introduced the character of the Virginian in his stories, "ratified" the cowboy's character; two Kansas men at Las Playas, New Mexico, reinforced the character the next year; and in that same year Dean Duke, the foreman of the Apache Tejo Ranch in Mexico, said things that "reminded" Wister of the Virginian. The Virginian, though, was a Wyoming cowboy. None of these men were that, and, aside from the innkeeper in Wyoming, all had been met *after* the creation of the character. The one cowboy to whom Wister obviously owed the greatest debt he never mentioned. This, of course, was George B. West, whose life had provided Wister with some of the inspirations for his Lin McLean stories as well. Wister's omission of the man who was his first and most impressionable western hero is striking. Two distinct explanations exist for Wister's failure to credit West: (1) Wister knew that to tie the Virginian too closely to a real individual would detract from the character's power over the imagination, and West so resembled the Virginian that little space for speculation could remain; (2) Wister had become disenchanted with West because of his undignified requests for help and the difficulties he had encountered when he got his ranch. (West himself assumed in later years that he was the inspiration for the character.)[63]

Upon publication of *The Virginian* pressure arose immediately for Wister to further define the enigmatic cowboy. Responding to Hamilton Wright Mabie, Wister said the Virginian embodied a "throb" he had felt far and wide in the land. He was a "son of the soil, whose passion and intelligence and character made him able at last to fight battles almost without need of captains, and then to disperse among his fields when it was over as simply as if nothing had happened." Such a character could only be latent in civilization; it required the frontier to bring him to perfection. "I don't know how he will stand the strain of the future.

With trusts to unman him and populism to turn him into a beast of destruction, his clean splendid self respect is in danger of being polluted on all sides," Wister said.[64]

The latter comment reflected Wister's more considered opinion; he no longer believed that the West could create a superior individual. And even though *The Virginian* glorified the West, it was the West that Wister described in his prefatory "Note to the Reader" as a "vanished world," accessible only in memory. Since those early days the land had deteriorated into a "shapeless state," a condition as "unlovely" as the period between winter and spring. In fact, Wister's overall pessimism about the general state of contemporary American society and his prejudices, including anti-Semitism, were clearly evident in the novel, a fact unnoted by reviewers. These aspects of the book, with almost no exception, appeared evident in the new material added in 1902. The drummers Wister detested as crude examples of the dollar society dominating the nation's culture, two of whom were Jews, were depicted with scorn in the opening pages. The Virginian himself demonstrated their supposed lack of intelligence when he duped one of them out of a bed at Medicine Bow when beds were scarce. The following morning, as the drummers stood at the wash trough, the tenderfoot narrator noted their unhesitating use of a degraded roller towel: "filth was nothing to them." Their accents and Jewishness he declared un-American, and the Virginian as well spoke of them and treated them disparagingly. The tenderfoot narrator, a thinly disguised Wister, possessed an "American" heart, and as he watched these salesmen he worried about the fate of his "native land." The promotion of values deemed "American" by Wister was one of the book's guiding themes. He told his mother that the "whole raison d'être" for *The Virginian* was its "nationality." Neither the narrator nor the Virginian cared for the tendency of American democracy to erase class distinctions; the narrator declared "true democracy and true aristocracy" to be the same. Actually, he went on to say, the intent of achieving American independence had been to give every man the right "to find his own level" and no more than that. The natural aristocracy that would emerge would be an improvement over Europe's artificial aristocracy.[65]

This "natural aristocracy" would arise through the evolutionary process of natural selection; both the Virginian and Molly Stark Wood represented the sort of superior species that would triumph when placed in a free setting removed from artificial props. The Virginian was clearly the "throwback" or atavism that Wister likened the cow-puncher to in his essay, "The Evolution of a Cow-puncher," in which the cowboy was compared to the heroic Anglo-Saxon knight. Molly, instead of fitting comfortably into the New England environment in which she was reared, had herself inherited the more vigorous instincts of an earlier day as a descendant of her Grandmother Stark of Revolutionary War times; she was therefore adventurous enough to go to Wyoming. This rugged individualism which the Virginian and Molly exemplified, and which Theodore Roosevelt so widely promoted, found its truest expression on the frontier where tradition and ancestry could not tilt the scales and where competition was quicker and fiercer. As the Virginian pointed out to Molly after her own confessions about the different capabilities of her students, men were *not* created equal. In the novel, Wister demonstrates the Virginian's own superiority: his ability to survive in competitions as varied as the telling of tall tales and a shoot-out on the streets, his triumph over Trampas, and his climb up the socioeconomic ladder from cowboy to acting foreman to foreman and ultimately to western entrepreneur.

Wister's comparison between the towns of the West and the unsettled areas around them suggested the disdain that he was feeling for the kind of civilization emerging there. Wherever a town arose it despoiled natural beauty. "Scattered wide, they [the towns] littered the frontier from the Columbia to the Rio Grande, from the Missouri to the Sierras. They lay stark, dotted over a planet of treeless dust, like soiled packs of cards. Each was similar to the next, as one old five-spot of clubs resembles another. Houses, empty bottles, and garbage, they were forever of the same shapeless pattern. More forlorn they were than stale bones." As the Virginian and the tenderfoot narrator depart for Judge Henry's ranch, the contrast of the vacant plains outside Medicine Bow is vivid. They pass "thick heaps and fringes of tin cans" and then reach the "clean plains" where they are bathed by "great, still air . . . pure as water and strong as wine." These comparisons came from Wister's new material, not from his earlier work.

If Wister's ideas about society were his more personal contributions to the book's content, the setting and many anecdotes came directly from his western experiences. The emergence of cattle thieves and the efforts to control them in the novel were inspired directly by events leading up to the Johnson County War. The description of Medicine Bow and the narrator's night there on a store counter came straight from the pages of Wister's 1885 journal; the description of Sunk Creek Ranch fit that of

205

the VR Ranch on Deer Creek; Judge Henry was Frank Wolcott, himself a justice of the peace; the narrator sometimes was mistaken, as was Wister, as an Englishman because of his clothing; Trampas was "Black" Henry Smith, the "bad man" Wister had vowed to catch, if only in words; Molly Stark Wood's fictitious relatives in New England were inspired by a Stark family Wister knew in Dunbarton, New Hampshire; the baby-swapping incident was patterned after the similar occurrence Wister had heard about in Texas; the frog story had been related to Wister himself; the "Balaam and Pedro" chapter, as already noted, centered on a traumatic event he had witnessed; and there were many other examples.[66]

The Virginian was not sufficiently complex to lend itself to extensive literary analysis, and the novel was not to profit from the passage of time. Too much of it—especially the short stories—represented Wister's thinly disguised fiction of real events he had experienced or heard about in the West. The two main characters, for all their appeal, are basically one-dimensional and, by today's standards, maudlin in their purity. Trampas, the villain, has no apparent motivation, and until Shorty's murder he gives little reason for the reader to dislike him. The aspect of the book that most lent itself to analysis was the clash between the cultural values of East and West.

Yet the response by readers to *The Virginian* was overwhelming; a tide of letters ensued and would continue throughout Wister's life. The book's elevating qualities assured its acceptance under the genteel standards of the day, but it was provocative and vigorous enough to distinguish itself from typical best sellers such as *Rebecca of Sunnybrook Farm*. Scores of readers wanted to know what horrible thing Balaam had done to Pedro. Rather than be explicit in responding, Wister generally referred them to the original version as it had appeared in *Harper's Monthly*. Many complained because the book approved of lynching under certain circumstances in Wyoming but declared the practice inappropriate in the South. Most readers who wrote simply told Wister how much they enjoyed the book. One commented that he had never read a book that "so took hold" of him, and he had never met between pages a man "whose character I would so greatly like to possess myself." Wister's aunt, Mrs. Caspar Wister, typified many sentiments by giving Wister her fervent thanks for not permitting "her" hero to die. "Had you done so I never could have been the same aunt to you." A significant number of readers wanted practical information about going West to find for themselves the kind of romantic existence Wister had described. Even Richard Harding Davis caught the fever, and he wrote: "I decided to go to New Mexico and Arizona on my own to get 'local color' at the fountainhead. So could you tell me where I ought to go to see cowboys, indians, army posts, and ranches." Davis did criticize Wister's title for its supposed glorification of Virginian qualities, insisting that the "pure" Virginian had disappeared after the Civil War. "The last time I saw a first family Virginian he was hitting a bell and saying 'Take two towels and a pitcher of water to 296.' " Now, Davis complained, Wister had told those Virginians that they were the only gentlemen left in the country. "That really hurt me terribly. But I did not allow it to spoil my delight in the book." "The Cow Puncher" or "The American," he thought, would have been better titles. Wister felt obliged to respond to Davis's comments, explaining that the title referred to nothing more than a man's name and agreeing that the people of the "new South" were "discredits to their species."[67]

Although Wister had neglected to send Henry James a copy of *The Virginian*, he did not forget to mail one to his cowboy friend Dean Duke. Duke savored the book save for "one exception and that a very serious one." He complained that in his nineteen years in the cattle business he had never seen in real life a cowboy call another one a "son-of-a-b———" without trouble resulting, usually a fight. "I wouldn't have a man in my outfit that would submit to being called that even in fun," he added. Wister answered that indeed he had seen the phrase used casually in Wyoming, and Duke consequently "rose off on the criticisms."[68]

Among the book's readers was a curmudgeonish University of Wyoming geology professor who was thoroughly familiar with the state's physical features and history. The professor never read novels; he considered them to be "nothing but a pack of lies." His friends urged him to make an exception for *The Virginian* because of its fidelity. Upon spraining his ankle, the professor relented and read the novel with great enjoyment until he reached the closing passages about the island honeymoon. He then threw the book across the room in disgust, saying: "The God damn liar! That stream wasn't stocked with trout until ten years after that time!"[69]

Harper & Brothers surely wrung their hands in despair at having invested so much time in developing Wister as a western writer and then seeing his greatest success achieved with a competitor. Yet Henry Mills Alden graciously congratulated Wister for his "well-deserved triumph" without a word of recrimination but only a hope to see once more his stories in the magazine which was "so closely associated" with his work.[70]

In August the cover of *Current Literature* carried Wister's photograph, and that same month he dined with President Roosevelt at Newport. He saw there "all the people I know of that world." One of the guests, the novelist Edith Wharton, recalled having played with him as a youngster at Vevey. Wister never had been to Vevey, but he calmly told her that he remembered it perfectly. (He did not like Miss Wharton; she was "shy, thin, watchful, & displeasing both in flesh & spirit.")[71]

On the same day of the President's party another milestone was passed: just three months after publication *The Virginian* reached 100,000 copies in print. William Roscoe Thayer noted the achievement with a spirited, tongue-in-cheek note.

> With regret we bid you farewell from the ranks of literature. 'The Virginian' has 'passed the 100,000 mark' and landed you in the company of Mary Johnston, Winston Churchill, the Rev. Sheldon of Topeka, Marie Corelli and Hall Caine. What a group!
>
> Ah, if you had only stopt short of the 100,000! Then you might still have felt yourself in the same clan with Shakespeare, Milton, Keats and Shelley.[72]

In fact, Wister evidently was worrying over the implication of this generous acceptance by the masses. Publisher Henry Holt, who heard of this concern, wrote to remind him to "get over thinking (if you really do) that your popularity is a sign of poor work." It would not be the last time, however, that such worries would be attributed to Wister.[73]

Holt was one of the many publishers who in this moment of triumph solicited Wister's future work. He proposed a series of biographies of leading Americans which he said only Wister could write. "What a stunning thing you could make of it," he said. In fact, shortly before publication of *The Virginian*, Wister had committed himself to Macmillan to write a life of Benjamin Franklin, and while he spurned Holt's proposal he agreed a month later to do a biography of Oliver Wendell Holmes, Sr., for Houghton and Mifflin. Richard Watson Gilder of *The Century* suggested that Wister go to Central America for the winter and "look a little into this scrap that is going on. . . . See a little about those canal routes and what the people in those countries are thinking about the United States." S. S. McClure solicited stories for his magazine, *McClure's*, imploring Wister to visit him at any time he was in New York City.[74]

Such demand inevitably meant better rates, and in early October he was writing an article for ten cents a word and feeling somewhat guilty. "I really think Weir Mitchell would be sick if he heard anybody he knew in Philadelphia got 10 cents a word. But then he does not know & nobody knows except you," Wister wrote to his mother. He was committed to another project which was "very good fun" but not otherwise rewarding—the writing of captions for "doggerel," as he called it, for a book of Remington's drawings. The relationship between the two men had cooled substantially, and so had Wister's opinion of Remington's art, as one of his private utterances indicated. "He is the most uneven artist I know which you find out very much when you come to extract verse from each drawing. Some are full of meaning & some empty as old cartridges."[75]

Wister was more pleased when Doubleday, Page & Company asked him to read Frank Norris's latest novel, *The Pit*, and give them his comments. But by the time Wister's complimentary comments had reached the Norris home, the thirty-two-year-old writer whom Wister so admired was dead, the victim of peritonitis, a perforated appendix, and gangrene. *The Virginian* had been the last book Norris read.[76]

Until mid-October the Wister family stayed in Saunderstown where Wister rode horseback, swam, exchanged visits with friends, and wrote. After riding for nine consecutive days he declared himself to be feeling better than he had any time since September 1896. The prospect of returning to Philadelphia, though, was dreary, for the city had "ceased to be a place for gentlefolk to live in."[77]

The year 1902 ended as Wister never had suspected it would. His previous successes and reputation had been nothing compared to the acclaim now accorded him. He was not merely a writer who had earned critical praise for his western stories; he was the idol of the popular crowd which he so disdained. He found himself deemed an instant expert on practically any subject, and United States Senator Albert J. Beveridge, chairman of the committee on territories, solicited and obtained his advice on affairs concerning the territories. The year was so busy that there was no time to contemplate things that deserved contemplation. In August, Judge Holmes confided something which was not yet public knowledge—the president had asked Holmes to become a justice on the United States Supreme Court. Wister's only comment on the matter when he wrote to his mother was "I saw Judge Holmes. He has been appointed to the Supreme Court of the U.S." The dramatization of *Lin*

McLean also was completed in 1902, but not to Wister's satisfaction. Already he was hearing recommendations that *The Virginian* be adapted for the stage. The idea seemed absurd at first—or so Wister claimed— for there seemed to be "about as much drama in it as in Robinson Crusoe." But he rationalized that it was "the fad to put every prominent book on the stage," and he quickly warmed to the idea.[78]

Chapter XI

"THE VIRGINIAN" ON BROADWAY
(1903–1904)

"HE LOOKS LIKE A MAN WHO COULD GET HIS LIVING WITH HIS HANDS if his brain failed him." So wrote a Rochester newspaper reporter after interviewing Wister in 1903. There was, the reporter continued,

> a suggestion of ruggedness about the tall, muscular, well-knit frame, although the flexible carriage has in it something of the actor. The face has determination written in every line and curve. It is the face of a fighter. The jaw is decisive. The eyes are rather stern in repose, but in conversation they become responsive to the mood of the speaker, now glinting earnestly, now twinkling quizzically, but always on the alert. They are the eyes of the man of the prairies—the restless eyes of men who are accustomed to sweep great distances and to whom the accuracy and quickness of sight means safety. He is essentially an out-of-doors man, a man who faced the wind and rain; who has felt the furnace's breath of the hot winds and the blast of the blizzard. A man's man is the summing up, and there you have the key to his character.

Such a description, rendered in glowing detail more suited for a character in a novel than for a real person, signified that the subject was a genuine twentieth-century celebrity—a man whose name the news media spread from coast to coast and whose every move was deemed worthy of mention.[1]

The suggestive power of his name was demonstrated at a diplomatic reception in the White House. When the introducer called out "Owen Wister" instant clamor arose among the assembled guests and, Wister wrote to his mother, "one or two ladies screamed!" He added quickly, "None fainted." As he was rushed about from one guest to the next he was amused and pleased to see that they all—from the English ambassador Sir Michael Herbert and Lady Herbert to a Salt Lake City editor's wife—became "intensely animated" over *The Virginian.* He saw many old friends, including former Harvard classmates, cabinet officials, and Army officers, and he met new ones, too, such as the political satirist

Finley Peter Dunne, known to newspaper readers from coast-to-coast as
"Mr. Dooley." Upon learning of Dunne's presence, Wister hurried to
him, introduced himself, and the two immediately began talking "with
much energy." After the crowd left, about a dozen chosen guests, including Dunne and Wister, remained for champagne. Roosevelt approached Dunne's table, where Wister was seated, placed his muscular
hand on the satirist's shoulder, and in a heavy Irish brogue quoted from
memory Dooley's well-known satirical description of the Rough Rider
"alone in Cubia." Dunne's face turned purple, but the president was
having fun, and he gustily concluded: "By George, that was bully. I did
enjoy that!"[2]

That evening was the first of four days in which Wister and Molly
were guests at the White House. The next morning at breakfast, Wister
decided to be frank and tell the president his candid opinion of Roosevelt's controversial choice of a black man to be collector of the port at
Charleston, South Carolina. The United States Senate had refused to
confirm the appointment of Dr. William Crum, but Roosevelt kept him
in office with interim appointments, an act that Wister said "had finished
him [Roosevelt] with those high spirited, sorely bruised people." Wister
concurred with his Charleston friends' outrage over the selection of a
black man for the position. Surprised, Roosevelt turned for support to
Molly Wister with her rich family heritage of social action as well as
her own record of endeavors in behalf of the Negro race. "Why, Mrs.
Wister. Mrs. Wister! . . . Why don't you see—why you *must* see that I
can't close the door of hope upon a whole race!" But Molly agreed with
her husband. The appointment, the Wisters contended, had brought
harm to the cause of the Negro because it created new animosities rather
than erasing old ones. Years later Wister would recall that after two
consecutive mornings of this painful discussion Roosevelt admitted that
he may have erred in the controversial appointment. The discussion was
not the last the two men would have over such matters, and Wister
again would criticize Dr. Crum's appointment by implication in his
next novel.[3]

The remaining "unforgettable" White House days included meals
with the presidential family and visits with important guests such as
Leonard Wood, the Henry Cabot Lodges, and Henry Adams, who lived
across the street at Lafayette Square. One of Wister's special thrills was
his discovery that the Roosevelt children had "read to rags" the copy of
The Virginian he had sent the family. The days had another reason for

being significant: Wister was the fourth generation of his family to stay at the White House. His great-great aunt, Miss Isabel Mease, went there during the presidency of James Madison; his grandfather Pierce Butler and his mother Sarah had been to the White House when Franklin Pierce was president.[4]

Not long after the visit many of the nation's newspapers recounted the story of Wister's introduction to the wife of a high government official. Upon the presentation, according to the published anecdote, a look of recognition dawned on the woman's generous features, and she eyed Wister with great interest. Wister, as the story went, stood first on one foot and then on the other, "after the manner of a successful literary man waiting for something complimentary to come." The lady beamed brilliantly and said with genuine feeling: "You know that it's very often hard to catch the names of people who are introduced to you, and some-times it's harder to remember them. But in your case it's so different. I really want to tell you, Mr. Worcester, how much I like your sauce!"[5]

The White House visit was an ego-satisfying interlude to Wister's current literary project—dramatization of *The Virginian* for the stage. His original belief that the book could not hold material for a theatrical production soon collapsed under the allure of Broadway. By December he had rejected several offers from dramatists to undertake the project himself. Sarah Wister, for once, encouraged him; her son had such a strong "dramatic instinct" that she had "very little doubt" of his success.[6]

Against his mother's strong advice Wister determined to include in the drama the vigilante lynching of the likable cowboy Steve and an-other man for cattle theft. Sarah Wister argued that such a scene, even if the lynching were not depicted literally, would "offend certain canons of taste." (She likewise had thought the lynching scene inappropriate for the novel.) Wister disagreed, citing as precedence the tragedy *Oedipus*, in which Oedipus rushes offstage to blind himself, then reenters sightless. This paralleled Wister's own projected lynching scene, for he was having the two rustlers judged and sentenced on stage and then led offstage for the hanging. "That scene as I have imagined it . . . will be rather terrific," he believed.[7]

In late March he finished the play and delivered it to the office of a powerful producer named Daniel Frohman. The continuing success of the novel made him hopeful, for he had learned from Macmillan that the book had sold another thousand copies on the previous day. "This is so powerful (and so economical) an advertisement that it would take a *very bad* play to discourage the Hebrew [Frohman]," he observed. Meanwhile, he was "awfully tired with writing & thinking," and he planned to "go easy" during the time before Frohman announced his decision.[8]

His mother continued to have problems with Butler Place, though, and it was impossible not to worry with her over the family home's fate. Much of the problem concerned disagreements with Aunt Fanny, who held partial ownership of the land. The "best thing" would be to find a buyer for the whole of Butler Place and sell it at the earliest possible date, he believed. Otherwise, he foresaw increasing difficulties with Fanny.[9]

Sarah Wister was in Charleston that spring. From there she reinforced her son's belief that Roosevelt had erred both in the Crum appointment and in having Booker T. Washington dine at the White House. The effect of these acts, she believed, could be seen in deteriorating manners of Charleston's Negroes, noticeable even in children. She related an incident involving a Charleston plantation owner named Pucking Alston, who was greeted on his arrival home from Washington, D.C., by his old body servant. "Well Mars Puck, you done see de President?" "Yes." "You shake hands with him?" "No." "You—[?] dine with him?" "No—I don't care to dine with a gentleman who has niggers to dinner." "Law now Mars' Puck you must 'scuse de President; him don't know niggers like you & I does."[10]

Wister thought he could discern another deleterious effect of Roosevelt's unpopular recognition of the two black men: an adverse effect on servant-master relationships. An incident in his own household reaffirmed his convictions. Molly had called in a new housemaid upon her tenth day on the job to assess her performance. "You have taken no interest in your work," Molly complained. "No, mum, I have not—not until to-day. To-day I have begun to take an interest." There had been no mockery in the new maid's voice; she had spoken in a "perfectly respectful and candid" fashion. Wister was amazed at such behavior. "It seems new. Quite new—to me." What the ultimate impact of such attitudes would be Wister could not guess. One thing was certain: he was not pleased.[11]

By May *The Virginian* had climbed to 187,000 in sales. A statement from Macmillan showed that in less than a year Wister's royalties had amounted to $29,935. "When the play comes out . . . I have no doubt that the sales on the book will take a fresh start," Macmillan editor George P. Brett declared.[12]

Meanwhile, two of the men identified with the character of the Virginian were not faring so well—Charles Skirdin had been fired from his job, and George West was encountering difficulties with the corporation over the ranch's operations. Skirdin had supervised a maintenance crew on the Philadelphia and Reading Railroad, and the colorful background and narrative powers that had so entranced Wister had done the same for others. Because his stories kept others from working he was relegated to sweeping floors. The demotion's timing was unfortunate, for Skirdin was engaged to be married. In the midst of such turmoil he apologized to Wister for not having seen him in a while. "You know how it is a fellow working and having a girl to go see it keeps one pretty busey [sic]." He still had to obtain a wedding "lyssence," a ring, and a new suit of clothing. Given this hint, Wister gave Skirdin a check for a wedding present which allowed Skirdin to buy a wedding ring, three suits, a hat, a pair of shoes, and other items. Skirdin professed not to realize what his friend had done for him until the cashier told him to endorse the check. "I felt as if I was wrong by taking it," he said. "Now Mr. Wister I don't know how to ever thank you for what you have done but I fear you have given to mouch [sic] for nothing if you will let me put it that way. I cant find words to express just what I would like to say." The generous gift also enabled Skirdin to make his first rental payment for a house at 1830 Brandywine Street. When the wedding ceremony occurred in April, Wister's dandified presence among the humbler spectators surely was conspicuous. Afterwards, Skirdin assured his friend of his eagerness for him to visit, for he would always leave his "latch string outside" for him. Three months after the wedding Skirdin became a motorman at wages of $2 to $2.25 a day, which was "a whole lot better than $1.90 a day from the Reading and Cleaner work." He had not yet read The Virginian, but he assured its author that as soon as he could visit a bookstore he would buy a copy.[13]

West's troubles with the corporation that controlled his ranch apparently stemmed from his lack of sophistication in business matters. He was ousted as president, his name was removed from the firm's title, and he was ordered to vacate the property. Wister's response to the unfortunate news is not available, but West's reply indicates that it was unsympathetic. "What you say about my being incapable of being president may be true." Thus, after a few years' relative prosperity West found himself once again in debt and no better off than ever. Wister's attitude evidently even further cooled the relationship which already had weakened over the years, and after one more exchange of letters the correspondence between the two men ceased altogether for sixteen years.[14]

A third friend to whom Wister felt he owed a debt for his western stories, Captain Frank A. Edwards, also approached him for assistance. For some twenty-five years Edwards had accepted without complaint military assignments in the West, while he watched others with political influence receive choice positions at posts of relative luxury. Now Edwards wanted Wister's advice—what should he do to procure a good assignment for himself? Wister, advising him to wait, broached the subject to Roosevelt, who remembered the captain with fondness and promised a reward. In the fall of 1903 Edwards received his reward—an appointment as military attaché at Rome. He sent Wister his warmest thanks for his "friendly talk" with the president.[15]

In May, having taken his family to Saunderstown for the summer, Wister and Frohman failed to agree upon the play's production. "I declined Frohman's terms, Frohman declined my terms," as Wister summarized it. What Wister disliked was a clause that permitted Frohman to delay production for a year and a half. Meanwhile, another less powerful producer had become interested in staging *The Virginian*, and before the month ended, Wister's script was in his hands. The man was Kirk La Shelle, a congenial man who had achieved some reputation with his previous staging of *Arizona*. Within a month, the two men had signed a contract. La Shelle agreed "to make a first class production" of the play before November 1, 1903. Wister was to render assistance "in the matter of dialogue, supervision of details in dress, manners and character usage." He would also go on the road with the play during its trial performances preparatory to a New York opening. La Shelle impressed Wister with his bold new ideas for the drama. "He has managed very ingeniously to change the babies without making it farce or horse play, and he has introduced Emily [the unusual hen]!! I did not see how he possibly could, but he has managed it with extreme cleverness." La Shelle had "picked the novel to the bones" and preserved much more of it than Wister had been able to. His dialogue, Wister thought, was not as good as his own, but La Shelle's construction was better, and the producer wanted Wister to write his own dialogue wherever he wished, subject only to editing. The role of the

Virginian was to be played by a slim, slow-talking, six-footer named Dustin Farnum. Farnum, thirty years old, had performed earlier in *Arizona*, and he looked the part of the Virginian as well as anyone could. There remained, however, one disappointment for Wister: La Shelle refused to stage the lynching scene because he thought it too repellent. Even that news could not dampen Wister's spirits. "I am as satisfied as I can be until the curtain comes down on a success," he wrote to his mother.[16]

During the time remaining before rehearsals, Wister, Molly, and the children, as well as the family parrot, enjoyed themselves in Saunderstown. A new Franklin stove replaced the old one and brought warm, new cheer to the nippy spring days. Their spirits and health, they were convinced, always improved when the family were in Saunderstown, or for that matter whenever one of their frequent changes occurred. They continued to see the La Farges almost daily, and only a short hop away in Boston many other friends awaited. On one such visit Wister encountered William James ("such good company"). James complimented him again on his Grant biography and on "Philosophy 4," which had been published by Macmillan as a short book. James flattered Wister still further by exclaiming, "You really have an extraordinary mind." Langdon and Marion Mitchell visited for several days. Mitchell had two plays of his own ready for the stage, and there was much to reminisce over as they swam, walked, and rowed on the Narrow River and played dominoes in the evenings. The Sergeant Kendalls were occasional guests, and the Wisters commissioned Kendall to paint for five hundred dollars a portrait of their son Owen. In August it was completed to their great satisfaction. When a statue of William Ellery Channing, Molly's illustrious ancestor, was unveiled in the Public Gardens opposite the Arlington Street Church in Boston to commemorate the hundredth anniversary of his ordination, all his descendants, including the entire Wister family, sat in the front pew to hear Harvard president Eliot speak. Physical exercise, always important to Wister's sense of well-being, was a daily routine in Saunderstown with rowing, walking, and horseback riding. There also were organized picnics which included water activities on the Narrow River.[17]

Amidst all these activities, Wister was writing a book about Saunderstown and vampires. "It must be Hawthorne *up to date*," he said, "that is, no imitation of him, but what he might do now, were he alive." The project further postponed his work on the biography of Oliver Wendell

Holmes, Sr., and in the fall Wister sought to break his contract. But Houghton Mifflin had announced the delay so many times that the firm was too embarrassed to cancel the work entirely, and Wister reluctantly agreed to honor his commitment after he finished his Saunderstown novel. As it turned out, neither the novel nor the biography ever would be completed.[18]

Wister's reading interests in mid-1903 were quite varied. He found Henry James's portrayal of American women in *The Wings of the Dove* "marvellous and masterly." He analyzed it for his mother as an artful story about "civilized complex perfidious brutality" in which the heart had disappeared to be replaced by the head and stomach. Sarah Wister gained his permission to forward his comments to James. Wister would have liked to send the comments himself, but considering himself still a beginner at writing novels, he felt it would have "seemed cheeky" to burden James with his own assessment. Two other authors attracted Wister's interest during the summer: Joseph Conrad and Jack London. They were "too rough and fronterian or buccaneerian" for Wister to recommend to his mother. Instead, he suggested some French plays which he knew she would enjoy.[19]

Saunderstown's idyllic life offered an additional bonus to Wister as a quiet retreat from his celebrity status. In midsummer, Edward Bok of the very successful *Ladies' Home Journal* tested Wister's desire for privacy by suggesting a candid photographic portrayal at his summer retreat. It would be part of a series including similar photographs of writers such as William Dean Howells and Mark Twain. At first Wister agreed, but it was against his principles, and within days he changed his mind and "resisted the vulgar temptation." The disappointed Bok responded: "I can't argue with a man who seeks to maintain his privacy: I like it too well myself. But, all the same, I am keenly disappointed, for I know there are thousands of women among our readers who would like to know in the way I proposed, the author of 'The Virginian.' "[20]

Another unique offer, which would have portrayed Wister's image to a widespread masculine audience, came three months later. The American Lithographic Company sought his permission to name a brand of cigars after him. There was no temptation here—Wister refused. However, he accepted with pleasure the request to speak at the laying of the cornerstone of the new Saunderstown public library. Saunderstown had grown immensely in Wister's affections, and the new library, built without a penny from Carnegie or any other wealthy benefactors, filled him with pride.[21]

Such an attractive, ocean side village was sure to appeal to others, and Saunderstown did. By the end of the summer Wister was discontented by what seemed to be hordes of uncultivated people. Moreover, a more literate family had come to Saunderstown—the Whartons, who brought with them their own friends to plague Wister's existence. "Since they have come to Saunderstown I must take prominent measures, or they'll be crawling over my piazza for the remainder of my life."[22]

Another diversion of the summer involved Upton Sinclair, living with his wife and infant child in a rude, combination shanty and tent outside Princetown, New Jersey. Sinclair, nearly penniless, was immersing himself in the Civil War material housed at Princeton University as he prepared to write *Manassas*. A resumption of correspondence began when Sinclair sent Wister a copy of his latest book, *Prince Hagen*, and a note: "One day last October I sat out upon a mountain meadow with a blanket, a Winchester, & the Virginian. And a deer came out in front of my nose and I never saw him; and when he saw me and ran, I never turned a hair—that's honest truth—& so much for the Virginian." Wister responded amicably, offering advice on subjects ranging from literary matters to the kind of nursery Sinclair should construct for his son. Sinclair, who had been converted less than a year earlier to socialism and who now was being subsidized by the socialist George D. Herron, soon began imploring the aristocratic Wister for financial aid, painting a horribly bleak picture of his family's existence. So desperate did the situation appear that in late August Molly Wister visited the Sinclairs for several hours to assess their needs. Upon returning home she sent supplies to ease their plight. But if Sinclair expected Wister to be of further help he obviously had misread him. In a "painful answer," Wister declined to assist Sinclair financially. Sinclair responded with a lengthy, self-pitying plea for just one hundred dollars. His shanty-tent home was muddy inside, his wife was miserable and exhausted, his son was cutting teeth and constantly howling, and in trying to improve their primitive dwelling Sinclair had severely mashed his finger with a hammer. Finally, he wrote, while they ate the meal that Sinclair himself had prepared under these conditions the baby vomited, whereupon Mrs. Sinclair threw herself into the middle of the muddy floor and exclaimed, "Oh how I *wish* I had Mrs. Wister in this hole tonight!" That desperate exclamation miraculously cleared the air, and the couple began pretending that Mrs. Wister were there, grandly showing her about their wretched dwelling while bursting with laughter at the contrast in life-styles. As for the requested one hundred dollars, Sinclair said it would be used to provide

> a thousand little *things* about a house—useless to a person who is, or thinks he is, inspired, but helpful to a woman who has to wait endlessly for the book to be born. The things are too homely to name—a pump, a sink, a rug, a blanket, a foot scraper (oh the mud in the tent!). . . . Can you spare it [$100] without depriving the others, and hurting yourself, for two years? If you can it will make these two years of travail much easier; and if the book does not sell I will take to store clerking, and will repay it as sure as I am honest, which I am.

He wanted a "fair chance," two years without the haunting specter of penury to write a book that would "shake men to the depths of their souls." If at the end of those two years he had not written such a book, Wister could "sell" him for debts. This he promised.[23]

Wister was not moved by this impassioned plea. He coldly told Sinclair that he already had had a "fair hearing" for his works; that he had published three books without significant response; that a spell of "distasteful work," such as clerking, to pull his family together economically would strengthen his literary vision; and furthermore that he was wallowing in "chronic self pity." Sinclair did not appreciate these harsh words. He now replied heatedly, defending himself on each accusation. In this fashion the once-friendly correspondence between the twenty-five-year-old, struggling, impoverished writer and the famous, affluent author from Philadelphia's highest social circles ended. The episode was not to be forgotten by either man, however.[24]

At the same time this round of correspondence was concluding, Kirk La Shelle in New York was assembling a cast for *The Virginian*. Wister's help was needed in this and in arranging a musical overture. At first Wister handled these duties from Saunderstown, reacting by mail to photographs of actors and actresses being considered and trying to find tunes for the overture and entr'actes. The plan, proposed by Wister, was to use nothing but American tunes.[25]

In late August the Wister family sailed to Manhattan, where Wister disembarked and checked into the Players Hotel to be of direct assistance with the play. Molly and the children continued on to New Jersey to visit cousins. Wister was pleased to learn that Dustin Farnum had followed his suggestion and spent time in Richmond to learn the proper dialect for his role as the Virginian. He seemed a certain success. Frank Campeau, as the villainous Trampas, was in Wister's mind the "real thing." But the woman who played Molly, a Miss Yorke, concerned him. The most that he hoped for was that she would "look right," for he felt that she would be unable to perceive what he somewhat astonishingly saw as an integral part of the character—that the high-minded teacher was actually "not quite a lady."[26]

The nation's president interrupted Wister's concerns over such matters by summoning him by telegram to Oyster Bay for a weekend. When Wister arrived, he found Roosevelt battling Grant La Farge on the tennis court with Mrs. Roosevelt as the only spectator. The intimacy of the occasion pleased Wister. "Nobody else, thank goodness, was spending the night. No statesmen or other notorious characters—just ourselves." That evening at dinner the men talked almost wholly of "game and hunting and the liars who are now writing about wild animals and their ways." Mrs. Roosevelt asked question after question about the dramatization of *The Virginian*, and the president flattered Wister by quoting passages from it and *Lin McLean*. Roosevelt was in fine form. Wister imagined he could observe a "power" growing in his brow which indicated a mysterious but healthy response to the demands of the office. After dinner the Roosevelt children persuaded Wister to sing their favorite songs until bedtime, and then Wister, La Farge, and Roosevelt continued to talk until midnight. "If it wasn't for my unfortunate conspicuous position," said Roosevelt, "I should attend the first night of 'The Virginian.'" The next morning after breakfast Wister resisted Roosevelt's importunities to stay longer for riding and swimming; he boarded the train with La Farge for New York and arrived in time for the 11 A.M. rehearsal.[27]

There he found, to his dismay, a crisis. La Shelle had been put to bed under threat of appendicitis. Surgery was scheduled within weeks. The future of the play, as well as the cast's job security, was at stake. But the crisis brought out the best in Wister. Not at all unfamiliar with theatrics, at least on an amateur basis, he conducted the rehearsal himself with authority on that day and on the days to follow. "I expected to find a professional rehearsal quite other than Dickey and Hasty Pudding. You couldn't tell them apart," he declared. La Shelle soon returned, his surgery having been delayed until early October after the play's opening, and he complimented Wister on the cast's considerable progress under his guidance.[28]

221

The relationship between author and producer might well have been strained, but the two had quickly developed an understanding and appreciation for one another. "He is an *extraordinary* person," said Wister of La Shelle, "a mixture of subtle critical talent & shrewd business sense, and all hands say—more honest & square than anybody." La Shelle, two years younger than Wister, had much in common with his collaborator. The producer had entered the theater after a successful career as a Chicago newspaper reporter, editor, and drama critic. His light opera, *The Princess Chic,* had won acclaim, and he had originated in 1895 the Frank Daniels Comic Opera Company. La Shelle had been born in Illinois, yet his grandfather John La Shelle had been a noted Philadelphia lawyer. Even the appearances of author and producer were similar. La Shelle's features, though more angular, were framed by a closely cropped beard, mustache, and slightly receding hairline, and were dominated by deep-set, penetrating eyes.[29]

As rehearsals continued, Wister and La Shelle constantly made adjustments in the script. Wister deferred to La Shelle, but believing that he had no small claim himself to theatrical knowledge, Wister developed some contrasting opinions. One concern which Wister subjugated for the moment was La Shelle's elimination of the lynching scene and his substitution of his own third act. A lynching, La Shelle explained in accord with Sarah Wister, would shock the audience unduly. "It was good in itself," Wister said of La Shelle's third act, "but coming after a very gentle second act (also Kirke's) it was monotonous." As the days went on, Wister became more and more convinced that his lynching scene was vital to the play's success, but rather than make an issue of it with his partner, he began once more to lie awake nights, tossing with worry.[30]

By day he kept busy with musical arrangements, costumes, and script revisions, as well as with assisting the ailing La Shelle with rehearsals. When Wister completed the overture he entitled it "American Medley." It included a tune written by La Shelle entitled "Young Lochinvar." Wister's own compositions served as introductions to the second, third, and fourth acts. They were entitled "Ten Thousand Cattle Straying," "Emily," and "Dawn of Love." Another of his duties was to authenticate the play's western aspects. From Dean Duke, that genial cowboy who now addressed Wister in letters as "Smiley," Wister sought to obtain genuine chaps for the actors. Failing to reach Duke in time he gave up and ordered satisfactory chaps from Montgomery Ward.[31]

A week before its September 30 opening in New Haven, Wister had convinced himself that "The Virginian" had box office appeal. "Unless some quite monstrous mischance happens, the play will make a very great success," he wrote to his mother. "It is a *play*, & not scenes strung together, & parts of it are very moving." Farnum was "marvelous" as the Virginian—so perfect that he looked as if the book had opened and he had stepped out of the pages. Wister's opinion of the actress who portrayed "Molly" had improved slightly. Miss Yorke was "all wrong" in the early parts—she lacked humor, and she played the light parts "heavily"—but she got "quite good" toward the end of the play. "The other characters are all adequate, and several much better than adequate," he said. But a few days after these judgments Molly Wister, now expecting another child, came with Molly Moss to New York to see a dress rehearsal. When Wister saw their scowls over the leading lady's performance his own criticisms reemerged.[32]

There was no time to replace her, even if La Shelle had agreed, and "The Virginian" opened as planned in New Haven before an audience packed with Yale students. Wister summed up the results succinctly for his cowboy friend Duke, whom he had implored unsuccessfully to join him for the road tour. "Big house. Acts 1 & 4 successful. Acts 2 & 3 cold. Girl fearful." On the second night the leading lady was worse, and on the third night she went "all to pieces." Later that evening La Shelle approached Wister and asked, "Do I look like shambles?" If so, he explained, it was because he had "shipped" Miss Yorke, who had cried pathetically at her dismissal. "You can say anything to me you like," La Shelle said to Wister. "It's my fault. I've been completely wrong." As Wister later told Duke, Wister "rose to the occasion" and insisted to La Shelle that it "wouldn't be healthy" if he were right all the time. Then they drank together and pondered anew the play's fate.[33]

The next morning Wister accompanied the cast to Boston, where another short run was scheduled. La Shelle and Dustin Farnum went to New York to find a new leading lady. They found her, an actress named Nanette Comstock, who was performing in a play due to close in several days. While Wister rehearsed the rest of the company in Boston, La Shelle and Farnum worked intensely with Miss Comstock in New York. A week later "The Virginian" resumed its run, and the new heroine assumed the role to the satisfaction of all.[34]

The Boston opening, however, did not promise much for the play's future. Despite kind words from his many friends, Wister became convinced that the play, as it stood, was a failure. The Boston critics thought so too—"damned the play up hill and down," as Wister summarized it. More than ever, he became convinced that his own third-act lynching scene was needed to inject some fire into the drama. La Shelle still did not agree. Wister decided not to force the issue, but he told his friend Grant La Farge of his concerns. La Farge prepared a letter for La Shelle, urging the adoption of Wister's third act to relieve a "flatness," and forwarded it to Wister for approval. Wister thanked his friend for his effort, but he elected not to send the letter to La Shelle.[35]

Two weeks later, just before La Shelle was scheduled for surgery, Wister approached him with a proposition. "I want my day in court. Let me put on that lynching act, written over again with some new ideas I've got, and then if it fails I have no kick coming." La Shelle agreed, and as the play moved from city to city in a series of one-night stands Wister tried to get his "lynching act" ready for substitution. With La Shelle gone, he soon concluded that the first and second acts also needed a "tremendous lot of overhauling." Enlisting the aid of stage manager John Stapleton, and assisted by whiskey and bromide, Wister commenced the job of massive overhauling. The cast rehearsed new material by day while they played the old version at night. A new first act presented in Geneva met "instant success"; the revised second act was performed satisfactorily before a Rochester audience; and in late November the revised third act containing the lynching scene was unveiled with "unqualified success." The dramatic lynching held the audience perfectly silent without even a cough to interrupt. Afterwards, the elated actors exclaimed to an even happier Wister that he had been right all along. "A better vindication no man ever got," Wister declared to Dean Duke.[36]

"I cannot conceive of any one in the world objecting to the way it deals with the lynching," Wister wrote to his mother in defense of the scene.

> The picture I have made is so remote (and even romantic!) in its atmosphere, and so utterly restrained in tone as to banish everything except the two points I worked for—the gallant fatalism of Steve, and the misery of The Virginian. I tell you when one of the cowboys says, "Steve, we don't want to do this. We wish it wasn't you," and Steve answers: "Why, it's all right. I played the game and I lost. There's no hard feelings"—there's a moment there when the play touches tragedy. It transfixes the audience anyhow—just that simple speech.[37]

Despite the act's success, Wister still feared that it would be scratched upon La Shelle's return. Learning of the enthusiastic audience reception, however, La Shelle wired his heartiest congratulations to Wister and wrote detailed instructions to Stapleton about scenery changes needed to accommodate the new act. La Shelle behaved, Wister observed, like the "direct and generous person" he was, for Wister knew that it "went *very* hard" with La Shelle to see his own third act dismissed.[38]

The success of the third act and the other modifications by no means signified an end to problems. Rewriting continued for the third act, and other script and acting adjustments had to be made. Wister himself suffered at least two spells of sickness because of the daily pressures. Nanette Comstock turned out to be as big a problem for the company as her predecessor. Miss Comstock's demanding personality caused the cast to dislike her intensely. Wister alone escaped her quick temper, but he saw that Farnum and Campeau both hated her. "So does the stage *director*; & the stage *manager* is afraid of her!" It was serious but also entertaining, and sometimes Wister went back to his hotel room to laugh by himself. In Buffalo, six weeks away from the opening on Broadway, Miss Comstock went to "pieces" and gave notice. Wister and the rest of the company were relieved at the news, despite their need for still another heroine, which they quickly found in Agnes Ardeck. So hectic, so diverting, so filled with the complications of human nature was the task of conceiving, casting, producing, and touring a play that Wister was certain the experience was "good for one highly interesting novel" at least and possibly education enough for him to write a play without assistance.[39]

The lengthy road engagements ended on December 3 in Erie, Pennsylvania. The twenty-eight member cast settled in New York City, and on January 5, 1904, "The Virginian" opened at the Manhattan Theater on Broadway and 33rd streets. Wister and La Shelle shared billing as "co-dramatists." If the novel had been a smashing success, the stage debut was merely a success, with much room for criticism. As the *New York Times* critic wrote, the nature of the story was such that it did not lend itself to consistent and well-ordered theatrical narrative. One shocking aspect was that the cowboys called one another "liar" and "cattle thief" as placidly, the *Times* critic noted, as people in the effete East ask the time of day. All the actors save the "new" Molly won praise from the *Times*. The reviewer singled out Farnum in particular as destined to be a star. Miss Ardeck was declared "the one failure" of the evening. A critic who had seen the play in New Haven and held little hope for it, now declared that the changes made on the road caused "vast improvement." "The Virginian," he wrote, "will never be a great play, but it is a good one, and I predict a fair life for it, especially in the popular priced houses, where melodramas of this order, with cowpunchers and the like, are always appreciated."[40]

The *New York Sun* dealt the harshest criticism of all, labeling the adaptation "extremely amateurish" and the music "impossible." The *New York Tribune* reviewer, "W.W.," gave a mixed notice—the play was "rather rough domestic melo-drama, but at least arouses memories of wild and careless nights in a . . . strange, grim, enchanting country." The *New York Evening Telegram* found it "not exceptionally strong." Another opinion came from Wister's mother. She found it "very amusing, striking, & picturesque," though "necessarily of faulty construction" because of its adaptation from a novel.[41]

While the stage version of *The Virginian* obviously was to be a mild success—if only because of the book's immense popularity—no one could predict its ultimate fate of becoming a favorite for generation after generation. After a four-month run in New York City the play continued on the road for more than a decade, bringing Wister weekly royalties of two hundred to three hundred dollars and some weeks even more. Its history would be one of frequent stage revivals, and in 1914 the youthful Cecil B. De Mille would produce the first of four movie versions of *The Virginian*. Ultimately, the character of the Virginian would be transferred to the medium of television for still another generation. It is impossible to calculate the effect of these many presentations for the American public.[42]

For Wister, one happy result of the stage version of the book was the fact that one of his musical compositions proved to be a commercial success on its own merits. His tune, "Ten Thousand Cattle Straying," was played as an introduction to the second act and sung on stage by Trampas. Published in sheet music by Witmark & Sons, the song was destined over the years to be reprinted in several collections of cowboy songs. Wister had written the lyrics and set them to a tune from a French opera (*Fra Diavolo*) while in camp in Wyoming in 1888. But for "The Virginian" he composed a new tune for his words and personally taught the song to Campeau.[43]

After the play's New York opening Wister's own work was over. Accordingly, he went home to Philadelphia and, as he described it, "smashed up in good shape." He spent a week in bed, four weeks on the sofa, and more than a month alone at a resort at Hot Springs, Virginia, where he rode horseback daily, breathed deeply of mountain air, swore off lemonade when he learned it was $1.50 a pitcher, and visited with fellow guests such as Langdon and Marion Mitchell. Mostly, however, his existence was welcome solitude. "One blessed thing about this enormous hotel is that one *need* see *nobody.*" That was what Wister believed he needed. "I must have this sort of thing periodically as I suffer in some spiritual way," he told his wife. Molly had stayed in Philadelphia with still another baby, William Rotch, named for her father. He was, according to Wister, "uglier than sin" and robust at 10 3/4 pounds. His parents would later call him Bill, but they now dubbed him "Weenty."[44]

Wister's Hot Springs vacation ended in late April when he became physically ill. He returned to Philadelphia, where he was found to have appendicitis, and was taken to Pennsylvania Hospital for an appendectomy. Press reports virtually placed him on his deathbed. The *San Francisco Chronicle*'s headline listed him in "critical condition." *The Hartford Courant* said the noted author was "lying between life and death."[45]

He remained in the hospital for nearly a month before going to the Corinthian Yacht Club at Marblehead, Massachusetts Bay, for another month of recuperation. By early June he felt well enough to sail all day, and in July he rejoined at Saunderstown the entire family—Molly, Marina, Owen, Fanny, and the infant Weenty. The children's patience at their father's long absence was rewarded three weeks later when he surprised them with a team of harnessed goats pulling a wagon. The sight of the animals, "Ned" and "Billy," made the children roll in the grass with wild excitement.[46]

Chapter XII

A NOVEL OF MANNERS
(1904–1906)

At the age of forty-four, his greatest success behind him, Wister was far from the young man who once reveled in the rough edges of western society. That part of the country forever would enchant him, yet no longer did he think that the best Americans would be those who arose in the unstructured West. That area's eager embrace of populist tenets demonstrated to Wister that the common man there was as susceptible to the ephemeral, vulgar, and cheap aspects of life as were the masses of the East. Life held few uncertainties for Wister; he now knew precisely where he stood; he knew exactly what he must do. And that was to strike in his own way against forces that degraded the best aspects of American culture.

His growing mood of despair was evident in many of his actions and comments. He joined and became a vice-president of the Immigration Restriction League, an organization dedicated to halting the invasion of alien blood now swamping the facilities at Ellis Island. He expressed his contempt for labor organizers in a signed editorial, "The Land of the Free," published by the *Saturday Evening Post*. He glorified the scab who crossed picket lines to keep workshops humming with activity. "He is the man who needs your backing now. . . . He is the human symbol of protest against tyranny." The public that embarrassed him by its adulation and requests for autographs caused him to send tart rejoinders. "You are most welcome to my autograph in response to your letter, which I shall keep as a chastening and instructive document; since, in twice miss-spelling my name it so admirably discloses the 'limits' of the collector's knowledge of his specimen." He believed the American climate to be inhospitable for the writing of fine literature, and he wrote in the *Bookman* that the nation was a desert for reading and writing worse than anywhere else where those arts were practiced. He wrote to his mother that nine out of ten American novels were "so thin in texture, so vacant of style, so vulgar in fibre, and so thread-bare commonplace in

229

general execution, not to speak of their ignorance of method" that he seldom could read more than a fourth of any that he started.[1]

He did not suffer gladly those fools he saw about him. When the editor of *Youth's Companion* requested an opportunity to buy a story, Wister bristled and reminded the man that in earlier days he had rejected two of his submissions. "The Youth's Companion must feel very confident of its allurements to return to me under these circumstances; I, however, have little inclination to repeat an experiment which has proved so unsuccessful." He was so proud of this calculated rejoinder that he sent a copy of his reply along with the editor's letter to the president. "Dear Theodore: You'll relish this," he wrote. Roosevelt responded in kind. "You must have felt that revenge was sweet when you sent your letter! I was immensely amused with it."[2]

The popular acclaim thrust upon him embarrassed him. Henry James had never faced such a situation, and Wister did not like to think he was cast from a different mold. The early western stories, he liked to think, had served a historical purpose and had won an audience from readers who appreciated authenticity. Now, however, he was an object of interest to people who had not even read his works. Certainly the success of *The Virginian* pleased him; yet it seemed to create within him a need to disassociate himself from the approbation of the masses.

The fact that, as Wister put it, *The Virginian* had headed the "foolish and meaningless list of 'best sellers'" naturally led George P. Brett at Macmillan to urge him to write another cowboy book. This was precisely what Wister would not do. Later he wrote of that decision: "I had written four volumes about the West; I expected to write more, but not just then; I wished to turn to other themes for a while, even if the box office receipts should fall away." Brett acquiesced. Despite the certain profits awaiting a new western book, Brett agreed that for the artist a change of pace would be beneficial.[3]

The idea for his next book came as Wister lay in his hospital bed recuperating from his appendectomy. It would be a novel of manners, the sort of book Henry James wrote, and its setting would be the American city that Wister had grown to love and that seemed so ripe for his theme—Charleston. He perceived this city as the one place in the nation where older values withstood the incipient effects of commercialism. The winter he and Molly had spent there while he completed *The Virginian* had left a "wonderful and sad impression" which had turned into a persistent longing to return. Charleston was one of the few cities that had retained "English-thinking, English-feeling, English-believing authenticity" and thereby had clung tightly to "George Washington and the true American tradition." For Wister the tragedy of the Civil War, aside from Abraham Lincoln, was Charleston—the subjugation of the sensitive spirit and society which had arisen there in antebellum days and which now stubbornly lingered on against great odds. "They had taken a splendid hand in the first making of our country and the civilization they had produced was altogether the most civilized in the United States," he believed. Moreover, he encountered there more and more people whose feelings, thoughts, philosophy, humor, faith, and attitudes toward life were like his own.[4]

The specific inspiration for the new novel's plot arose from an incident in Charleston a friend had told Wister about. A young man had ordered a wedding cake at the Women's Exchange (a place where Wister and Molly had eaten while on their honeymoon), then had cancelled the order. Wister's mind raced over the rich possibilities behind that cancellation, and he imagined an elaborate tableau for an excursion into Charleston society with approving commentaries on its social structure.[5]

The more he thought of the possibilities, the more "ravenous" he became to create this book which he believed would possess more depth than *The Virginian.* He considered it such an important undertaking, though, that he dared not begin it until he had regained his strength from the appendectomy. He walked and swam daily, visited with friends such as Langdon and Marion Mitchell and Flos and Grant La Farge, and played with the ever-growing family menagerie. The children loved animals, and Wister indulged them. They kept in Saunderstown two billy goats, three rabbits, a crow, a parrot, and, briefly, Weir Mitchell's bulldog before banishing it because of its late-night howling. In a nearby field, Marina found a "hideous but happy" one-eyed kitten which immediately replaced the dog. There were also improvements to be made to the property. Wister, in high spirits over the physical exertion, worked on fences and planted trees. "I'm beginning to feel more elastic, & the children don't bother me one particle," he declared as August arrived. "They fight like a whole monkey house about every seven minutes, and I don't mind it at all." A month earlier he could not have tolerated it, and two months earlier a slamming door would have unnerved him. More placid hours were spent with Langdon Mitchell reading aloud a biography of Edgar Allan Poe. To Wister, Poe's life was totally unenviable; he could find absolutely nothing in it to admire. Poe seemed to have lied on "every important occasion of his life." Wister's own life seemed so pleasant during this summer in Saunderstown that he predicted he would be "pretty well restored" when the family returned to Philadelphia in the fall.[6]

Almost every day something occurred to remind Wister of the continuing impact of *The Virginian*. Usually it was money. Every week he received returns of two hundred dollars or more from the theatrical version, whose road show engagements showed no signs of faltering. The 1904–1905 season opened in Brooklyn, and its itinerary after that included towns along the East Coast, throughout the South, and into the Midwest and Canada before closing for the summer. Royalties from the book continued to be substantial; sales for the twelve months previous to the summer of 1904 earned him just over ten thousand dollars. The emotional impact of the book on the reading public continued to be manifested through letters. One faithful reader, W. B. Cameron, who in 1899 had urged Wister to put the Virginian into a volume all his own, named his son Owen. J. W. Redington, Wister's friend from Heppner, Oregon, wrote to say that he had been attracted by a large crowd in a San Francisco bookstore and had found that the commotion was over two big stacks of *The Virginian* in paperback at the bargain prices of eighteen and twenty-three cents. Such comments as the following gave testimony to the book's appeal: "I read it three weeks ago & am reading it ever since—opening and starting any and everywhere, and finding it all delightful. I have always enjoyed Western stories, but never any as much as this." Another kind of public comment which forever would be part of Wister's life was the occasional news story identifying the model for the character of the Virginian. From San Francisco came a report that the "original," a Mexican ranch manager named John Henry Hicks, had married a schoolteacher. "Mexican friends sent him [Hicks] a box of a dozen dolls, dressed to represent characters in Wister's history." A man from Urbana, Illinois, wrote to ask if it were true that "Trampas" lived in Butte, Montana, and to add that he had heard while on a trip there that Trampas had vowed to shoot either Wister or the man who played the part of the Virginian when the drama played there.[7]

In mid-August Harvard president Charles W. Eliot asked Wister to join the English faculty. "The addition to the department of a comparatively young man, who has been successful as a writer, would be a good thing for the College," President Eliot wrote. Such positions were not easy to obtain, but Wister declined it. It was the most prestigious of many offers he received during the summer. He considered the *New York Herald*'s proposition that he write a story to represent the opposite end of the social scale. "You're not real good unless *both* the New York Herald *and* President Eliot want you," he observed.[8]

Wister wanted no offer to deter him from the major work that he felt lay ahead. As preparatory exercises he wrote several short pieces, the best one being an anonymous appreciation of Henry James for the *Atlantic Monthly*'s Contributors' Club. In August he began the novel in earnest, taking as a title the name of the cake ordered by the young man in Charleston, the "Lady Baltimore." He worked slowly at first, following his normal practice of composing a first draft in pencil in a tiny, neat hand, then rewriting it before giving it to a typist. From the typescript he made further alterations, then had it typed a last time. *Lady Baltimore*, so different from his earlier books, tired him physically to write, but from the beginning he thought it "remarkably good," and his writing pace quickened. "I find that my slender theme developes [*sic*] more fluently than I had anticipated, and I am quite surely making a picture of Charleston which no other fellow would approach! I don't feel modest about it in the least." By late September, remarkably, he was half-finished. News of his progress soon reached beyond the bounds of Saunderstown and the Macmillan office. Henry M. Alden wrote to express his special eagerness to serialize the book in *Harper's*, but Wister declined. Instead, he accepted a five-thousand-dollar offer from the *Saturday Evening Post*.[9]

So hard did he work on *Lady Baltimore* through late summer and early October that he suffered a relapse of his old nervous malady. A September visit to Philadelphia, taken before he had fully recovered from the appendectomy, seemed to Wister the cause of his deterioration. Thus, he decided not to return to Philadelphia for the winter; he did not feel capable of responding to the social demands there. Even in Saunderstown, though, his situation worsened. Sleep became tortured and then next to impossible. The president invited him to the White House, but he declined even this because of his physical condition. The accuracy of the nickname that Frederic Remington had bluntly given Wister a few years earlier, "Nerve Cell," now was all too apparent. In this agitated state of mind, Wister ceased all writing in December.[10]

What he needed, he felt, was solitude. Wister went alone to the Hotel Brighton in Atlantic City to find privacy, vowing not to leave until he escaped his "perfectly unreasonable and infernal state of depression." Through Christmas and the New Year he remained, one of hardly more than a half-dozen guests, doing nothing but eating, walking, and gazing into the sea until at last he felt capable of attempting to write a few pages. He believed that if he only could complete the novel, no matter how painful or difficult, he would recover his mental health. At times the solitude in this off-season bored him, but then he would remember "the curse of no sleep" or of earlier "incessant dreams." At these moments he became thankful for the improved sleep he now was enjoying and for the "several pages" he was adding to the nearly finished book.[11]

By mid-January he had completed the first draft of *Lady Baltimore*, and he felt well enough to go south to Camden, South Carolina, to polish it, stopping en route at the White House for dinner. Alone in Camden, he stayed at the Court Inn and commenced a regular schedule prescribed by Jack Mitchell, who had assumed the burden of caring for his father's patient. His regimen included horseback riding and daily massages. Weir Mitchell wrote to assure Wister that if he would live exactly as Jack prescribed he would be fit for the work he desired, and his bodily discomforts would cease.[12]

About a week after his arrival in Camden, George Brett came to visit and to inquire discreetly about his progress on *Lady Baltimore*. Brett sat patiently for hours while his prize author read to him aloud the first draft in its entirety. Wister watched carefully for clues to his editor's reaction, and afterwards he told his mother that Brett sat "in a ceaseless smile" as he listened. One wonders if Wister saw only what he wanted to see, for although Brett did pronounce the subject new and its treatment superb, he cautiously suggested that Wister "look out about some phrases which sound like Henry James." Wister proudly relayed this comment to his mother, urging her to "tell my elder brother Henry this."[13]

Henry James at this very moment was in America—back after an absence of nearly twenty-five years. His very presence seems to have prompted Wister to emulate James's difficult style. Sarah Wister, now seventy years old and more than thirty years removed from those happy days she had spent with the young, unknown James in Rome, felt "out of it." Their relationship had shifted dramatically, she realized, and she even thought James not at all happy to see her.[14]

As he heard of James's visits along the East Coast from his mother, Wister's urge to see him grew more intense. The inevitable meeting finally occurred in Charleston, where on a warm and radiant day Wister showed the city—as he viewed it—to James. This pleased James, for as he later wrote in *The American Scene*, Wister "blessedly lifted" the analytic burden that James normally forced upon himself. James, without naming Wister, described his host as a man who knew the South intimately and who made him distinctly "feel" the city of Charleston because of his "bright critical candle." The two strolled for hours, made social calls to the great houses, wandered through an old cemetery, contemplated Fort Sumter from the distance, stopped at St. Michael's Church, and entered the Women's Exchange where James pronounced the "Lady Baltimore" cake a "most delectable compound."[15]

James, of course, took a keen interest in Wister's current literary effort. He listened, as had Brett, to Wister read aloud the opening chapters of his manuscript. "Look here," Wister naively said upon finishing, "while I was reading my stuff aloud, Augustus [the novel's narrator] now and then sounded remarkably like you. That'll never do." James, Wister recalled nearly twenty-five years later, responded pleasantly, "Well, my dear Owen, may I in all audacity and sincerity ask what could Augustus better sound like?" James did offer one important suggestion. Charleston should be given a fictitious name. The city was too small and well defined, unlike London or Paris, for its real name to be used, and Wister's personal ties to the town were too obvious. "Invent some charming other name for it—you'll find swimming much freer," James said. Wister substituted for Charleston the suggestive name of "Kings Port." That done, he made no further effort to conceal the city's identity. Even the book's illustrator, Vernon Howe Bailey, visited Charleston to sketch scenes that could be identified easily by anyone familiar with its landmarks.[16]

A month after James left, Wister ended his own stay in Charleston and joined Molly in nearby Beaufort for a short vacation. Molly rarely left the children alone, and, as if confirming her fears, the children became sick with scarlet fever. The vacation had to be ended early. A six-week quarantine was placed on the 913 Pine Street house, but Molly went inside to care for the children. Wister retreated temporarily to Miss Sophie's house, lamenting that Molly would never leave the children again. This was the third time she had done so, and on each occasion a serious illness had occurred.[17]

Wister departed Philadelphia once more, returning to a favorite place in the Appalachians—Hot Springs, Virginia. He continued there the recovery program prescribed by Jack Mitchell. Mitchell urged him to delay extensive work on *Lady Baltimore* until after an elaborate program of physical exercise. Wister followed the advice, and completion of the novel was postponed further while he exercised heavily every morning, walked an hour each day before noon, rode horseback for less than fifteen miles every afternoon, and relaxed with a thorough massage every evening. Horseback riding, even more so than before, became a special pleasure. Wister even toyed with the idea of buying his favorite horse there, riding it the 150 miles or so to Washington, and shipping it from there by rail to Philadelphia and by sea to Boston, where he would join the horse and ride triumphantly into Saunderstown.[18]

By May 1 he felt his strength returning and his persistent cough, the most "violent" he had had for years, disappearing. Molly, very patient about her long-absent husband, reminded him by letter that he must still expect occasional bilious attacks. That was all the more reason for regaining strength. "They won't come often or last long when you're in good condition."[19]

Another very patient person was George Brett, who waited in puzzlement for the overdue *Lady Baltimore*. He already had arranged for simultaneous American and English publication, but he could get no idea when his firm's prize author might turn over the manuscript. "I suppose I must not ask you as to how nearly the work on the book is finished," Brett gingerly offered, "but if you can give me any information on this point pray do so as I must make my announcements sufficiently in advance of its appearance to handle it properly." Wister's advance on royalties, ten thousand dollars, was ready too, awaiting only his decision as to whether to take it all at once or to receive monthly payments.[20]

In June he was back in Saunderstown with his family, now recovered themselves, where his program of exercise continued. A new addition to the household was a young medical student, recommended by Jack Mitchell, who massaged Wister regularly, watched over the children, and acted as a correspondence secretary. His presence gave Wister and Molly added time together. They rode daily on "George" and "Bessie," their favorite horses, although horseback riding in Saunderstown was getting to be a problem because of the increasing and disruptive presence of the motorcar. All in all, the constant riding, the evening massage, and the relative tranquility of Saunderstown gave Wister faith that his recovery would continue.[21]

In late July he felt well enough for several vigorous activities. The Chapmans arrived by yacht for a week's visit, and Wister joined them on an excursion to see Julia Ward Howe in Newport. When he learned that a new road coming through Saunderstown would be curved rather than straight he wrote a petition, carried it around the community for signatures, and succeeded in having the route altered into a straight one. It was an exhilarating appearance in the public arena. His most important personal accomplishment, however, was at last finishing *Lady Baltimore*. The approaching deadline for *Saturday Evening Post* serialization had left him little choice, for the installments began with the October 28, 1905, issue and continued through the last week of January.[22]

Shortly before the first episode appeared, Wister, back in Philadelphia, suffered a relapse. He announced it to his mother: "This morning I am very much troubled. I am much less well than when I wrote you last. If it goes on, I shall fail in a serious business obligation. I can't come with the children to-morrow for I'm really not up to facing the prospect of any other responsibility." What the "business obligation" was is not known, but by early December Wister had returned to New Jersey for several weeks to recover with his favorite remedy—solitude.[23]

Back in Philadelphia his mental equilibrium was threatened again. An irate professor of zoology at Cornell University named Burt G. Wilder confronted him in the mails, charging him with racism in a segment of *Lady Baltimore*, which was appearing serially in the *Saturday Evening Post*. The charge was too serious to dismiss lightly, for the book had not yet appeared, and its integrity might be jeopardized. The disputed section concerned an incident in which the narrator Augustus encounters a vague sort of scientist described as a "collector" who demonstrates the similarity between the ape and the Negro by comparing bone structures in their skulls. The skull of a Caucasian displayed by the collector is distinctly different. "The picture which they thus made spoke more than all the measurements and statistics which he now chattered out upon me," Augustus noted. The collector underscores the point: "Have you now learned someding [*sic*] about skulls, my friend? Will you invite those Boston philanthropists to stay home? They will get better results in civilization by giving votes to monkeys than teaching Henry Wadsworth Longfellow to niggers."[24]

The zoology professor, who held a doctor of medicine degree, asked Wister for his source of information. Wister responded with false confidence, "It incorporates no special knowledge, but only information of the ordinary kind which is to be found in any museum of anatomy or academy of natural sciences." Such naive "documentation" infuriated Dr.

Wilder. He had been comparing skulls of apes and men since 1859, he wrote, and "a child would unhesitatingly separate the men from the apes." If Wister did not notify him of a retraction within a reasonable period of time, Dr. Wilder threatened to fulfill his scholarly duty and seek "to arrest the further diffusion of the scientific error and the politic venom that characterize the passage."[25]

Wister instructed his clerical assistant to reply cautiously for him. The assistant wrote that the passage was not based merely upon Wister's own observation, although, "it seems to him that what he has personally observed would warrant it." Nevertheless, Mr. Wister had asked him to advise Dr. Wilder that he would "at the earliest opportunity investigate the matter." If upon investigation he found the observation in error he would "take every step in his power to set the matter right."[26]

Along with millions of other Americans, four decades after the Emancipation Proclamation, Wister still assumed the black man to be inferior and found evidence of this in the shape of the skulls. A prominent body of "scientific" ethnology supported the belief, one that had originated in 1839 when Dr. Samuel George Morton of Philadelphia published the book *Crania Americana* and claimed distinctions in skulls based on years of study. Late nineteenth-century doctrines based on evolutionary thought reinforced a belief among many, Northerners and Southerners, that the black men were not only a race different in anatomy and physiology but also an inferior race struggling for survival. Wister felt no need to inform himself specifically on the issues Dr. Wilder raised. He merely ordered his assistant to locate "scientific matter to weave into the dialogue." As a result, instead of eliminating the unfortunate and inaccurate passage, Wister compounded the error by making his allegations more specific. His "revision" added details to support further the alleged similarities between the skulls of the Negro and of the ape, describing now "the contours of vaulted skull, the projecting jaws, and the great molar teeth." For the moment Dr. Wilder made no further protest. He awaited a time of his own choosing, which would come five years later.[27]

In April, *Lady Baltimore* at long last appeared in the nation's bookstores. Critics paid scant attention to the author's approval of the South's discriminatory practices against the black race, although the *New York Evening Post*'s reviewer noted that a reader could smile at Wister's introductory disavowal of his characters' prejudices against the "colored race." Many critics did point, however, to the book's contrast between the vulgar, commercialized life of the East and the gracious, well-ordered culture of the South. While few of the eastern critics cared to score Wister on this point, a reviewer in Charleston surely surprised him. "However pleasing the adulation of the manners and customs of the town," the critic wrote in the *News & Courier*, "it is distinctly cruel to have it written down that it is a sepulchre of memories and not a living, breathing reality of these commercial times." Moreover, Wister's impolite criticisms of his own eastern part of the nation left "a very bad taste" in the reviewer's mouth. Nobody had expected Wister to be unkind to his own region, the reviewer wrote, and it was not necessary to the completeness or charm of the work for him to do so. The subterfuge of using "Kings Port" for Charleston could not in any way disguise the true identity of the city. The illustrations and descriptions of Charleston were so accurate, according to the *Philadelphia Inquirer*, that the reason for the pseudonym was "inexplicable except that it pleases the whim of the author."[28]

Despite such comments, reviewers from throughout the nation with few exceptions praised *Lady Baltimore*. They viewed the author's departure from his previous writing style and subjects to be a mark of his versatility. George Brett was convinced that in revising the novel Wister had eliminated "as if by magic" all traces of James's style. Yet if Brett was convinced, almost no one else was, for many reviewers commented upon the style's resemblance to James's. Some criticized it for this reason. None were quite so blunt about it as the *Springfield* (Massachusetts) *Republican*, which headlined its review, "Another Novelist Falls Under the Spell of Henry James." The anonymous critic asked, "Who would have thought it possible for the author of 'The Virginian' to be infected?" Indeed, the abrupt shift in subject matter alone surely puzzled faithful readers who had been nurtured in his western realism.[29]

Still, *Lady Baltimore* almost instantly appeared in the nation's bestselling book lists. In June it was cited as the most popular book in the land, and in the following months it vied with *The Jungle* by Upton Sinclair (who at last was receiving the public recognition he so earnestly had sought) and with Winston Churchill's *Coniston*.[30]

In Charleston the "Owen Wister Lady Baltimore" cake became a thriving industry: cakes were shipped to places throughout the nation. Sylvia Emerson, a friend, told Wister that in Boston the Lady's Exchange had so many orders for the "Owen Wister Lady Baltimore" that they could not fill them all. The Okemo Cake Kitchen Company in Newton

Center, Massachusetts, added three new loaf cakes to its price list: "the Lady Baltimore," "the Round Owen Wister," and "the Square Owen Wister." Perhaps the supreme compliment came when J. Mahlon Duganne composed a musical score, the "Lady Baltimore Waltzes," and Jos. W. Stern & Co. of New York City published the sheet music.[31]

By May some 71,000 copies of *Lady Baltimore* had been sold; Wister's first royalty payment amounted to $11,250. The book undeniably was one of the season's most popular novels. Yet to write a best-selling novel in 1906 was not at all the same as to have written a best-selling novel a few years earlier, Brett told Wister. The public was not buying books with the same enthusiasm. "The fact, however, has been established that 'Lady Baltimore' is the most successful novel of its time at present, and it has, I think, done for your reputation, in the way of enhancing it, all that I expected it to do." Brett anticipated that the book would "go on in . . . a perfectly steady manner . . . for some years to come."[32]

Wister could not have been happier over the book's reception. He confided to M. A. De Wolfe Howe that in his opinion he had "got off very easily" for he had indulged himself "outrageously" in writing it. "[I] said everything that came into my head, and mostly of a disagreeable nature; and I also kicked down stairs every method of appeal by which I had hitherto reached my audience." He had thought that "probably thirty-six people" would read it and "twenty-seven would be unable to finish it."[33]

United States Senator Henry Cabot Lodge liked the book "extremely." He wrote to Wister that "all that you say of the yellow rich warms my heart and is not only realistic but strong and impressive." Their views of the Negro appeared identical, Lodge said, although he personally faulted the South for not giving a chance to the "occasional negro" who was a good citizen. Still, despite the affection he claimed to share with Wister for the South, Lodge stressed that sympathy should blind neither of them to the fact that the North had saved the nation and carried it forward.[34]

The best and most penetrating criticism of *Lady Baltimore* came privately and directly from the White House. Wister's literary retreat from the strenuous life might have been expected to win less praise from Roosevelt, and indeed the president did not especially admire this book—but clearly for other reasons. For one thing, Charleston had been a particular thorn to Roosevelt because of its hostile reaction to his appointment of the Negro, Dr. William Crum, to be collector of the port. Wister irritated the president by including in *Lady Baltimore* a thinly disguised version of the incident, portraying in sympathetic tones a customs house official of established social stature who was embarrassed and chagrined at having to serve under a black man.

The president's response came just two weeks after Wister had spent the night at the White House. On that occasion, at Roosevelt's insistence, Wister had entertained guests by playing the piano and singing popular ballads. The president had startled the guests, who included the French ambassador, by joining in the merriment himself and cutting "a few capers on the polished floor." There had been no evidence then of Roosevelt's hostile reception of the book.[35]

Now, though, in a fourteen-page letter on White House stationery, he reacted so vehemently against *Lady Baltimore* that it is surprising the friendship survived. Roosevelt castigated the book most emphatically for its sweeping generalizations about the societies of the North and the South. It was no more than "a tract of the times," he wrote, and "a capital error to make your swine-devils practically all northerners and your angels practically all southerners." The clear implication, Roosevelt protested, was that the "swine-devils" were representative of the overwhelming majority of the North. A far more effective approach, he argued, would have been to delineate between the best and worst Northerners; then Wister could have attacked with purpose the vulgarity and greed of those who deserved it. As for Wister's southern "angels," Roosevelt listed specific incidents and generalizations to demonstrate that in fact they had developed "traits of a very unhealthy kind." Southerners sent men to Washington, he claimed, who were less valuable than northern men, who were not as efficient, and who exaggerated the common American tendency of using bombastic language, failing in performance to live up to it.

> Your particular heroes, the Charleston aristocrats and their kinsfolk in the up-country . . . have never made good their pretensions. They were no more to blame than the rest of the country for the slave trade of the colonial days, but when the rest of the country woke up they shut their eyes tight to the horrors, they insisted that the slave trade should be kept, and succeeded in keeping it for a quarter of a century after the Revolutionary war closed, they went into secession partly to re-open it. They drank and dueled and made speeches, but they contributed very, very little toward anything of which we as Americans are now proud.

As for the grievances felt in the South as a result of Reconstruction, Roosevelt felt that the area had brought these upon itself and deserved not a particle of sympathy.[36]

Roosevelt agreed with Wister that Negroes as a race and in mass were "altogether inferior to the whites." Yet the "latest scientific theory" showed that their skulls were closely akin to those of the white man and differed markedly from those of the Mongolians. "Your views of the negro are those expressed by all of your type of Charlestonian. . . . They are only expressed in their entirety to those who don't know the facts." While southern politicians decried the black man as unfit to vote on one hand, they nevertheless insisted that their representation include both blacks and whites. "Your Charleston friends lead this outcry and are among the chief beneficiaries, politically, of the fraud and violence which they triumphantly defend." Any talk that the Negro had degenerated since the Civil War was the "veriest nonsense," Roosevelt claimed. His own appointment of Dr. Crum as collector of the port, a matter over which he and Wister already had disagreed, had been made only after the people of that city had assured him that Crum was one of the "best citizens." Those same guarantors of his merits then had turned about and had "hysterics" over the appointment.

> When I have tried to fall in with the views of the very southern people, which in this volume you seem to be upholding, the results have been worse than in any other way. These very people whose views you endorse are those who have tried to reintroduce slavery by the infamous system of peonage.

Southerners and especially Charlestonians outdid all others in being "slavishly afraid" of expressing opinions contrary to those of their neighbors, Roosevelt wrote.

> They shriek in public about miscegenation, but they leer as they talk to me privately of the colored mistresses and colored children of white men whom they know. Twice southern senators who in the Senate yell about the purity of the white blood, deceived me into appointing imposters whom I found had colored mistresses and colored children.[37]

Actually, Roosevelt continued, the "best people" of the South supported him in such actions as the tumultuous appointment of Crum, as well as in his decisions to have lunch in the White House with Booker T. Washington and to close the Indianola, Mississippi, post office rather than to buckle under pressure to remove the postmistress he had appointed there. The Southerners who supported him in these actions, he claimed, were in truth the courageous ones, rather than the hypocritical aristocrats of Charleston. Yet in *Lady Baltimore*, Wister had dealt these brave and lonely Southerners a body blow in their uphill struggle against uninformed majority opinion. In closing, Roosevelt said he had written "as I should only write to a dear friend," and why could not Wister "get on here soon and spend a night or two?" Yet, having concluded on this amiable note, he could not resist returning to *Lady Baltimore* in a lengthy postscript.

> As a tract on the social life of the North . . . it really seems to me to be about as inaccurate as they [*sic*] are; and what is more, it produces the very feeling which makes men followers of David Graham Phillips, the Hearst writer, and of [Upton] Sinclair, the socialist, and which makes them feel that there is no use of trying to reform anything because everything is so rotten that the whole social structure should either be left alone or destroyed.[38]

In addition to the president's fury, there is evidence that Wister's circle of East Coast friends also lamented, though privately, his transgressions in *Lady Baltimore*. Winthrop Chanler sent Roosevelt a harsh assessment of the novel, causing the president to comment that Chanler's criticisms contained much that he wished he could have written to Wister but had not had the heart to. "I was really sorry to have him [Wister] write this book, because his other work has been so very, very good," he told Chanler. "I guess there is a good deal in what you say about Dan's not being a man of the world." The rumor among this set of friends was that one of their own members, Woodbury Kane, had been the model for the entirely unsympathetic Northerner.[39]

No record exists of Wister's response to Roosevelt's vigorous criticisms, but twenty-two years later he reproduced the letter in full in the preface to *Lady Baltimore* for his collected works. For this new edition of the book he followed Roosevelt's criticisms—as he had done in "Balaam and Pedro"—and "moderated the diatribes of Augustus in several places." Augustus's comments, he finally realized, had been "far too sweeping." Yet, Wister wrote, Augustus's views of "certain social, political, and commercial aspects of our country strike me as true then, if overstated, and more true to-day, provided the sense of proportion be kept. But I didn't and don't agree with Mr. Roosevelt about the negro and about Reconstruction."[40]

As president, Roosevelt's own public acts concerning race relations had earned him almost nothing but abuse. The Booker T. Washington, Crum, and Indianola affairs had prompted his southern critics and others to attack him as a champion of the black race. Yet, in the same year that he criticized *Lady Baltimore*, he summarily discharged "without honor" three entire companies of black infantry soldiers for a shooting spree in Brownsville, Texas, perpetrated by a dozen or so soldiers. For this precipitous act, which punished innocent as well as guilty, Roosevelt earned the enmity of many others.

In addition, Wister's western friends found nothing to cheer them in the author's neglect of their part of the country. Dean Duke good-naturedly rebuked his friend from San Francisco several days after he heard about Wister's entertaining with his music at the presidential dinner.

> Smiley, you're headed the wrong way. Come back to the cow outfits and write about real life with cussing in it. You may go and get chummy with a lot of those good old Eastern Brothers & Sisters, but the first time you forget and keep your hat on in the house they will not only be fairly scandalized, but among themselves later they will knock your ancestors. Come back to the Cowpunchers, Smiley, they sure liked you—even if you did play the piano.[41]

The West was at this point little more than a fond memory, and two weeks after receiving Duke's letter Wister boarded a Cunard line passenger ship for England. Aunt Fanny's daughter, Alice, was to wed, and Wister was to give away the bride so that her father, a minister, could help perform the ceremony. He had time to spend a weekend at Rye with Henry James, and the two of them dined with Edith Wharton. James appeared "very lonely," but his life at the quaint seaside town of Rye was totally ordered, a way of life he seemed to like best.[42]

Back in Philadelphia good news awaited. Sales of *Lady Baltimore* continued strong; Wister was approached about the possibility of dramatizing the novel for the stage; a German translation of the book was underway; and a flattering review had arrived from the other side of the world—Australia. On still another note, the dramatic version of *The Virginian* opened in August in its fourth season on the road. Its handsome profits were continuing, but when Wister attended a performance he concluded that the new actor who portrayed Steve was not suited for the part. Wister warned the producer that the play was in danger of "falling to pieces" unless the situation was corrected. Dustin Farnum and Frank Campeau continued to perform superbly in their original roles.[43]

The only misfortune Wister could count was the disastrous 1906 earthquake in San Francisco which temporarily deprived him of some $1,050 in annual income from his street railroad investments. He complained of this loss to his mother and then had second thoughts. He wrote to assure her that in fact he was "quite rich."[44]

In Saunderstown, where the family went in the fall, his daily life continued to prove satisfying. He purchased a Shetland pony for the children which kept Marina, a promising horsewoman, happy from dawn till dark. Another addition to the menagerie was a pet mockingbird named "Gabriel" which cheered the family daily with its singing. Henry James sent greetings from England and wished that he, too, could be sitting in that "graceful ring" in Saunderstown with the Wisters, La Farges, and Mitchells.[45]

If Saunderstown ever got dull, New York City or Oyster Bay offered diversion. In November Wister joined the staff of Harper & Brothers and William Dean Howells in celebrating Henry Mills Alden's seventieth birthday, and later that month he returned to New York City to stay with John Jay Chapman for the opening at the Lyric Theater of Langdon Mitchell's new play, *The New York Idea*. Mitchell's British-born wife, the former Marion Lea, whose theatrical aspirations had previously disgusted Wister, surprised him by looking quite lovely and performing better than ever. He predicted that the play would achieve certain success and that the Mitchells would have "the time of all their lives" during its Broadway run. "No subsequent success can ever be like the first. They will revel in the play, and the people they'll see, the clever half reputable people,—and neither of them will save one penny." His estimation of the play was correct, for *The New York Idea* soon would be hailed as an important event in American dramatic history for its innovation in daring to portray divorce laws in satirical fashion.[46]

Visits with the Roosevelt family at Oyster Bay were as fun as ever. On one occasion Alice Roosevelt had as a guest her friend Mary Harriman, daughter of railroad magnate E. H. Harriman, a bitter foe of Roosevelt's because of the president's trust-busting activities. After the visit, Wister returned to New York City by train with Miss Harriman and expressed his happy surprise to learn that she preferred the study of deep-sea life to the society her mother enjoyed at Newport. "Harriman is a thief, a pirate, a Wall Street gambler, a vast industrial tyrant, who hates Roosevelt for his attacks upon corporations," Wister observed, "and here's his daughter the friend of Roosevelt's daughter, and, so far as they know her, a remarkable and admirable person. But the queer thing is, *she* must know the relation between her father & the President."[47]

Before the year ended, Wister found himself once again at odds with Roosevelt. This time the disagreement arose over the Spelling Reform Association's move for the nation to adopt simplified spellings— "dropped" and "chased" would become "dropt" and "chast," and scores of other words would be spelled the way they sounded. The idea appealed to Roosevelt's direct approach to problems. He ordered the government printer to use new spellings for some three hundred words, and when Congress convened he sent them his annual message in simplified spelling. A wave of protest arose throughout the nation for his defiling of the English language. Congress challenged Roosevelt's directive for simplified spelling too, and he withdrew the order—but not until wits such as "Marse Henry" Watterson of the *Louisville Courier* had stung him. "Nothing escapes Mr. Rucevelt. No subject is tu hi for him to takl, nor tu lo for him to notis," Watterson wrote. Roosevelt seemed to enjoy the spirited arguments. Wister joined the opposition himself, writing a satire for the *Saturday Evening Post* entitled, "How Doth the Simple Spelling Bee." Macmillan published the article as a short book the next year. If only the president had asked him in advance about this move, Wister told his mother, he would have done his utmost to dissuade Roosevelt from "such folly."[48]

Part Three

THE CURMUDGEON

Chapter XIII

IN THE PUBLIC ARENA
(1907–1908)

FOR SEVERAL YEARS NOW THE TEMPTATION HAD BEEN GROWING in Wister to assert himself as an authority on public affairs. Occasionally he had yielded to this urge, but he realized that if he were to be more effective he needed to develop a "platform presence." The undeniable failure that had marked his public reading at the opening of the new Symphony Hall in Boston still haunted him, and he made a 1907 New Year's resolution to become a better public speaker. "I can speak fairly well," he told his mother, "but it has always frightened me & made me so wretched. I want . . . to overcome this, & feel entirely at ease on my legs." To force himself to work on his resolution he accepted three speaking engagements for January and February.[1]

The first engagement was in the nation's capital, a banquet marking the fiftieth anniversary of the American Institute of Architects. Wister set his fears aside and spoke without notes on "Literature and Music" to a distinguished audience in the Willard Hotel which included William Howard Taft, Elihu Root, Speaker Joe Cannon ("a venerable buffoon"), Thomas Nelson Page, and the Reverend E. E. Hale. The talk, he felt, was "well received," and he claimed that it removed all fears for his next speech in Boston.[2]

The occasion for the Boston address was a dinner to honor the prominent lyricist of "The Battle Hymn of the Republic," Julia Ward Howe. As so often was the case, Wister privately was caustic to his mother about the event, which he labeled "preposterous." The other speeches, in his opinion, were of "a driveling imbecility that would disgrace Germantown or Tioga." The water was tepid and the food "slim and mean." Of those present, Wister knew only Miss Howe and four others. This was not *his* Boston.[3]

The third speaking opportunity came in February when the orator who was to give the George Washington birthday address at the University of Pennsylvania unexpectedly cancelled. Wister agreed to replace him. It was stipulated that the address concern Washington, a figure Wister professed to know nothing about. He worked diligently in his determination to get at the essence of the Founding Father's personality. The more he worked, the more excited he became. His notes soon swelled out of all proportion to the size of the task before him. Washington's strong character made a profound impression upon him as he learned of acts such as Washington's assuming responsibility for educating his nieces and nephews and not dining without guests at his table for twenty years. This kind of behavior Wister admired; it seemed to be vanishing all too soon from the modern world. When Wister had finished writing his speech he sent a copy to his mother, who made careful corrections in style.[4]

When the day arrived, Wister donned academic regalia, received an honorary doctor of laws degree, and then delivered his carefully prepared speech at a measured pace as if he were addressing a few intimate acquaintances instead of a crowd of several thousand. The speech won high acclaim, and as a result Wister felt satisfied that he had made great progress in living up to his New Year's resolution. He was ready now for assuming a broader role as an oracle.

Meanwhile, the city of Boston redeemed itself in his eyes when he went there in early March with Molly to commemorate at Sanders Theatre the centennial anniversary of Longfellow's birth. This time it was a "perfect occasion." Wister sat with Molly on the front row with Harvard president Charles W. Eliot, Charles Eliot Norton, Bliss Perry, Sarah Orne Jewett, Julia Ward Howe, Charles T. Copeland, and the governor of Massachusetts.[5]

In April he again went to Hot Springs, Virginia, to join Langdon Mitchell for four weeks at the Homestead resort. He had more than relaxation in mind, for he intended to use his time to convert his Washington speech into a book. Wister plunged deeply into the writings of Washington as well as into those of the first president's contemporaries. As he read he developed an intense dislike for the republican Thomas Jefferson, and he vowed to construct a "corrosive paragraph" about the famous Virginian. "Among other things, he seems to have been a liar," Wister wrote to his mother in Italy. As was his constant custom, Wister also kept up with his correspondence, sending Henry James ("My blessed H.J.") a lengthy letter filled with details of his mother's health, people and places of mutual interest, and complaints of American servants who "grow daily more infernal." Hot Springs itself was so "richly indigenous" that Wister mulled over the possibility of writing a novel about it and its resorts. A good title—if Henry James agreed—seemed to be "The Waters of Babel." Midway in his visit Molly arrived, daring to come without the children, for a vacation of her own. She had been busy in the municipal political race in Philadelphia—supporting as had Wister the reformist City Party—and relaxation was overdue. But once again she cut short her vacation. Problems in the Unitarian Church summoned her there. As for Wister, even Theodore Roosevelt's invitation to accompany him to the opening of the Jamestown Exposition could not budge him from his favorite spa. But he did manage to have the invitation delayed so that he could visit the White House for a weekend en route to Philadelphia.[6]

This he did, finding Roosevelt at what seemed to be the peak of his career. Roosevelt had thrived on the controversy erupting from his efforts to bring J. P. Morgan, James J. Hill, Edward H. Harriman, and giant railroads and corporations to public accountability. In this battle he already could claim victory, Wister thought.[7]

Naturally, he solicited the president's own ideas concerning George Washington and his era, and he learned happily that Roosevelt thought even less of Jefferson than he did. In fact, Roosevelt scarcely allowed Wister's mild protestations in Jefferson's behalf. Roosevelt would grant Jefferson only "a wholesome fundamental belief in the conception of the Republican Government, and nothing more."[8]

Sarah Wister suggested that her son's hostility toward the author of the Declaration of Independence was inherited from his father. Not so, Wister countered.

> I never liked his [Jefferson's] bad manners in the White House— slippers &c—nor was I ever in sympathy with his political creed as opposed to Hamilton's—but none of this gave me any dislike for the *man*. That has come from reading of his insincerity toward the long-trusting and slow-suspecting Washington, and his wholly groundless disparagement of Patrick Henry when Henry was dead.

He urged his mother to reread carefully the Declaration of Independence. He felt certain that she would agree that it contained many phrases which "mean little, or nothing" and that the fame of the document resulted solely from the momentous event with which it dealt.[9]

There were plenty of other diversions for Wister these days besides visits to the White House and immersion into the thoughts and actions of the Founding Fathers. In Saunderstown a new house, designed by

Grant La Farge, was going up for the Wister family. It was to be smaller than their present Saunderstown home, but still spacious with three stories, plenty of bathrooms, a study, a playroom for the children, and a guest suite apart from the main house. In Cambridge, where Wister's Harvard class celebrated its twenty-fifth reunion in June, a special treat awaited. The Hasty Pudding Club revived Wister's *Dido and Aeneas* and performed it to commemorate this first operetta in the club's annals. Notes from Kirk La Shelle came frequently about the stage version of *The Virginian*, in which a young actor named William S. Hart had replaced Dustin Farnum. Farnum had declined La Shelle's offer of a ten-year contract with top pay of four hundred dollars a week during the last two years. La Shelle lamented that Farnum was turning out to be "like all other actors"; there was "no actor in the world whom you can depend on, after he has made a hit." Frank Campeau remained loyal as the villain Trampas, however, and along with Hart he continued to satisfy thousands of playgoers.[10]

Wister began in 1907 a rambling, philosophical correspondence of several years' duration with Charles Francis Adams, whose father and grandfather both had served as president of the United States and whose father had been ambassador to England. Their letters covered a wide range of subjects, especially educational theory. The changes that had occurred in Wister's outlook were reflected in his response to Adams's query as to what Wister thought of Eliot's elective system at Harvard. As a young man, Wister had debated the subject vehemently with his parents in favor of freedom of choice; now he was "utterly opposed" to the elective system. The obvious fallacy of the scheme, in his opinion, was that students would avoid intellectually demanding subjects. He had shown those tendencies himself as an undergraduate, he acknowledged, but his mother and father had asserted their control. Now he expressed gratitude for their attitude, for without it he would have "worked as little, played as much as possible, and graduated not only pretty ignorant (which I am now) but also without any mental edge or coherence." He believed that the main ingredients of education should be history, philosophy, and ancient and modern languages. "Before anything and everything else, a man should know what the human race has said, and done," he said.[11]*

---

* In the correspondence, Adams related to Wister what Dr. Oliver Wendell Holmes had told a woman who had asked him what the proper time was to begin a

Less than three weeks later, these thoughts fresh on his mind, an opportunity arose for Wister to talk about education to an even greater audience. Byron S. Hurlbut, dean of Harvard College, asked him to present a "short, informal address" at the scholarship meeting in December. The entire meeting, including the presentation of awards, would last no more than an hour. Wister accepted the invitation eagerly. He had nearly half a year to ruminate on the topic. Meanwhile, he would finish his book on Washington.[12]

The Washington volume was too brief, more of a snapshot of the man than a biography. Yet Wister was far more painstaking in this research than he had been in his other short biography on Ulysses S. Grant. "I am working very slowly in hopes of doing a really fine thing," he explained. In August he went to Avon by the Sea, New Jersey, for the solitude that seemed necessary to finish the work properly. He felt under great stress—it seemed that his book had to approach the greatness of Washington—and contrary to his usual practice he rewrote practically every word.[13]

Wister had been planning upon the book's completion to write a biography of Lincoln, but he now told the firm's M. A. De Wolfe Howe that financial needs required him to write more commercial material. Dividend payments from two of his sources of income had been suspended, and he faced substantial expenditures for his new house in Saunderstown. Thus, his plan was to write a collection of short stories and a novel.[14]

He dated the preface on the Washington book on October 20, entitling it *The Seven Ages of Washington.* Now he began preparing for his upcoming talk at Harvard. Dean Hurlbut had stipulated a short, informal talk, but Wister conceived a much more ambitious and, as it turned out, foolish goal. He was inspired by a report from the United States Secretary of Agriculture stating that America had supplied the world enough foodstuffs for a $444 million surplus in balance of trade. This achievement in agriculture seemed to contrast sharply with the impoverishment of American intellectual life, which instead of exporting knowledge, borrowed heavily from Europe. If the balance of trade in foodstuffs could be measured, Wister thought, then so could the balance of trade in learning. He determined to do just that in as precise

child's education. "Well, madam, about 250 years before it is born," Holmes was said to have replied. (Adams to Wister, February 4, 1907, Box 13, Owen Wister Papers.)

a manner as possible, a parlous task. He began examining every field of learning in an effort to determine the acknowledged masters. He wanted to know which American scholars attracted students from the world over, and which were recognized as the supreme authorities in their chosen subjects. He examined twenty-six branches of learning including physics, botany, psychology, Egyptology, Romance languages, economics, astronomy, chemistry, American history, mathematics, pathology, archaeology, philology, art history, semetic philosophy, and others. He compiled his own list of masters from throughout the world in these fields, then wrote to "several educators of note" for their appraisals of his choices. His sweeping conclusion was that "no American University possesses one single teacher of undisputed preeminence." And, one week before Christmas, this is what he told the professors and honor students of Harvard and the friends, relatives, and former schoolmasters of the prizewinners at the annual meeting of the Award of Academic Distinctions. They had not bargained for a talk such as this, but there was little they could do now but sit quietly and listen as the state of American knowledge was deprecated by a famous American author.[15]

"Balance of trade in food products for the year 1907, 444 millions; balance of trade in scholarship, minus 100 per cent," Wister bluntly declared. He acknowledged his host institution to be foremost among American universities, but the distinction lost its luster entirely when viewed in Wister's appraisal of America's overall backwardness in scholarship. There were, of course, certain American men of "education, enlightenment, and character," and Wister named a few of them: Henry C. Lea, Horace Howard Furness, S. Weir Mitchell, Josiah Willard Gibbs, and Charles Eliot Norton. But of the forty-three preeminent scholars in the twenty-six branches of knowledge outlined, just three were Americans, and none of them were absolutely foremost in their fields.*

The task before the audience, Wister said, was to bring American scholarship to the level of American agriculture. It could be done if financial support and the necessary freedom of research were given. "Does this lesson not stare us in the face? Do we not see that if American brains can take our desert wastes of earth and fill them with crops of golden wheat, American brains can also take our desert wastes of scholarship and fill them with a crop of high authorities to whom

* The honored American scholars were Maurice Bloomfield of Johns Hopkins in Sanskrit, Albert Michelson of Chicago in physics, and Theodore Richards of Harvard in chemistry.

Europe will turn with admiration?" The speech was, to Wister, a patriotic message which urged Harvard men and Americans to do their utmost for the good of the country. It came when the glorification of college athletics and a growing preoccupation with business, not yet respectable in academic circles, seemed more than ever on the verge of crowding out all recognition of scholarly achievement.[16]

To Wister's astonishment his speech prompted a wave of criticism and conflict. He had intended to promote American scholarship by criticizing the nation's emphasis on material progress and its neglect of the intellectual. Few took the speech in that spirit. News stories throughout the nation reported his negative assessment of American scholarship. One spokesman after another arose to rebut—and occasionally to defend—his harsh appraisal. He had omitted, it was pointed out, such distinguished individuals as the psychologist G. Stanley Hall, Stanford president David Starr Jordan, and even his friend William James (who perhaps was present in Sanders Theatre for the speech).* "Wister is a nice fellow, but then, you know, he's a literary man," chided Nicholas Murray Butler, president of Columbia University, in a widely repeated comment. "He [Wister] was less than just to his own university . . . and, whether what he said is true or not, it is at best only half the truth," the *Boston Congregationalist* charged. Wister was accused, too, of a breach of etiquette in making such remarks to a Harvard audience. It amounted to "innate cruelty," wrote Boston's *Zion Herald*. The *Brooklyn Daily Times* declared the speech to be "the greatest shock this rather complacent centre of learning has received in many years." The *Milwaukee Sentinel* wondered in print why Harvard had chosen a "popular novelist" to make the speech. "Perhaps Yale may be moved by this innovation to choose, say, a press humorist for a similar office, by way of trumping the lead of her competitor."[17]

There was little doubt but that the speech offended Harvard's scholars. Mindful of the fact that Wister had been an invited guest, they muted their criticisms. Dean of Arts and Sciences Le Baron Russell Briggs wrote to Wister to say that everyone agreed that the speech was "noteworthy," but he pointed out that "no two persons' estimate of the greatest scholars the world over in all the principal departments of learn-

---

* Perhaps it was to make amends for having omitted William James from his speech that two weeks later Wister wrote to him to praise his new book, *Pragmatism: A New Name for Some Old Ways of Thinking.* "No piece of intellectual reading that I have done for many years has excited me so much and delighted me," he wrote. The letter, dated January 10, 1908, is in the Houghton Library, Harvard University.

ing will be the same; and men will always disagree about the wisdom of estimating living men to their faces." However, if such estimating were to be done, Briggs said, "nobody could have done it in a better spirit." A *Harvard Bulletin* editorial proved similarly diplomatic. "Admitting that what he [Wister] said may have an element of exaggeration, he was, nevertheless, right beyond a doubt in stating that the intellectual, is wholly disproportionate to the material output of our country." William James wrote, "What a row your Sanders Theatre address has made!" The speech was a "very fine thing," James declared, but he thought Wister had been "a bit too definite in rating individuals." Of course, he acknowledged, this is what had brought so much attention.[18]

Wister's position was not without support. The *Boston Transcript* credited him with prompting a wholesome reexamination of American scholarship which, for example, had caused Princeton president Woodrow Wilson to say that the American university had "missed the true inner meaning of education." The *Charleston News* rallied to his support too. "He has done a great public service in showing where 'American scholarship' stands when not compared with itself." Despite the "storm of protesting comment" that must be unpleasant for him, the *Providence Tribune* knew Wister could stand up to it because the remarks "would not have made such a commotion if there had not been a large measure of truth in them."[19]

Yet the controversy did trouble Wister. He defended his comments to a reporter from the *Philadelphia Public Ledger*, saying he had spent "many weeks" in preparing the list; he had consulted with knowledgeable scholars; and, as for his own qualifications, he pointed to his Harvard degree and to the fact that he had graduated tenth in his class of 180. "What I meant by my little joke about the balance of trade in knowledge between Europe and America—and there is no question as to where the balance lies—was that Europe does not have to come over to America to sit at the feet of its scholars. The balance of trade is on the other side of the Atlantic."[20]

Wister listed his own reasons for America's backwardness in scholarship. A greater portion of young men now went into brokers' offices instead of into the learned professions; a generation had died in the Civil War; child labor was a "formidable foe" against higher learning; "ring politicians" sought to keep the voters uneducated and malleable for their own purposes; and the modern college hero was the football player instead of the scholar. The argument that football playing developed "big men in after life" seemed particularly fallacious to Wister, and he pointed out that Abraham Lincoln, Ulysses S. Grant, Cornelius Vanderbilt, and John Jacob Astor had prospered in practical life without the aid of football. (The sport was based on "vanity" and the "female lust for gore," he claimed.)[21]

In short, conditions for academic excellence simply were lacking in America. The rewards to be gained were insignificant in money and in social recognition. Despite these amplifications, the speech—intended to ignite a spark for the nation to support its scholars in grander style—had instead cast Wister in the role of enemy of American scholarship.[22] The debate he had started, regardless of the wounds suffered, aroused his aggressive instincts even further. He now was ready to join his friend Roosevelt in the arena of politics.

Philadelphia's local political scene, dominated by the Republican Party, long had been earmarked by "bossism." A flurry of reformism in 1905 and 1906, which Wister and his wife had supported with contributions and work, had loosened only momentarily the iron grip of the local GOP faithfuls. Wister, nominally a Republican himself, refused to identify with the local organization because he believed it to be thoroughly corrupt. As a result of the reform movement of 1905 and 1906, he had been inspired to write a muckraking article for *Everybody's*, "Keystone Crime; Philadelphia Corrupt and Contented," which examined unethical tactics of the local Republicans. "My whole soul was stirred," he said later of what he had learned, and he realized that there were "some duties I owe to those about me besides writing books."[23]

This sense of duty was prodded more specifically when a City Party official called on him at his office at 328 Chestnut Street. The City Party wanted to draft Wister as its candidate in the Seventh Ward for the Select Council. Most of the voters in the Seventh Ward were black. As Wister would recall some twenty years later, the request so startled him that the visitor had to repeat it. "That's perfectly ridiculous. I should make no sort of select councilman. I've no training," Wister remembered replying. The City Party official assured him that there was not the "slightest chance" he would win, but insisted that it was necessary to have a good candidate for the sake of maintaining the organization of the reformist City Party. (The ward was acknowledged to be tightly held by the Republican machine which dominated city and state politics. United States Senator Boies Penrose, with whom Wister had hunted in Wyoming, was the acknowledged kingmaker of that organization.) Despite the overwhelming odds against his election, Wister agreed to be the City Party candidate.[24]

The announcement that one of the nation's most famous novelists was running for political office warranted headlines across the nation. His candidacy shocked staid Philadelphia. A newspaper feature asked: "Why is Owen Wister running for office? Why is this most distinguished member of one of Philadelphia's patriarchal and patrician families seeking election to Select Council from the Seventh Ward? Why is this big, genial American, who has found fame and fortune in authorship, waging a red-hot campaign as a City party candidate in a ward bottled and corked by the Gang and locked away in its dark cellar of civic degradation?" In answer to such questions, Wister told an inquiring reporter that recent revelations about corruption in Pennsylvania had convinced him that he must not shirk his citizen's duty. He claimed no interest in a political career, for "book-writing" was his work, and even if the race proved futile he at least would have "kept alive and strengthened" the principles of the City Party. Outside his house a new blue and yellow City Party flag gaily signaled the occupant's commitment to the cause of civic reform.[25]

Two weeks after his decision to run he made his first speech before a large crowd of independent voters who greeted him at Assembly Hall with loud, sustained applause. As one newspaper account stated, he "plunged into the heart of his subject like an experienced politician and stump speaker." He stressed the need for a renewal of reform principles, and he charged the "bosses" with raising taxes but not providing services in return. "Figures show that there has been nearly $125,000,000 increase in assessments in four years. Have we taxpayers got our money's worth of the revenue from this? Are Philadelphia's schools up to date? Are her streets clean? And now they talk of raising the tax from $1.50 to $2."[26]

Despite the attention he inevitably received in an active campaign, Wister remained an underdog. The newspapers wrote of a whirlwind campaign involving house-to-house canvassing. A colorful wagon bedecked with such signs as "Stop the Coin Clippers in Councils" and "No Tax-eating by Contractors" paraded daily up and down the Seventh Ward streets southwest of Independence Hall, urging a vote for Wister. But the campaign manager for his opponent Seger boasted that if Wister won as many as five hundred of the expected four thousand votes, he would move out of the Seventh Ward. His confidence seemed aptly placed, for the Seger political machine was an effective one among the ward's predominantly black voters.[27]

This effectiveness particularly irritated Wister, for he was convinced that Seger's black partisans supported him because of bribes instead of logic. It was the policy of the "organization," Wister charged in a handbill, to "keep as many voters as possible, especially colored voters, in ignorance." He blamed the "organization," a word he ultimately stiffened by shortening to "gang," with bringing to the ward "dirty streets, dirty water, dirty air, and dirty politics." He was "sick and tired" of seeing substantial rises in real estate tax assessments with no visible returns. The futility of the race for Wister was epitomized by an elderly black man quoted by the *Philadelphia Daily Evening Telegraph*: "Mistah Wistah am a gen'men of de highest quality. He represents de essence of de 'ristocrats, and am a mighty fine man. But he can't get us no jobs like Mistah Seger."[28]

When Wister spoke to a group of Negroes in an upstairs meeting room someone placed a box of free cigars at the top of the stairway. He subsequently was "exposed" for using cigars as bribes, although a black newspaper, *The Pilot*, sought to exonerate him from any association with the cigars and quoted him as saying in the speech that he had "no jobs to offer, none to promise and no promises for the colored man for his personal benefit." Up and down the ward Wister campaigned in this forthright manner with a message that the voters did not necessarily want to hear. He spoke in "stinking halls amid rank tobacco smoke to dirty niggers and dingy whites." Wherever he went he was cheered by an accompanying band of supporters. As the campaign progressed he found it "extraordinarily good fun."[29]

"The only issue in the 7th Ward campaign is the issue of HONESTY," he proclaimed as the February election day approached. A campaign leaflet stated:

> Honesty may be stated in subheadings, such as, Police out of Politics, Protection of Property, Firemen out of politics. No Blackmail assessments, Decent Streets, Up-to-Date Schools, Clean Water, Cheap Gas. Honesty covers all these. Honesty also covers JUSTICE to our 3000 colored voters, instead of GANG ENSLAVEMENT by vote purchase or threat. I invite those who believe in honesty to vote for me. I invite those who don't to vote for the Gang. I want the support of none who deems this 7th Ward should be the sanctuary of gamblers, crooks and ill-fame.[30]

Sweeping charges such as this won him no support from influential organs like the *Philadelphia Inquirer*, which declared that Wister, "a writer of romance," knew nothing about such matters. His mistake, the newspaper editorialized, was in thinking that the people of Philadelphia wanted to hear that their government was the rottenest in the union. The muckraker's day had passed, and the "dreamy and romantic Mr. Wister" made little impression because "the man who is eternally defaming and tearing down and never building up is not wanted."[31]

An aristocratic Philadelphian who despised labor, who favored tighter controls over immigration, who was an innate conservative, who thought the black race inferior, and yet who campaigned as a reformer may seem today to be an odd sort. Yet Wister fit an established mold for elitist reformers of the era, described by Richard Hofstadter as the old-family, college-educated class that had deep ancestral roots in local communities, belonged to patriotic societies and the best clubs, staffed the boards of philanthropic and cultural institutions, and led movements for civic betterment. Such people, and certainly this would include Wister, had a sense that their rightful role of leadership in American life had been preempted by the agents of the new corporations, the corrupters of legislatures, the buyers of franchises, and the allies of the political losses. Surely Wister was influenced more immediately by Molly, whose aggressive involvement in civic and educational issues placed her family within the camp of urban progressives who through municipal politics were seeking to restructure the social order to fit their own priorities of specialization, education, and bureaucratic order.[32]

As his gentlemanly station in life seemed to dictate, on election morning Wister slept his usual number of hours, ate a hearty, relaxed breakfast, and leisurely cast his ballot at 9:30 A.M. When reporters asked him if he had voted for himself he acknowledged only that he voted for City Party candidates. Afterwards, he strolled to his campaign headquarters at 915 Lombard Street, just a block from his house on Pine Street, and conferred with his supporters. Then, dressed fashionably in a fur lined, Persian lamb–collared coat, he drove in his automobile to the twenty-seven districts of the Seventh Ward, where receptions awaited. His opponent's election-day actions stood sharply in contrast. Seger appeared at his own polling place as soon as it opened at 7 A.M. and cast the first ballot there. Then, surrounded by his supporters, he walked rather than rode into the remaining districts.[33]

Wister was not surprised by the results at the end of the day. He lost by a 5 to 1 margin. Seger had 3,458 votes; Wister, 646. The "gang" had maintained its domination throughout the city. Wister accepted defeat graciously and predicted that ultimately his cause would triumph and graft would be expelled from public affairs. "I was never more hopeful than now," he said to a reporter in his home. In view of the one-sided returns, the reporter asked, on what could he base his optimism? Wister's response was: "The better classes are growing discontented. When they become fully aroused, and I believe they will arrive at that point suddenly, graft will be dealt a fatal blow." For the moment, however, he blamed the "best people" of Philadelphia for failing to vote and for permitting by default the election of unfit men. "If by not going to the polls they allowed men to go in office that rob the city, are they not morally guilty of the crimes of the grafters?" The answer seemed obvious to Wister, and he continued, "For years the rich young men of Philadelphia have been a dormant mass." Until recently, he acknowledged, he would have included himself as one of those privileged few. His evident sincerity led the reporter to describe him afterwards as a "man with a new conviction" whose voice was steady and forceful and who was determined to work until his ideals were reached.[34]

The nation's press was not so sympathetic in its coverage. Once again Wister found himself the target of their sharpest barbs. "Novelist Owen Wister tried politics in Philadelphia and the expected votes on his side proved to be largely fiction," wrote the *Canton* (Ohio) *Repository*. An editorial cartoon in the *Pittsburgh Gazette Times* entitled "A Tenderfoot in the Bad Lands" portrayed an astonished Wister being thrown rudely on his posterior by a bucking horse labeled "Politics" while a smiling Theodore Roosevelt, seated comfortably on another horse, looked on. More sympathetic was the *Milwaukee Journal*, which noted that Wister's opponent was "the wise and seasoned veteran of a hundred ward contests and a cog in one of the most powerful machines in the country for delivering the goods on election day."[35]

Despite the prediction by the Philadelphia reporter that Wister was determined to move forward in a new capacity as a politician, Wister never stood for public office again. There may have been more sting in defeat than he acknowledged. Not long afterwards he urged Roosevelt not to accept an invitation to Philadelphia's celebration of "Founders Week" because it was sponsored by the "corrupt and criminal organization" in control of the city. He also reproached the president for having spoken recently at the unveiling of the new Capitol at Harrisburg.

Roosevelt assured Wister that he would not be in Philadelphia for Founders Week, but as for declining to visit any state capital, governor, or legislature, that was not realistic.[36]

Wister's brief flurry with reform politics led Henry James to join him in lamenting the "deplorable & disgusting" state of the nation's public affairs. The question was not whether thievery and corruption existed, James wrote to Wister, but how to measure its extent. Lying, cheating, and stealing were so universal that candidates were praised nowadays for the mere virtue of being honest. The only things remaining in life that he believed in, James said, were art and friendship. Even science had played "straight into the hands of the Swindlers."[37]

If disappointed in politics, Wister still could win praise for his writing. *The Seven Ages of Washington*, just published, was—despite Wister's announced intentions—little more than an apotheosis of the man at seven stages of his life. Still, most reviewers agreed with Henry James that the book was "vivid & charming . . . with great art & much taste." Henry Adams, perhaps as fine a historian as James was a novelist, also sent his compliments on the book. Yet its limitations soon were recognized by the reviewer for the *American Historical Review*. The reviewer, John Spencer Bassett, wrote that the portrait revealed Wister's "crude historical knowledge" and contained many statements inconsistent with themselves. Even the author's avowed reason for having written—the ordinary biographer of Washington had presented a "frozen image" of the man—was said to be a mistaken one. The informed reader would find Wister's work "unreliable," and the uninformed reader would be given "an erroneous view." Even Wister's style was said to contain "crude expressions." In short, this study of Washington, no less than the predecessors which Wister criticized, was "idealized beyond reality."[38]

Such an assessment, printed in an academic journal of limited circulation, did little to tarnish Wister's favorable image as fostered in more popular publications such as the *Bookman*. Here, Edward Clark Marsh, in appraising the entire body of his work, declared Wister to be "the accredited social historian of the Western frontier," as well as the leading American writer of comedy. "I doubt if a survey of the total of American fiction would reveal a sustained comedy to place beside *Lady Baltimore* for grace and strength, for the insight and the spirit that will awaken thoughtful laughter," Marsh wrote. The quality that stood out saliently in all of Wister's writings, according to Marsh, was his American patriotism. The critic saw no need now to measure the intrinsic value of his work, for "all that can safely be said is that he is not through with literature." (In fact, however, Wister virtually *was* "through with literature." But no one could have suspected that.) In the formal portrait accompanying Marsh's article Wister looked, as always, the picture of health. He gazed confidently from his chair into the camera lens and looked rather regal in his light suit, vest, and high collar. He appeared to be far younger than his forty-eight years. His appearance, as well as his writing, was, as Ford Madox Hueffer wrote in England, "distinctly American."[39]

Still another milestone was passed in June 1908. Sarah Butler Wister, undoubtedly the most important influence on her son's life, died at Butler Place. Death came as no surprise: she had been seriously ill for several months. Within hours Wister sent the sad news to Henry James because he wanted her friend "to hear at once . . . straight from me." For three days Sarah lay in state at Butler Place for her friends and relatives to see and to mourn. Wister recalled his grandmother Fanny Kemble's observation that Sarah's gifts had been "utterly squandered" in Philadelphia, that she "was fitted to grace a high state in the brilliant and great world." The news stories inevitably described her as Owen Wister's mother and Fanny Kemble's daughter, and the injustice of such an epitaph tempted Wister to write the papers to set it right. But he did not, for he decided that those who knew Sarah Wister already knew of her distinction, and those who didn't did not matter.[40]

One practical aspect of Sarah's death was that her only son became the owner of Butler Place. The Wister family accordingly moved from Philadelphia's crowded city streets to the spacious country estate in Germantown. The place remained as attractive as ever, especially to the four children, ages four to nine. The lemon, citron, and oleander trees Fanny Kemble had planted in red wooden tubs still were there, cared for by the same gardener who now had served three generations of the family. A collection of ponies permitted the children to gallop happily around the drive encircling the main house and up and down the lawn between the double avenue of maples also planted by Fanny Kemble. In the hallway hung two framed letters from George Washington to Pierce Butler, Sr. The parlor walls were adorned by five portraits of the Kemble family thespians. The "Morning Room," in which Sarah Wister had written and conversed with the cultural gods, was converted into a bird room, where various finches and canaries and Wister's pet mockingbird, Gabriel, were caged. It was in the happy surroundings of Butler

Place that the children would remember their father playing the piano and singing to them "with gusto in his clear, ringing voice." The music ranged from Offenbach's light operas to Wister's own composition, "Ten Thousand Cattle Straying." Their favorite tune, though, was "Here I come, Dum de Dum, I'm a Plum, Dum de Dum, My appearance puts others on the bum."[41]

The same year of Sarah Wister's death Charles D. Skirdin reappeared in Wister's life, this time under unpleasant circumstances. Skirdin, whose bravery had so impressed Wister years earlier in Arizona Territory, had become a Philadelphia policeman. In November, however, he was called before a coroner's jury on a charge of first-degree murder. Skirdin had been assigned to a notoriously rough section of the city to cope with a gang of hoodlums. After a series of confrontations, he encountered resistance when he attempted to make the youths disperse. Shouts and shoves ensued, and Skirdin became so alarmed that, as he later would testify, he fired twice into the ground in self-defense. One youth, James Bradley, fell to the ground mortally wounded, evidently struck by a ricochet. Skirdin said he had been convinced that the gang would have killed him had he not fired warning shots. A score of witnesses, most of them friends of the dead youth, contradicted him, claiming that Skirdin had shot the young man deliberately and without provocation. As the hearing progressed, the gang milled about outside the courtroom, muttering threats of retribution if justice were not done. It was under these circumstances that Wister, answering the summons of his friend Skirdin, entered the courtroom to testify in his behalf. Wister's testimony, as a newspaper reported, was "brief and to the point." He described how he had met Skirdin in 1893 at Fort Bowie, Arizona, when Skirdin was a corporal in the United States Cavalry and assigned as Wister's guide. His courage and faithfulness, Wister said, had made a deep impression. "That man embodies all the characteristics of the hero of my novel, 'The Virginian,'" Wister told the jury. "While no person was the actual prototype of the character, Skirdin, more than any man, embodies the type. . . . I often hunted with him and he was absolutely fearless, but exceptionally quiet and peace-loving."[42]

After thirty minutes' deliberation the jury returned to the courtroom and declared that there was no substance to the charge of first-degree murder. Skirdin would not have to stand trial. Wister and city officials rushed to congratulate him; Skirdin thanked them through a tearstained face; the dead youth's mother collapsed into the arms of her two daughters at the supposed injustice of the decision.[43]

The impact of Wister's testimony, as far as his own life and career were concerned, was that for the first and last time he had identified an individual as a prototype of the Virginian. The fact that the character of the Virginian actually had been introduced in his fiction *before* he ever met Skirdin was forgotten, as were the restrictions imposed by Wister's comment that Skirdin merely embodied the type—not that he actually provided the inspiration. It was not a distinction that Wister sought to explain, for Skirdin was a true friend, and Wister quite deliberately had connected him to his literary creation. The result was that Skirdin hereafter would be identified erroneously as the man who had inspired *The Virginian.* As the *Philadelphia Evening Telegraph* reported three years later, "When Wister was forecasting about for a hero in 'the Virginian,' he found a good subject in his guide [Skirdin]."[44]

Skirdin also found himself being quizzed by reporters about Wister as a Westerner. He told the *St. Louis Star* that Wister was a "good rider" and not at all like most eastern gentlemen who went to the West and "put on superior airs." Asked if he thought he himself was "the Virginian," Skirdin could say only that he did not know. He had not read the book. To the St. Louis newspaper reporter Skirdin certainly *appeared* to be like the character. He was tall, wiry, and strong; he had the "loose, easy gait" of the Westerner; his face was rugged and doubtless handsome at an earlier age; and his eyes were "softly blue" and his expression gentle.[45]

Not long after Skirdin's hearing Wister heeded a call from the president to bring his entire family to the White House for lunch during the first week of January 1909. For the occasion the two boys and two girls dressed in white piqué suits and dresses and all wore their dark hair shoulder-length. In this elegant attire they slid back and forth on the East Room's polished floor, marveled at the pistol that the president's bodyguard, Major Archie Butt, quietly showed them, and dined afterwards on lamb chops and rice. Dessert was for them a disappointment: they were offered shiny red apples.[46]

This was to be Wister's last visit to the White House, for the president's days there were approaching an end. William Howard Taft was inaugurated in early March, and Roosevelt departed on an African safari. Roosevelt and Wister had gained prestige and power simultaneously; henceforth, they would be on the outside looking in, both in politics and in literature.

Chapter XIV

TRIBULATIONS
(1909–1914)

"WHAT WITH ELECTRICITY, AND STEAM AND JOURNALISTIC ENTER-
PRISES," Charles Francis Adams wrote to Wister in 1908, "the whole
world now occupies the stage at once. The babel of voices is deafening."
The age of the masses had begun. No longer would the educated and
privileged bestow fame and prestige; that power was shifting to the mass
public. Adams and a perceptive few recognized this fact. Leaders in government, business, journalism, education, and religion more and more
were seeking approval from the popular crowd, not from the elite few.
Genteel habits such as dressing for dinner were being forsaken. Class
distinctions noted in everyday clothing were disappearing. Wister did not
approve. As a young man he had rebelled from many of his parents'
unyielding guidelines for conduct; now he firmly supported the old code.
He had a deep sense that the country already had crossed a dividing line
over which it never could return. In common with John Jay Chapman—
and they discussed the subject often—Wister thought he detected increasing signs of materialism and intellectual laziness, and he detested
that fact. The democratization of the American political system through
broadened suffrage and direct election of United States senators had made
government worse instead of better, Wister thought. Jews, Catholics,
and working classes whose numbers included many eastern and southern
European immigrants were gaining, to his dismay, in power and influence just as the authority of the landed gentry declined. The new age
was not one that Wister could accept.[1]

The neurasthenia which so frequently plagued Wister and those of
his social class was a classic symptom of difficulty in accepting these
changes. As one contemporary neurologist explained it, the necessary
adaptation drained much nervous energy. Vertigo, headaches, depression,
and heart palpitations were common complaints among genteel families.
Life, as historian Stow Persons has pointed out, in fact was not easy for
the leisure class, for they bore "a heavy burden of cultural responsibilities

at the same time they were attempting to perpetuate the elaborate uses of gentility."[2]

Wister, having issued a vigorous protest against a resurrected proposal to institute a federal income tax, took to bed once more in the spring of 1909 with "nervous dyspepsia." According to a Philadelphia newspaper, he was "seized by illness" and suffered extreme physical weakness and nervous depression. For the remainder of the year he did little but dedicate himself to recovery. By his own estimation he spent one of every three days in bed, isolated from the children and entertained primarily by the singing of "Gabriel," his pet mockingbird. His writing abruptly ceased; for the next three years his only new work to appear in print was a sixteen-line poem in *Harper's Monthly.*[3]

Wister could not have been cheered by a news story originating in early summer 1909 at a national conference in Baltimore on the status of the Negro, where one of the key speakers was his old nemesis, Professor Burt G. Wilder of Cornell University. Before a distinguished audience which included such men as John Dewey, Wilder ridiculed Wister's view of the Negro. He told the audience in detail of his exchange with Wister over his absurd contrast in *Lady Baltimore* of a Caucasian's skull with those of a Negro and an ape. "A more monstrous perversion of facts I do not remember to have seen," exclaimed Professor Wilder. Despite evidence he had personally presented the novelist to show that the Negro skull and the Caucasian skull were similar instead of distinct, Wilder said the novelist had persisted in a mistaken belief that the skulls of the Negro and the ape were closer. The press gave wide coverage to Wilder's comments; Wister offered no defense. Years later, either Molly Wister or one of the children, upon finding a newspaper clipping describing the controversy, inscribed on it: "Is it possible that you could have done this thing? For your sake, I hope not."[4]

Molly, an unusually sturdy and efficient woman, once again held the household together to permit her husband his frequent isolation and recovery periods. Somehow, she not only managed to be mother, wife, and the director of household affairs, but also continued her civic endeavors in a manner befitting a descendant of William Ellery Channing. While this aspect of her life had worried Wister early in their marriage because it violated the traditional role he envisioned for his wife, he had grown to accept it. Molly served as chairperson of the Philadelphia Civic Club's state committee on civics, and she was on the board of the Playgrounds Association of Philadelphia. She led a statewide campaign to clean up streets and yards, to plant trees, to force merit appointments for policemen and firemen, to install street lights, to insure wholesome public drinking water, to improve the quality of schools, and to organize the women of the state to further these goals. She initiated and led a Civic Club drive to persuade the Philadelphia School Board to adopt a new curriculum. Her goal was to integrate vocational studies with academic training, rather than to offer the former as an afterthought in the concluding semester of a student's school year. In brief, Molly wholeheartedly joined in the movements by urban progressives to institute civic and educational reforms. Despite the pressures of her demanding life, she, in contrast to her husband, never seemed to suffer illnesses or nervous exhaustion. Her steadiness was an important factor in her husband's successes.[5]

In February 1910, Wister, Molly, their youngest son William Rotch, and a nursemaid departed for California on a leisurely train trip through the Southwest. When the nursemaid, a Miss Morgan, became ill in El Paso they stopped there for a few days. The waiter at the hotel restaurant both amused and insulted Wister by asking him each night if he would have a "demy tass," explaining pointedly, "coffee, you know." "I do not understand why my talk and appearance should lead him to suppose I know nothing & have been nowhere, but by encouraging this impression I learn a great deal from him," Wister observed. One afternoon, sitting on a bench in the sun outside the library, Wister watched with delight as two boys tied a string to a rubber snake, concealed themselves, and terrorized passersby by pulling the snake across their paths. Wister laughed "so disgracefully" at the boys' successes that he had to leave for fear of being implicated.[6]

Soon after, Wister checked into the Loma Linda Sanatorium near San Bernardino, California—a quiet, beautiful place with a marvelous view of the Redlands Valley and the San Bernardino Mountains. The sanatorium was operated in strict fashion by Seventh-Day Adventists. Their special diet had no meat but many substitutes, as well as ample fruits, fresh vegetables, olives, honey, and milk. Another part of the routine was a series of hot and cold baths, steam baths, and "electric light baths." At the end of his allotted three weeks, Wister was highly pleased with his progress.[7]

Not long after his return in midsummer to Butler Place, however, it became clear that Wister still was not fully recovered from his mysterious malady. Even though magazine editors clamored for his work (the

New York Sun described him as one of a handful of authors who earned one thousand dollars for a single story*), he simply could not concentrate. The muckraking *Hampton's Magazine* implored him to write a series of stories, and publisher Benjamin B. Hampton promised to "get back of them and push them" if only Wister would write the series. But Wister could not comply. His main concern was full recovery. He wanted to feel rested each morning instead of tired, he declared. Recovery, he prayed, would permit him to throw away the aromatic ammonia and veronal upon which he was beginning to rely more and more. As he continued to despair of recovery at home in Philadelphia he concluded that once again he should take a rest cure away from friends and family.[8]

Perhaps, he thought, the old magic of Wyoming would work. He arranged to stay at a ranch owned by S. W. Aldrich east of Yellowstone National Park near the tiny town of Ishawooa. In August, accompanied by a young companion named Walter Smith, Wister traveled across the continent by train to get there. Reporters who learned that the famous author was passing through their towns clamored for interviews, but Wister invariably refused. In Minneapolis a persistent female reporter lingered for forty-five minutes, but he outwaited her. Wister, so he said privately, was embarrassed to be seen because he had gained weight, and he especially wanted no ladies to see him.[9]

On the eve of his arrival at the Aldrich ranch, Wister spent the night at a hotel in Cody, Wyoming, owned by none other than Colonel William F. "Buffalo Bill" Cody. Buffalo Bill was not on the premises of his Irma Hotel, but his sister, a Mrs. Dekker, and her henpecked husband Louis were there as managers. Wister told Molly by letter what the noisy Mrs. Dekker said—in a rush of words—as soon as she saw the author the morning after his arrival.

> I'm just going to introduce myself without waiting a bit longer. I didn't yesterday because they said you were tired and didn't want to see people but you don't look tired a bit and I want to tell you how much I like your book and Looey, K'em here! K'em here, Looey. I want to introduce you to . . . er . . . what's the name, please?[10]

At the Aldrich ranch, where eastern boarders frequently stayed, Wister immediately adopted his old routine of sleeping outdoors in a

---

* The others were Sir Arthur Conan Doyle, Sir Gilbert Parker, William Dean Howells, Robert W. Chambers, Rex Beach, Jack London, and Richard Harding Davis. High above these was Rudyard Kipling, who earned as much as $2500 for a short story.

tent. He did not feel strong enough at first for horseback riding, so he exercised by walking short distances and fishing. At first Wyoming could generate no magic. Wister even suffered from homesickness. The sight of Molly's handwriting made him so lonesome, he claimed, that he nearly cried. "The only thing that can atone for the separation," he told her, "is that I shall come home a long way on the road to health & strength, if not completely well—& be able to do some of my share in the responsibilities of our life." Molly handled an uncommonly large share of their mutual responsibilities, he acknowledged, and the best way to repay her was to "regain health & cease to be so useless and such a care."[11]

What were the causes of these mysterious ailments that so frequently plagued Wister? How necessary were his rest treatments? In the absence of physical evidence, it is impossible to speak with authority, but Americans of the upper classes in the late nineteenth and early twentieth centuries seemed preoccupied with nervous ailments. They thought they knew the causes, and the man who best described them was a physician named George M. Beard, who in 1881 published *American Nervousness: Its Causes and Consequences*. Beard placed the blame primarily on modern civilization, and those who suffered nervous disorders because of it were not "muscle-workers," but the relatively few "brain-workers" who carried the responsibility for civilizing the nation and preventing its regression to barbarism. The advent of new forces in modern life—such as the invention of watches and the resulting strains caused by a desire for punctuality, the telegraph which now permitted more business to be conducted in less time, and energy-draining noises brought about by the industrial age—placed far greater burdens on the nervous system than ever before. "The capacity of the nervous system for sustained work and worry has not increased in proportion to the demand for work and worry that are made upon it," Beard wrote, and the result was a proliferation of nervous disorders as never before seen. He further theorized that instances of neurasthenia would multiply as modern civilization progressed and imposed even more loads on man's finite nervous system. Wister never wrote directly of such theories, but as a writer he felt an ongoing need to keep his nervous system as free from outside interferences as possible if he were to do his work. Up to this point in his life he had shown no ability to discard the hypochondria that his mother had warned him about as a child. Suppositions such as Beard's, accepted widely as fact, conveniently provided Wister with a "factual" basis for his hypochondria.[12]

Wister's program of restoration for this illness started slowly. After a couple of hours of fishing, the stones in the river hurt his feet; climbing took away his breath; mild activity caused every bone in his body to ache. Inevitably, though, a good night's sleep restored him. He reasoned that if his muscles were growing stronger, surely a gain in "nerves & vitality" would follow. He wrote to John Jay Chapman in early September that he could feel the fountain of health "stirring deep inside me." Walter Smith cautiously reported to Molly that "Mr. Wister is gradually improving." One sign of progress, Wister boasted, was that he had not used aromatic ammonia since the train left Chicago, and he slept well at night without the help of veronal.[13]

Wyoming seemed overrun with Easterners. Parties of hunters with packhorses constantly filed into the mountains. In earlier years Wister sometimes had not seen a single other party while hunting. Now there were so many that it seemed "they'd be as likely to shoot each other as game."[14]

Soon, however, Wister began to adjust emotionally to the new environment, enjoying conversations with the Aldriches and their other boarders. He heard lurid gossip about drinking problems of previous eastern boarders, and he assumed that most natives around the Aldrich ranch figured that he, too, was an alcoholic in retreat.[15]

His own retreat was not in as remote a place as he had expected, for he soon learned that William James's son was staying seven miles up the river. Young James was a "nice boy," and he gave the sad news that both his father and his uncle, Henry, were in wretched shape. The brothers were together now at Chocorua, sharing their bad health. The day after Wister relayed the news of their illnesses to Molly he received a letter from "poor Henry James," feeling better himself but especially worried about William.[16]

September brought unusually frigid air to the northern Rockies, and Wister surrendered his tent for a log cabin. Smith came in at 7:45 A.M. each morning to light a small stove before his employer washed and dressed. "The log cabin is full of chinks through which daylight can plainly be seen, and as I sleep with the door wide open to the world I think I really get as much fresh air, if not more, than I did in the tent," Wister wrote to Molly. He was confident that his routine of exercise and constant fresh air would be exactly what Jack Mitchell preferred for him, and he used more tranquil moments to read English classics like *Canterbury Tales* and Edmund Spenser's *The Faerie Queene*.[17]

Back home, Molly was uncertain what plans to make for the family during the winter. Would her husband be with them or not? Wister replied that there was little doubt but that he would have to be away. "Just assume that, and go ahead with your plans," he told her. He did intend to return briefly in November, and he vowed that he would be in better shape at that time than he had been for years. Afterwards, he would spend the winter much closer to home—Charleston, Summerville, or Ashville—so that occasional visits would be possible. "It is plain to me," he told her, "that my business is to get well. I can be of no use to you or any one until I do, and until I am able to take up my profession again and publish something important, I shall be blue and without peace of mind." His progress thus far gave reason for high spirits even after the past two rough years, he assured her.[18]

It required two weeks for a letter to go between Wyoming and Philadelphia, but Molly was determined to keep her husband involved in household decisions. Should a former servant be rehired? Yes, Wister answered, but only as a waiter because the family's "irregular way" of living would cause his deterioration as it had for everybody else. Should the children keep a pet monkey? Yes. What should be done with the royalty checks from Harper & Brothers and Macmillan? For all these questions Wister gave precise instructions.[19]

The greatest problem to emerge during his absence concerned Butler Place. The spread of Philadelphia's suburbs now threatened it on all sides. Molly was confronted directly by the City of Philadelphia, which wanted to build a street through the property. Wister began sending desperate telegrams to oppose the move, and his correspondence with Molly became dominated by discussion of the problem and advice on what she should do. He feared that Butler Place would no longer be habitable because a housing development surely would follow the new street; taxes would be raised; sale of the property would become inevitable. "Unless we can go on living there in some degree of peace and privacy, I must sell, and it is of very material importance indeed that I get the highest price I can," Wister declared. If it were to be sold he could accept no less than ten thousand dollars an acre; if it should be assessed for taxes at that price he could not afford to keep it. Moreover, the house was in disrepair; it needed gas or electricity; it was defenseless against burglars; it needed a new drainage system; and the area was growing noisier and more crowded with undesirable people and things. The problem was still complicated by the fact that some of the land surrounding Butler Place was owned jointly with Aunt Fanny. "It is desperately annoying and hampering to own property in common with people who live a mile off; but when they're across the sea words fail to characterize the situation," Wister proclaimed in exasperation.[20]

For her part, Molly wanted to continue living at Butler Place for as long as possible because of its advantages for the children. She was willing to act as forcefully as she possibly could to preserve the property's integrity, but she suggested that the present emergency required her husband's return so that he could handle it himself. Meanwhile, she would seek a postponement of final action by the council. Agitated though he was, Wister declined to return unless it were certain that what he might accomplish would be more beneficial than his physical recovery. "Short of being able to do something that you and Flood [the attorney representing the Wisters] can't do, my presence at home would be an injury to us all, for I would break down to a certainty." He had dreaded, since at least 1896, the certain prospects of city streets crossing the Butler Place domain, and his father on his death bed had worried that Sarah Wister would have to face the problem. It was clear that Butler Place obstructed the suburban growth of Philadelphia. "As it is not we who have the political influence but those who will be benefitted by the opening of the streets, our position is not very strong & can't be made so," Wister said.[21]

The crisis presently subsided. For the moment the property would remain inviolate, but Wister still favored selling it. Molly presented a list of reasons as to why they should remain there, no matter what. Wister reluctantly agreed. "Only one of my reasons against it remains— money. If I can afford it, there is nothing more in the way; and I suppose the only means to find out if I can afford it is to try it."[22]

Despite the turmoil over Butler Place, Wister felt stronger. "If I continue to improve at the present rate, I am almost certain I need not go away for the winter," he wrote home. Molly was skeptical, having seen too many sudden illnesses, but Wister reassured her, "Why nothing but calamity would keep me from being with you & the children at Christmas."[23]

A man who could ride horseback for fourteen miles, without resting, on two consecutive days, as Wister did at the end of November, certainly was not far from being in prime physical condition, and his emotional state was improving too. He began and completed a short story, a simple tale entitled "The Drake Who Had Means of his Own," about some strange-acting ducks he watched from his cabin window. On December 6 he left the ranch as promised, but the closer his train carried him to the East, the worse he felt. In Chicago he got off the train to spend several days in a hotel bed. Whatever it was that plagued him was to remain with him, for after arriving home he was unable to resume his normal writing pace. He learned that Aunt Fanny had died in England. A week later on Christmas day a cousin died in Philadelphia. Wister was so depressed that four days after Christmas he still had not opened any of his presents. "The mechanical details of daily existence are a good thing at these times, if one can attend to them," he wrote to John Jay Chapman. Despite his depression, the short story he managed to write in Wyoming about the ducks enabled him a few months later to bring out a collection of short stories, the first of which had been written in 1900. It was entitled *Members of the Family*, and he dedicated it to Philadelphia's Shakespearean scholar and physician, Horace Howard Furness.[24]

In the early summer of 1911, Wister had recovered sufficiently to depart with Molly and the children for the West and never-to-be-forgotten adventures. The itinerary included an automobile trip between Wyoming and California. From July 7 until July 30 they were "imprisoned" in Salt Lake City by the illness of one of the children. It was "a perfectly horrible place, all asphalt, heat, and Mormons." Then they went to the first of many dude ranches soon to dot the Jackson Hole, Wyoming, area—the JY Ranch at Phelps Lake—for a three-month stay. Five days after their arrival, a telegram announced the death of Molly's father, and, as fate so often seemed to dictate to her on vacation, she returned to Philadelphia, leaving the rest of the family behind. Reunion came later in Idaho, where the family crossed into Yellowstone National Park to camp for a week before driving their two wagon teams back to the JY Ranch. The visit, certainly for the children, was like nothing they ever had experienced. The beautiful Teton country and the western characters there held boundless fascination. The four children—Mary Channing, 11; the twins Owen and Fanny, 9; and William Rotch, 7—had a log cabin of their own next to their parents' cabin. They fished, hunted, rode, hiked, and enjoyed the breathtaking scenery. On one "superbly beautiful day," September 20, three of the four children celebrated simultaneous birthdays. For celebration, Wister took all the children by horseback to the Snake River, which they forded, and then they caught twenty-four fish amid great excitement. Nearly fifty years later the memory of that remarkable summer seemed as fresh as ever to Fanny.

> Mostly we rode, I bareback for miles each day. Fording Snake River, loping through the sagebrush with no trail, we went into the foothills as far as our laboring horses could climb. We were not too young to be stunned with admiration by the Tetons, and we loved the acres of wild flowers growing up their slopes. . . . We were not awed by the wilderness, feeling that the Grand Teton was our own mountain and the most wonderful mountain in the world, and the Snake River the fastest, longest river in America. We could ride all day and never get past the Tetons. When we returned to the ranch in the late afternoon, we would ride up the brief slope and suddenly Phelps Lake would appear in front of us.

The children intently studied the ranch's colorful and wrinkled wrangler, for they knew he was the "real thing"; they learned from their father to dry fly-fish in the cold, clear streams; and they came to disregard the dead flies so often found between their flapjacks at breakfast. They nursed to life a wounded mouse hawk, given up for dead, and in late summer they rode far up into the foothills to watch the first slain elk being skinned. With snow in September it was time to return to Philadelphia.[25]

The stay had been at least as invigorating for Wister as for the children. Inspired to establish a permanent link to this land which had meant so much to him, he purchased a 160-acre tract within walking distance of the JY Ranch. During this happy time he outlined a new novel. Tentatively entitled "The Star Gazers," it was to be, like *Lady Baltimore*, a novel of manners about a flirtatious female astrologer who brought chaos to a respectable circle of friends. One of the characters would be Augustus from *Lady Baltimore*. He took a risk with the plot—the ending he planned was not a happy one. To write it otherwise would be a demeaning concession to the popular crowd which demanded happy endings and which "positively forbids the American girl to be anything but an angel of purity in the novelist's hands." And he certainly did not intend to sacrifice art for the sake of the masses—he feared he already had committed that sin.[26]

At a stopover in Denver en route home, Wister bemoaned this state of affairs to a newspaper reporter in the lobby of the Brown Palace Hotel. Why should American novels end happily when life so frequently did not? "Real life," he said, "is deep in its contrasts of light and shadow." The best source for plots could be found in the daily newspaper, he asserted. American literature's fundamental need, he believed, was to portray reality and truth.[27]

As for himself, Wister told the reporter that his health now was restored. He had conceived of plots for several novels during his western visit, and he was departing the next day with his family for Philadelphia, where he hoped to produce a novel within a year. The reporter noted "a jovial twinkle" lurking in the famous writer's brown eyes. He described Wister as a picture of perfect health, "bronzed by constant intercourse with Ol Sol . . . his eyes reflect the health-giving sunshine and vast freedom of camp life and mountain climbing."[28]

Wister, indeed, had prospered in the West, and his return to Philadelphia came too soon to please him. In October he was back at the JY Ranch for a serious hunting trip. Accompanying a group of other men, he rode deep into the Wyoming mountains near the Idaho and Utah borders. It was a hunting trip he never would forget, for on October 13 the Associated Press and United Press both—erroneously—reported his death! Molly Wister assumed the story to be true and boarded the first available train for Wyoming.* In a story bearing a Cleveland dateline (indicating that the story's origination was far from the site of the alleged death), the United Press declared that "Owen Wister, the novelist, died in the state of Wyoming to-day. His wife, who was attending the Federation of Women's Club at Erie, is being rushed there on a special train." There was no information as to the "cause" of death, but the stories and headlines dramatically portrayed Molly Wister's futile effort to reach her dying husband's bedside. "Although the train averaged a mile a minute death was the speedier and won the race," proclaimed the *Findlay* (Ohio) *Courier.* A Boston newspaper announced that Wister had died not in Wyoming but in Cleveland. The *Philadelphia Evening Times* announced the death at the top of page one in a banner headline and hinted at a natural cause of death by writing that Wister had suffered in recent years from "nervous dyspepsia." Many other stories alluded to recent illnesses which had limited his work.[29]

Wister's family and friends obviously were shocked. Only one East Coast newspaper, published on October 13, acknowledged the possibility of error. Observing that the death report might not be true, the *Philadelphia Evening Bulletin* quoted members of Wister's family and his friends as saying that they had not been notified of his death. The

---

* Wister incorrectly dates the false report as September 11 in *Roosevelt: The Story of a Friendship.*

Sacramento Star, having the West Coast advantage of extra hours before its deadline, summarized a confused state of knowledge in its headline: "Is Owen Wister, Novelist, Dead?" The story said that "every fresh report only adds to the mystery of the situation." By the end of the day confirmation had come that Wister was alive and well, and the error of the premature obituaries was reported in newspapers the next morning. Wister himself furnished his own proof of survival. Paraphrasing Mark Twain's comment under similar circumstances, he was quoted as saying that not only was he alive, he was "not even in bad health."[30]

Twenty years later Wister recalled his own discovery of the mistaken report, perhaps exaggerating:

> Quite unaware of my loss, I travelled for several days as I don't know who, vaguely puzzled by the atmosphere that my arrival anywhere created; until the hotel clerk at Ogden refused to give me a parcel addressed to me and left there by my order. He explained to me that I was no more. He called witnesses to prove it. They had all read it last week.[31]

Who was responsible for the error never was definitely determined, but the story evidently originated from the very meeting Molly had been attending in Erie. An innocent remark had been made there that Mrs. Wister's father had died recently. Somehow in the retelling, her father, William Rotch Wister, became Owen Wister, and a reporter accepted the story without checking. The ensuing wire service reports were received and published by newspapers throughout the country. They had no reason to doubt the report's authenticity and no way to confirm it.[32]

Two weeks after the incident Wister was home again, still disturbed about the "two or three bad days" caused by the incident. "It is interesting and enlightening at best to get the world's private opinion of one from the bland and appallingly frank obituaries in the newspaper," he remarked, "but extremely distressing when you know that your friends and relatives may be accepting the news of your death and when you are unable to contradict the reports." One of the worst aspects had been the instant assessments about his place in the contemporary world of literature. Wister had not been placed in the forefront of the nation's living authors. In fact, the comments, it seemed to him, had been couched in a "faintly patronizing tone."[33]

All in all, despite its unfortunate aspects, the year had not been entirely bad for Wister. He had had an invigorating rest in Wyoming with his family, and he had purchased land there. *Members of the Family* had been published to favorable reviews. A new edition of *The Virginian* had come off the presses containing a new and longer dedication to Theodore Roosevelt as well as illustrations by both Remington and Charles Russell. The stage version of *The Virginian* had continued to draw crowds in its eighth year, and this as well as the book had brought handsome royalties. Magazines such as the *Saturday Evening Post* had clamored for Wister's work.[34]

Such a man could afford to speculate in financial affairs, something Wister was not inclined to do. But in an atypical move he decided that an investment in southern California real estate was certain to pay rich dividends, and he bought a half interest in 3,298 acres for $25,000. The co-owner was a Californian named Ed Fletcher, who was to subdivide this property and manage it for twenty-five percent of the net profits. Wister put five thousand dollars down and agreed to pay the remaining sum in annual installments of four thousand dollars at six percent interest. Known as El Cajon Ranch, the property was in the Del Mar vicinity of San Diego.[35]

Wister had not been much concerned in recent months with politics, but as the 1912 presidential campaign loomed, his interest revived. What especially intrigued him was the possibility of Roosevelt's return to the White House to rescue the nation from William Howard Taft. Early in 1912 Roosevelt announced his candidacy. In April he toured the East Coast in a whistlestop campaign. Wister agreed to introduce him in Philadelphia when he spoke at the opera house, and the author joined the campaign train at Coatesville for the trip into Philadelphia. The night of the speech, the Wister family was escorted proudly to the opera house in the family brougham behind a bay team of horses named Parsifal and Siegfried. As Fanny Wister recalled later, the experience of being led by a policeman into the auditorium through the excited, overflow crowd and seated in a grand tier box near the stage was "electrifying." Wister and Roosevelt, both in formal attire, sat together on the stage, facing the largest crowd Wister ever had addressed. There was no amplification, and he shouted his introduction of Roosevelt: "He knows that dollars are needful, but he does not think dollars more sacred than men. He stands for no governing class. He stands for a 100 millions of American people. His battle is against the secret inner circle of privilege that would defraud these American people & turn the very Constitution that they made into a weapon for their destruction." The evening was declared a great success, and Wister earned much of the credit.[36]

Yet the events of that controversial, memorable presidential election did not please him. While he publicly supported Roosevelt and felt that his friend had acted properly in leading his famous walkout from the Republican National Convention to found the Progressive Party, Wister lamented the resulting turmoil and preferred that Roosevelt run under the GOP banner. As Wister confided to a friend in the summer, Roosevelt unfortunately was committed by some of his followers to "say so many and such extreme promises of reform" that he could not possibly fulfill them all. Deep inside, Wister "almost hoped" that former Princeton president Woodrow Wilson would win, and when news of Wilson's election eventually came in November Wister privately considered it a "positive relief!"[37]

Instead of actively working for Roosevelt in the summer of 1912, Wister looked forward to western travels and a return to his Jackson Hole property so that he could build a ranch house. First, though, he went in June to Williams College to be awarded an honorary doctor of letters degree together with Oliver Wendell Holmes, Jr. Wister suggested that the shorter the comments made about him the better. "Were you to confine it to a single phrase: 'author of The Virginian,' I should be more than content," he wrote in advance to one of his hosts. Another academic honor, one accompanied by the promise of a significant amount of work, came that same month. He was elected to the Board of Overseers at Harvard, the governing body of the university. This was no honorary title; it meant semiregular visits to Harvard and extensive amounts of committee work.[38]

Finally, in July, Wister and Molly left the children behind and went West. They first visited San Diego and Santa Barbara, where they spent some two weeks and looked over the Del Mar real estate investment. While they were there, the *San Diego Union* reported a rumor that the famous author was gathering material for a new novel with a San Diego setting. The novel was "expected to equal in popularity 'The Virginian' and 'Ramona' combined." Actually, a novel with a San Diego setting was the furthest thing from Wister's mind.[39]

The couple's next stop was Jackson Hole, where, following a pattern set by mountain men of years past, they had a rendezvous with their children. The family's German governess and Negro houseman had accompanied the children to the JY Ranch. For the many Westerners who never before had seen a black man, the Negro was the object of profound curiosity. He was especially needed, for there was a house to be built—the Wisters' own two-story log cabin on a sagebrush clearing.

They worked, all of them, aided by the inspiring view of the snowcapped Tetons just visible over the surrounding aspen and birch forest. They ate and slept at the JY as they hammered and sawed by day, and long before the interior could be completed they moved into their new house.* Ironically, now that Wister at long last had his own Wyoming house, the state's magic seemed to have disappeared for him. "Strangely and rather sadly, my longing for Wyoming & the roughing it is gone," he wrote to Chapman. It seemed now too ordinary; too many people were there.[40]

In the fall, the family returned to the East for Wister to confront a much-delayed challenge: writing. Having dropped his projected novel about the woman astrologist, he now was considering three other possibilities. "The Fixed Star" described the ups and downs of a theatrical couple; "Dividends in Democracy" gave a picture of Philadelphia's changing society from the old order to the new; and "The Marriages of Scipio" told of the old cowpuncher, Scipio Le Moyne, who had survived his own era but could not adjust to the new civilization. On a visit to Sagamore Hill to see Roosevelt, who was on a break from campaigning, Wister and the Bull Moose candidate talked not of politics but about Wister's literary career and his dilemma as to which book to write. Roosevelt urged him to write all three, but to start with the Philadelphia book.[41]

Wister, working in a new office at 1004 West End Trust Building, followed the advice, at least beginning the book. "I want *horribly* to complete the novel," he wrote to Mark A. De Wolfe Howe. Instead, though, he acquiesced to the many demands on his time that always came in Philadelphia.[42]

He could not decline, for example, to address a meeting of the Shakespeare Society of Philadelphia (founded in 1851 as a result of readings given by Fanny Kemble) in memory of that quiet, scholarly Shakespearean expert and physician, Horace Howard Furness. Dr. Furness, whose deafness obliged him to carry a silver ear trumpet and who persisted in wearing buckled shoes long past their time, had died in late summer. Wister had always been especially fond of Dr. Furness, and he wrote to Chapman that the news made him feel "as if I could not go on." Wister's speech was to be long remembered and quoted in the city, not for what he said about Furness but for his cynical comment about

---

* The Wister cabin has since been disassembled by the National Park Service, moved to Medicine Bow, Wyoming, and reconstructed as a tourist attraction.

the lack of mutual esteem in his own City of Brotherly Love as contrasted to Boston. "When a Bostonian hears that a fellow Bostonian has distinguished himself, he exclaims: 'Quite natural!' When a Philadelphian hears that a fellow Philadelphian has distinguished himself, he exclaims: 'Quite impossible!' "[43]

In June of 1913, with Molly at the age of forty-four expecting the couple's sixth child, the Wisters settled into their home at Saunderstown for the summer. This time tragedy awaited.

On Sunday, August 24, Molly went into a difficult labor. A daughter was born amidst complications. Wister wrote to Henry James the next day: "Yesterday morning at ten, died my wife, suddenly, after childbirth. . . . The case was a dangerous one, but the danger was believed quite over. Then the heart could not hold out against the shock; and after being thought safe, she died in an hour." The surviving daughter was named Sarah Wister.[44]

There was inescapable and tragic irony in the fact that it was Molly, the strong presence who held the family together during her husband's frequent melancholia and illnesses, who died. The shattering effect of her loss on the young children, and upon Wister, is not difficult to imagine.[45]

Her death received wide coverage in the newspapers, for not only was she married to a famous novelist, but also was in her own right an important Philadelphian. Her many civic and educational accomplishments were recalled, as well as her noted ancestors William Ellery Channing and James Logan, the latter secretary to William Penn and one of the signers of the Declaration of Independence. "There is no woman in this city more widely known and respected throughout the country in every walk of life than Mrs. Wister. . . . Indeed, I can think of no woman who could less be spared and whose death will leave a greater void, not in one place, but in many," wrote *Philadelphia Public Ledger* columnist Sallie Wistar.[46]

Theodore Roosevelt comprehended Wister's loss. Thirty years earlier he had lost his first wife under the same circumstances, when Alice was born, and on that same day his mother had died. Having learned of Wister's continued depression more than six weeks after Molly's death, Roosevelt sent a warm, handwritten note: "Dan, it *must* not kill you. You *must* live for your children's sake, and for the sake of their mother who loved you and them so. . . . Be brave . . . face the darkness fearlessly, for whether it be light or dark you must bear yourself well in the Great Adventure."[47]

Before the year ended, the Philadelphia School Board had named a school for Molly, changing the Zachary Taylor School at 8th and Parrish streets to the Mary Channing Wister School.* The following year the Philadelphia Civic Club, which she had cofounded at the age of twenty-three with Cornelia Frothingham, devoted a fifty-five page issue of its *Bulletin* to memorials to Molly. She had been such a fine woman that a decade later John Jay Chapman seriously suggested to Wister that his mysterious illnesses had been caused by the strain brought to his conscience from living with a superior woman.[48]

Life for Wister did go on, of course. There were governesses and servants to help with the children and house, and Molly's sister assumed a mother's role for her nieces and nephews. In fact, Wister thought the children fared better emotionally than he. They seemed to conspire to help him over the difficult period instead of vice versa. He was eager to "gain enough command" of his mind to resume writing, but meanwhile a number of affairs kept his mind occupied. As president of the Harvard Club in Philadelphia, he was master of ceremonies at its fiftieth anniversary festivities. He spoke at the Julia Ward Howe School, in sight of Butler Place, and told his young audience how as a boy he had roamed the area when it was known as York farm, once tumbling into a duck pond full of thick green water the consistency of pea soup. When French playwright Eugène Brieux got off the train in Philadelphia to make a speech, Wister, wearing a bowler, vest, and bow tie, was there to greet him. Henry James continued to correspond, complaining now of "chronic & very active *angina pectoris*" and detailing the pulling of his teeth for his health's sake. The exchange of letters which had gone on for so many years with Chapman continued, and a new, intense correspondence began with his Boston friend, Robert Grant, over the jurist's novels and their mutual service on the Harvard overseers' English Department committee.[49]

Another diversion—and it was no more than that—was the fact that *The Virginian* was to be presented in yet another dimension for its continually expanding audience. The Lasky Company had obtained rights to create a motion picture version of the drama, and a young new director named Cecil B. De Mille had been given his first solo assignment for

* Fifteen years later, in 1928, a memorial tablet was placed in her honor at the school.

making the film. De Mille, fortunately, had Dustin Farnum to repeat his stage role. (In accepting the film assignment Farnum had made a startling statement: he was giving up the stage for motion pictures.) De Mille faced the same problem in the film that Wister had dealt with in the stage play—how to portray the lynching. De Mille's solution, a successful one, was to show the shadows of the hanging bodies rather than the gruesome sight of the victims themselves.[50]

Wister paid scant attention to the movie; he was concerned about the delay in completing his novel about Philadelphia. He decided to send his first hundred pages to the ever-patient George Brett at Macmillan for an opinion. Brett was ecstatic, overly so, but he obviously wanted to encourage his author. "I wish you could see your way to sending me the rest of the novel as far as it is done. . . . It is magnificent."[51]

But Wister was not ready to finish it—"the doctor seriously forbids me from writing a word." Instead, he decided to go to Europe, where he had not been in years. On May 2 he sailed in company with Agnes Irwin and his friend and physician Jack Mitchell, each going separate ways upon arrival. While there, he visited with Henry James, his godmother Lady Musgrave (Jeanie Lucinda Fields), and other friends in England, France, and Germany. In Nauheim, where he stayed at length, he enjoyed an orderly routine of baths, walks, and concert-going, and on most evenings he rode the train to Frankfurt to attend the opera. For five days he took German lessons, but since his opinion of the German people was low he decided it was not worth the effort. He made the notation that most of the Germans he encountered were "quite as usual: swine."[52]

Wister certainly had a far keener interest in European affairs than most Americans, yet he appeared hardly conscious of the turbulent mood on the continent in the summer of 1914. In Nauheim he saw a zeppelin floating quietly above as military maneuvers took place on the ground below. The martial significance escaped him. Neither did it mean anything to him—or so he later claimed—when he walked into his hotel at Triberg in the Black Forest on June 28 and read on the bulletin board, amidst an excited crowd, about the assassination of a royal couple whose names he did not recognize. Only later did he recall that a tall, grey-haired man commented gravely to those around the bulletin board, "That is the match which will set all Europe in flames." Nearly a month later an old woman in England asked Wister if he thought Austria would declare war on Serbia. He did not know what she meant, nor why war might be contemplated. When he departed by ship from London on

August 1, the war that had been declared involved only Austria-Hungary, Serbia, and Russia. Yet the restlessness evident on London streets did not escape his notice, and when his homeward-bound ship reached the open seas, the wireless brought daily news of hostilities on the continent. By the time the ship was four days out to sea, England and Germany were at war. The ship lights now were doused, and for two days the dark vessel sped silently through thick fog with two German cruisers not far behind. "I slept in my clothes," Wister recalled later, "but could not understand the agitation of a stewardess about our German pursuers—they were said to be two. What could they do to a passenger ship but take us to the nearest German port?" The stewardess corrected her American passenger's naiveté. "Oh, sir, you don't know them. They'd send us to the bottom of the sea." Wister did not believe her. Within two days the ship had reached an escort, and the voyage into New York continued without incident. Ultimately, the very ship on which he had been a passenger was sunk in the Mediterranean by a German submarine.[53]

Within weeks, Wister heard from Henry James, who passionately damned the German aggression. "The German crucifixion and whole treatment of the utterly harmless and innocent Belgium is an atrocity that cries aloud for some future penalty from the gods." The visit with Wister in July seemed to him part of another era; now there was the real possibility of "a world annihilated and lost altogether."[54]

Perhaps the war seemed far away and unimportant to most Americans, but to Wister, whose life had been touched in such fashion, it now became a personal obsession. For the next four years, he was to be absorbed by his determination to alert fellow Americans to the war's dangers. The novel about Philadelphia was put away for good, never to be touched again.

Chapter XV

THE CURMUDGEON UNVEILED
(1914–1923)

ALL EUROPE MOBILIZED, AND AMERICANS WATCHED FEARFULLY as President Wilson instructed them to be impartial in thought and deed. Impartiality was difficult for most people, as news photographs and headlines graphically described the Huns' invasion of neutral Belgium, and the air was filled with lurid atrocity stories. By the end of August, alarmed by the bellicose German general Friedrich von Bernhardi's book, *Germany and the Next War*, and by works of the pan-German historian Heinrich von Treitschke, Wister had become convinced of the "guilt and perfidy" of Berlin and Vienna. Neutrality in a conflagration that threatened the civilization from which he drew strength was impossible. And as President Wilson continued to remain aloof from the war, Wister's contempt steadily increased. The times, he was convinced, called for a man of action—a Theodore Roosevelt. Roosevelt himself publicly advocated neutrality, but there were oceans of difference between his views and Wilson's. Roosevelt pleaded military preparedness. "When giants are engaged in a death wrestle, as they reel to and fro they are certain to trample on whomever gets in the way," he said. The nation must be strong to prevent this from happening, he insisted.[1]

Despite his growing alarm, Wister could do little but fret impatiently about the world situation. In early February 1915, however, he received an invitation to speak at Trinity College's spring commencement exercises in Durham, North Carolina. He sensed an opportunity. Having declined the college's invitation on three previous occasions, he now responded to Trinity's president that only one subject stirred in him a desire to speak. This was the impression he had gathered of Germany during his summer there before the outbreak of war. "If such a subject appeal to you, I could make an address out of this into which I could put something more than a perfunctory interest." Trinity's president, W. P. Few, readily consented. Wister dropped all plans for fiction to work on his address.[2]

287

In June, accompanied by Jack Mitchell, he went to Durham to deliver his talk, "The Pentecost of Calamity." It amounted to a passionate indictment of an alleged Prussian indoctrination program which since 1870 had proclaimed the creed of a super race and super state, silencing all dissenters, and which had prepared the nation for this "wild spring at the throat of Europe." And now there prevailed in Germany "a hospital case, a case for the alienist; the mania of grandeur, complemented by the mania of persecution." After the speech, a local newspaper regretted that another speaker had not been selected who could have talked about a more interesting subject. But a month later when the *Saturday Evening Post* published the address, it was greeted with wide acclaim. George Brett saw potential for a book, and Wister agreed. In August an expanded version of the speech, written while he was spending the summer in California, appeared. The slim volume, which managed to be 148 pages long only because of wide margins and ample spacing, immediately caught the public's fancy. It provided an uncomplicated explanation of the German character that made understandable such acts as the sinking of the *Lusitania*. By year's end the book had gone through twelve printings and had sold 46,000 copies. Before demand slacked, it had gone through twenty-seven printings in the United States and had been translated into French, Dutch, Italian, and Japanese.[3]

Wister's explanation was slick and simplistic, full of generalities and, as it developed, packed with undocumented and doubtful assertions. Nevertheless, it appeared to many to be the right document for the tense, emotional moments prior to the United States entry into the war. *The Pentecost of Calamity* stopped short of urging a declaration of war, but the implication was clear that involvement was inevitable if the cause of humanity were to be served.[4]

Despite the book's numerous shortcomings, which today seem so obvious, praise came quickly and from influential sources. The outpouring of letters filled Wister's mailbox and briefly matched those inspired by *The Virginian*. "A very brilliant book," United States Senator Henry Cabot Lodge wrote. William Dean Howells found it "extraordinarily good, very calm, fine, just, and illuminating." "Clear and accurate," wrote the *New York Times*. Theodore Roosevelt, although he preferred a more emphatic call to action, called the work "admirable" and of great service to the nation. Harvard's Charles W. Eliot read the book "with great admiration and satisfaction," wishing only that Wister had recommended a definite path of action. Had he done so, Wister wrote back to Eliot, he would have urged fortification of both the Atlantic and Pacific coasts and the issuance of a protest that Germany had violated the Hague Convention, but he would not have recommended training and equipping an army.[5]

While sympathy for the Allies clearly prevailed in America despite the official stance of neutrality, there was a vociferous pocket of pro-German dissenters. These people were not swept up by the *Pentecost*'s emotional message, and as they began to challenge many of the book's assumptions Wister found himself on the defensive. He had stated unequivocally that the "cities of the Rhine" had celebrated the sinking of the *Lusitania* by dismissing school. An American reader with a German surname demanded by letter to know Wister's authority for the statement. Wister responded that his source was the "leading daily morning papers of New York and Philadelphia." These newspaper accounts, it turned out, were wrong, for the Germans had been celebrating a national holiday which coincidentally fell on the same day as the sinking of the *Lusitania*.[6]

Another instance in which *Pentecost* failed to survive critical scrutiny was revealed by Wister's claim that the University of Chicago "stopped the mouth of a Belgian professor who sought to present his native land's case in public." The university's dean of faculties called Wister's statement "radically at variance with the essential facts," and the dean of the Graduate School of Arts and Literature asserted that the claim was "utterly unfounded." Wister had to acknowledge that his "only source for the statement" was the word of the professor himself. It soon became clear that the statement was wrong. The book's several discrepancies alarmed Wister so much that he asked Brett to publish a new edition which would include amendments and citations of the sources for his information. Brett declined. To do so would be an injustice to the fifty thousand readers who already had bought the book, he believed.[7]

Years later, Howard Mumford Jones and Richard M. Ludwig would declare *Pentecost* to be "virtually a classic . . . [which] persuaded Americans that Germany was wrong." In the mid-1930s Walter Millis less charitably described *Pentecost* as "that dreadful piece of dripping invective." The book, most assuredly, was propaganda and little else. Its meteoric rise in popularity was a reflection not of merit, but of the rampant anti-German sentiment stirring in the nation.[8]

If the excitement generated by *The Pentecost of Calamity* were not enough, Wister became embroiled at the same time in another contro-

289

versy, this one over an acerbic article he wrote for the *Atlantic Monthly* bemoaning the inferiority of American literature. Entitled "Quack-Novels and Democracy," it appeared as the lead article in the June issue. Wister argued that America's most successful novels were nothing more than quackery. Indeed, he claimed, they were not novels at all; they were formula packages marketed like patent medicines. Slick merchandising beguiled the masses into elevating mediocre books to the best seller lists, and America's critics were too timid to do anything but praise these popular successes. The result was a genuine lowering of American literary tastes, and Wister did not refrain from naming individual authors who were responsible for it: Harold Bell Wright, Robert W. Chambers, and Upton Sinclair. Wister's conclusions meant, for him, that the commercialization of American life which had upset his family so much in the nineteenth century now had triumphed even in literature.[9]

The *Atlantic Monthly*'s editor, Ellery Sedgwick, had been right when he triumphantly told Wister to "just watch for its [the article's] smegmatic effect on contemporary letters." Wister's observations, indeed, created a literary stir with point and counterpoint appearing in many of the nation's most prominent publications. Meredith Nicholson, seeking in the October *Atlantic* to rebut Wister's arguments, called the article an act of inhumanity "unworthy of a good sportsman."[10]

Upton Sinclair was furious, for Wister had singled him out particularly as an American writer who catered to the popular crowd by creating stereotypes. In a personal letter, Sinclair chastised Wister for quoting unfairly from his "least impressive" book, *The Metropolis*. While acknowledging Wister's high idealism in attacking corruption in Philadelphia politics, Sinclair observed that in literature he appeared to be a reactionary. "Every age has its cheap popular writers, Mr. Wister; its quack novelists like Marie Corelli and Harold Bell Wright. Every age also has its leisurely and politic critics who lament the decadence of present-day literature, and are unaware of great revolutionary forces that are changing the thoughts of the world about them." Sinclair also chose this opportunity to chide Wister by claiming that the older author had failed to visit him in New Jersey as promised a dozen years earlier at a time when Sinclair desperately needed encouragement.[11]

Embroiled by day in what seemed to be one controversy after another, at home Wister presented an entirely different figure to his children. During the day he frequently charmed them with his own tunes, playing and singing with joyful abandon at the big grand piano downstairs at Butler Place. Late in the evening, past their bedtime, they drifted to sleep upstairs to the sounds below of their father's expert renditions of Wagnerian opera. To them, music and their father were inseparable. They were too young to know that he was an especially troubled man these days, worried over his inability to move ahead with his fiction. He confided to John Jay Chapman that the things he had written lately were "rotten," and he assessed his problem as slothfulness and a will that was too weak to tackle anything hard.[21]

As the war continued in Europe, and the United States appeared no closer than ever in aiding the Allies, Wister's temper began fraying even further. So did Roosevelt's, whose star, having fallen since his 1912 loss, now was being rehabilitated. The ex-president's loud attacks blasting Wilsonian neutrality grew more withering, and Wister, still under Roosevelt's orbit, despised Wilson more than ever. Neither could Chapman abide the policy of neutrality. His intense and uncompromising spirit remained as undiminished as the day he had plunged his hand into a bed of coals as a Harvard law student. Now he urged Wister to use his wide reputation by joining him in starting a petition signed by prominent individuals that would force Wilson to speak out against Germany's invasion of Belgium. Wister readily agreed to speak out on the war—indeed, he already had done so—but the idea of the petition was dropped when Chapman, perhaps with tongue in cheek, said his wife had persuaded him that he was "old & excitable" and should limit his activities to his "little essays on what not."[13]

Wister did not drop his own determination to speak out more forcefully against Wilson, whom he labeled an "obscure teacher of history." He did so in his own way in a scathing sonnet entitled "To Woodrow Wilson, Feb. 22, 1916." Nothing Wister did in his life ever evoked a greater or more immediate storm of protest. The poem, widely reprinted, was a vicious attack upon Wilson's character. It linked him with "public cowards, hypocrites, poltroons."

> Not even if I possessed your twist in speech,
> Could I make any words (fit for use) fit you
> You've wormed yourself beyond description's reach;
> Truth, if she touched you, would become untrue.
>
> Satire has seared a host of evil fames,
> Has withered emperors by her fierce lampoons;
> History has lashes that have flayed the names
> Of public cowards, hypocrites, poltroons.

You go immune. Cased in your self-esteem,
    The next world cannot scathe you, nor can this;
No fact can stab through your complacent dream,
    Nor present laughter, nor the future's hiss.

But if its fathers did this land control,
    Dead Washington would wake and blast your soul.[14]

The timing for this devastating attack now seems strange, occurring just after Wilson had reversed his previous position and had advocated American military preparedness to insure a strong defensive posture. Yet this action, in turn, had disturbed some neutralist Democratic leaders, who protested that the president was pushing the nation toward war. Wilson's reaction to the neutralist Democrats infuriated Wister, who called the president's explanation a "revocation." That, together with the unsettling news about the beginning of the siege at Verdun, caused Wister to vent his emotions. Just two days after he wrote the startling sonnet, it appeared in the *New York Times*, and then in newspapers throughout the country.[15]

The reaction was instantaneous, widespread, and often vindictive. A man from Ohio wrote, "I wonder whether in all of Philadelphia there is not some stout heart who will take his dog lash and whip you until you whimper out an apology, not to President Wilson, but to the outraged citizenship of the United States." A Georgian commented: "What a pity you were not a passenger on the Lusitania. What, oh what kind of an American are you? Certainly not the kind portrayed in the Virginian." Even longtime friends like Henry D. Sedgwick told Wister that "you take my breath away," although he added diplomatically that what disturbed him most was that the president of the United States "should appear in this way to so many citizens. In an eight-line poetical response, the *Boston Transcript* thought it to be "A sorry state of things, alas, / When Owen's muse brays like an ass!'"

Despite the tempest, Wister would not admit to any second thoughts at all about the poem's suitability. And Roosevelt, predictably enough, "entirely approved" of the poem. "Do not mind at all what the mushy brother-hood say of it; it's going to last. The people will in the end be glad that the foremost man of letters speaks of the Buchanan of our day as it is right to speak."[16]* The next time Roosevelt saw Wister he

---

* The reference to "Buchanan" was to President James Buchanan and his failure to prevent southern states from seceding from the Union prior to the Civil War.

gustily exclaimed that "the only trouble with that sonnet was that it wasn't half severe enough." It was a comment that he would make every time he saw Wister during the few remaining years of his life.[17]

Instead of shrinking under the weight of widespread criticism, Wister submerged himself even more deeply in his effort to prick America's conscience into supporting the Allies. One of his most conspicuous moves was to join a committee of twelve distinguished Americans who, as Chapman had suggested earlier, gathered signatures of some five hundred leading citizens to proclaim publicly their sympathy for the Allies. Among Wister's fellow committee members were Josiah Royce, William Dean Howells, Ralph A. Cram, William R. Thayer, Bliss Perry, Robert Grant, and others, including politicians, railroad presidents, bankers, journalists, clergymen, and professors. In April the petition, in the form of an open letter to the Allies, was released for publication in newspapers in Europe and America. "Our judgment supports your case, and our sympathies and our hopes are with you in this struggle. In saying this we are confident that we are expressing the convictions and feelings of the overwhelming majority of Americans." A month earlier a German submarine had torpedoed the passenger ship *Sussex*. An official break in relations with Germany appeared imminent. In the aftermath of such news, the petition's impact was not nearly as great as it would have been several weeks earlier.[18]

Roosevelt himself was not satisfied with merely encouraging others to act—he longed to get into actual combat. He plotted to raise a "Roosevelt division of mounted infantry" to lead into battle, drawing up lists of prospective officers and even performing command problems along the north shore of Long Island. In late spring of 1916, Wister joined thirty-five other professional writers in a campaign to recruit Roosevelt as a candidate for the presidency. Meeting at the Players Club in New York City to plan their strategy, they contended that the present international crisis made Roosevelt's election "essential to the welfare of the country."[19]

The expected rush to join their movement did not materialize. The committee quietly dissolved from public view, but not before Wister became involved in an acrimonious exchange over the petition with the colorful and longtime editor of the *Louisville Courier-Journal*, "Marse" Henry Watterson. In a humorous editorial, Watterson lampooned these "d—d literary fellers" as vagabonds. Such a writer might be "as exquisite as Winston Churchill and Owen Wister–but if he contrived by his insinuating charm, his smooth exploitation of his possibilities, to secure a place, let us say on the Courier-Journal, he would lose his job in a week." Watterson mailed Wister a copy of the editorial. As a young man Wister once had confessed that he lacked a sense of humor about himself. In this fifth decade of his life he was in no mood to accept such comments in humor, so he fired back a response chastising Watterson's "insolence" in sending the editorial to his attention. Watterson used Wister's letter to type his own comment on the bottom half: "I had actually fancied you a gentleman. You appear to be not even a person of sense, or intelligence. The article was written in the best of good humor and sent as a matter of courtesy." Days later, Wister sent a telegram which was anything but conciliatory. "In letter of June fifth, for insolence substitute impudence." Watterson, on the same day, sent a further note. The *Courier-Journal* had been promoting Wister's work for years, he said, and recently had declared *The Pentecost of Calamity* superior to all other war publications. "How could you take offense at such a skit, or get grumpy with me of all men? . . . Brace up, old man, and take punishment smilingly, though in this instance honor not attack was intended."[20]*

Wister was not through yet with Woodrow Wilson. His reelection, Wister was convinced, would be disastrous to the nation's welfare, so he spent much of his summer gathering material for a final blast against the incumbent president. The article appeared in *Collier's* under the title, "If We Elect Mr. Wilson." Wilson had clipped the American eagle's wings and had caused rotten eggs to be thrown at the American flag, Wister wrote. It was, by Wister's own admission, a "venomous" article, but he was convinced that the times demanded venom.[21]

Wister's eagerness for war did not at all please his godmother, Mrs. Jeanie Lucinda Fields (Lady Musgrave) of England, who lamented the extraordinary loss of life the war was bringing to Europe. When the Zimmerman note revealed Germany's offer to Mexico to regain Texas, New Mexico, and Arizona, making war seem certain, she told her godson that "surely . . . you are satisfied." His "hatred" of President Wilson was unfair, she wrote, because the president's first duty was to his own country, and he required an unmistakable mandate from the people before he could declare war. When Germany resumed unrestricted submarine warfare, and the United States at last declared war, Wister's godmother wrote, "You will rejoice." As for herself, she lamented America's

* Almost a year later, true to his word, Watterson heartily complimented Wister upon a book he had just read—*The Seven Ages of Washington*.

entry into the war because it meant a "widening of the loss of life." A year later, Lady Musgrave's son was killed when he lead a sortie over Europe.[22]

With war a reality, there was little more for Wister to do save encourage the heartiest American participation. This he did, aiding the government in its landmark campaign to mold public opinion. Wister and other writers, actors and actresses, educators, ministers, and people from all walks of life joined in this monumental effort which was headed by George Creel's Committee on Public Information. Wister was an eager participant in these propaganda activities. He wrote for the Committee an answer to the claim that the true purpose of the United States in the war was to conquer the world and exploit its markets. For the National Security League, Wister wrote 320 words on the topic, "What the Victory or Defeat of Germany Means to Every American." "After the crumbled ruins of Belgium, France, England—New York and Chicago and all the rest . . . after Europe's butchered children and violated women—ours." Music played an official part in the war effort as never before, both at home and abroad, and Wister composed words and music for a sprightly song that was distributed to song leaders in the Army and Navy. In addition, he wrote an article about the value of teaching American soldiers to sing. He wrote so many short articles for the defense effort that he had almost no time for longer works. At times his enthusiasm ran wild. Editors for *American Magazine* requested that he temper a passage in an article for them in which he alleged that certain unpatriotic books played the Kaiser's game as well as if they were spies. "I am afraid it may be libelous," an editor complained.[23]

Such loose talk dealt misery to great numbers of innocent Americans who came under suspicion of disloyalty for the most trivial of reasons—perhaps no more than a German surname. Spies were assumed to be lurking everywhere; citizens were asked to keep their eyes and ears open and to report disloyal utterances or suspicious activities. German-born Americans especially suffered, and the hysteria inspired to a large degree by the Creel Committee soon enveloped one of Wister's oldest and dearest friends, Henry Lee Higginson.

Now in his eighties, Higginson was still the energetic force behind the Boston Symphony Orchestra. The situation there was a difficult one. The very able conductor of the orchestra, Dr. Karl Muck, was a German citizen whose sympathies naturally lay with his native land. The orchestra's approximately one hundred performers included twenty-two German citizens. The reason for this was that Major Higginson, determined that his symphony be second to none, had recruited musicians in Europe. He now decided to retain the German musicians, even after the United States entry into the war. To remove Dr. Muck and the musicians would be ruinous to the quality of the symphony, Higginson reasoned. He resolved that as long as the German musicians conducted themselves honorably and engaged in no improper activities they would continue to perform. The orchestra thus continued with its 1917 obligations despite raised eyebrows and some complaints.[24]

Serious trouble arose, however, in Providence, Rhode Island, when on the afternoon of a scheduled evening performance, four citizens demanded that the symphony play "The Star-Spangled Banner" as proof of the organization's patriotic commitment. There was no time to rehearse the piece; the music was not available; and it could not be played that evening. As a result, the story spread that Dr. Muck had refused to play "The Star-Spangled Banner." Pressures arose for Higginson to insure that this patriotic tune, not yet officially the national anthem, be a standard part of all future concerts. In this time of trouble Higginson turned to Wister for support. "I can see no reason why Dr. Muck should play the national anthem, for of course he is not on our side," Higginson wrote to Wister. "The whole purpose of my letters is to ask your friendly word and assistance if occasion should require it." He soon needed it in Philadelphia. Even though Higginson agreed to play "The Star-Spangled Banner" at the conclusion of the concert, doubts arose as to whether the orchestra would even be permitted to perform in Philadelphia. Higginson privately told Wister that if the orchestra were forbidden to perform in Philadelphia, the group would never return to that city. What Wister did is uncertain, but he evidently worked diligently to assure the performance's success not only in Philadelphia but also in Washington. Higginson afterwards thanked Wister for his "energetic and splendid work" for the orchestra. "Philadelphia & Washington have treated us very well & now we'll try NYork & Brooklyn. . . . Thank you, thank you." Mrs. Higginson sent her thanks too.[25]

Rumors continued to spread, however, that Dr. Muck was doing more than merely conducting a symphonic orchestra; he was also guilty of acts disloyal to the nation. "This hounding of him and me is exhausting," Higginson wrote to Wister. The Department of Justice conducted an investigation and declared Muck innocent of any objectionable conduct. Still the stories and protests continued, and a scheduled concert tour through the Midwest in early 1918 had to be abandoned because of the furor. At last Higginson told Muck that he would be terminated—on May 4, the date of the season's last concert. Higginson, disgusted that public opinion could force a decision dictated by political rather than artistic considerations, vowed to relinquish his long and distinguished sponsorship of the orchestra. And this he did with the season finale, thus ending on a very unfortunate note his immense contributions to symphonic music not only in Boston but also in America. Meanwhile, Dr. Muck was arrested in late March and interned as an alien enemy before he could finish the musical season.[26]

A year later Higginson died, and only then did Wister publicly reveal his own conviction that his aged friend had been foolish in supporting Dr. Muck. This he did in a tribute to Higginson in the *Harvard Alumni Bulletin*. Muck, Wister wrote, was "a base, disloyal scoundrel." Yet Higginson's fine character, he wrote, had been proven by his obstinate but chivalric persistence in stubbornly defending a man known by everyone but him to be totally unworthy.[27]

These years, despite the trauma of the European conflict and his personal involvement in controversial matters, brought for Wister a more relaxed pace of life. For one thing, he abandoned all pretenses of serious work on a novel. He had no need to worry about earning a living. Dividends from his stocks and bonds alone in 1918 amounted to $47,642, and combined with royalties and miscellaneous sources his total income equalled $55,205, an especially comfortable sum for the day. He briefly developed a keen interest in golf, his calendar for March 1918 showing that on one ten-day stretch he played on eight occasions. His children were showing signs of independence and adulthood. Marina and Owen Jones had visited Africa in 1910. Owen had attended private schools— Haverford in New York and then St. Paul's. His father carefully corrected spelling errors in letters sent home. Marina was blossoming on the violin. Another son, Carl, was already ten years old. Only the youngest child, Sarah Butler, whose mother had died at her birth, was cause for worry. She had begun to show evidence of worsening retardation.[28]

One untoward event, more bothersome than tragic, occurred in August 1917 when Wister's young French valet disappeared in Wyoming with many of Wister's possessions. The valet, a French Army veteran named Charles Bret, packed about one thousand dollars worth of Wister's clothes in his employer's luggage and fled to Boston, where he rented a suite of rooms at the Hotel Savoy and posed alternately as a count and as Wister himself. After a week there, the valet transferred his operations to fashionable Swampscott, continuing his pose and fooling several young society ladies. Finally, though, his bad checks caught up with him, and he was arrested one day as he drove up to the Swampscott hotel in a hired limousine. Wister suggested that charges against the handsome young man be dropped if he would reenter the French Army. Brett preferred to stand trial. Wister urged in court that the punishment not be unduly severe, and Bret was sentenced to prison for one year.[29]

Wister was not so lenient in his feelings against Germany. As the war news brightened and the end grew near, Wister feared that the Germans would find a way to escape harsh peace terms. What he really wanted was a "reckoning that will settle their hash." He wrote two hundred words on the subject for the Defense League.[30]

In Wister's mind, Roosevelt by now had regained the luster he had lost as a result of the 1912 presidential race; once more the ex-president was the "moral leader of the United States." Wister went to Sagamore Hill in October for a leisurely visit with him. He stayed there for three or four days, and the two men let their minds ramble leisurely not only over the daily news from the war front but also over their memories of the old West. They talked openly and honestly, and Roosevelt confided his belief that he had been blessed with "only a second-rate mind." Wister was beginning to wonder now if his poetic blast at Wilson had not been in bad taste, but Roosevelt insisted that it had been entirely appropriate and that the passage of time more and more vindicated the poem's harshness. As enjoyable as the visit was with such intimate exchange, Wister sensed sadness, for Roosevelt was not well. Days later, on the eve of Roosevelt's sixtieth birthday, Wister decided that the time was appropriate to salute his longtime companion, and he did so in a twenty-one line poem entitled "To T.R. Oct. 27, 1918." He wrote:

> You noblest servant in our land.
> None lives that matches your good deeds;
> May all your years the tale fulfill;
> No eye so plainly sees our needs—
> Our captain once, our pilot still.[31]

Roosevelt's response was the last letter he ever wrote to Wister. "My dear Dan, I shall keep the poem to serve as my undeserved epitaph." Three months later he was dead. A chapter in Wister's life, and indeed in the nation's life, closed much sooner than anyone had expected.[32]

There was another, bigger milestone for the nation—the war ended two months before Roosevelt died. Wister commented in his pocket calendar, written in microscopic hand: "News that war ends. 2 P.M. The most vertiginous hours I have ever lived." Wister's involvement was far from over, however. His anger toward the Germans remained. Two days after the war's end he sent a note to Mark A. De Wolfe Howe concerning the brief biographies Howe was preparing of Harvard men who had fallen in the war. If Howe harbored any thoughts about including Harvard men who had fought and died on the German side, Wister wanted him to know that he strongly opposed the idea.[33]

Wister's concern over postwar problems caused him to break a string of summer visits to the West. Dean Duke wrote to complain of his priorities, "You have your close associations in that far-off Eastern part of the map and, naturally, being constantly in touch with them they appeal to you most." This appealing Westerner, as always, had a way with the pen that belied his lack of formal education. "Those dear youngsters of yours that climbed on my lap at your home at 913 Pine Street and called me Uncle Duke are grown now and have long ago forgotten the lonely cowman that once invaded your home and was made a better man by having their dear arms turned about his neck." Duke recalled, too, how the Wisters' maid had been afraid to straighten the cowboy's room after she saw the six-shooter and the bottle of whiskey he had placed on his dresser. He was, on the day he wrote Wister, fifty-one years old, and he had been called "the old man" since becoming the riding boss on the Owyee Ranch at the age of fifteen![34]

Another, even older, western friend, George B. West, soon wrote a similar letter to Wister from his new home in Seattle, Washington, where he had moved in 1909 after a dispute with his partners in the West-Lovering Cattle Company.* West had not corresponded with his eastern friend in sixteen years. He wrote, "Wister: I want you to remember this, that with all my faults I love you as I did long years ago, and shall always want to see you when you come to Seattle."[35]

George Brett wished that once again Wister would devote some time

* West had been warned by his cattle associates that if he did not leave Wyoming he would be shot, whereupon he was given a horse and buggy and escorted to the train depot. This is the story as recalled by his nephew, George M. West, in an interview in Seattle on August 17, 1978. West first appeared in the Seattle city directory in 1911, where his occupation was listed as fisherman. The following year his occupation appeared as department store "floorman"; in 1914 as a solicitor; and in the next several years as "manager of the Wintonia Hotel." By the 1930s he owned three apartment houses.

to writing about the West, for the public's interest in that subject remained undiminished. Indeed, it had been whetted by the film industry's vivid and successful portrayals of western dramas, including Cecil B. De Mille's 1914 production of *The Virginian*. If Wister did not attempt another western novel, he did at least seek to capitalize on the western interest by selling motion picture rights for *Lin McLean*, *Red Men and White*, and *Members of the Family* to movie producer Benjamin Hampton, a former magazine editor and tobacco executive. None of these books would be filmed. A year later, in 1920, Wister, Kirk La Shelle's widow, and Famous Players–Lasky Corp. once again sold the motion picture rights to *The Virginian*, this time to movie idol Douglas Fairbanks for $55,000, Wister receiving 4/18 of that sum.[36]

Despite the obvious market for western stories, that part of Wister's literary life was for the most part finished. His attention remained riveted on Europe and the critical postwar issues there. The question on most minds was what to do about President Wilson's drive to join the League of Nations. While the idea was "a star to hitch our wagon to," as Wister publicly said, the star needed to be viewed more clearly before any hitching was done. Voting provisions in the draft, which seemed to surrender American sovereignty, caused Wister to oppose United States participation. His hatred for Wilson remained undiminished. He wrote to Barrett Wendell that he had never yet read anything of Wilson's that had substance. "So help me God, never yet have I read a sentence of his in which anything was said, unless it was plagiarized." And even then Wilson spoiled the other fellow's thoughts with his clumsy attempts to rephrase them, Wister added.[37]

What interested Wister more than the League was a subject he first had written about during the war—that of Anglo-American relationships. In "The Ancient Grudge," appearing in *American Magazine*, he urged that Americans should immediately discard any vestiges of enmity toward England and firmly ally themselves with that country against Germany. To explore this theme more fully, Wister determined to sail to Europe, but war-imposed restrictions on travel remained, and the State Department denied him permission to go. The English ambassador, Lord Reading, mindful of the favorable impact of *The Pentecost of Calamity*, intervened in his behalf, and the State Department acquiesced, issuing a passport. On March 1, 1919, Wister sailed for London on the *Celtic*, and for the next six months he toured England and the continent. Battle sites such as Belleau Wood, Soissons, Saint-Mihiel, Argonne, and

Verdun especially attracted him. His publicly announced purpose—along with the support of people like John W. Davis, the American ambassador to England, and General John Joseph Pershing in Paris—opened many doors. In England he dined almost nightly with prominent government officials and titled individuals. Invariably he peppered them with questions about Europe and its future. Lord Northcliffe, "a very fascinating one," who as a young British press tycoon named Alfred C. Harmsworth had popularized the newspaper for the masses, impressed Wister as a man who liked power, but who preferred evil to good. "We talked of Hearst! who wants social recognition in London for Mrs. Hearst!! and in *exchange* promises to be *good*!!! Dear Dear Dear what things I am hearing." Wister recorded these comments in his journal. In Constantinople he visited Henry L. Morgenthau, former ambassador to Turkey, and his opinion of him was not so high. In fact, it repeated the anti-Semitism that first had surfaced in *The Virginian*. He wrote of Morgenthau: "He's a Jew and that's what seems to be the matter. Slightly oily in voice & manner."[38]

When Wister returned in June, he spent the next few months in a "sustained heat" writing a book on the premise that American citizens had an "inherited and carefully fostered hate of Great Britain" dating from the Revolution. To demonstrate his point, he sought to show how American history textbooks presented a distorted view of Great Britain. This realization of a longtime anti-British indoctrination first came to Wister during the war when he had become irritated upon hearing "the man in the street" gripe about England's lack of performance on the battlefield. With this book, just as with *Lady Baltimore*, Wister was acutely aware that he risked making enemies.[39]

In mid-1920 the book appeared under the title of *A Straight Deal or The Ancient Grudge*. It infuriated many people—none more so than a spokesman from the Friends of Irish Freedom, Daniel T. O'Connell, who wrote a twelve-page pamphlet under the organization's imprint entitled *Owen Wister, Advocate of Racial Hatred: An Unpatriotic American Who Seeks to Destroy American Traditions*. In Peterborough, New Hampshire, *A Straight Deal* was removed from the public library at the request of a board member who was a prominent state politician and friend of Irish freedom. Such critics could be discounted because of their obvious biases, but serious analysts justifiably noted that Wister's work lacked historical objectivity. As in *The Pentecost of Calamity*, his hatred of Germany was undisguised. That nation, Wister wrote, was at

heart "an untamed, unchanged wild beast, never to be trusted again."
As the reviewer in the *Athenaeum* noted, this kind of language was distinctly reminiscent of the "stunt" press. "In fact, our 'stunt' press is at
present less extreme, less hysterical, less violently silly than Mr. Wister."
The book, as the *Bookman*'s reviewer observed, was "a product of war
psychology" in which "passion and hate and ignorance presided at its
birth." Harold Stearns believed *A Straight Deal* was proof that the literary mind should be "forbidden to express itself on political affairs on
pain of the immediate destruction of all it has ever written." Even Wister's friend and attorney, Francis B. Biddle, felt obliged to be frank
about the book's faults. "I felt, when I finished your book, that your
hates were stronger than any longing for good will and peace."[40]

Wister remained undaunted. He already was working on the third
of what was to be a trilogy of war-inspired books. This book's themes
were to be "the plight of France, the deed of Germany, and [the] inevitable path ahead of the United States." It was to be entitled *Neighbors
Henceforth*.[41]

Before he could finish it, however, Wister would have to return to
Europe, and before going there he had places to go and people to see in
his own country. One such person was Senator Henry Cabot Lodge of
Massachusetts, flush from having led the fight to keep the United States
out of the League of Nations. Wister spent several days at Lodge's Washington home, where he and the senator concurred in their viewpoints
about current affairs and, evidently, their ideas about the mental makeup
of Jews. In a note written afterwards, Lodge told Wister that he had
observed "what Lowell said about the Jewish trait of playing with
phrases and theories, regardless of facts." Lowell was Abbott Lawrence
Lowell, the Harvard president who had unsuccessfully sought to institute
a quota system to limit the number of Jewish students.[42]

One matter to which Wister paid close attention during 1920 was
the campaigning of the two presidential candidates, Warren G. Harding
and James M. Cox. When Harding emerged unexpectedly as the candidate of the Republican Party, Lodge (who had supported Calvin Cool-
idge and then Leonard Wood before shifting to Harding) described him
for Wister as a man of "most attractive personality." He was "very
agreeable . . . open-minded, liberal, and sensible, and so far as I know,
and I think I know a great deal about him, there is not a speck on his
character anywhere." In deciding between Harding, who stayed on his
front porch in Marion, Ohio, and Democratic candidate Cox, who as-

sumed Wilson's advocacy of the League of Nations, Wister had no difficulty. He preferred Harding.[43]

In December, the fierce reviews on *A Straight Deal* not yet abated, Wister departed once again for Europe to complete his research for *Neighbors Henceforth*. His plan, as before, was to visit officials and battle sites. A friendship he had developed with Sir Campbell Stuart, Lord Northcliffe's able assistant, grew closer on this visit. Stuart did all within his power to introduce Wister to prominent government officials. One individual Wister met was Harold Macmillan, future prime minister of England. Lord James Bryce supplied him with fresh ideas about the Treaty of Versailles and implored Wister not to quote him. "Good gracious, I never quote anyone!" Wister replied. It was France, however, that was his primary concern on this visit. Wister's anti-German and his pro-Ally sentiments, widely known, caused French hospitality to be just as cordial as in England. "They tell me that your reception in Paris will be mentioned in the literary histories after the manner of Petrarch's satisfactory visit to Rome," Ellery Sedgwick, editor of the *Atlantic Monthly,* wrote to him. Of particular assistance in Paris was André Tardieu, intimate adviser to Premier Georges Clemenceau, who managed the difficult feat of giving Wister a "white-hot half hour" of Clemenceau's busy schedule. "Heavens, what a man," Wister wrote of Clemenceau in his journal. "I came away feeling as if I had conversed with Vesuvius." At eighty years of age, the walruslike premier was as "vital and volcanic" as Roosevelt had been at forty. More important to Wister, Clemenceau seemed to ratify what he himself had been saying about the need for harsh peace terms. Wister observed that it would be difficult to make a hundred million people agree with the two of them, but "plenty of my class understand it," he assured Clemenceau.[44]

When he interviewed public officials Wister never neglected to ask his favorite question: How was it that the German army was allowed to return home with its arms and banners? No one could answer the question to his satisfaction. Neither did Germany's postwar attitude commend itself to him. "Germany is showing herself to be the liar, the sneak, the whiner, & the bully that she has been all along. A contemptible people."[45]

One grave he particularly wanted to inspect was that of Theodore Roosevelt's youngest son, Quentin, who had been shot down over a battlefield. As a tot in the White House, Quentin had been one of the First Family's children Wister had entertained by his singing and piano playing. Now, en route to Quentin's burial site, Wister saw men at work at Nesle digging up bodies of American soldiers from their graves to be sent home to their families. The upheaval of these beautiful, solemn cemeteries distressed Wister. His feelings about its impropriety were heightened when he learned that many of the bodies were torn and misshaped beyond recognition. Far better, he thought, for the dead soldiers' remains to rest in tranquility at a lovely site than to be dug up and shipped to America for burial in a family plot where in not many years they might be forgotten. He drafted a four-hundred-word letter of protest over the practice of "exploiting mothers' grief to put money in certain pockets" and sent it to the American Legion and the Paris bureau of the *New York Times*. The *Times* reproduced the letter on the front page of its April 15 edition in America. Wister's unguarded words constituted a shocking document for parents of the war dead. Sadder even than the sites of ruined towns and forests, he wrote, "is the sight of our cemeteries, from whose peaceful decent dignity the bones of our soldiers who fought together and fell together in France are daily being torn up." The war dead had been buried quickly because of extenuating circumstances, he pointed out. "There were no coffins—there could be none. Bodies were sometimes wrapped in blankets and sometimes put in baskets. Mud has filled these baskets and in winter has frozen to a hard cake. Those who take this mass up often place the basket on top of a stove to melt the mud off and find something left to send to America." And that was not the worst aspect of the situation, for he claimed that once in the United States "piles of these poor fragments of human beings lie at Hoboken unclaimed. They have been dragged there from the soil their sacrifice made sacred. . . . Now many go to Potter's Field. . . . Can nothing stop this hideous mockery of the living and the dead?" Accompanying Wister's letter was one from the former American ambassador to Italy, Thomas Nelson Page, who in far less vivid words voiced the same opinion.[47]

The question raised was a difficult one for those parents whose sons' bodies lay far away in European cemeteries they probably never would see. Their anguish was compounded by Wister's morbid description of masses of mud being heated so that odd bits of bones could be retrieved from the muck. A flurry of vehement pro and con discussions arose. Once again, Wister's penchant for overstatement made him vulnerable to charges of overemotionalizing the issue. A *New York Times* reporter visited the Graves Registration Bureau at Hoboken, New Jersey, to view those "piles" of unclaimed human fragments. He found solemn rows of coffins in a great shed "as quiet as a cathedral," guarded day and night by sentries and watched over by Army chaplains "to see that every possible honor" was paid their memory. A captain in charge of the Bureau told the reporter than only two out of 14,852 bodies returned from Europe had been unclaimed—one of these already had been buried with military honors at the National Cemetery in Arlington, Virginia, and the second was to be sent there shortly. The national commander of the American Legion, Colonel F. W. Galbraith, Jr., vehemently declared in "brusque soldier language" that the Legion would never allow the body of a returned soldier to be buried in Potter's Field. The national president of the Bring Home the Soldier Dead League called Wister's remarks "cowardly propaganda" and the "worst illustration of heartlessness yet published." The father of one dead soldier labeled the letter "ghoulishly shocking." It was only natural and proper, these men and others argued, for grieving parents and relatives to want the remains of their loved ones returned home. In fact, according to a government survey, nearly seventy percent of the parents wanted their sons' bodies returned.[48]

Yet United States War Department officials seemed pleased that Wister had expressed a sentiment with which they agreed but that they could not promote. Their statements clearly indicated a preference that the dead soldiers should remain in Europe. They acknowledged that they would follow the wishes of all parents and would return the bodies at government expense. Others added knowledgeable support of Wister's position, as well as authentication of his ugly description of the conditions of the bodies. The *New York Times* urged Americans to follow Wister's advice and leave their war dead in the peace and dignity of the French countryside. While the impassioned letter did not win many new friends for Wister, or enhance his reputation for objectivity or accuracy, it served the useful purpose of focusing national attention on the matter and causing parents to examine in a new light the question of what to do with their war dead.[49]

In August, Wister returned to the United States, having been gone eight months instead of the two he had planned. On the day he stepped onto the New York harbor he noted on his calendar that he already had a "bad blank homesick feeling for Europe." It was a feeling he would not lose for the remainder of his life. Henceforth he would make frequent journeys there to enjoy the culture that he believed commercialism and the rise of the masses had made impossible for America.[50]

The image that Wister projected now to the American public was an entirely different one from that he had held as author of *The Virginian*. The *Rochester* (New York) *Herald*, which had so warmly described him in a lengthy feature a decade earlier, hailed his return to American shores by calling him the author of "an American hymn of hate." He should find things in Washington to his liking, the brief item continued, because Woodrow Wilson had left the White House. A month later the newspaper described him as "the most contemptible scribbler that the war had developed outside Germany."[51]

Wister's public utterances had fallen into a pattern characterized by bitterness. As a result, a significant part of the public that once had adored him no longer did. One man, complaining of Wister's recent "scandal-mongerish" style, warned that he was among the many readers who had known and enjoyed Wister's talents but now believed the author was "making grave mistakes, not only for your own reputation, but towards a malignant spirit which is all too manifest in our country today."[52]

Interesting news of a personal nature awaited Wister upon his return. He learned that his son Owen Jones, a junior at Harvard, had achieved hero status for saving a boy's life on the Charles River. Young Wister had dived into the water from a shell to rescue a fourteen-year-old boy who was enmeshed underwater in eel grass. Newspapers had given wide coverage to the event.[53]

The only pressing burden awaiting Wister was to write *Neighbors Henceforth*. He completed the job on Decoration Day in 1922 in Philadelphia. This volume lacked the venom that had marked *The Pentecost of Calamity* and *The Straight Deal*, perhaps because the war was further removed in time. Its subject—the need for postwar Allied cooperation—did not attract readers in an age already preoccupied with the good times of the 1920s. The book's critical acceptance was mostly favorable—the *New York Times* applauded the author's "new and very human viewpoint"—but the reading public was not interested in it. As soon as the book was issued, as Wister later observed, it "immediately expired." Wister did not regret having made the effort, though, for gathering the information in Europe had been an experience he declared he would repeat gladly if it were possible.[54]

Chapter XVI

ENTANGLEMENTS
(1923–1938)

THE WAR'S END USHERED IN A NEW AGE, and new American writers: Ernest Hemingway, F. Scott Fitzgerald, John Dos Passos, Gertrude Stein, Eugene O'Neill, Sherwood Anderson, E. E. Cummings, and T. S. Eliot. Owen Wister, age sixty in 1920, had not published a volume of fiction since 1911 when a collection of his stories appeared as *Members of the Wedding*. He no longer even mentioned a next novel; he had no plans to write one. He had long since recognized an unpleasant fact—his greatest talent had been the short story. Every lengthy work of fiction he had done save for the lackluster *Lady Baltimore* had been in essence, if not in fact, a collection of short stories loosely tied together. His most faithful readers—those who treasured his western stories and above all *The Virginian*—did not follow him into nonfiction. For them and for many others he was a forgotten man.

"Are you alive[?] Oh I hope so," a woman from Maine asked Wister in a letter. Another wrote in 1925 to say that she was astonished to have learned just the previous week that he was alive—she had read his premature obituary in 1911 and never learned the truth.[1]

Indeed Wister was alive—very much so—and unlike earlier days he at last was free from illness. He was an even more unusual mixture of ingredients now than ever before. He was the thick-waisted, graying, and genial gentleman who lounged around the fires at the Philadelphia Club and chatted freely with old and new friends about times gone by and current events. He was careful not to neglect his lifelong friendships, making especially sure he attended meetings at the Tavern Club in Boston. He was an international traveler who between 1919 and 1938 sailed to Europe on fourteen occasions, usually accompanied by one or more of his children. He remained, of course, a writer, one who tended now in his work to be reminiscent about old friends and past experiences. He also produced some new western tales and poetry, and he undertook a corporate history and a book-length appreciation of wines.

307

Finally, he was an aging curmudgeon, quick to render a tart judgment on events of the day, a tendency that continued to embroil him in public debate.[2]

It was this tendency to get involved—whether it be in innocent committee work or in public controversy—that provided Wister with an excuse from prolonged writing. Chapman, in his blunt fashion, warned him in 1922 that he should not permit himself to be trapped for as long as a single hour by any organization or effort that bored him, and also that he should fret less about his sons who were nearing manhood. "You are still under the harrow & you *must get out*," Chapman told him. Chapman was right. When General John J. Pershing spoke at the Tavern Club, it was Wister who traveled to Boston to introduce him; when Georges Clemenceau came to America to address the American Committee for Devastated France, it was Wister who introduced him. When Upton Sinclair was proposed for a Nobel Prize, it was Wister who stepped forward to oppose him. Whenever an introduction to a book was needed, a committee member or chairman sought, it was Wister to whom his friends turned for help. He enjoyed the work; he chose not to seek relief from the harrow.[3]

One of the duties was his service as an overseer at Harvard, a task he performed from 1912 to 1925. In March 1923 Wister addressed his fellow overseers shortly after Harvard president Abbott Lawrence Lowell's unfortunate effort to establish a quota system to reduce the number of Jewish students. Wister chose to defend Lowell in a speech calculated to touch sensitive nerves. "Jews are perfectly free to found colleges of their own," he said bluntly. The goal at Harvard, he declared, was not to exclude all Jews but to seek a "quantity and a quality that will mix with us, and become Americans, as certain well known Jews in several of our cities have done." That excessive numbers of Jews seemed undesirable was evident in the actions of students at a Virginia school who, according to Wister, took pains to "run them out" because the Jews annoyed others. A second potential problem Wister addressed was the Negro question, but here the concern was not so great, Wister felt, because the "black belt" of the South was far away. He also reminded the audience that "there are Hampton, Tuskegee, and other colleges where Africans are taught those things for which their brains are adapted." Just what those brains were capable of doing, he said, was demonstrated by seven thousand years of history. Wister also doubted the wisdom of new freshman dormitories at Harvard that sought to democratize beginning students by requiring all of them to live there during their first year. In his view, the mandatory dormitories had the negative effect of creating a more diluted Harvard than that poured into his veins.[4]

All these observations melded into one overall concern which had been close to the top of Wister's agenda since the turn of the century: the displacement of the "American" way of life by aliens and alien ways. Russians, Poles, and Italians were all—so Wister stated—below the average American in intelligence; yet for twenty-five years the nation had been diluting its basic Anglo stock by receiving these strangers with open arms. Australia and Canada had set proper examples by placing quotas on undesirable immigrants. "The cuckoo is a perfectly good bird, but he is not a bird of my feather, and I don't want his eggs on my nest," Wister summarized to the Harvard audience. The fact that the speech, filled with material that today would be highly controversial, created hardly a stir was more a commentary on the climate of the times than on Wister's inability to create headlines on the occasion.[5]

There were other battles waiting. While Wister ardently disapproved of Prohibition, like many Americans he had been too preoccupied with the war to seriously oppose its enactment. Now he publicly joined hands with the Association Against the Prohibition Amendment. To express his feelings in his own way he wrote a scathing and scintillating "dry opera" in three acts entitled *Watch Your Thirst* for the Tavern Club. Reminiscent of *Dido and Aeneas,* its conflict centered on the battle between a "wet" king and his "dry" queen. Performed by members of the Tavern Club in 1924, the musical was so successful that it was revived for performances in 1927 and 1933.[6]

In another controversy Wister found himself again under attack. The New York commissioner of accounts condemned the use of Wister's books in the schools because they allegedly contained anti-American propaganda and besmirched American values with their pro-British stances. Such was Wister's bounty for being identified as an Anglophobe.[7]

He was the protagonist in yet another matter—Butler Place continued to be threatened by urban growth. The property surrounding the once-spacious estate had been reduced to seventeen acres by 1924, with housing developments on all sides. When the city opened Sixteenth Street from Olney Avenue to Nedro Avenue, Wister sued for damages. The trial lasted three days. The jury personally inspected the property, and finally it ruled against Wister by concluding that rather than decreasing the property's value the street enhanced it by at least five thousand dollars. For Wister this was the final blow. He began looking for a new house.[8]

Yet another war-related controversy involved Wister in a debate of national dimensions. Wister placed himself in the seemingly untenable position of opposing aid for starving children in Germany. The debate arose innocently enough when General Henry T. Allen, chairman of the executive committee for the American Committee for Relief of German Children, asked him to join the effort to prevent the "wholesale starvation" of German children by serving on Philadelphia's subcommittee. Wister declined, not perfunctorily but through an open letter that highly criticized the relief body's function. It was reprinted with accompanying news stories throughout the land. In effect, Wister accused the committee of gross distortion. Americans sent to investigate the question of food shortages, he claimed, had reported that a fine harvest had supplied ample grain, that Germans in need of food numbered a hundred thousand, not millions, and that only "fat stuffs" were scarce. This latter shortage, he wrote, had been alleviated already by a huge shipment of American hogs. The absurdity of the notion of relief for German children was underscored by Germans who were "buying prodigially the most expensive French wines and the latest Paris fashions." All this, Wister confessed, was hearsay to him, but what was not hearsay were the "expensive Swiss hotels crowded with German profiteers, conspicuous for their eating, their drinking, and their jewels," which Wister personally had seen. "May I not suggest that before asking American help, you invite these German profiteers to look after their own flesh and blood?" he asked.[9]

Four days later General Allen responded publicly with statistics indicating that three million German children were suffering from a lack of food and that the German people were doing fifty times as much for their relief as all other sources combined. Wister answered by saying that reports on Germany were conflicting and that nobody seemed to be calling attention to France's needs. A flurry of editorials and letters resulted, and once more Wister's mailbox overflowed with critical letters. One adjunct squabble which developed was between Wister and George Sylvester Viereck, editor of the *American Monthly*. Their entire exchange was reproduced in that journal. An amusing aspect of the debate was that all but the first of the seven letters exchanged were written by the secretaries of the two men. Neither deigned give the appearance of personal involvement.[10]

Such contretemps could not be avoided by a man who inevitably preferred to take positions opposite to conventional wisdom. His disdain for the masses and their preferences was suggested indirectly by Edgar Rice Burroughs, who commented in his widely read column that he understood Wister deplored having written *The Virginian.* Wister protested that indeed he was proud to be its author. It was a fact, however, that when asked his own preferences among his literary creations he cited not *The Virginian,* but three short stories, "Philosophy 4," "Padre Ignacio," and "The Right Honorable the Strawberries."[11]

"Padre Ignacio" had been published in 1900 and "Philosophy 4" in 1901, just before *The Virginian.* Wister claimed a special fondness for "Padre Ignacio" because it dealt not with frontier action, as did so many of his earlier works, but with a priest's personal debate about whether or not to yield to his desire to return to the culture of Europe and to abandon his ministry among the simple and uneducated Indians. It thus explicitly involved the conflict between civilization and frontier, and also the struggle between duty and pleasure. Having chosen, after much inner turmoil, to return to Europe after twenty years among the Indians, the padre changes his mind just before the boat departs because of the arrival of a last letter from a dying youth, the same youth who earlier had prompted Padre Ignacio's yearning to leave. Even though the decision to stay seems right, it is clear that the padre's sustenance of the mind will continue to come not from his surroundings but from music and books which arrive periodically from Europe.[12]

"Philosophy 4" was a rather innocuous tale about two carefree Harvard students who hire a bookish, boring fellow student to prepare them for a philosophy examination. As it turns out, the two students, who seem hardly to care one way or another, make a higher exam grade than their tutor because they are witty and imaginative, and their tutor can do no more than recite facts learned from books. The story caused some stir in Boston when it appeared in 1901 because of its depiction of Harvard students engaging in questionable behavior and using improper language, but Wister insisted on the story's fidelity as it had been based on an actual incident—when he was an undergraduate—involving a good friend (Robert Simes).[13]

The best of the three, "The Right Honorable the Strawberries," was written some twenty-five years later, appearing first in *Cosmopolitan* in November 1926. The tale was loosely based on a true anecdote related years earlier to Wister by Amos W. Barber, governor of Wyoming. It

311

concerned a young Easterner who came to Fort Fetterman (renamed "Drybones" in Wister's fiction), lapsed into dissolution through his gambling, and was run out of town. Wister transformed the tenderfoot into a winsome, youthful Englishman of aristocratic background who had been disowned by his family but who still received a regular remittance from them for living expenses. Helped especially by a cowboy named Chalkeye, he attempts for a while to integrate himself into the life and customs of Drybones. Success at this effort appears at hand, but somehow it cannot be achieved, and "Strawberries," as the cowboys nickname the Englishman, begins participating in nightly card games at the hotel with the town's gamblers. He loses regularly until finally he reverts to the practice that caused his banishment from England—cheating. So thoroughly does he degenerate that he even cheats the very cowboys who have befriended him. When Chalkeye learns of a plot to kill Strawberries, he arranges a ruse to get the youth out of town, only to be shot and killed himself. The story ends when years later the narrator (obviously Wister), having heard of the Englishman's purposeless wanderings over the West, encounters him once more in Drybones, now a ghost town. In a poignant ending, Strawberries suggests and the narrator agrees that he was not the man that Chalkeye was.

What Wister portrays in the story is the utter incompatibility of the two societies represented. Strawberries' conversion, despite his ability to ride and his mastery of other skills of the cowboys' art, is a failure. The gulf between the two civilizations is too broad. Separated from his native civilization, Strawberries is unable to adapt to the new western setting, and without one or the other he is doomed.

A common thread through all three of these favorite stories of Wister's is the inability of individuals to adapt successfully to new settings. In "Padre Ignacio," the priest accepts a voluntary exile to an Indian mission because he is too liberal to get along satisfactorily with his European church hierarchy. Then he similarly is unable to achieve mental serenity in the frontier because of his yearning for the culture of Europe. In "Philosophy 4," a bookish student who can parrot the textbooks for his professors makes a lower grade than his two pupils because the exam questions require an imaginative, thoughtful response rather than a mere recitation of facts. He is incapable, despite his sharpness, of changing his approach. And in "The Right Honorable the Strawberries," the Englishman is unable to adjust himself to the culture of Drybones.[14]

Did Wister prefer these stories, did he use this theme so frequently in his western writing, because of the resemblance to his own story? His decision to leave Paris as a musical student came, ultimately, not because of his father's opposition (his father at the end had approved Wister's continued stay) and his mother's instability, but because he had admitted to himself that he was too conventional to fit that style of life. Next came Wister's failure to adjust to a career in business in Boston; neither did his choice of the law as a profession satisfy him. For a while the West had seemed to him to be an answer, for here everyone was adapting and creating a new setting which would shed old shibboleths and produce a new type of individual. These hopes evaporated as well, and when Wister at last accepted, appreciated, and began to relish his own eastern heritage, the urge within him to write such stories faded, and his productivity nearly ceased altogether.

Now, in the mid-1920s, the significance of his greatest work, *The Virginian*, could be viewed with some perspective. "I doubt whether you realize the quantity of its importance as a contribution to American history," Philip A. Rollins, a Princeton University historian who specialized in cowboy lore, wrote to Wister. The book, the play, the film versions, and a host of imitators had painted an indelible portrait of the cowboy as characterized by Wister for millions of Americans.[15]

The impact of this enduring work surfaced at times in unsuspecting ways, such as the christening of the world's largest locomotive as *The Virginian*. When Douglas Fairbanks met Wister's sister-in-law, Mrs. Jansen Haines, in Hollywood, he demonstrated for her the various poses he would take as the Virginian. He seemed obsessed with the idea, yet he confessed sadly that he really was too small to play the role, even though he had bought motion picture rights. The character, he acknowledged, not only was too large in stature for him, but also was too sharply defined as a soft-talking, easy-going individual.[16]

Thus, when in the summer of 1923 the second movie version of *The Virginian* was filmed in the High Sierras, not Fairbanks but an actor named Kenneth Harlan played the title role. Florence Vidor portrayed Molly, and Russell Simpson took the part of Trampas. The filming required six weeks of work in a remote area nearly eight miles from telephone or telegraph. To supply the three hundred or so people involved, fifty mules hauled in ninety tons of goods; fifty steers were slaughtered and cooked; and an entire mountain village was constructed for the crew. The filming was not without mishap. Harlan accidentally shot himself in the street duel scene, halting production for a week. Two pack mules fell to their deaths, slipping off narrow mountain trails. Before Christmas 1923, the finished silent movie, released by Preferred Pictures, was showing to avid western fans throughout the nation. It introduced the Virginian to still another generation of Americans.[17]

Fairbanks wrote to Wister to express his dismay that he had not been involved in the movie. He never lost his fascination for the book or for its author. Three years later, when the two met for the first time in person in Rome, Fairbanks turned to his Italian escort and said, "This man has influenced my life more than any other man, I'd rather see him than anything here except Mussolini!"[18]

Claimants for the honor of having served as the original model of the Virginian continued to surface. Wister, quietly amused, never publicly disputed any of them. None of the publicized models could make a claim with any legitimacy. One individual widely reported to be the original Virginian was Edwin B. Trafton, an early settler of the Teton Basin country. In August 1922 Trafton was drinking a soda in downtown Los Angeles when he dropped dead. A note found in his pocket, addressed "To Whom It May Concern" and signed by a special agent of the United States Department of Justice, proclaimed Trafton as Wister's model for the Virginian. The item was reproduced in newspapers throughout the country, and when the *Los Angeles Times* wired Wister for his comments, he refused to reply. Privately, however, he declared the claim to be "bosh." It is likely that he had met Trafton in Wyoming, but there is no record of it.[19]

The same year another newspaper article from Methow Valley in Washington declared Milton Storey to be the Virginian, and his wife the model for Molly Stark. Wister's private comment was "nonsense." Another account, with an even more unlikely claimant for the honor, emerged in 1924 when the former governor of Puerto Rico, E. Montgomery Reily, wrote to ask if the assertion by his former chief of police that he was the model for the Virginian were true. The man since had been discharged for bootlegging. Other claims were equally farfetched.[20]

A different kind of indication of the book's lasting hold on the public came later that year from a Massachusetts man. He wrote to Wister to say that he had read *The Virginian* 141 times.[21]

Domestic affairs consumed an increasingly large portion of Wister's attention. He had sold his Jackson Hole ranch not long after Molly's death, but he still had to be watchful over the declining condition of Butler Place, of 913 Pine Street, of his speculative property in San Diego, and of the summer place at Saunderstown he called Crowfield. When he advertised for a caretaker to look after Crowfield he painted a quaint picture of his life there. "I sell a little milk and a few pigs and depend upon my kitchen garden for my summer vegetables and upon some crops, and I desire to raise apples in a small way." Saunderstown remained a favorite gathering place for the Wister children, who now were becoming adults.[22]

In the fall of 1920, Marina turned twenty-one, happily leaving the supervision of the aunt who had taken over a principal role in the rearing of the children after their mother's death. Marina received an inheritance of seventy-five thousand dollars, which assured her of an annual income of four thousand dollars to five thousand dollars. She had developed a taste for art, encouraged by her father who believed that she had his own mother's keen critical sense. Foremost, though, Marina wrote poetry. In 1920 she won the Browning Medal for her poem, "The Sea." Four years later Macmillan published the first of several volumes of her poetry entitled *Helen and Others*, dedicated to her mother's memory.[23]

Owen II, Bill, and then Carl followed their father to Harvard. Owen did well and went on to law school while Carl, who had trouble with mathematics, was less happy there and did not complete his studies. The youngest child, Sarah, remained in New England under special care, crippled and retarded, until she died in late 1935 after an appendectomy.[24]

In late 1924 Wister realized his desire to buy a big house with suitable grounds as a substitute for Butler Place. It was a brick house on Bryn Mawr Avenue priced at $135,000, surrounded by nine acres, and concealed from the road by woods. It had three floors, eight bedrooms, three servants' rooms, a library, and a croquet ground. Wister dubbed his new home "Long House."[25]

Still, wanderlust too was an indelible part of Wister, and he spent about as much time in Europe, Saunderstown, and other places as he did in Philadelphia. In 1924 he visited Europe twice, the first time touring Spain during May and June with Henry Sedgwick, enjoying fine food, wine, and art. The Fourth of July found him sailing home aboard the *SS Minnetonka*, where he presided over a shipboard concert and gave a talk on the significance of the holiday. By September he had left the United States again for England. He was to forgo a European trip in 1925, but, with the exception of 1932, every year thereafter through 1936 would find him on the continent for a period. On one of his visits he met the eccentric Joseph Conrad, who brushed aside Wister's invitation for dinner. It was, for Wister, a "dissolving view" of this writer of sea stories, for the mere request to dine greatly agitated Conrad. "Next month next month not now not now," Conrad replied.[26]

Other American writers, to whom Europe was new and fresh, found inspiration on Paris's Left Bank. Their Europe was not the land Wister knew or appreciated. His was the Europe of privilege, of scenes described by Henry James. These new writers' fresh works only reinforced Wister's own literary decline, and his former partner in cynicism, H. L. Mencken, described Wister's eclipse in this way: "Put Owen Wister, say, against [William Dean] Howells; it is a wart succeeding Ossa." Coming from one of the few critics who had dared praise "Quack Novels and Democracy," this was an especially bitter cup for Wister. He would not forget it.[27]

Actually, Wister already was working on another set of short stories with western settings, his first return to the genre since 1911. Senator Lodge, who along with Oliver Wendell Holmes, Jr., constituted Wister's link to the nation's capital, was "delighted" to hear this news. "The tragedy of the cowboy is over," Lodge wrote, "but it is very desirable that that picturesque creature in our national life should be written up as you can write it up." There was little that Wister could add at this point to his established portrait of the cowboy, however, and a series of distractions delayed completion of the stories.[28]

When a group of individuals protested that medical experiments performed on animals constituted cruelty and sought to stop the practice, Wister felt obliged to respond vigorously. The result appeared in a newspaper feature service as "Your Child's Life—Or a Guinea Pig's?" Identified as "the Famous Novelist"—his perennial label—Wister cited numerous medical experiments with animals that had forwarded research and aided mankind. He repeated the theme a few months later in his introduction to Earnest Harold Baynes's *Animal Heroes of the Great War* (1925), and he won praise from the *New York Times* for his "savage indictment of folly and malice blown large by fanaticism." Wister also accepted an invitation to write the preface to a book by artist Charles Russell, whose stature as a western interpreter rivaled that

316

of Remington's, but who especially endeared himself to Wister for having been a genuine cowboy.[29]

St. Paul's School still held his allegiance, and he did not hesitate when asked to write the preface to a prospectus for a campus war memorial. This gave Wister another opportunity to reflect on the national character. He recounted recent "blunders" in foreign policy and called them the result not of improper character but of "undisciplined emotion and untrained reflection." While he observed that the spread of knowledge could not keep pace with the increasing birth rate, he thought "training" might help season some of the base emotions that improperly swayed legislation decade after decade. No, he had little hope for the elevation of common America; he had had little since the dawning of the twentieth century. The voice of the people, he believed and wrote, was more frequently the voice of the madhouse than that of God. "No Ship of State," he stressed, "has ever yet been captained by the steerage and escaped the rocks."[30]

Finally, in 1928, his new collection of short stories appeared under the title of *When West Was West*. After a long hiatus from western literature, Wister in these stories related his mature conclusions concerning the meaning of the western experience. This was exemplified especially in "The Right Honorable the Strawberries" which, after its initial appearance in *Cosmopolitan* in 1926, had been honored through its selection for Edward O'Brien's *The Best Short Stories of 1927*. Another one of Wister's best stories, "At the Sign of the Last Chance," also was included in *When West Was West*. The setting once again was Drybones, and again the characters included cowboys, miners, and gamblers, but now Drybones was nearly a ghost town, the Old West merely a series of memories recalled by the players around the card table at the Last Chance Hotel. The card players come to recognize in their rambling discussions that the Last Chance has outlived its time, and following an old English custom about which they have just learned, they take down the sign late at night and bury it with ceremony alongside the creek. For Wister, the West that he had known and loved had long since ended; now came its end in his own literary statement.[31]

In September of 1928 a publishing event occurred which was of great significance to Wister: Macmillan issued an eleven-volume collection of his works. Each book contained a new preface by Wister telling of the general circumstances in which the book had been written. He answered a recurring criticism of years past that he, after all, never actually had been a cowboy. His response was reprinted in many news-papers. "Shouldn't these acute thinkers also remind us that the author of Othello wasn't a nigger, the creator of Sherlock Holmes isn't a detec-tive, and that the man who painted Vesuvius had never seen a volcano?"[32]

After publication of the collection, Wister retreated to a lodge near Yellowstone National Park with his son Carl to await the reviews. His earliest *Harper's* stories, praised at the time of publication for their realis-tic treatment of fresh subjects, long since had been forgotten under the influence of the romanticized *The Virginian*. Now many critics expressed surprise at the striking directness of his short stories. William Curtis, writing in *Town & Country*, said he had disliked *The Virginian* for its "saccharine" and "melodramatic" qualities, but now he apologized for not having recognized the author's "true work," his realistic short stories. In the comments of many others, though, there was an implication that as a writer Wister was outdated. "Because my 'method' ripened in the Victorian era, and not when Sherwood Anderson's did . . . I'm over," Wister commented wryly. "It's like the music-show Jews declining to hear any songs in 6-8 time." Sales lagged so much that Macmillan sought Wister's permission to sell individual copies rather than the en-tire set. He declined.[33]

Still, interest in *The Virginian* itself hardly had lagged in the twenty-six years since its publication. The book now was in its sixteenth edition. Between May 1928 and May 1929 it sold 33,986 copies, an unusually fine showing for any book even in the first year of publication. The per-son who was fortunate enough to own a first edition of *The Virginian* could boast of a market value of $150.[34]

Wister's own position as a western monument was assured, despite latter-day critics. A 1928 historical map of Wyoming listed Medicine Bow as the site for much of the action in *The Virginian*, and by 1933 postcards depicting the Goose Egg Ranch, where the baby swapping allegedly had occurred, were being sold to tourists. The result was that relic-seekers stripped the real Goose Egg of everything removable. As the years ensued, other episodes from the book achieved similar distinc-tion, and a hotel by the name of *The Virginian* sprang up in Medicine Bow, thereby alleviating the need for anyone else to sleep on a store counter. One of the eleven major peaks in the Grand Tetons already had been informally dubbed as Mount Wister, and a suggestion arose in the late 1920s that the federal government officially recognize this desig-nation. (This was done on February 24, 1939.) In 1929 the Roosevelt

Memorial Association presented Wister with a gold medal for recording "for all time the character and atmosphere of the 'wild West' during the last quarter of a century" as well as catching for posterity "the passing figure of the cowboy."[35]

Another honor came in Boston: election as president of the Tavern Club. The club had become an institution since Wister, as a young counting clerk, had become a charter member and William Dean Howells had been its first president. Club members greeted their new president at his inaugural dinner with an eight-stanza poem. Typical were these verses, summarizing in a few words Wister's feats:

> Whose music shames the nightingale?
> Who spins a ripping Western tale?
> Who made the German people quail?
> Dan Wister!

Wister's response was a rambling, reminiscent presidential address recalling good times and interesting guests of the past. Serving as president was a burden he relished, although he pointed out that all seven of his predecessors had lived within thirty minutes from the club, and he was eight hours away.[36]

Few things, if any, did Wister cherish more than good friends, and the Tavern Club had been a rich source for many of those friendships throughout his adult life. The fact that so very many of his friends had been lifelong acquaintances was itself a compelling statement of the tightly knit circles with which Wister was associated. One friend, George Waring, who had returned to New England after several decades in the Methow Valley in Washington, saluted Wister for the qualities that endeared the author to so many. Both had reached the age of sixty-eight, and Waring told Wister that of all the men he had known, Wister received the utmost credit for having deliberately made himself a "consistently high minded & able man." Ellery Sedgwick, who along with his brother Henry also had known Wister for all of his adult life, gave Wister another kind of compliment. "When your obituary is written, there will be plenty said about your talents and your distinguished name in the world, but I am afraid no one will mention your kindness and sympathy to young authors. If you are in hopes of a Christian Heaven that passport will get you there."[37]

Sedgwick's exclamation probably had been prompted by a note from Wister asking if Sedgwick knew where Wister might reach the new young American writer, Ernest Hemingway. "Were I thirty, that's the way I should wish to write," Wister had exclaimed to a friend, praising in particular *The Sun Also Rises* and the short story "Fifty Grand." Hemingway, pleased when he soon heard of Wister's comments, visited Wister at Shell, Wyoming, in 1928 with his second wife. Along with Wister's son, Carl, the foursome enjoyed themselves by fishing in the Snake River, shooting prairie dogs with a pistol from a car, exploring the Tetons, and discussing the new novel Hemingway now was working on, *A Farewell to Arms*. Hemingway genuinely appreciated Wister as well as his talent. "Saw old Wister, sweet old guy, writes damned well too," he told Waldo Peirce after his visit.[38]

The two writers planned another rendezvous that fall in Paris, and although it was delayed until spring 1929, the two men began a correspondence that lasted for several years in which Wister played elder statesman and Hemingway assumed the role of solicitous apprentice. Wister deprecated himself as "damaged goods" at the age of sixty-eight, but the younger writer would have none of it—if Wister were damaged goods Hemingway hoped that he could be just as "damaged" at the same age. In offering criticisms of Hemingway's work, Wister expressed fear that he might seem too harsh. Hemingway urged him to "always go the limit"—only an amateur would be offended. In fact, he insisted to Wister that "you have always had much greater talent." Hemingway told his editor, Maxwell Perkins, that Wister's "The Right Honorable The Strawberries" was "a lesson to our generation in how to write."[39]

Early in 1929 Perkins agreed, at Wister's request, to send him galley proofs of *A Farewell to Arms*. Revisions still were being made, and Wister sent his own suggestions directly to Perkins, praising the work's literary merit. Learning meanwhile that Hemingway was having a momentary financial crisis, Wister dispatched him an impromptu personal check for five hundred dollars. Hemingway returned the check uncashed with profuse thanks; *Scribner's Magazine* had made early payment for first serial rights to *A Farewell to Arms* and had rescued him already. Privately, Hemingway was furious to learn that Perkins had sent the galleys to Wister without his permission, and he was irritated that Wister had criticized his use of profanity. Hemingway's ruffled feelings were soothed early that summer, though, when he and Wister got together twice in Paris, and Wister praised the novel's new ending. On the morning after the second visit, Hemingway wrote to Perkins: "His last words were last night—Don't touch a thing. He is nice and damned kind and generous."* Hemingway apologized to Perkins for his earlier outburst over the galley proofs. Perkins thanked Wister, meanwhile, for the older author's knowledgeable criticisms and for serving as an ally in helping to deal with the sometimes difficult Hemingway. Perkins also used Wister's praise in the book's promotional campaign.[40]

It was at this time that a third film version of *The Virginian* was seen in the nation's movie houses. A tall, laconic actor named Gary Cooper, appearing in his first "talkie," took the title role. Others in the cast included Walter Huston as Trampas, Richard Arlen as Steve, and Mary Brian as Molly. Two years later when Cooper played in the film version of *A Farewell to Arms*, Hemingway sent Wister a telegram observing that the two of them now had something else in common— Gary Cooper portraying both their literary creations.[41]

Meanwhile, Wister glowed once more with anticipation over a new writing project of his own: a personal biography of Theodore Roosevelt. As early as 1920 Mrs. Roosevelt had given her "dear adopted Dan" permission to use her late husband's letters. Wister intended not only to portray the man that he had known and admired, but also to reproduce the atmosphere of the intimate American society to which he and Roosevelt belonged—that is, the close circle of eastern friends whose common interests focused around family, Harvard, wealth, and heritage. Whether such a book would interest outsiders Wister professed not to know—or particularly to care—but he wanted to describe the setting from which a man like Roosevelt could emerge. It was a bygone era, but to Wister it had been a rewarding and much-yearned-for time.[42]

He entitled his book *Roosevelt: The Story of a Friendship*. In it, he portrayed Roosevelt from the moment he had first seen the future president as an undergraduate in the boxing arena at Harvard. Wister wrote of other friends too: John Jay Chapman, Winthrop Chanler, Grant La Farge, Henry Adams, Oliver Wendell Holmes, Jr., Amos French, and Frank Frost. The manuscript was completed at the end of 1929. Upon reading it, George Horace Lorimer of the *Saturday Evening Post* agreed to pay Wister fifteen thousand dollars for the opportunity to publish

* In 1956 Hemingway singled out Wister as one of only a handful of writers he had ever known whom he personally liked. "He was the most unselfish and most dis-interested and the most loving. When my father shot himself and things were not good at all and I was making trust funds and having to discipline my bitch mother and put it all out of my head and do the re-write on A Farewell To Arms . . . he wrote me and sent me a very huge check and said for me not to have any money worries and he would back me all the way." (Carlos Baker, ed., *Ernest Hemingway: Selected Letters, 1917–1961* [New York: Charles Scribner's Sons, 1981], p. 862.)

six excerpts. In the book, Wister included the entire text of the letter Roosevelt had sent him excoriating him over *Lady Baltimore* and its views of the South. Lorimer decided to omit the letter because, he told Wister, it would "hopelessly damn" Roosevelt's memory in that part of the country.[43]

By early summer of 1930 the book had been printed and bound, initial orders taken, and copies shipped across the nation for distribution. At this point Wister sailed to Europe for six months, content to let the book appear in his absence. As George Brett at Macmillan was planning to leave on his own well-deserved vacation, a crisis erupted. A woman in Charleston, South Carolina, having learned in advance of an unfavorable description of her in the book, threatened to sue Wister and Macmillan for libel if it appeared.[44]

The threat could not be taken lightly, for the book accused the woman of having led a life of deception. If this were erroneous, she stood to collect substantial damages. The characterization of her appeared in a lengthy anecdote describing an alleged hoax that she had played on Roosevelt, when, as president in 1902, he visited the Charleston Expedition. Wister, too, was in Charleston at the time, completing *The Virginian.* The official presidential reception committee had decreed that Roosevelt would visit no private homes in Charleston, for it did not seem fair for him to honor just one or two of the many worthwhile homes and families. Yet, according to Wister's account, the woman in question —a recent arrival who was neither by birth nor tradition a Charlestonian —lured Roosevelt into her home by passing off one of her elderly servants as a former slave who would die happy if only he could serve the president a cup of tea. Decent Charleston, realizing what was happening but unable to stop it, was shocked and disgusted at the woman's successful ploy. So was Wister, but he did not reveal the truth to Roosevelt until long after.[45]

The threat of litigation came at an awkward time, for publication was announced, and the books were distributed and ready to sell. No easy remedy was in sight. Urgent cables trailed Wister all over Europe, failing to reach him. Macmillan officials held hurried conferences with Wister's children and attorneys, and the result was a decision to call back all distributed copies, prevail upon Wister to write a new section as a substitution, and then to print a "new" first edition.[46]

News of the month-long postponement of the widely anticipated book quickly surfaced, but the reason was not revealed and the press began to speculate. A news story sent across the nation by Associated Press reported a rumor that the Macmillan Company had "formally demanded" that all copies be returned for revisions because the family of the late Woodrow Wilson strenuously objected to critical statements about him attributed to Roosevelt. Owen Wister II, contacted in lieu of his absent father, refused to comment to the press. Brett, finally reaching Wister in Europe, assured him that the attention "ought to be good publicity for the volume." And indeed it was, for when the revised edition soon appeared it sold out almost immediately, and a new printing commenced. A month after the recall, the original editions, too, had been repaired and were ready once more for distribution.[47]

If readers were expecting a serious analysis of Roosevelt they surely were disappointed. The book was, as the subtitle indicated, no more than "the story of a friendship." Wister relied heavily upon his memory for its contents; he recreated whole conversations from years past; and the only documentation included was the reproduction of numerous letters. Still, the book revealed many intimate moments, including a passage that through the years would be quoted time and time again. This was Wister's recollection of an evening at the White House when Roosevelt exclaimed in exasperation that he could either be president or he could attend to his daughter Alice, but he could not do both.[48]

The book won considerable praise and attention from reviewers as well as from friends, and Edward S. Martin, both friend and critic, told Wister that it revealed Wister and John Jay Chapman to be "incurable aristocrats." Wister responded that Jack, of course, certainly was an aristocrat, but as for himself—"how about my cowboys?"[49]

Wister's most recent book did not, however, prevent a California newspaper editor from declaring the author to be an example of a person who accomplishes something early in life and is remembered for that and for nothing else. Now, at the age of seventy, Wister was "merely the author of 'The Virginian,'" and publishers issued his other books just to be billed as "by the author of 'The Virginian.'" Such notices did not escape Wister's attention, and this one reached him in France. He quickly reacted to the item by writing to the editor, "I can't be sorry, [for] you have provided several people with so hearty laugh and will continue to provide others." The editor's remarks conveyed, Wister told him, an "unintended revelation of yourself." The chastised editor hurriedly answered that he actually was Wister's admirer—he had in his possession not only *The Virginian* but also *Philosophy 4*, the memorial edition of *Roosevelt: The Story of a Friendship*, and now a letter from Wister himself to remind him that "even the great and distant may be annoyed."[50]

Wister's own moments of despair were not helped by such remarks —which were all too frequent these days—or by the Crash of 1929. In the fall of 1930 he returned from Europe thoroughly disgusted at the economic turmoil and convinced that the nation's own excesses had created the problems. Now, Wister said, he could understand how intelligent people of the Middle Ages could wall themselves away from the world and turn to prayer and gardening.[51]

He had not been home long, though, when his spirits were cheered by a remarkable testament to the power of *The Virginian*. A Colorado rancher, having deliberated twenty-five years over the matter, wrote Wister a warm, lengthy letter describing the book's influence over his own life. The novel had caused him to leave the East and move to the West to become a rancher, and ever since then the book had sustained him. He read it twice each year, and once he had even played Trampas in an amateur production of the play. Now he had a feeling deep in his heart that

> when I die and go to Heaven, perhaps after I have fixed fences up there for a few years they'll give me a vacation and let me come back to the Wind River Country for awhile so Mandy [his wife] and me can ride horseback over that section apicking out a ideal spot for a new ranch. Some afternoon we might catch glimpses of the Virginian and Molly ariding ahead of us. And then meby we would see you fishing along a creek or asitting in the shade awriting a story. On our way back we'd pick you up and the three of us would ride back to Judge's Ranch, where you'd make us acquainted with everybody and we'd spend the evening. When it got late we'd start back to Heaven and then meby change our minds and stay right there forever provided you stayed with us.

Such a letter deserved a warm answer, and Wister gave one, an act which prompted another response from the rancher.[52]

"No letter you ever wrote fetched more happiness to anyone," he said. He and his wife had declared a holiday on the ranch, put on their dress clothes, read the letter over and over, and sat talking for more than an hour as they watched the sunlight leave Pike's Peak.

> Mandy said to me after a long silence, "I didn't know a letter from a stranger could make anyone as happy as this one did you." I looked straight at her and said "It couldn't." So thanks for your letter Mr. Wister

and its our hope that no fences bar you from the Range of Good Health for many years to come and always.[53]

A few months later a letter of an entirely different nature evoked a furious reaction from Wister. Ernest S. Greene and a committee of some twenty distinguished Americans proposed that Wister, as a member of the American Academy of Arts and Letters, join them in their petition that Upton Sinclair be awarded the Nobel Prize. Wister was outraged. Sinclair was an avowed Socialist, an exponent of everything Wister detested, and a man whose every action had disgusted him since they had corresponded some thirty years earlier. He absolutely refused to consider the idea. He told Greene that Sinclair advocated communism, that his morals were abhorrent, his views "flighty and chemerical, his writing purely journalistic, and sensational publicity his chief desire." For some unchivalrous reason, Greene forwarded Wister's intemperate reply to Sinclair himself at his home in Pasadena, California. The letter incensed Sinclair, who in his own white heat of fury sent a bitter reply to Wister. Could this be the American literary aristocrat's idea of courtesy and fair play? Sinclair said he was not a communist, he was a socialist, and the blurring of that distinction made it obvious that Wister had not even read his works. However, Sinclair said, the primary purpose for writing was not to defend himself but to remind Wister of the time twenty-eight years earlier when Wister had declined to assist him at a moment of desperate need. Sinclair, referring to himself in the third person, painted an emotional picture of himself as a semistarving, unknown writer living on thirty dollars a month in two small tents with a wife and an ill child, while struggling to do the research for *Manassas*, his Civil War novel.

There was a popular and prosperous novelist [Wister] living not far from him [Sinclair], and the younger man, not knowing the world very well, was moved to send the great man one of his crude, early books. Receiving a letter of encouragement from the older man, he was moved to write again, and reveal the dreadful conditions in which he was situated. . . . They were close to starvation. . . . The popular and prosperous novelist wrote that he was deeply sympathetic to the young writer's purposes, and that he and his wife would come to call. That, of course, caused great excitement in the young writer's family, and the promised visit was eagerly awaited—but in vain. The young man wrote once or twice to remind the great man of his promise, but if any answer was received it was a polite evasion. The young man struggled on by himself; building a little cabin, partly with his own hands, where he and his wife and baby continued to exist upon that $30 per month. The wife came close to suicide and the baby close to death from pneumonia. But "Manassas" was written and in due course published.

If Wister had kept his promise and called upon the younger writer, giving needed support, Snclair might never have "grown up to be what you call 'an advocate of Communism.' " Instead, the younger writer might have followed in the steps of his ancestors and become a naval officer. But such had not happened, and here they were—Wister, a man of "wealth and fashion, the arbiter of accepted letters, the holder of academic honors, the recipient of all the dignified publicity you desire; and I, the author of 'The Brass Check,' lied about and suppressed, obliged, when my cause is in peril, to seek what you sneer at as 'sensational publicity.' " Sinclair concluded with a ringing cry, calculated to upset Wister all the more, for the collapse of the established social order and the triumph of socialism.[54]

For Wister, this impassioned letter only indicated anew Sinclair's perfidy, and he told him so bluntly in a rejoinder. Sinclair had conveniently neglected to say that Mrs. Wister indeed had visited him and his family, and that she afterwards had sent them an accumulation of household supplies. With this letter the correspondence ended, both men remaining firm in their convictions that the other represented a menace to society. Sinclair did not receive the Nobel Prize.[55]

"It's not my world anymore," Wister observed as the twenties neared an end. What kept him going, he said, were his children. They were graduating from college, marrying, and having children. Fanny was the first to marry. In 1928 she was wed to Walter Stokes, a Philadelphia banker who loved fox hunting and who at forty-two was considerably older and calmer than the high-spirited Fanny. He was, in Wister's opinion, "very nice looking, with the *right* sort of look—most pleasant voice—makes an excellent cocktail." Fanny's twin, Owen Jones, graduated from Harvard in 1927 after a stint characterized by his father as "obscure." Afterwards, Owen studied law at the University of Pennsylvania and then joined the Biddle law firm in Philadelphia. Bill graduated from Harvard and married in 1929 in the face of his father's opposition. Within a few months, though, Wister decided he had been wrong in opposing the match. Bill soon entered business in New York City. Carl followed his father and older brothers to Harvard, but unlike them he was not happy there, and he withdrew. Marina, the eldest child and unmarried as the 1930s dawned, published her second volume of poetry in 1930, *Night in the Valley*. Her father was convinced that she would not marry a "conventional" man, and in 1933 she met an unconventional man in Santa Fe, New Mexico, named Andrew Dasburg, a forty-four-year-old artist and holder of a Guggenheim Fellowship. Born in Paris, Dasburg had twice won first prize at the Carnegie Institute's International Exhibition. By 1933 Wister, seventy-three, was grandfather to three children.[56]

Other chapters began closing in Wister's life. A Wyoming man wrote to say that the author might enjoy a return to Fort Washakie, which was lovelier than ever, but Wister said he did not ever want to see it or any part of that country again because they held too much nostalgia for him. Still, he could say that after a full life of seventy-three years he had never enjoyed anything more than those camping days in Wyoming.[57]

Old friends were dying, and invariably it was Wister who wrote memorials for them. His other writing consisted almost entirely of reminiscing. Younger authors and men of letters were beginning to venerate him as one who had been friends with such people as Henry James, William Dean Howells, Mark Twain, and Oliver Wendell Holmes, Jr. Wister began sorting out his personal papers, adding notes of clarification when necessary.[58]

The hardest loss came in late 1933 when John Jay Chapman died. Doctors had feared cancer, surgery confirmed their suspicions, and a month later he was dead. Just as Wister had been there to console Chapman after he had held his hand in the burning coals, he was there now on his dying day. These two men, almost miraculously, had maintained a close friendship throughout their lives, even when Chapman's acerbity had at one time or another alienated practically every other close associate. Wister had spent Chapman's last day in the hospital consoling and helping the Chapman family, performing what Chapman's son Chanler described as "a grand piece of rescue work." Soon Wister paid tribute to Chapman in an article for the *Atlantic Monthly*.[59]

He might well have taken Chapman's death as a signal to slow down himself, but he stayed as busy as ever—perhaps busier. He served as president of the Library Company of Philadelphia, one of whose founders was Benjamin Franklin, and when it celebrated its 200th anniversary on April 21, 1932, Wister was the inevitable speaker. He also was chairman of the trustees of the Mutual Assurance Co., known as the Green Tree, insurers of homes against fire, and in 1935 he began writing a history of the company. Such activities did not prevent a regular schedule of golf or trips to Europe.[60]

As president of the Tavern Club he began planning in early 1934 a grand fiftieth anniversary for the membership. Almost every Monday throughout the summer and fall—save for a five-week stay in France—he traveled to Boston for a Tavern Club meeting, and on November 1, 1934, the long-anticipated celebration took place. Members wore green, red, yellow, blue, or purple waistcoats; fifty-year medals were presented to Wister and other charter members; Wister recited a poem and presided over the entire joyous occasion. The high point was the presentation of Wister's comic opera, *Watch Your Thirst*, the satirical musical that he had revised the previous year. "A supreme success," he privately noted in his pocket calendar. Having served now as president for five years, he resigned shortly after the anniversary.[61]

Wister managed to muster the willpower to decline an offer to be president of the Harvard Alumni Association. A growing disenchantment with Harvard helped him refuse. He and Chapman mutually had been dismayed at what they considered Harvard's inability or unwillingness to teach English properly. Because of this disgust Wister even refused to preside over a dinner of the Harvard Associated Clubs in Philadelphia. The college's downfall, he thought, had begun when Charles Eliot had introduced the elective system. In so doing, he believed, Eliot merely had anticipated the popular tide, and the result for higher education everywhere was chaos.[62]

A poignant letter came in 1934 from the man who so many years before had guided him in his Wyoming hunting adventures—George B. West. It was only the second letter West had written to Wister in the past thirty years, the other having come fourteen years earlier when West had declared that with all his own faults he still loved Wister as he had "long years ago." The unfortunate West once again had encountered adversity. "I think of you every day," West wrote, "when I go about my work as a janitor in an apartment house." During his years in Seattle he had managed to acquire three apartment houses, one at a time, and to create a comfortable life for himself and his wife. But the Depression caused him to lose all three of his properties, reducing him to his present difficult circumstances. He told Wister that he had lost fifty-five thousand dollars to a "chiseler" and that his eyesight was failing. Despite these unguarded comments to a friend he had not seen for many years, in Seattle West exhibited to his family and acquaintances an unusual formality far removed from the cowboy life of Wyoming. Every day of the week he donned coat and tie, vest, and an old-fashioned celluloid collar. A nephew who saw him frequently could not recall, years later, a single instance in which his uncle had not been attired in this manner.* West told Wister that many of his friends were asking him why he did not write a sequel to *The Virginian.* "They all think it would be a good seller—I suppose it would come after I have passed away?" As far as West was concerned, there was no question about it— he himself was the Virginian. Ironically, this man, whose supposed lack of self-control had brought a breach in his relationship with Wister, never publicly claimed the honor. Only his close friends and relatives heard the story.[63]

During this decade of the 1930s music reemerged as an essential part of Wister's life. Perhaps even now he regretted the lost opportunity for a musical career, especially when he heard the Tavern Club's loud applause for *Watch Your Thirst.*

In 1933 he wrote to John A. Lomax, the first man to collect folk songs from the cattle country, and asked him how he spelled "dogie" in "Git Along Little Dogies." Wister had been uncertain about it since that day forty years earlier when he had copied the song's first five stanzas exactly as a Texas cowboy had sung them on Fitzhugh Savage's West Texas ranch. Lomax answered the question and countered with his own request: would Wister send the musical annotations for the "dogie song" as he had recorded them in 1893? Lomax wanted to include it in his collection as "most probably the earliest record of what I consider the most typical of all cowboy songs." Wister faithfully forwarded the information, and Lomax observed that Wister had obtained from that Brady City cowboy "the best extant copy of 'Git Along Little Dogies.' "[64]

What prompted Wister's curiosity about the spelling of "dogie" is unknown, but he now was busily composing his own music. He set music to several Shakespearean songs and sent them to G. Schirmer, Inc., where the editors were surprised to see the name of Owen Wister appended to such serious music. When they sent the songs for evaluation to an outside expert, Dr. Percy Goetschius, their opinion was reinforced, for Goetschius reported, "They are remarkable in every best sense; so finely conceived, so effective; and written with a command of technic that

---

* West lived to the age of ninety, dying in Seattle on November 9, 1951, where his remains were cremated. His wife, Mabel, died on March 7, 1956. The couple had no children.

would do honor to any master." It was, he confessed, a revelation to learn that the author of *The Virginian* was an accomplished composer. The result was that the Schirmer firm chose three of the pieces to list in their winter catalogue: "Winter's Song," "Sigh No More, Ladies," and "Blow, blow, thou winter wind." C. Engel, Schirmer's editorial contact with Wister, sent him a congratulatory note. "For a long time I had come to regard you only as an eminent writer; then I woke up to the fact that you are also an excellent musician." Would Wister now be willing to write an article about his "musical experiences and connections" for the *Musical Quarterly*? The answer was yes, and in the article, entitled "Strictly Hereditary," Wister gave a revealing portrait of his childhood and of his youthful pursuit of a musical career.[65]

Perhaps his return to musical competition at this stage in his life indicated the extent of his revulsion at what was happening in American society. If he had been disturbed before, the Crash of 1929 and the ensuing Depression further darkened his despair. There is no indication of the extent to which the plunging stock market affected his own fortune, although since his assets largely were in stock surely the result was calamitous, though far from ruinous. Still, it was not the widespread financial distress that bothered Wister so much as the lack of resiliency and absence of taste he perceived in America. By now, he reasoned, the American character may have "rotted too deeply to be helped by adversity." It was so low, he wrote in the summer of 1932, that "things in politics, justice, finance, and crime, which not very long ago would have sent up a flame of indignation, happen just about every week without raising a ripple." Americans had used their minds just twice in history, he thought—during the Revolution and during the Civil War—and at this present moment of crisis the nation's leaders had failed pitifully. "From Henry Ford up through Owen Young to Hoover, our household gods have uttered a string of oracular imbecilities right along, one on top of another." And with this failure there was no one remaining to set things right, for Wister, since he had been "old enough to observe and think," had not believed universal suffrage to be the answer. In fact, he had confided to Chapman that he could not forgive Theodore Roosevelt for working toward the direct election of United States Senators.[66]

When Theodore's cousin, Franklin Delano Roosevelt, sought to unseat the incumbent Herbert Hoover in the fall of 1932, Wister could not generate enthusiasm for either candidate. For that matter, he did not care for Al Smith either—all three men gave him a "pain."[67]

With Roosevelt taking office in 1933, many Americans of the privileged classes shuddered in disgust with each New Deal measure. Wister tolerated New Deal legislation with far less patience than most. He suffered quietly until the beginning of Roosevelt's second term, when the president announced his intention to alter the structure of the Supreme Court through his "court-packing plan." Wister was enraged.

When an impromptu national committee emerged to battle the plan, Wister was named honorary chairman of the Pennsylvania subcommittee. The organization gave itself a fancy title—the Citizens National Supreme Court Protective Committee of The Defenders, Inc.—but it was called simply "the Defenders." A series of local rallies were held during the spring of 1937, and on May 6 Wister sent out an appeal for funds, imploring "every patriotic American" to aid the Defenders in their battle to save the Constitution from this assault by the White House. In Philadelphia a public rally was announced for May 10.

Wister little realized it, but his appeal for funds placed him again in a storm center of controversy. The Pennsylvania State Department of Welfare and the state attorney general had warrants issued for the arrest of Wister and two other officials of the Defenders on the day of the rally. Their "crime" was nebulous indeed: failure to secure a license for soliciting funds. The motive for the warrants was further suspect since Democrats occupied the seats of power in Pennsylvania state government. Before the evening meeting could take place, officers found and arrested the two other officials, Louis M. Bailey and John B. Carrigan, and placed them behind bars. They could not locate Wister, but an officer publicly proclaimed that if Wister appeared at the meeting that night he too would be arrested.

Some two thousand people gathered that evening for the rally at the Academy of Music. On the platform sat four United States Senators, all Democrats, to share the speaking duties: Pat McCarran of Nevada, Josiah W. Bailey of North Carolina, Peter G. Gerry of Rhode Island, and Royal S. Copeland of New York. Wister dramatically walked into the auditorium and onto the stage in full view of every spectator in the house. George W. Norris, chairman of the meeting, declared that if anyone offered a prize for the "most stupid inane petty spite" that could be devised, the state's attorney general would win it. "We have not yet been Russianized to the point where a group of self-respecting citizens cannot assemble to hear members of the U.S. Senate discuss an important issue," he said. Wister sat unmolested throughout the meeting. The ludicrousness of the situation already had become clear to state officials, and now they backed away from their previous position and clamored to deny all responsibility for the arrests. A photograph of Wister at the meeting appeared the next morning on the front page of the *Philadelphia Inquirer* under the caption, "They Won't Be 'Russianized.' " Wister was quoted as saying he was "not sure just what I've done." His attorney, Benjamin H. Ludlow, arranged for a 10 A.M. meeting that morning to surrender his client to the authorities.[68]

By now, of course, the surrender was moot. All charges were dropped, and officials issued apologies to Wister and to the two other representatives of the Defenders. A deputy attorney general accepted full blame for the arrest warrants, saying he had not known that the Defenders actually had sent the required application and fee for a solicitors' permit in advance by registered mail. Pennsylvania Attorney General Charles J. Margiotti and Secretary of Welfare John D. Pennington denounced the untimely arrests as unfortunate mistakes. Wister proved entirely amiable to the whole affair, relishing the new adventure that had awaited him in jail at the age of seventy-six. He characterized himself to reporters as a "near-convict."[69]

Despite such high jinks, Wister continued to write. He described for *Harper's* his brief acquaintance with Mark Twain; he wrote for the same publication of the halcyon days of Yellowstone National Park; in the *Atlantic Monthly* he recalled his friendship with William Dean Howells. He also was working slowly on the history of the Green Tree and on a new book—an appreciation of wines for which he took copious notes during his European travels.[70]

His pieces on Twain and Howells caught the attention of an eastern critic who was engaged in a lengthy study of American letters: Van Wyck Brooks. Brooks now was preparing a volume on New England from 1865 to 1915, the second in his series. The two men began corresponding, Wister happily responding to Brooks's endless questions about writers he had known. Finally, Brooks accepted Wister's invitation to visit him at his home. There, on a Saturday night in April 1937, they sat for hours, Wister fascinating not only Brooks but also a handful of invited guests with his personal recollections of Howells, Henry James, Henry Adams, and many others. "What I wouldn't give—along with hundreds of other readers—for a book of those reminiscences," Brooks later told his host.[71]

"The tenement which I have inhabited for 77 years is somewhat out of repair," Wister told another literary friend, Edward S. Martin. Yet he was not ready to take to his armchair. In early August he sailed with his son Owen to France, where they stayed until October. He could look about him, though, and know that his own body must be wearing out. He counted off each of his old friends' funerals. In 1937 alone, six of them died. He told intimates that he was sensing his own "diminished energy." A contemporary, Henry D. Sedgwick, visiting Wister in May 1938, thought he saw a ruddy glow; Sedgwick declared that compared to Wister he was a "stagnant, old slug." If Wister looked the picture of health, he did not feel it, although he thought that "with the help of a telescope" he could see health and strength, and he was crawling toward them with "half the speed of a tortoise."[72]

This was not to be the case. In early July 1938, as was his custom, he repaired to his summer home at Saunderstown. There, surrounded by his children and grandchildren, he celebrated his seventy-eighth birthday. A week later he was struck with a cerebral hemorrhage. On the next day, July 21, 1938, the life of this extraordinary American ended.

Notes

ABBREVIATIONS

OWP Owen Wister Papers, Manuscripts Division,
     Library of Congress
OW   Owen Wister
SBW Sarah Butler Wister
OJW Owen Jones Wister
MW   Molly Wister
HL   Houghton Library, Harvard University

CHAPTER I. A GENTLEMAN BORN (1860–1878)

1. OW to SBW, August 29, 1882, Box 8, OWP.

2. Ernest Newman, *The Life of Richard Wagner*, 4 vols. (New York: Alfred A. Knopf, 1933–46), 4: 568 and Chapter 36, passim.

3. OW to SBW, August 29, 1882, Box 8; OW to OJW, September 30, 1882, Box 101; OWP.

4. Margaret Armstrong, *Fanny Kemble: A Passionate Victorian* (New York: Macmillan Co., 1938), pp. 1-2; Herschel Baker, *John Philip Kemble: The Actor in His Theatre* (Cambridge: Harvard University Press, 1942), pp. 4-5.

5. Armstrong, *Fanny Kemble*, pp. 4-6; Baker, *John Philip Kemble*, pp. 3-18; Percy Fitzgerald, *The Kembles: An Account of the Kemble Family*, 2 vols. (London: Tinsley Brothers, n.d.), passim.

6. Armstrong, *Fanny Kemble*, p. 7.

7. Fanny Kemble's journal was published as *Journal of a Residence in America* (Philadelphia: Carey, Lea & Blanchard, 1835); Pierce Butler's views are given in *Pierce Butler's Statement, Originally Prepared in Aid of His Professional Counsel* (Philadelphia, 1880).

8. Frances Ann Kemble, *Records of Later Life* (New York: Henry Holt and Co., 1882), pp. 105-6, 143; Frances Ann Kemble, *Further Records, 1848–1883* (New York: Henry Holt and Co., 1891), p. 346; Armstrong, *Fanny Kemble*, pp. 316-17.

9. S. Weir Mitchell, "Memoir of Owen Jones Wister, M.D.," speech, December 2, 1896, Box 48, OWP; Harry M. and Margaret B. Tinkcom, Grant Miles Simon, *Historic Germantown: From the Founding to the Early Part of the Nineteenth Century* (Philadelphia: American Philosophical Society, 1955), p. 56; Owen Wister, notes entitled "A Wister Meditation, 1727–1927," p. 7, Box 85, OWP; Dorothie Bobbe, *Fanny Kemble* (New York: Minton, Balch, & Co., 1931), p. 266.

10. Note, Fanny Kemble to SBW, n.d., 1860, as quoted in Ben Merchant Vorpahl, *My Dear Wister: The Frederic Remington–Owen Wister Letters* (Palo Alto: American West Publishing Co., 1972), p. 4; Bobbe, *Fanny Kemble*, p. 269; Kemble, *Further Records*, p. 335.

11. SBW to Lady Musgrave, March 19, 1863, December 20, 1863, Box 7, OWP. (Lady Musgrave, wife of Sir Anthony Musgrave, was OW's godmother. Born in the United States, she was the daughter of David Dudley Field, a prominent lawyer, and the niece of two more illustrious Fields—Stephen J. Field, United States Supreme Court Justice for thirty-four years, and Cyrus K. Field, the inventor.)

NOTES

12. Wister, "A Wister Meditation," p. 8, Box 85; Charles J. Wister to OW, March 30, 1865, Box 3; OWP.
13. SBW to Lady Musgrave, May 26, 1865, Box 7, OWP.
14. Ibid.
15. Pierce Butler II to OW, August 20, n.d., Box 2, OWP.
16. OW to Miss Ethel Small, February 6, 1925, Box 36, OWP; Bobbe, *Fanny Kemble*, p. 98; Kemble, *Records of Later Life*, p. 10; Fanny Kemble Wister, ed., *Owen Wister Out West: His Journals and Letters* (Chicago: University of Chicago Press, 1958), pp. xi-xii, 5-6.
17. Wister, ed., *Owen Wister Out West*, pp. 4-5; OW to Miss Ethel Small, February 6, 1925, Box 36, OWP; Owen Wister, "Strictly Hereditary," *Musical Quarterly* 22 (January 1936), p. 2; Kemble, *Further Records*, p. 166.
18. SBW to William Dean Howells, March 11, 1875, William Dean Howells Papers, HL.
19. Mitchell, "Memoir of Owen Jones Wister, M.D."; School Reports, Box 92, OWP; Anna Robeson Burr, *Weir Mitchell: His Life and Letters* (New York: Duffield & Co., 1929), p. 283; Ernest Earnest, S. *Weir Mitchell: Novelist and Physician* (Philadelphia: University of Pennsylvania Press, 1950), pp. 73, 136.
20. Notes prepared by Wister, Box 85, OWP.
21. Wister, ed., *Owen Wister Out West*, p. 6; Newman, *Life of Richard Wagner*, 4: 267; Kemble, *Records of Later Life*, pp. 263-64; Wister, "Strictly Hereditary," pp. 2-3.
22. Owen Wister, *Neighbors Henceforth* (New York: Macmillan Co., 1922), pp. 8-9.
23. Ibid., p. 9; OW to SBW, August 28, 1870, April 23, 1871, February 26, 1871, January 29, 1871, Box 7, OWP.
24. Wister, *Neighbors Henceforth*, pp. 9-10; OW to SBW, February 7, 1871, Box 7, OWP.
25. OW to SBW, February 26, 1871, March 5, 1871, Box 7, OWP.
26. Ibid., August 28, 1870, Box 7; notebook entry, August 7, [1882], Box 90; OW to SBW, April 27, 1871, Box 7; OWP.
27. The letter from Wister's master, W. F. Bickmore, is included with OW's letter to SBW, March 20, 1872, Box 7; OW to SBW, June 12, 1872, Box 7; OWP.
28. OW to SBW, November 29, 1871, March 13, 1872, Box 7, OWP.
29. Kemble, *Further Records*, p. 52.
30. Leon Edel, *Henry James*, 5 vols. (Philadelphia: J. B. Lippincott Co., 1953–72), 2: 84-85.
31. Ibid., 2: 108-22; Leon Edel, ed., *Henry James Letters, 1843–1875*, vol. I (Cambridge: Belknap Press of Harvard University Press, 1974), p. 318.
32. Edel, *Henry James*, 2: 118-22; the quotation from "The Solution" also is given in Edel, *Henry James*, 2: 122.
33. Ibid., p. 118.
34. Mitchell, "Memoir of Owen Jones Wister, M.D."
35. William D. McCrackan, "St. Paul's School," *New England Monthly* 16 (June 1897), pp. 415-32; Norman B. Nash, *Henry A. Coit (1830–1895): Educator, Leader, Pioneer—A Great American Schoolmaster* (New York: Newcomen Society in North America, 1950), passim; Owen Wister, "Dr. Coit of St. Paul's," *Atlantic Monthly* 142 (December 1928), pp. 757-62.
36. OW to SBW, September 14, 1873, October 24, 1873, November 30, 1873, Box 7; OJW to OW, November 19, 1873, Box 6; OWP.
37. OW to SBW, October 24, 1873, March 2, 8, 1874, Box 7, OWP.
38. Ibid., November 30, 1873, March 8, 1874, Box 7; Owen Wister, "My Maiden Effort," manuscript in Box 56; Owen Wister, "Down in a Diving Bell," *Horae Scholasticae* 7 (November 1873), Box 54; OWP.

336

39. OW to SBW, April 9, 1876, March 19, 1876, May 28, 1876, Box 7, OWP; Twain's story appeared in *Atlantic Monthly* 37 (June 1876), pp. 641-50.

40. OW to OJW, July 23, 1874, Box 6, OWP.

41. Kemble, *Further Records*, pp. 354-55.

42. OW to Fanny Kemble, November 22, 1874, Box 2; OW to SBW, September 25, 1875, January 30, 1876, Box 7; OWP; Julian Mason, "Owen Wister, Boy Librarian," *Quarterly Journal of the Library of Congress* 26 (October 1969), pp. 201-4.

43. OW to SBW, n.d., 1875, June 26, 1875, Box 7, April 24, 1877, Box 8, OWP.

44. SBW to OW, October 2, 1875, Box 7, OWP.

45. Owen Wister, "Rockaway," *Horae Scholasticae* 9 (November 6, 1875); Wister, "A Fable," ibid., 9 (January 22, 1876); OW's remarks about his fiction are in an article he wrote for a special seventy-fifth edition of the *Horae* entitled "Poetry at St. Paul's," appearing on pages 229-35 of that June 1, 1935, issue. A copy of the newspaper is in Box 54, OWP.

46. OW to SBW, February 4, 12, 1877, Box 8, OWP.

47. Ibid., May 23, 1875, Box 7, OWP.

48. Ibid., April 9, 1876, May 9, 23, 1875, May 7, 1876, February 20, 1876, March 26, 1876, April 2, 1876, Box 7, OWP.

49. Ibid., November 12, 19, 1876, October 11, 1876, Box 7, April 29, 1877, Box 8, OWP.

50. Ibid., [September 1877], Box 8, OWP.

51. Ibid., November 25, 1877, Box 8, OWP; Owen Wister, "John Jay Chapman," *Atlantic Monthly* 153 (May 1934), pp. 529-31; Richard B. Hovey, *John Jay Chapman: An American Mind* (New York: Columbia University Press, 1959), pp. 10-12; M. A. DeWolfe Howe, *John Jay Chapman and His Letters* (Boston: Houghton Mifflin Co., 1937), p. 22.

52. Kemble, *Further Records*, p. 207; OW to SBW, April 4, 1877, Box 8, OWP.

53. OW to SBW, February 25, 1877, Box 8, OWP.

54. Ibid., March 25, 1877, Box 8, OWP.

55. Ibid., April 8, 15, 1877, Box 8, OWP.

56. Ibid., May 2, 1875, Box 7; R. S. Miniturn to Wister, May 17, 1878, Box 30; OWP.

57. OW to SBW, May 23, 1875, November 5, 1876, Box 7, OWP.

58. Ibid., December 2, 9, 1877, March 31, 1878, Box 8, OWP.

59. OW to OJW, April 16, 1876, OJW to OW, October 21, 1876, Box 6, OWP.

60. Ibid., October 27, 1877, November 6, 1877, Box 6, OWP.

61. Kemble, *Further Records*, pp. 107, 356, 114, 111.

62. Ibid., p. 157.

63. Ibid., pp. 156, 166.

64. OW to SBW, January 28, 1877, February 4, 1877, Box 8; OJW to OW, January 31, 1877, Box 6; OWP.

65. SBW to OW, October 25, n.d., Box 12, OWP.

66. Joseph H. Coit to OW, May 17, 1878, Box 16; Edward D. Tibbits to OW, May 31, 1878, Box 36; OWP.

CHAPTER II. HARVARD, CLASS OF '82 (1878–1882)

1. Samuel Eliot Morison, *Three Centuries of Harvard, 1636–1936* (Cambridge: Harvard University Press, 1936), p. 342; Samuel Eliot Morison, ed., *The Development of Harvard University Since the Inauguration of President Eliot, 1869–1929* (Cambridge: Harvard University Press, 1930), pp. xlii-xliii, liv, 112-13; *Secretary's Report, Class of 1882*, Harvard Archives, Nathan Marsh Pusey Library, Harvard University.

NOTES

2. OW to SBW, September 26, 1878, Box 8, OWP; Owen Wister, *Roosevelt: The Story of a Friendship, 1880–1919* (New York: Macmillan Co., 1930), p. 3.

3. OW to SBW, November 17, 1878, Box 8, OWP.

4. Ibid., April 27, 1878, January 13, 1878, October 20, 1878, December 16, 1878, Box 8, OWP.

5. Ibid., n.d., [1878], Box 8, OWP.

6. Ibid., January 13, 1878 [probably misdated, apparently 1879], Box 8, OWP.

7. OJW to OW, November 7, 1878, January 23, 1879, Box 6, OWP.

8. OW to OJW, n.d., Box 6; OW to SBW, n.d., 1878, Box 8; OWP.

9. Cleveland Amory, *The Proper Bostonians* (New York: E. P. Dutton & Co., 1947), pp. 261-63; OW to SBW, February 24, 1878, n.d., 1878, Box 8; Edward D. Tibbits to OW, February 19, 1880, Box 36; OWP.

10. OW to SBW, n.d., 1878, Box 8; OW to Henry G. Chapman, Jr., December 30, 1878, Box 16; OWP.

11. OW to SBW, Easter Day, 1879, Box 8, OWP.

12. Wister, *Roosevelt*, pp. 4-5.

13. OW to SBW, October 14, 1879, November 30, 1879, Box 8, OWP.

14. Ibid., June 11, 1880, March 8, 1881, Box 8, OWP.

15. Morison, *Three Centuries of Harvard*, p. 424.

16. Wister, *Roosevelt*, pp. 9, 11-12.

17. Ibid., pp. 13-14.

18. OW to OJW, May 2, 1880, Box 6, OWP.

19. Ibid.; OJW to OW, May 5, 1880, Box 6, OWP.

20. Wister, *Roosevelt*, pp. 15-16, 20-21.

21. OW to SBW, May, n.d., 1881, December 12, 1881, November 19, 1881, Box 8, OWP.

22. Ibid., n.d., 1880, Box 8, OWP; Hovey, *John Jay Chapman*, p. 15.

23. Howe, *Chapman and His Letters*, p. 25; OW to SBW, March 20, 1881, Box 8, OWP.

24. OW to SBW, May 25, 1881, May 1, 1882, Box 8, OWP.

25. Bliss Perry, *Life and Letters of Henry Lee Higginson* (Boston: Atlantic Monthly Press, 1921), pp. 299-300; Owen Wister, "Where the 'Ought' Comes in," [1920], Box 61, OWP.

26. Wister, "Where the 'Ought' Comes in."

27. OW to SBW, October, n.d., 1881, Box 8, OWP.

28. Ibid., September 28 [1879], October 19, 1880, April 25, 1881, November 15, 19, 1881, Box 8; OW to OJW, n.d., Box 6; OWP.

29. OW to SBW, Easter Day, 1879, June 11, 1880, October, n.d., 1881, Box 8, OWP.

30. Ibid., November 15, 1881, Box 8; J. J. Chapman to OW, April 13, 1882, Box 16; OWP.

31. Thomas Bailey Aldrich to OW, November 17, 1881, Box 13, OWP; Owen Wister, "Beethoven," *Atlantic Monthly* 49 (February 1882), p. 242.

32. OW to SBW, Easter Sunday, [1880], Box 8, OWP.

33. Ibid., January 30, [1882], Box 8, OWP.

34. Program dated April 9, 1880, Box 96; *Dido and Aeneas* File, Box 63; OW to SBW, May 10, 1881, Box 8; OWP.

35. The words are printed on a sheet in Box 89, OWP.

36. *Dido and Aeneas* File, Box 63, OWP.

37. J. J. Chapman to OW, April 13, 1882, Box 89; clippings, n.d., Box 63; OWP.

38. *New York Herald*, April 14, 1882, clipping, Box 89; clipping, n.d., Box 63; OWP.

39. *Dido and Aeneas* File, Box 63, OWP.

40. OW to SBW, May 1, 1882, Frances Ann Kemble to OW, October 21, 1882, Box 8, OWP.

41. Wister, ed., *Owen Wister Out West*, p. 8.
42. OW to SBW, May 9, 1882, Box 8, OWP.
43. Owen Wister, "An Inquiry into the Future of the Opera," Box 81, OWP.
44. OW to SBW, n.d., 1882, Box 8, OWP; Morison, ed., *Development of Harvard University*, p. 113.
45. Notebook entry, n.d., Box 90, OWP.

CHAPTER III. THE EUROPEAN JUDGMENT (1882–1883)

1. Notebook entry, July 5, 1882, Box 90, OWP.
2. Ibid., July 16, 1882, Box 90, OWP.
3. Ibid.
4. Ibid., July 24, 1882, Box 90, OWP.
5. OW to OJW, September 30, 1882, Box 101, OWP; Henry James, as quoted in Edel, *Henry James*, 3: 53.
6. Notebook entry, July 24, 1882, Box 90; OW to OJW, September 30, 1882, Box 101; OWP.
7. Notebook entry, July 30, 1882, Box 90, OWP.
8. Ibid., August 1, 1882, Box 90, OWP.
9. OW to OJW, September 30, 1882, Box 101, OWP.
10. Notebook entries, August 7, 9, 1882, Box 90, OWP.
11. Ibid., August 8, 9, 1882, Box 90, OWP.
12. Ibid., August 22, 1882, Box 90; OW to SBW, August 21, 1882, Box 8; OWP.
13. Notebook entry, September 27, 1882, Box 90, OWP.
14. OW to OJW, September 30, 1882, Box 101, OWP.
15. Martin Cooper, *French Music: From the Death of Berlioz to the Death of Fauré* (London: Oxford University Press, 1951), passim.
16. SBW to OJW, October 23, 25, 1882, Box 101, OWP; Nathan Haskell Dole, *Famous Composers*, rev. ed. (New York: Thomas Y. Crowell Co., 1925), p. 666.
17. OW to OJW, October 25, 1882, Box 101, OWP.
18. SBW to OJW, October 23, 1882, Box 101, OWP.
19. Ibid.
20. OW to OJW, October 25, 1883, Box 101, OWP.
21. Ibid.
22. Ibid.
23. Ibid.
24. OW to OJW, January 9, 1883, Box 101, OWP; Wister, *Roosevelt*, p. 22.
25. Edward Lockspeiser, *Debussy: His Life and Mind*, 2 vols. (New York: Macmillan Co., 1962–65), 1: 56-57; Wister, "Strictly Hereditary," pp. 4-5.
26. Programs for the events are in Box 89, OWP; OW to J. J. Chapman, January 19, n.d., HL.
27. [Sarah Wister], "Paris Classical Concerts," *Atlantic Monthly* 53 (June 1884), pp. 739-53.
28. SBW to OJW, March 25, 1883, Box 101; program dated March 29, 1883, Box 89; OWP.
29. OW to SBW, December 17, 19, 1882, n.d., 1882, Box 8, OWP.
30. Ibid., December 17, 19, 29, 1882, Box 8, OWP.
31. OW to OJW, December 13, 1882, Box 101, OWP.
32. Ibid.
33. OW to OJW, October 14, 1882, Box 101, OWP.
34. Ibid.
35. Edel, *Henry James*, 3: 53.
36. SBW to OJW, March 25, 1883, Box 101, OWP.
37. OW to OJW, December 13, 1882, Box 101, OWP.
38. Ibid.

39. OJW to OW, December 30, 1882, Box 101, OWP.
40. Ibid.
41. OW to OJW, January 9, 1883, Box 101, OWP.
42. Ibid.
43. Ibid.
44. Ibid.
45. Ibid.
46. Wister, "Strictly Hereditary," p. 6.
47. Ibid., p. 7.
48. Ibid.
49. Ibid.

Chapter IV. A Boston Stopover (1883–1885)

1. Perry, *Henry Lee Higginson*, pp. 273-76; Wister, *Roosevelt*, pp. 26-27.
2. Perry, *Henry Lee Higginson*, p. 270.
3. OW to SBW, December 13, 21, 1883, Box 8, OWP.
4. Ibid., January 16, 1884, Box 8, OWP.
5. Ibid., December 21, 28, 1883, Box 8, OWP.
6. Ibid., February 15, 1884, Box 8, OWP.
7. William Dean Howells, *A Woman's Reason* (Boston: James R. Osgood and Co., 1884), p. 142.
8. OW to SBW, February 8, 1884, Box 8, OWP.
9. Ibid., September 24, 1984, Box 8, OWP.
10. Ibid., February 8, 1884, April 26, 1884, Box 8, OWP.
11. Wister, *Roosevelt*, p. 23; OW to SBW, June 21, 1884, Box 8, OWP.
12. OW to SBW, n.d., 1884, April 5, 1884, March 26, 1884, Box 8; George Waring to OW, March 20, 1884, Box 37; OWP.
13. OW to SBW, September 29, 1884, December 22, 1884, Box 8, OWP.
14. Ibid., January 12, 1885, Box 8, OWP.
15. OJW to OW, January 6, 1884, Box 6, OWP.
16. OW to OJW, January 8, 1884, Box 6, OWP.
17. OJW to OW, January 10, 1884, Box 6, OWP.
18. OW to OJW, July 23, 1884, September 2, 1884, OJW to OW, October 9, 1884, Box 6, OWP.
19. OW to SBW, October 13, 1884, Box 8, OWP.
20. Ibid., July 12, 1884, Box 8, OWP.
21. OW to OJW, July 23, 1884, Box 6, OWP.
22. OW to SBW, March 26, 1884, Box 8, OWP.
23. Joseph H. Coit to OW, July 2, 1884, Box 16; OW to Dr. Henry Coit, August, n.d., 1884, Box 15; OWP.
24. Joseph H. Coit to OW, July 2, 1884, Dr. Henry Coit to OW, July 8, 1884, Box 16, OWP.
25. OW to Dr. Henry Coit, August, n.d., 1884, Box 15; Dr. Henry Coit to OW, September 1, 1884, Box 16; OWP.
26. Joseph H. Coit to OW, October 16, 1884, Box 16, OWP.
27. Sherman Evarts to OW, September 18, 1884, Box 19, OWP.
28. Owen Wister, "The Creed of a Charter Member," speech, n.d., Box 52, OWP; Mildred Howells, ed., *Life in Letters of William Dean Howells*, 2 vols. (Garden City: Doubleday, Doran & Co., 1928), 1: 391.
29. OW to OJW, September 2, 1884, Box 6, OWP.
30. Owen Wister, "William Dean Howells," *Atlantic Monthly* 160 (December 1937), p. 707; OW to SBW, December 22, 1884, Box 8, OWP.
31. Wister, "William Dean Howells," p. 712.
32. Robert L. Hough, *The Quiet Rebel: William Dean Howells as Social Com-*

mentator (Lincoln: University of Nebraska Press, 1959), p. 29; Walter J. Meserve, Introduction to William Dean Howells, *The Rise of Silas Lapham* (Bloomington: Indiana University Press, 1971), p. xvi.

33. OW to SBW, February 25, 1885, April 14, 1884, Box 8, OWP.
34. Ibid., April 14, 26, 1884, Box 8, OWP.
35. Wister, *Roosevelt*, p. 23.
36. OW to SBW, April 5, 1884, Box 8; OJW to OW, April 23, 29, 1884, July 23, 1884, Box 6; OWP.
37. OW to OJW, August 26, 1884, September 2, 1884, January 7, 1885, Box 6, OWP.
38. Ibid., August 20, 1884, Box 6, OWP; Wister, *Roosevelt*, pp. 27-28.
39. OW to J. J. Chapman, April 15, [1885], HL.
40. Ibid., April 30, [1885], HL.
41. OW to Howells, May 21, [1885], HL.
42. Ibid., June 1, [1885], HL; Wister, *Roosevelt*, p. 23.
43. OW to Howells, June 1, [1885], HL.
44. Wister, *Roosevelt*, p. 28; Earnest, *S. Weir Mitchell*, pp. 80-86; Burr, *Weir Mitchell*, p. 244.
45. Wister recorded Dr. Mitchell's remarks eight years later in his Texas journal under an entry listed as "Miscellaneous Items: At the Hot Springs," Box 1, OWP.

CHAPTER V. DISCOVERY (1885)

1. OW to SBW, June 30, 1885, Box 1; notebook entry, July 2, 1885, Box 1; OWP.
2. Copies of the poem and the "confession" with notations are in Box 85, OWP.
3. Notebook entry, July 3, 1885, Box 1, OWP.
4. OW to SBW, July 4, 1885, Box 8, OWP; Wister, ed., *Owen Wister Out West*, entry for July 6, 1885, p. 31. Citations of letters and journal entries which are reprinted in *Owen Wister Out West* refer to that work rather than to the original journals at the University of Wyoming in Laramie or to the transcripts which are in Box 1, OWP.
5. H. H. Bancroft, *The Works of Hubert Howe Bancroft*, vol. 25, *History of Nevada, Colorado, and Wyoming, 1540–1888* (San Francisco: History Company, 1890), pp. 659-806 passim; Charles A. Guernsey, *Wyoming Cowboy Days* (New York: G. P. Putnam's Sons, 1936), p. 68; Robert G. Athearn, *High Country Empire: The High Plains and Rockies* (New York: McGraw-Hill Book Co., 1960), pp. 140-42.
6. G. Edward White, *The Eastern Establishment and the Western Experience: The West of Frederic Remington, Theodore Roosevelt, and Owen Wister* (New Haven: Yale University Press, 1968), pp. 48, 122-23; Earl Pomeroy, *In Search of the Golden West: The Tourist in America* (New York: Alfred A. Knopf, 1957), passim.
7. OW to SBW, July 4, 1885, Box 8, OWP; "Sketch of Road from Fort Fetterman, Wy. T. to Fort Fred Steele, Wy. T.," 1968, C.Q.M. Office, Dept. of the Platte. A copy of this map is at the Wyoming Pioneer Memorial Museum, Douglas, Wyoming.
8. OW to SBW, July 4, 1885, Box 8, OWP.
9. Ibid.
10. John Clay, *My Life on the Range* (Chicago: privately printed, 1924), p. 143.
11. John Rolfe Burroughs, *Guardian of the Grasslands: The First Hundred Years of the Wyoming Stock Growers Association* (Cheyenne: Pioneer Printing & Stationery Co., 1971), p. 165; Clay, *My Life on the Range*, p. 142; Wister, ed., *Owen Wister Out West*, July 16, 1885, p. 34, August 1, 1885, p. 37. A former employee of Wolcott's who helped him put the ranch together in 1878 described him in even less flattering terms as a "hardboiled rascal who would cheat his men out of their

wages." This account appears in "The Autobiography of Otho Henry Durham," in *Tales of the Seeds-Ka-Dee* (Denver: Sublette County Artist's Guild, Big Mountain Press, 1963), as quoted in Burroughs, *Guardian of the Grasslands*, p. 165. A suggestion that the Irwins may have partly owned the ranch is in a letter from Sarah Wister to her son thirteen years later in which she said that the only summer he had not suffered an illness in the West was the one he spent on the Irwins' ranch. SBW to OW, September 30, 1898, Box 10, OWP.

12. OW to SBW, July 6, 1885, Box 8, OWP; OW to J. J. Chapman, July 17, 1885, HL.

13. Wister, ed., *Owen Wister Out West*, July 10, 1885, p. 32, July 19, 1885, p. 36; OW to SBW, July 24, 1885, July 10, 1885, Box 8, OWP.

14. OW to SBW, July 10, 1885, Box 8; OW to Mrs. Eleanor Jay Chapman, August [1885], Box 15; OWP; Wister, ed., *Owen Wister Out West*, July 7, 1885, p. 32.

15. OW to SBW, July 15, 1885, Box 8, OWP.

16. OW to Mrs. Eleanor Jay Chapman, August [1885], Box 15, OWP; Wister, ed., *Owen Wister Out West*, July 10, 16, 1885, pp. 32-33; OW to SBW, July 17, 1885, Box 8, OWP; OW to J. J. Chapman, July 17, 1885, HL; Neal Lambert, "The Western Writings of Owen Wister: The Conflict of East and West" (Ph.D. diss., University of Utah, 1966), pp. 3-4.

17. Notebook entry, July 21, 1885, Box 1, OWP.

18. Ibid., July 28, 1885, Box 1, OWP.

19. OW to Eleanor Jay Chapman, August 20, 1885, Box 15, OWP.

20. Wister, ed., *Owen Wister Out West*, July 16, 18, 1885, pp. 34-35.

21. OW to J. J. Chapman, July 17, 1885, HL.

22. Notebook entry, July 18, 1885, Box 1, OWP.

23. OW to SBW, July 24, 1885, Box 8, OWP; Wister, ed., *Owen Wister Out West*, July 19, 21, 1885, pp. 35-37.

24. Notebook entry, August 6, 1886, Box 1; OW to SBW, August 6, 1885, Box 8; OWP.

25. OW to SBW, July 15, 1885, Box 8, OWP.

26. OW to Eleanor Jay Chapman, August 20, [1885], Box 15, OWP.

27. Ibid., August 20, 24, [1885], Box 15, OWP; Wister, ed., *Owen Wister Out West*, August 6, 1885, p. 38.

28. Wister, ed., *Owen Wister Out West*, July 18, 1885, p. 35, August 6, 1885, pp. 38-39; OW to J. J. Chapman, July 17, 1885, HL.

29. Wister, ed., *Owen Wister Out West*, August 6, 1885, p. 39.

30. OW to SBW, August 20, 29, 1885, Box 8, OWP.

31. Clay, *My Life on the Range*, p. 144.

CHAPTER VI. AN UNCERTAIN SCHOLAR (1885–1888)

1. Morison, ed., *Development of Harvard University*, pp. 491-95, 507.

2. OW to SBW, October 6, 1885, Box 8, OWP; Hovey, *John Jay Chapman*, p. 39; Owen Wister, "John Jay Chapman," *Atlantic Monthly* 153 (May 1934), p. 533; OW to J. J. Chapman, July 17, 1885, HL.

3. OW to SBW, October 15, 1885, December 5, 1885, May 25, 1886, Box 6, OWP.

4. Francis Biddle, *Mr. Justice Holmes* (New York: Charles Scribner's Sons, 1943), pp. 70-71; OW to SBW, February 20, 1886, April 25, 1887, Box 8, OWP.

5. OW to SBW, August 20, 1885, December 24, 1886, Box 8, OWP.

6. Howe, *Chapman and His Letters*, p. 51; Hovey, *John Jay Chapman*, pp. 44-46.

7. OW to SBW, n.d., 1887, Box 8, OWP.

8. Ibid., November 16, 1885, November 28, 1887, Box 8, OWP.

9. Ibid., November 16, 1885, Box 8, OWP.

NOTES

10. Sanford E. Marovitz, "Owen Wister: An Annotated Bibliography of Secondary Material," *American Literary Realism: 1870–1910* 7 (Winter 1974), p. 9; "Recent Fiction," *Independent* 39 (September 29, 1887), p. 1231; OW to OJW, May 29, 1887, Box 6, OWP.
11. OW to SBW, December 23, 1886, Box 8, OWP.
12. "Republican Opera," *Atlantic Monthly* 59 (April 1887), pp. 568-71; OW to SBW, [spring], 1887, Box 8, OWP.
13. OJW to SBW, March 9, 1886, Box 6; OW to OJW, December 5, 1885, Box 6; OWP.
14. OW to OJW, May 7, 1888, May 26, 29, 1887, Box 6, OWP; Wister, ed., *Owen Wister Out West*, p. 42.
15. OJW to OW, June 1, 1887, OW to OJW, June 4, 1887, Box 6, OWP.
16. Wister, ed., *Owen Wister Out West*, pp. 44-46.
17. Ibid., pp. 46-47.
18. Ibid., p. 47.
19. OW to SBW, n.d., 1887, Box 8, OWP.
20. Owen Wister, "Old Yellowstone Days," *Harper's Monthly* 172 (March 1936), p. 472; Wister, ed., *Owen Wister Out West*, pp. 43, 47-48.
21. Wister, ed., *Owen Wister Out West*, p. 50.
22. Ibid., p. 51.
23. Ibid.
24. Ibid., pp. 54-56.
25. Ibid., pp. 48, 56-57; George M. West to Mrs. Park C. Hayes, August 21, 1934, the original of which is in the possession of West's nephew, George M. West, Seattle, Washington.
26. Wister, ed., *Owen Wister Out West*, opposite p. 114.
27. Writers' Program of the Work Projects Administration, *Wyoming: A Guide to Its History, Highways, and People* (New York: Oxford University Press, 1941), pp. 408-9.
28. Wister, "Old Yellowstone Days," p. 471.
29. Wister, ed., *Owen Wister Out West*, pp. 59-60.
30. Ibid.
31. Ibid.; Wister, "Old Yellowstone Days," p. 475.
32. Wister, ed., *Owen Wister Out West*, pp. 60-61.
33. Ibid., p. 61.
34. Ibid.
35. OW to OJW, June 25, 1887, Box 6, OWP.
36. Wister, ed., *Owen Wister Out West*, p. 64; OW to SBW, November 28, 1887, Box 8; West to OW, October 13, 1887, Box 37; OW to OJW, March 5, 1888, Box 6; OWP.
37. OW to OJW, January 27, 1888, Box 6, OWP.
38. West to OW, October 13, 1887, Box 37, OWP.
39. Ibid.
40. OW to SBW, May 28, 1888, Box 8, OWP.
41. Robert Louis Stevenson to OW, February 10, 1888, Box 35, OWP.
42. OW to OJW, January 27, 1888, March 5, 1888, Box 6, OWP.
43. Wister, ed., *Owen Wister Out West*, p. 64.
44. Ibid., pp. 65-67.
45. Ibid., p. 67.
46. Ibid., p. 79; Owen Wister, "When the Lightning Struck," mss., January 20, 1899, Box 61, OWP, published as "An Electric Storm on the Washakie Needles," *Science* 28 (December 11, 1908), pp. 837-39.
47. Ibid.
48. Wister, ed., *Owen Wister Out West*, p. 85.
49. Ibid., pp. 85-86.

NOTES

CHAPTER VII. WESTERN STORYTELLER (1889–1892)

1. Wister, ed., *Owen Wister Out West*, p. 11.
2. Certificate of admission to bar, Box 87; OW to Frances Ann Kemble, May 7, 1889, Box 9; OWP.
3. Oliver Wendell Holmes, Jr., to OW, March 30, 1889, April 14, 1889, Box 23, OWP.
4. OW to Frances Ann Kemble, May 7, 1889, Box 9, OWP.
5. OW to SBW, November 6, [1888], Box 8, OWP.
6. *The Dragon of Wantley* was published in 1892 by J. B. Lippincott Co., Philadelphia; OW to SBW, May 28, 1889, July 15, 1889, Box 9, OWP.
7. OW to Frances Ann Kemble, May 7, 1889, OW to SBW, July 15, 1889, Box 9, OWP; Wister, ed., *Owen Wister Out West*, pp. 89-90.
8. OW to SBW, July 15, 1889, Box 9, OWP.
9. Ibid., May 28, 1889, Box 9, OWP.
10. Ibid., August 20, 1889, Box 9, OWP.
11. Ibid.
12. OW to SBW, August 20, 1889, September 7, 1889, Box 9, OWP.
13. Ibid., September 7, 1889, Box 9, OWP.
14. Ibid., October 14, 1889, Box 9, OWP.
15. Ibid.
16. Notebook entry, October 10, 1889, typescript in Box 1, OWP.
17. Wister, ed., *Owen Wister Out West*, pp. 90-91; Helena Huntington Smith, *The War on Powder River* (New York: McGraw-Hill Book Co., 1966), pp. 121-34.
18. Wister, ed., *Owen Wister Out West*, pp. 90, 91.
19. Ibid., p. 92.
20. Papers relating to the Putnam Nail Company case are in Box 89, OWP; Wister, *Roosevelt*, p. 28.
21. Sergeant Price to OW, March 5, 1891, Babel I (the first in a series of Wister scrapbooks), Box 40, OWP; Wister, *Roosevelt*, p. 28.
22. West to OW, January 26, 1890, March 2, 9, 1890, August 27, 1890, January 30, 1891, March 14, 1891, Box 37, OWP.
23. Wister, *Roosevelt*, pp. 28-29; Wister, ed., *Owen Wister Out West*, p. 114.
24. Wister, ed., *Owen Wister Out West*, pp. 98, 102-3, 113, 114.
25. Ibid., pp. 97-98.
26. Ibid., p. 98.
27. Ibid., pp. 104-10.
28. Ibid., pp. 110-11.
29. Ibid., pp. 112-14.
30. Ibid., pp. 117-18; Smith, *War on Powder River*, pp. 254-58.
31. Wister, ed., *Owen Wister Out West*, pp. 118-20.
32. Ibid., p. 125.
33. Ibid., p. 128; OW to SBW, August 31, 1891, Box 9, OWP.
34. Wister, ed., *Owen Wister Out West*, pp. 119-20, 130.
35. Ibid., pp. 12-13.
36. Ibid., p. 29; Owen Wister, "Preface—Thirty Years After," *The Writings of Owen Wister: Lin McLean* (New York: Macmillan Co., 1928), p. ix; newspaper interview with Wister in *San Francisco Bulletin*, n.d., [1902], Box 96, OWP; Wister, *Roosevelt*, pp. 29-30.
37. Owen Wister, "Hank's Woman," *Harper's Weekly* 36 (August 27, 1892), pp. 821-23; Wister, ed., *Owen Wister Out West*, p. 106; *Sixth Report of the Secretary, Harvard Class of 1882*, Harvard Archives, Nathan Marsh Pusey Library, Harvard University; Owen Wister, "Preface," *Members of the Family* (New York: Macmillan Co., 1911), p. 17.
38. Owen Wister, "How Lin McLean Went East," *Harper's New Monthly Maga-*

zine 86 (December 1892), pp. 135-46; Wister, *Roosevelt*, p. 72; Lambert, "Western Writings of Owen Wister," pp. 122-23.

39. OW to SBW, October 17, 1892, November 14, 1892, Box 9, OWP.

40. Henry Mills Alden to OW, January 28, 1892, Box 45, OWP; Wister, ed., *Owen Wister Out West*, p. 20; Wister, *Roosevelt*, p. 30.

Chapter VIII. In Search of Material (1892–1895)

1. An exceptionally complete scrapbook maintained by Wister concerning the Johnson County war is in Box 47, OWP.

2. West to OW, May 6, 1891, November 21, 1891, February 14, 1892, March 13, 1892, April 6, 21, 1892, May 13, 30, 1892, Box 37, OWP.

3. Clipping in OW's scrapbook from the April 17, 1892, issue of *Philadelphia Times*.

4. Hubert E. Teschemacher to OW, July 6, 1892, Box 36; Amos W. Barber to OW, September 22, 1892, Box 14; OWP.

5. Smith, *War on Powder River*, passim.

6. Notebook entry, July 11, 1892, Box 1, OWP.

7. Ibid.; White, *Eastern Establishment and the Western Experience*, pp. 129-30.

8. George T. Watkins, "Owen Wister and the American West" (Ph.D. diss., University of Illinois, 1959), p. 312, as quoted by White in *Eastern Establishment and the Western Experience*, p. 129; Wister, ed., *Owen Wister Out West*, p. 167.

9. Notebook entry, July 6-14, 1892, Box 1, OWP.

10. Owen Wister, "The White Goat," in Caspar Whitney, George Bird Grinnell, and Owen Wister, *Musk-Ox, Bison, Sheep and Goat* (New York: Macmillan Co., 1904), pp. 262-64.

11. Notebook entry, October 11, 1892, Box 1, OWP; and Wister, ed., *Owen Wister Out West*, pp. 138-39.

12. OW to SBW, November 14, 1892, Box 9, OWP.

13. Appointment book entry, November 2, 1892, Box 84, OWP.

14. OW to SBW, October 17, 1892, Box 9, OWP.

15. Notebook entry, December 2, 1892, Box 1, OWP; Wister, ed., *Owen Wister Out West*, pp. 146-47.

16. Hale Harrison to OW, October 31, 1892, Box 45, OWP; Mrs. Helen Peck Smith to OW, December 6, 1892, Box 45, OWP; Wister, *Roosevelt*, p. 33; OW to SBW, November 14, 1892, Box 9, OWP.

17. A copy of the December 3, 1892, *Literary World* review is in Box 45; OW to SBW, November 9, 1882, Box 9; criticisms from friends concerning *The Dragon of Wantley* are in Box 46; OWP.

18. Owen Wister, "Preface—A Best Seller," *The Writings of Owen Wister: The Virginian* (New York: Macmillan Co., 1928), p. x; *Atlantic Monthly* (writer of letter not identified) to OW, June 7, 1892, Charles D. Lanier of *Cosmopolitan* to OW, December 13, 1892, Box 45; notebook entry, October 8, 1895, Box 45; OWP.

19. Newspaper clipping, n.d., 1894, Box 46, OWP. Wister's dating of his abandonment of law is in a biographical sketch at the end of *Philosophy 4* (New York: Macmillan Co., 1909).

20. MW to OW, November 24, 1892, Box 45; programs dated April 26, 1893, and March 22, 1893, Box 89; OWP.

21. Francis Michael to OW, October 20, [1892], Box 45; a notation by Fanny Butler Kemble on the libretto of the opera described its ultimate fate, Box 64; OWP.

22. John I. White, "Owen Wister and the Dogies," *Journal of American Folklore* 82 (January-March 1969), pp. 66-69; Owen Wister, "Catholicity in Musical Taste," *Harper's Monthly* 72 (November 1893), pp. 650-55.

23. Wister, ed., *Owen Wister Out West*, pp. 150, 152-57; Wister, "Preface," *Writings of Owen Wister: The Virginian*, p. x.

NOTES

24. West to OW, August 14, 1892, November 26, 1892, December 25, 1892, Box 37; February 24, 1893, May 4, 1893, June 25, 1893, Box 38; OWP.

25. Wister, ed., *Owen Wister Out West*, p. 164; notebook entry, June 16, 1893, Box 1, OWP.

26. Wister, "Preface," *Writings of Owen Wister: Lin McLean*, p. ix; appointment book entry, June 17, 1893, Box 84, OWP; notebook entry, June 18, 1893, Box 1, OWP; Wister, ed., *Owen Wister Out West*, p. 165.

27. Henry Pault to OW, June 20, 1893, Box 45, OWP.

28. Wister, ed., *Owen Wister Out West*, p. 196; Owen Wister, "Balaam and Pedro," *Harper's Monthly* 88 (January 1894), pp. 293-307.

29. OW to William Dean Howells, June 7, 1892, Charles D. Lanier to OW, December 13, 1892, Box 45; notebook entries for 1893, Box 89; OWP.

30. Wister, "Preface," *Writings of Owen Wister: The Virginian*, p. xi.

31. Wister, *Roosevelt*, p. 34.

32. Wister, "Preface," *Writings of Owen Wister: The Virginian*, p. xi.

33. Wister, ed., *Owen Wister Out West*, p. 166; Charles Scribner's Sons to OW, July 17, 1893, Box 34, OWP.

34. Alden to OW, June 27, 1893, Box 45, OWP; J. Henry Harper, *The House of Harper: A Century of Publishing in Franklin Square* (New York: Harper & Brothers, 1912), pp. 606-7; Wister, ed., *Owen Wister Out West*, p. 167.

35. Wister, *Roosevelt*, pp. 29-30; Wister, ed., *Owen Wister Out West*, pp. 167-68; Alden to OW, July 14, 1893, Box 45, OWP.

36. Wister, ed., *Owen Wister Out West*, p. 168.

37. OW to SBW, March 5, 1893, Box 6, OWP; Wister, ed., *Owen Wister Out West*, p. 170.

38. OJW to OW, July 27, 1891, OW to SBW, March 5, 1893, Box 6, OWP.

39. Wister, ed., *Owen Wister Out West*, pp. 170-71.

40. Notebook entry, July 9, 1893, Box 1, OWP.

41. Wister, ed., *Owen Wister Out West*, pp. 174-75; the calling cards are in Box 45, OWP.

42. Wister, ed., *Owen Wister Out West*, pp. 182-83.

43. Marta Jackson, "Frederic Remington," *The Illustrations of Frederic Remington* (New York: Bounty Books, 1970), p. 9.

44. Ibid.

45. Owen Wister, "Preface—Twenty-Eight Years After," *The Writings of Owen Wister: Hank's Woman* (New York: Macmillan Co., 1928), pp. ix-xii; Owen Wister, "The Promised Land," *Harper's Monthly* 88 (April 1894), pp. 781-96; Owen Wister, "A Kinsman of Red Cloud," *Harper's Monthly* 88 (May 1895), pp. 907-17.

46. Wister, ed., *Owen Wister Out West*, pp. 183-84.

47. OW to Frank A. Edwards, July 23, 1893, August 3, 1893, as quoted in Fanny Kemble Wister, ed., "Letters of Owen Wister, Author of *The Virginian*," *Pennsylvania Magazine of History and Biography* 83 (January 1959), pp. 7-10.

48. *St. Louis Star*, January 3, 1909, clipping, Box 87, OWP; Wister, ed., *Owen Wister Out West*, pp. 204-5.

49. Wister, ed., *Owen Wister Out West*, pp. 189, 190, 192; OW to SBW, October 30, 1889, Box 9; appointment book entry for October 21, 1893, Box 84; OW to SBW, November 1, 1889, Box 8; OW to SBW, November 5, 1893, Box 9; OWP.

50. Wister, ed., *Owen Wister Out West*, p. 192.

51. Wister, ed., "Letters of Owen Wister," pp. 15-16, 9-10; Francis Michael to OW, August 9, 1893, Box 29, OWP.

52. The prospectus is in Box 45, OWP; advertisement, *Harper's Monthly* 87 (November 1893); *Pittsburgh Bulletin*, November 18, 1893, clipping, Box 45, OWP.

53. George G. Goodman to OW, December 18, 1893, Frederic Remington to Wister, n.d., [1893], Remington to OW, November 11, [1893], Box 45, OWP.

54. Roosevelt to OW, April 20, 1894, Box 45; May 26, 1894, Box 33; OWP.

55. Notebook entry, December 31, 1893, Box 1, OWP.

56. Wister, ed., "Letters of Owen Wister," p. 16.

57. Notebook entry, July 1893, as quoted in Vorpahl, *My Dear Wister*, p. 36; Stow Persons, *The Decline of American Gentility* (New York: Columbia University Press, 1973), pp. 276-85.

58. Wister, ed., "Letters of Owen Wister," p. 18.

59. *Harper's Weekly* to OW, May 1, 1895, Box 46, OWP. The poem appeared in the May 18, 1885, edition, p. 460.

60. Notebook entry, June 28, 1893, Box 1, OWP; Theodore Roosevelt, "What Americanism Means," *Forum* 17 (April 1894), p. 202; Roosevelt to OW, April 20, 1894, as quoted in Wister, *Roosevelt*, p. 36.

61. Remington to OW, January 10, 1894, Box 45, OWP.

62. Owen Wister, Introduction, *The Writings of Owen Wister: Red Men and White* (New York: Macmillan Co., 1928), p. ix; Owen Wister, "The Evolution of the Cow-Puncher," *Harper's Monthly* 101 (September 1895), pp. 602-17; Peggy and Harold Samuels, *Frederic Remington: A Biography* (Garden City: Doubleday & Company, 1982), pp. 218-20.

63. Oliver Wendell Holmes to OW, August 21, 1893, Box 23, October 9, 1892, Box 45, OWP; *San Francisco Examiner*, July 15, 1894, clipping, Box 46, OWP; "Literary Notes," *New York Tribune*, July 1, 1894, as quoted in Marovitz, "Owen Wister: An Annotated Bibliography," p. 10; OW to SBW, April 15, 1894, March 3, 14, 1894, Box 9, OWP.

64. Wister, ed., *Owen Wister Out West*, pp. 201-2.

65. "Frontier Notes," notebook, 1894, Box 1, OWP; Wister, ed., *Owen Wister Out West*, pp. 204-5.

66. Wister, ed., *Owen Wister Out West*, pp. 207-8; Edwards to OW, January 7, 1894, Box 19; musical program, June 8, 1894, Box 45; OWP.

67. Notebook entry, June 25, 1894, Box 1; William Hills to Wister, May 15, 1894, Box 45; OWP; Sidney G. Fisher, "Owen Wister," *Writer* 7 (September 1894), pp. 130-31.

68. OW to SBW, June 25, 1894, Box 9, OWP; Wister, ed., *Owen Wister Out West*, pp. 208-13.

69. Wister, ed., *Owen Wister Out West*, pp. 211-12.

70. Ibid.

71. OW to Mrs. Frank A. Edwards, August 25, [1894], as quoted in Wister, ed., "Letters of Owen Wister," p. 25.

72. Appointment book entry, July 6, 1894, Box 84, OWP; "Has Come Out in the West," *San Francisco Examiner*, July 15, 1894, clipping, Box 46, OWP.

73. Wister, ed., *Owen Wister Out West*, pp. 222-23.

74. Unsigned letter, n.d., [1894], Box 46, OWP.

75. Wister, ed., *Owen Wister Out West*, p. 200; OW to Sarah Orne Jewett, December 2, 1897, HL.

76. Remington to OW, August 10, 1894, as quoted in Vorpahl, *My Dear Wister*, p. 41; OW to Mrs. Frank A. Edwards, August 25, 1894, as quoted in Wister, ed., "Letters of Owen Wister," pp. 25-26.

77. OW to Roosevelt, [April 1895], Box 33, OWP; Wister, *Roosevelt*, p. 40.

78. Samuel L. Clemens to OW, August 4, 1895, Box 46, OWP; untitled talk by Wister, n.d., Box 50, OWP; Owen Wister, "In Homage to Mark Twain," *Harper's Monthly* 171 (October 1935), pp. 547-56.

79. Skirdin to OW, May 2, 1895, Box 35, OWP.

80. Horace Scudder to OW, May 29, 1894, Box 45; appointment book entry, April 4, 1895, Box 84; H. L. Nelson to OW, September 20, 1895, October 28, 1895, Box 46; OW to SBW, October 6, 1895, Box 9; J. H. Trens [?] to OW, November 27, 1894, Box 46; Alden to OW, January 3, 1895, Box 46; *Louisville Courier-Journal*, December 22, 1894, clipping, Box 46, OWP.

81. Wister, ed., *Owen Wister Out West*, p. 227.
82. Ibid., pp. 229, 245, 246, 226.
83. OW to SBW, May 24, 1895, Box 9, OWP.
84. Wister, ed., *Owen Wister Out West*, pp. 248, 249.
85. OW to SBW, August 9, 1895, Box 9, OWP.
86. Wister, "Preface," *The Writings of Owen Wister: Red Men and White*, p. vii.

CHAPTER IX. FAME AND MARRIAGE (1895–1898)

1. See Wister's notations on his poem, "The Pale Cast of Thought," Box 85, OWP.
2. See the summary of reviews in Marovitz, "Owen Wister: An Annotated Bibliography," pp. 11-15.
3. William Dean Howells, "Life and Letters," *Harper's Weekly* 39 (November 30, 1895), p. 1133; Theodore Roosevelt, "A Teller of Tales of Strong Men," *Harper's Weekly* 39 (December 21, 1895), p. 1216.
4. *Cincinnati Tribune*, March 11, 1896, clipping, Box 42, OWP; Wister, "Preface," *Writings of Owen Wister: Red Men and White*, pp. xii-xiii.
5. Entries, October 15 and 16, [1895], in section entitled "A Postscript" and in notebook entitled "Journal and Notes 1895," Box 89, OWP.
6. Ibid.
7. Ibid.
8. Notebook entries, October 3, 7, ibid.
9. Notebook entries, October 9, 10, ibid.
10. Notebook entry, October 12, ibid.
11. Notebook entry, October 15, ibid.
12. Notebook entry, October 17, ibid.; Wister, *Roosevelt*, pp. 51-52.
13. See the note Richard Harding Davis appended to a clipping, "Town Topics," August 29, 1895, Box 46; entry, October 8, [1895], in notebook entitled "Journal and Notes 1895," Box 89; OWP.
14. Hamlin Garland to OW, January 4, 22, 1896, OW to Garland, January 23, 1896, Kipling to OW, February 20, 1896, Box 42; Babel III, Box 42; OWP.
15. Entry, October 17, [1895], in notebook entitled "Journal and Notes 1895," Box 89, OWP; notebook entries, September 27, October 16, 17, [1895], ibid.; OW to SBW, October 6, 1895, Box 9, OWP; Owen Wister, "A Journey in Search of Christmas," *Harper's Weekly* 39 (December 14, 1895), pp. 1181-85.
16. The menu for the dinner is in Box 42; undated newspaper clipping in letter from J. Henry Harper to OW, December 17, 1895, Box 22; entry, October 17, [1895], in notebook entitled "Journal and Notes 1895," Box 89; OWP.
17. George P. Brett to OW, February, n.d., 1896, January 29, 30, 1896, Box 42, OWP.
18. Langdon Mitchell to OW, n.d., [1895], Box 3; Mitchell, "Memoir of Owen Jones Wister, M.D."
19. Entries, April 9, 15, 30, May 5, July 27, 1896, in notebook kept at sea, Box 9, OWP; Wister, "Preface," *Members of the Family*, p. 18.
20. SBW to OW, May 20, 1895, OW to SBW, May 27, 1895, Box 9, OWP.
21. West to OW, January 3, 8, 23, May 3, September 4, 1894, February 23, 1896, Box 38, OWP.
22. OW to SBW, April 9, 1897, Box 10, July 13, 1897, Box 54, March 16, 1897, July 13, 1897, May 28, 1898, Box 10, OWP.
23. Ibid., July 13, 1897, n.d., [1897], Box 10, OWP.
24. Various appointment book entries, late 1890s, Box 84, OWP.
25. Program dated January 15, 1896, Box 42; "Poets of the Pegasus," *Philadelphia Bulletin*, February 15, 1896, clipping, Box 42; untitled, *Saturday Evening Post*, clipping, March 15, 1902, Box 40; OWP.

NOTES

26. OW to SBW, March 6, 1897, Box 10, OWP; Owen Wister, *Lin McLean* (New York: Harper and Bros., 1897), dedication page.

27. Owen Wister, "Sharon's Choice," *Harper's Monthly* 95 (August 1897), pp. 447-57; "Notes," *Nation* 65 (August 12, 1897), p. 131.

28. Alden to OW, June 22, 1897, Box 22; OW to SBW, July 3, 1897, Box 10; OWP.

29. OW to SBW, August 18, 31, 1897, Box 10, OWP.

30. Frederic Remington, *Drawings* (New York: R. H. Russell, 1897); J. Henry Harper to OW, May 18, 1897, Box 22, OWP.

31. *Boston Herald*, November 27, 1897, clipping, *Boston Globe*, November 30, 1897, clipping, Box 42; *Rochester Post Express*, August 31, 1897, clipping, Box 86; OWP.

32. *Lexington Morning Herald*, February 20, 1898, as quoted in Marovitz, "Owen Wister: An Annotated Bibliography," pp. 16-17; *Manchester Guardian*, December 2, 1897, clipping, Box 43, OWP; "Novel Notes," *Bookman* 7 (May 1898), p. 254; "As Howells Sees Fiction," *New York Sun*, February 6, 1898, clipping, Box 43, OWP.

33. J. J. Chapman to OW, March 25, 1897, Box 16; Dean Duke to OW, November 16, 1897, Box 18; OWP.

34. Harper and Bros. to OW, November 22, 1897, Box 22, OWP.

35. Roosevelt to OW, December 13, 1897, Box 43, OWP.

36. The 1898 calendar in Box 5, OWP, has a notation which indicates January 1, 1898, as the date of engagement; William Rotch Wister to OW, January 7, 1898, Box 10, OWP.

37. Isaac J. Wister to OW, January 22, 1898, Box 3; OW to SBW, March 3, 9, 1898, Box 10; OWP.

38. SBW to OW, February 27, 1898, OW to SBW, March 3, 1898, Box 10, OWP.

39. OW to Winthrop Chanler, April 6, 1898, HL; *Philadelphia Item*, April 24, 1898, *Philadelphia Record*, April 22, 1898, *Philadelphia Bulletin*, April 21, 1898, clippings, Box 86, OWP.

40. OW to SBW, May 24, [1898], May 3, [1898], April 24, [1898], Box 10, OWP.

41. Ibid., April 24, [1898], May 3, [1898], Box 10, OWP; Wister, *Roosevelt*, pp. 101, 103.

42. Wister, *Roosevelt*, pp. 101, 103; OW to SBW, May 3, [1898], Box 10, OWP; MW to SBW, as quoted in Julian Mason, "Owen Wister: Champion of Old Charleston," *Quarterly Journal of the Library of Congress* 29 (July 1972), p. 165; OW to SBW, May 18, [1898], Box 10, OWP.

43. OW to SBW, May 24, [1898], Box 10; J. J. Chapman to OW, July 16, 1898, Box 16; OW to SBW, May 3, [1898], Box 10; OWP.

44. George Waring to OW, April 26, 1898, Box 37, OWP.

45. OW to SBW, May 3, [1898], August 2, 1898, OW to SBW, August 28, [1898], Box 10, OWP.

46. MW to SBW, August 11, 1898, OW to SBW, August 28, [1898], Box 10, OWP.

47. OW to SBW, August 28, [1898], Box 10, OWP.

48. Eva A. Remington to OW, n.d., 1898, as quoted in Vorpahl, *My Dear Wister*, p. 229; Frederic Remington to OW, n.d., [1898], Box 33, OWP.

49. SBW to OW, September 4, 1898, Box 10, OWP; MW to SBW, August 12, 1898, as quoted in Vorpahl, *My Dear Wister*, p. 236.

50. OW to SBW, September 16, 1898, May 24, 1898, Box 10, OWP.

51. Ibid., September 19, 1898, Box 10, OWP.

52. Ibid., September 30, 1898, Box 10, OWP.

53. Ibid., September 16, 1898, Box 10, OWP.

NOTES

CHAPTER X. OVERNIGHT CELEBRITY (1899–1902)

1. Note, December 31, 1898, Box 87; OW to SBW, March 28, 1899, Box 10; OWP.

2. OW to SBW, June 17, 1899, Box 10, OWP; Owen Wister, "Padre Ignazio," *Harper's Monthly* 100 (April 1900), pp. 692-703; the *New York Tribune* article, April 14, 1900, is enclosed in a letter from OW to SBW, April 20, 1900, Box 11, OWP.

3. OW to SBW, June 3, 1899, Box 10, OWP; E. S. Martin, "This Busy World," *Harper's Weekly* 43 (July 8, 1899), p. 665.

4. OW to SBW, August 9, 1899, Box 62, August 4, 1899, Box 10, OWP.

5. Ibid., July 22, 1899, August 31, 1899, Box 10, OWP.

6. Ibid., June 12, 17, 1899, Box 10, OWP.

7. Ibid., September 20, 26, 1899, October 23, 28, 1899, Box 10, OWP.

8. Ibid., October 31, 1899, Box 10, OWP.

9. Ibid., n.d., 1899, Box 10, OWP; Earnest, *S. Weir Mitchell*, p. 128.

10. Harper and Bros. to OW, May 31, 1899, A. V. S. Anthony of Harper and Bros. to OW, June 5, 1899, Box 43; M. A. DeWolfe Howe to OW, October 21, 1899, Box 24; OW to Howe, October 31, 1899, Box 24; OWP; OW to Howe, October 29, [1899], HL.

11. Among those publishers who approached Wister were Outlook, Doubleday & McClure, D. Appleton, L. C. Page & Co., and Brown and Co. Their letters are in Box 43, OWP. OW's determination to help Harper and Bros. out of their difficulty is announced in a note in Box 43, OWP. J. Henry Harper to OW, December 1, 1899, Alden to OW, December 1, 1899, Box 43, OWP.

12. Wister, *Roosevelt*, p. 29; SBW to OW, March 27, 1900, OW to SBW, March 30, 1900, SBW to OW, April 1, 1900, OW to SBW, April 3, 1900, Box 11, OWP.

13. Owen Wister, *The Jimmyjohn Boss* (New York: Harper and Brothers, 1900), p. ix; OW's accompanying note to the dedication is in Box 43; a summary of reviews appears in Marovitz, "Owen Wister: An Annotated Bibliography," pp. 19-21; *Minneapolis Tribune*, June 9, 1900, clipping, Box 47; OW's observation about the small number of buyers for *The Jimmyjohn Boss* is in Box 43; OWP; Wister, "Preface," *Writings of Owen Wister: Hank's Woman*, p. viii; Eugene Exman, *The House of Harper: One Hundred and Fifty Years of Publishing* (New York: Harper & Row Publishers, 1967), p. 195.

14. OW to Howe, January 13, 1900, HL; Howells to OW, May 30, 1900, OW to Howells, June 2, 1900, Box 47, OWP; Perry, *Henry Lee Higginson*, p. 312; OW to SBW, August 9, 1900, Box 11, OWP.

15. *Philadelphia Press*, February 4, 11, 1900, clippings, Box 43; *New York Times*, February 25, 1900, clipping, Box 43; *New York Times*, March 4, 1900, clipping Box 43; OWP.

16. Notebook entry, August 12, 1900, Box 89, OWP.

17. Ibid., August 15, 1900, Box 89, OWP.

18. Undated newspaper clipping from the mid-1930s, Box 96, OWP.

19. OW to SBW, August 23, 27, 1900, Box 11; Owen Wister, "The Horse and His Destiny," *Boston Transcript*, September 5, 1900, Box 47; OWP.

20. OW to Charles Eliot Norton, October 9, 1900, [October 1900], HL.

21. OW to SBW, September, n.d., 1900, Box 11, OWP; a copy of the poem accompanies OW's October 9, 1900, letter to Norton, HL.

22. OW to SBW, April 20, 1900, Box 11, OWP; *Boston Journal*, October 15, 18, 1900, *Boston Courier*, October 20, 1900, *Boston Daily Advertiser*, October 18, 1900, clippings, Box 47; OW's comment concerning the notices also appears in Box 47; OWP.

23. Owen Wister, *Ulysses S. Grant* (Boston: Small, Maynard & Co., 1900); Owen Wister, "Preface—Success and the *Cash-Box*," *The Writings of Owen Wister:*

NOTES

U. S. Grant and The Seven Ages of Washington (New York: Macmillan Co., 1928), p. v.

24. Miss A. Torbell to OW, February 3, [1900], Box 43, OWP; OW's comment is found on Miss Torbell's letter.

25. OW to SBW, July, n.d., 1900, Box 11, OWP.

26. Ibid., April 5, 1901, Box 11, OWP.

27. See program dated December 4, 1900, Box 47; documents dated November 2, 1900, April 23, 1900, Box 32; OW to SBW, June 7, 1901, May 27, 1901, Box 11; *Boston Transcript*, February 23, 1901, clipping, Box 48; William James to Mrs. Henry S. Whitman, February 5, 1901, Box 25; OWP.

28. Roosevelt to OW, March 11, 1901, Box 41; OW to SBW, June 28, 1901, Box 11; OWP.

29. OW, by memory, quoted Roosevelt: "I can't know that I have the ability, but I do know that I have the will, to carry out the task that has fallen to me." Wister, *Roosevelt*, p. 86. Roosevelt to OW, September 14, 1901, Box 33, OWP.

30. *Philadelphia Press*, September 22, 1901, clipping, Box 56, OWP; Owen Wister, "Theodore Roosevelt: The Sportsman and the Man," *Outing* 38 (June 1901), pp. 242-48.

31. Roosevelt to Richard Watson Gilder, September 21, 1901, reprinted in Elting E. Morison, ed., *The Letters of Theodore Roosevelt*, 8 vols. (Cambridge: Harvard University Press, 1951–54), 3: 149; Roosevelt to OW, November 2, 1901, ibid., p. 187.

32. "The Game and the Nation," *New York Times*, February 21, 1901, clipping, Box 48, OWP.

33. Upton Sinclair to OW, April 3, 1901, Box 34, OWP.

34. OW to SBW, July 14, 1901, December 16, 19, 1901, Box 11, OWP.

35. Ibid., August 11, 1901, April 5, 1901, Box 11, OWP; Owen Wister, "Preface—Our Inveterate Family," *The Writings of Owen Wister: Safe in the Arms of Croesus* (New York: Macmillan Co., 1928), p. x; Owen Wister, "Philosophy 4," *Lippincott's* 68 (August 1901), pp. 193-217; Alden to OW, April 29, 1901, Box 22, OWP.

36. OW to SBW, April 21, 1901, Box 11, OWP; Owen Wister, "In a State of Sin," *Harper's Monthly* 104 (February 1902), pp. 453-69.

37. Owen Wister, "To the Reader," *The Virginian: A Horseman of the Plains* (New York: Macmillan Co., 1902; Boston: Houghton Mifflin Co., 1968), p. 3.

38. Wister, "Preface," *Writings of Owen Wister: The Virginian*, p. xiii.

39. OW to SBW, July 14, 1901, December 8, 1901, Box 11, OWP.

40. J. Henry Harper to OW, November 12, 1901, Box 22; OW to SBW, December 8, 1901, Box 11; Brett to OW, November 13, 1901, Box 28; OWP.

41. OW to SBW, December 8, 1901, Box 11, OWP; Sanford E. Marovitz, "Romance or Realism? Western Periodical Literature: 1893–1902," *Western American Literature* 10 (Spring 1975), pp. 48-49; *Saturday Evening Post*, May 3, 10, 1902.

42. Wister, *Roosevelt*, p. 95.

43. OW to SBW, February 9, 1902, Box 11, OWP; Wister, "Preface," *Writings of Owen Wister: The Virginian*, p. xv. In Wister, ed., *Owen Wister Out West*, OW is quoted as having said he worked forty days instead of fourteen. This is an error, as shown by the original letter from OW to his mother, February 9, 1902, Box 11, OWP.

44. Wister, *Roosevelt*, p. 103; White, *The Eastern Establishment and the Western Experience*, pp. 138-44; Joe B. Frantz and Julian Ernest Choate, Jr., *The American Cowboy: The Myth and the Reality* (Norman: University of Oklahoma Press, 1955), p. 148.

45. OW to SBW, February 9, 1902, Box 11, OWP.

46. Wister, *Roosevelt*, pp. 87, 99-100.

47. Charles D. Skirdin to OW, January 18, 1902, Box 35, OWP.

48. West to OW, June 19, 1898, March 8, 1900, April 14, 1900, July 21,

NOTES

1901, Box 38, OWP; Molly Stenberg to Mrs. George M. West, June 29, 1959, in possession of the Wests of Seattle; Wister, *Roosevelt*, p. 70.

49. West to OW, July 21, 1901, Box 38, OWP.

50. Wister, "To the Reader," *The Virginian*, pp. 3-4.

51. OW to SBW, May 3, 1902, Box 11, OWP; OW to Oliver Wendell Holmes, May 19, 1902, as quoted in Wister, ed., *Owen Wister Out West*, p. 16.

52. Advertisement in unidentified Philadelphia newspaper, July 13, 1902, *New York Sun*, June 26, 1902, clippings, Box 79, OWP; *New York Times Saturday Review of Books*, June 21, 1902, p. 427; *Current Literature* 33 (August 1902), p. 242; William Morton Payne, "Recent Fiction," *Dial* 33 (October 1902), p. 242; "Chronicle and Comment," *Bookman* 15 (August 1902), pp. 513-14; all reviews quoted, except when specified, from Morovitz, "Owen Wister: An Annotated Bibliography," pp. 23, 25, 27.

53. OW to SBW, June 17, 1902, Box 11, OWP.

54. Ibid., June 30, 1902, Box 11, OWP.

55. Wister, "Preface," *Writings of Owen Wister: The Virginian*, p. ix; OW to SBW, July 2, 1902, Box 11, OWP.

56. OW to SBW, July 1, 2, 3, 1902, Box 11, OWP.

57. Roosevelt to OW, May 29, June 7, 1902, Box 33, OWP; OW to Roosevelt, June 10, 1902, as quoted in Wister, ed., *Owen Wister Out West*, p. 16.

58. OW to SBW, August 2, 5, 1902, Box 11; *New York Tribune*, August 26, 1902, clipping, Box 79; OWP.

59. Henry James to OW, August 7, 1902, Box 25, OWP.

60. OW to SBW, August 23, 1902, July 5, 8, 1902, Box 11, OWP.

61. Ibid., July 5, 1902, Box 11, OWP.

62. H. W. Boynton, "Books New and Old," *Atlantic Monthly* 90 (August 1902), pp. 277-81; Frantz and Choate, *The American Cowboy*, p. 158.

63. Wister, "Preface," *Writings of Owen Wister: The Virginian*, p. xiv.

64. OW to Hamilton Wright Mabie, June 4, 1902, Correspondence of Hamilton Wright Mabie, Library of Congress.

65. Wister, *The Virginian*, pp. 33, 26, 31, 93, 91; OW to SBW, August 5, 1902, Box 11, OWP.

66. C. F. M. Stark to OW, January 14, 1904, August 30, 1902, Box 79; OW to SBW, May 23, 1901, Box 11; OWP.

67. OW to Miss Edith Miller, July 14, 1902, Box 30; various letters from readers are in Boxes 78 and 79; Charles Dartemann to OW, September 19, 1902, Box 78; Mrs. Caspar Wister to OW, September 9, [1902], Box 3; Richard Harding Davis to OW, February 1, [1902], Box 18; Richard Harding Davis to OW, November 1, 1902, Box 18; OWP. OW's response to Davis is quoted in John M. Solenstein, "Richard Harding Davis, Owen Wister, and *The Virginian*: Unpublished Letters and a Commentary," *American Literary Realism* 5 (Spring 1972), pp. 122-33.

68. Duke to OW, July 7, 1902, October 16, 1902, Box 18, OWP.

69. The professor was W. C. Knight, and the incident was related to OW in a letter from Horace Elmer Wood II, October 14, 1931, Box 79, OWP.

70. Alden to OW, October 17, 1902, Box 23, OWP.

71. OW to SBW, August 29, 1902, Box 11, OWP.

72. Ibid.; William Roscoe Thayer to OW, September 4, 1902, Box 23, OWP.

73. Henry Holt to OW, September 17, 1902, Box 23, OWP.

74. Richard Watson Gilder to OW, December 16, 1902, Box 15; Henry Holt to OW, June 20, 1902, Box 23; OW to Houghton Mifflin Co., July 3, 1902, Box 23; Houghton Mifflin Co. to OW, March 14, 1902, July 29, 1902, Box 40; OWP.

75. OW to SBW, October 30, 1902, August 20, 1902, Box 11, OWP.

76. Mrs. Frank Norris to OW, n.d., [1902], Box 79; J. O'H. Cosgrave to OW, October 30, 1902, Box 18; OWP.

77. OW to SBW, October 14, 1902, Box 11, OWP.

78. Senator Albert J. Beveridge to OW, December 2, 6, 1902, Box 14; OW to SBW, August 13, 1902, Box 11; J. Henry Harper to OW, October 14, 1902, Box 22; A. Kauser to OW, July 29, 1902, Box 26; Brett to OW, June 9, 1902, Box 28; OW to SBW, July 1, 1902, Box 11; OWP.

CHAPTER XI. "THE VIRGINIAN" ON BROADWAY (1903–1904)

1. "Author and Playwright," *Rochester Post-Express*, November 17, 1902, clipping, Box 86, OWP.
2. OW to SBW, January 9, 1903, Box 11, OWP; Wister, *Roosevelt*, pp. 106-14; Owen Wister, "Visit to White House," Box 61, OWP.
3. Wister, *Roosevelt*, pp. 116-18; Wister, "Visit to White House."
4. Wister, "Visit to White House"; Wister, *Roosevelt*, p. 106.
5. Undated article in *New York Commercial Advertiser*, as quoted in *Kansas City* (Mo.) *Independent*, May 30, 1903, clipping, Box 81, OWP.
6. SBW to OW, March 20, 1903, Box 11, OWP.
7. Ibid., March 30, 1903, July 8, 1902, OW to SBW, April 1, 1903, Box 11, OWP.
8. OW to SBW, March 27, 1903, Box 11, OWP.
9. SBW to OW, March 15, 1903, OW to SBW, July 8, 1902, June 3, 1903, May 27, 1903, Box 11, OWP.
10. SBW to OW, March 15, 1903, Box 11, OWP.
11. OW to SBW, March 21, 1903, Box 11, OWP.
12. Brett to OW, May 20, 1903, annual statement from Macmillan, April 30, 1903, Box 28, OWP.
13. George F. Baer to OW, April 2, 1903, Box 14; Skirdin to OW, March 26, 1903, April 24, 1903, July 25, 1903, Box 35; OWP.
14. The notice to West from the Lovering Land and Livestock Co. is enclosed in a letter from West to OW, August 9, 1903, see also West to OW, September 12, 1903, Box 38, OWP.
15. Wister, *Roosevelt*, p. 77; Frank A. Edwards to OW, October 27, 1903, Box 19, OWP.
16. OW to SBW, May 27, 1903, June 26, 1903, Box 11; Sherman Evarts to OW, May 28, 1903, Box 19; Memorandum of Agreement, June 25, 1903, Box 89; OWP.
17. OW to SBW, May 9, 1903, July 1, 24, 1903, August 15, 17, 25, 1903, August, n.d., 1903, June 3, 1903, Box 11, OWP.
18. Ibid., July 24, 1903, Box 11; Houghton Mifflin to OW, October 28, 30, 1903, Box 23; Alden to OW, August 5, 1903, Box 40; OWP.
19. OW to SBW, April 1, 1903, August 25, 1903, SBW to OW, April 5, 1903, Box 11, OWP.
20. Edward Bok to OW, July 1, 3, 1903, Box 26, OWP.
21. American Lithographic Co. to OW, January 4, 1904, Box 13; OW to SBW, September 14, 1903, Box 11; OWP.
22. OW to SBW, September 14, 1903, Box 11, OWP.
23. Sinclair to OW, May 23, [1903], August 22, 1903, Box 34, OWP.
24. OW's comments are quoted by Sinclair in an undated response in Box 34, OWP.
25. OW to SBW, August 5, 25, 1903, Box 11, OWP.
26. OW to Duke, April 23, 1904, Box 18; OW to SBW, August 5, 1903, Box 11; OWP.
27. OW to SBW, September 14, 1903, Box 11, OWP.
28. Ibid.
29. Ibid.; *The National Cyclopaedia of American Biography* (New York: James T. White & Co., 1904), vol. 12: 185-86.
30. OW to Duke, April 23, 1904, Box 18, OWP.

31. Ibid.

32. OW to SBW, September 24, 1903, Box 11, OWP.

33. OW to Duke, April 23, 1904, Box 18; OW to SBW, September 23, 1904, Box 11; OWP.

34. OW to Duke, April 23, 1904, Box 18, OWP.

35. Grant La Farge to OW, October 13, 1903, La Farge to La Shelle, October 12, 1903 (not sent), Box 79, OWP.

36. OW to Duke, April 23, 1904, Box 18; OW to SBW, December 4, 1903, Box 11; OWP.

37. OW to SBW, December 4, 1903, Box 11, OWP.

38. Ibid.

39. OW to SBW, Thanksgiving Day, 1903, November 7, 1903, Box 11, OWP.

40. *New York Times*, January 6, 1904, p. 2; N. Orwin Rush, Introduction, *The Virginian: A Play in Four Acts* (Tallahassee, Florida: n.p., 1958), p. iv.

41. *New York Sun*, January 6, 1904, clippings, Box 67; SBW to Hamilton Aidé, January 31, 1904, Box 11; OWP.

42. The royalty figures come from Box 67, OWP; Ima Honaker Herron, "Owen Wister as Playwright," *Southwest Review* 47 (Summer 1962), pp. vi-vii.

43. "Notes and Queries," *Western Folklore* 26 (October 1907), pp. 269-71; OW to Duke, April 23, 1904, Box 18, OWP.

44. OW to Duke, April 23, 1904, Box 18; OW to SBW, March 20, 1904, Box 11; OW to SBW, March 22, 1904, Box 3; OW to SBW, February 18, 1904, Box 11; OWP.

45. Newspaper clippings about Wister's illness are in Box 86, OWP.

46. OW to SBW, May 21, 1906, July 30, 1904, Box 11, OWP.

CHAPTER XII. A NOVEL OF MANNERS (1904–1906)

1. The officers of the Immigration Restriction League are on a list dated November, 1903, in Box 24, OWP; *Saturday Evening Post*, editorial, October 29, 1904, clipping, Box 44, OWP; OW to C. Gallup of Overlook, New York, December 4, 1905, Box 22, OWP; Owen Wister, "Chronicle and Comment," *Bookman* 18 (November 1903), p. 234; OW to SBW, July 17, 1905, Box 11, OWP.

2. William H. Riding to OW, September 19, 1904, Box 33; Roosevelt to OW, October 18, 1904, Box 33; OWP.

3. Wister, *Roosevelt*, pp. 245-46.

4. Owen Wister, "Preface—Cake and Critics," *The Writings of Owen Wister: Lady Baltimore* (New York: Macmillan Co., 1928), p. viii; Wister, *Roosevelt*, pp. 103, 246-47.

5. Wister, "Preface," *Writings of Owen Wister: Lady Baltimore*, p. viii.

6. OW to SBW, July 30, 1904, August 3, 4, 1904, October 13, 1904, Box 11, OWP.

7. The 1904–05 season schedule is in Box 67; royalty statement from Macmillan Co., July 25, 1904, Box 87; W. B. Cameron to OW, July 1, 1899, February 26, 1905, Box 15; J. W. Redington to OW, June 1, 1904, Box 32; Sylvia Emerson to OW, January 4, 1906, and enclosed clipping, Box 19; Charles B. Stewart to OW, September 27, 1905, Box 36; C. K. Fuller to OW, March 28, 1904, Box 21; OWP.

8. Charles W. Eliot to OW, August 16, 1904, Box 19; OW to SBW, August 29, 1904, Box 11; OWP.

9. "Mr. James's Variant," *Atlantic Monthly* 94 (September 1904), pp. 426-27; Reginald Wright Kauffman, "Writers in Philadelphia To-Day," *Book News* 24 (September 1905), p. 3; OW to SBW, August 25, 1904, September 26, 1904, Box 11; Alden to OW, November 16, 1904, Box 23; *Saturday Evening Post* to OW, October 10, 1905, Box 87; OWP. The installments appeared in the *Saturday Evening Post* in issues dated October 28, 1905, through January 27, 1906.

10. OW to SBW, December, n.d., 1904, October 7, 1904, Box 11, OWP.

11. Ibid., December, n.d., 1904, Box 11, OWP.

12. Wister, *Roosevelt*, pp. 244-45; Mitchell to OW, January 26, 1905, Box 3, OWP.

13. OW to SBW, January 21, 1905, Box 11, OWP.

14. Ibid., February 5, 1905, Box 11, OWP; Burr, *Weir Mitchell*, pp. 322-24.

15. Henry James, *The American Scene* (New York: Charles Scribner's Sons, 1946), pp. 408, 410, 412-13, 416.

16. Wister, "Preface," *Writings of Owen Wister: Lady Baltimore*, pp. viii-ix.

17. OW to SBW, March 26, 1905, Box 11, OWP.

18. OW to MW, April 11, 19, 1905, Box 4, OWP.

19. Ibid., May 1, 1905, MW to OW, n.d., [1905], Box 4, OWP.

20. Brett to OW, April 21, 1905, Box 28, OWP.

21. OW to SBW, June 26, 1905, July 1, 1905, Box 11, OWP.

22. Ibid., August 1, 1905, Box 11; *Saturday Evening Post* to OW, October 10, 1905, Box 87; OWP.

23. OW to SBW, October 2, 1905, December 9, 1905, Box 11, OWP.

24. Owen Wister, *Lady Baltimore* (New York: Macmillan Co., 1905), p. 171.

25. Burt G. Wilder to OW, December 20, 1905, with Wister's quotation repeated by Wilder in his letter to OW, December 29, 1905, Box 69, OWP.

26. Copy of unsigned letter to Burt G. Wilder, January 3, [1906], misdated as 1905, Box 69, OWP.

27. Samuel George Norton, *Crania Americana; or, A Comparative View of the Skulls of Various Aboriginal Nations of North and South America, to which is Prefixed an Essay on the Varieties of the Human Species* (Philadelphia: J. Dodson, 1839), as quoted by George M. Frederickson, *The Black Image in the White Mind: The Debate on Afro-American Character and Destiny, 1817–1914* (New York: Harper & Row, 1971), pp. 74-78. OW's revisions are on the installment as it appeared in the *Saturday Evening Post*, Box 69, OWP; Wister, *Lady Baltimore*, p. 171.

28. *New York Evening Post*, April 7, 1906, clipping, Box 70; *Charleston News & Courier*, April 15, 1906, clipping, Box 70; *Philadelphia Inquirer*, April 16, 1906, clipping, Box 70; OWP.

29. Brett to OW, February 15, 1906, Box 28; *Springfield* (Mass.) *Republican*, April 15, 1906, clipping, Box 70; OWP.

30. "Chronicle and Comment," *Bookman* 24 (January 1907), p. 440.

31. Sylvia Emerson to OW, n.d., Box 19; the Okemo Cake Kitchen Company menu is in Box 40; the musical score is in Box 70; OWP.

32. Statement of account, June 15, 1906, Box 28; Brett to OW, June 19, 1906, Box 28; OWP.

33. OW to Howe, October 29, 1906, HL.

34. Lodge to OW, April 30, 1906, Box 27, OWP.

35. J. J. Jusserand, *What Me Befell* (Boston: Houghton Mifflin Co., 1933), p. 271; OW to MW, April 7, 1906, Box 4, OWP.

36. The entire Roosevelt letter, April 27, 1906, is reproduced in both Wister, *Roosevelt*, pp. 248-57, and in Wister, "Preface," *Writings of Owen Wister: Lady Baltimore*, pp. xii-xxv; the original letter is in Box 33, OWP.

37. Ibid.

38. Ibid.

39. Roosevelt to Winthrop Chanler, June 23, 1906, in Morison, ed., *Letters of Theodore Roosevelt*, 5: 311.

40. Wister, "Preface," *Writings of Owen Wister: Lady Baltimore*, p. xi.

41. Duke to OW, April 12, 1906, Box 18, OWP.

42. OW to MW, June 4, 1906, Box 4; OW to SBW, May 10, 22, 23, 1906, June 15, 1906, Box 12; OWP.

43. Brett to OW, September 6, 1906, Box 28; OW to SBW, June 23, 1906, July 14, 1906, September 16, 1906, August 26, 1906, Box 12; OWP.

44. OW to SBW, September 16, 1906, October 18, 1906, Box 12, OWP.

45. Ibid., September 27, 1906, Box 12; Henry James to OW, August 22, 1906, Box 25; OWP.

46. OW to SBW, November 14, 26, 1906, Box 12, OWP; Allan Gates Halline, *American Plays* (New York: American Book Co., 1935), p. 457.

47. OW to SBW, August 26, 1906, Box 12, OWP.

48. Watterson's quote is from Stefan Lorant, *The Life and Times of Theodore Roosevelt* (Garden City: Doubleday & Co., 1959), p. 498; OW to SBW, October 31, 1906, Box 12, OWP.

CHAPTER XIII. IN THE PUBLIC ARENA (1907–1908)

1. OW to SBW, January 3, 1907, Box 12, OWP.

2. Ibid., January 10, 1907, Box 12, OWP.

3. Ibid., January 17, 1907, Box 12, OWP.

4. Wister, "Preface," *Writings of Owen Wister: U. S. Grant*, p. vii; OW to Henry James, May 1, 1906, HL; OW to SBW, February 3, 21, 1907, Box 12, OWP.

5. OW to SBW, March 6, 1907, Box 12, OWP.

6. Langdon Mitchell to OW, April 12, 1907, OW to SBW, April 15, 16, 28, 1907, March 18, 1907, Box 12, OWP; OW to Henry James, May 1, 1907, HL.

7. OW to SBW, March 16, 1907, Box 12, OWP.

8. Ibid., May 18, 1907, Box 12, OWP.

9. Ibid.

10. OW to SBW, February 15, 21, 1907, March 25, 1907, Box 12; La Shelle to OW, January 14, 1905, Box 26; OWP.

11. Charles Francis Adams to OW, February 4, 1907, OW to Adams, May 20, 1907, Box 13, OWP.

12. B. S. Hurlbut to OW, June 5, 1907, Box 40, OWP.

13. OW to SBW, May 18, 1907, August 15, 1907, Box 12, OWP.

14. OW to Howe, August 20, 29, 1907, HL.

15. The speech, "Our Country and the Scholar," is reproduced in its entirety in the *Harvard Bulletin* 10 (December 25, 1907), pp. 1-3.

16. Ibid.

17. Butler was quoted in the *Muncie* (Indiana) *Star*, December 24, 1907, clipping, Box 86; *Boston Congregationalist*, January 11, 1908, clipping, Box 86; *Brooklyn Daily Times*, December 19, 1907, clipping, Box 86; *Milwaukee Sentinel*, December 21, 1907, clipping, Box 86; OWP.

18. LeBaron Russell Briggs to OW, December 20, 1907, Box 14, OWP; "Recognition of Scholarship," *Harvard Bulletin*, December 25, 1907, p. 4; William James to OW, January 19, 1908, Box 25, OWP.

19. *San Francisco Town Talk*, February 22, 1908, clipping, Box 86; *Charleston News*, January 9, 1908, clipping, Box 49; *Providence Tribune*, December 22, 1907, clipping, Box 86; OWP.

20. "Owen Wister Discusses American Scholarship," *Philadelphia Public Ledger*, January 5, 1908, clipping, Box 86, OWP.

21. Ibid.

22. OW to William James, January 10, 1908, HL.

23. Untitled clipping, n.d., Box 86, OWP.

24. Wister, *Roosevelt*, pp. 266-67.

25. Newspaper clipping, n.d. [February 1908], Box 85, OWP.

26. *Buffalo Times*, February 10, 1908, clipping, Box 85; *North American*, February 7, 1908, clipping, Box 86; "Wister Makes First Speech; Hits Bosses," *North American*, February 7, 1908, clipping, Box 85; OWP.

NOTES

27. Untitled clipping, n.d., Box 86, OWP.

28. Handbill entitled "To the Voters of the Seventh Ward," Box 86; *Philadelphia Daily Evening Telegraph*, February 18, 1908, clipping, Box 86; OWP.

29. Wister, *Roosevelt*, p. 267; *The Pilot* comment quoted in the *Boston Transcript*, February 15, 1908, clipping, Box 86, OWP.

30. Campaign handbill, Box 85, OWP.

31. *Philadelphia Inquirer*, February 18, 1908, clipping, Box 86, OWP.

32. *Philadelphia Press*, February 19, 1908, clipping, Box 86; undated clipping, Box 86; OWP; Richard Hofstadter, *The Age of Reform* (New York: Vintage Books), p. 137; Robert H. Wiebe, *The Search for Order: 1877–1920* (New York: Hill and Wang, 1967), pp. 169-71; Gerald W. McFarland, *Misgivings, Morals, & Politics: 1884–1920* (Amherst: University of Massachusetts Press, 1975), p. 7.

33. Undated clipping, Box 86, OWP.

34. Ibid.

35. *Providence Journal*, February 22, 1908, *Canton Repository*, February 21, 1908, *Pittsburgh Gazette Times*, February 20, 1908, *Milwaukee Sentinel*, February 23, 1908, clippings, Box 86, OWP.

36. Wister, *Roosevelt*, pp. 269-70.

37. Henry James to OW, February 2, 1908, Box 25, OWP.

38. Ibid.; Henry Adams to OW, March 20, 1908, Box 13, OWP; John Spencer Bassett, "Reviews of Books," *American Historical Review* 13 (July 1908), pp. 911-12.

39. Edward Clark Marsh, "Representative American Story Tellers: Owen Wister," *Bookman* 27 (July 1908), pp. 458-66.

40. OW to Henry James, July 6, 1908, HL.

41. Wister, ed., *Owen Wister Out West*, pp. xii-xiii.

42. *Philadelphia Press*, November 28, 1908, clipping, Box 44; *St. Louis Star*, January 3, 1909, clipping, Box 87; *North American*, November 28, [1908], clipping, Box 44; OWP.

43. *Philadelphia Press*, November 28, 1908, *North American*, November 28, 1908, clippings, Box 44, OWP.

44. *Philadelphia Evening Telegraph*, July 22, 1911, clipping, Box 44, OWP.

45. *St. Louis Star*, January 3, 1909, clipping, Box 87, OWP.

46. Wister, ed., *Owen Wister Out West*, pp. xii-xiv. The luncheon is misdated in this book as having occurred in 1908.

CHAPTER XIV. TRIBULATIONS (1909–1914)

1. C. F. Adams to OW, December 11, 1908, Box 13, OWP.

2. Persons, *Decline of American Gentility*, pp. 290, 292.

3. Henry Cabot Lodge to OW, April 29, 1909, Box 27, OWP; untitled clipping, n.d., Box 86, OWP; *Philadelphia Evening Bulletin*, October 13, 1911, clipping, Box 48, OWP; W. B. Cameron to OW, June 23, 1911, Box 17, OWP; OW to MW, October 13, 1910, Box 4, OWP; notation by OW on letter from J. F. Deal to MW, October 6, 1905, Box 4, OWP; poem entitled "Serenade," *Harper's Monthly* 121 (June 1910), p. 37.

4. *Baltimore Sun*, June 1, 1909, p. 6, clipping, Box 87, OWP.

5. Letter from MW, n.d., Box 4; MW to Cree T. Work, Denton, Texas, July 30, 1909, Box 4; MW to Adolph S. Ochs, January 17, 1910, Box 4; OWP.

6. OW to MW, March 8, 1910, Box 4, OWP; OW to J. J. Chapman, September 3, 1910, HL.

7. OW to William Allen White, William Allen White Papers, Box 12, Library of Congress.

8. *New York Sun*, December 2, 1911, clipping, Box 44; Benjamin B. Hampton to OW, July 28, 1910, Box 40; OW to MW, August 20, 1910, Box 4; OWP.

9. OW to MW, August 8, 1910, Box 4, OWP.

NOTES

10. Ibid., August 21, 1910, Box 4, OWP.
11. Ibid., September 13, 1910, August 18, 1910, Box 4, OWP.
12. George Miller Beard, *American Nervousness, Its Causes and Consequences* (New York: Putnam, 1881), pp. 96-113, 133-38, as reprinted in Alan Trachtenberg, ed., *Democratic Vistas, 1860–1880* (New York: George Braziller, 1970), pp. 238-47.
13. OW to MW, September 9, 11, 25, 1910, August 20, 1910, Box 4, OWP; OW to J. J. Chapman, September 3, 1910, HL.
14. OW to MW, September 25, 1910, Box 4, OWP.
15. Ibid., September 13, 1910, Box 4, OWP.
16. Ibid., August 21, 1910, Box 4, OWP.
17. Ibid., September 13, 15, 1910, Box 4, OWP; OW to J. J. Chapman, September 3, 1910, HL.
18. OW to MW, October 2, 1910, August 30, 1910, n.d., 1910, Box 4, OWP.
19. Ibid., September 19, 22, 1910, October 13, 1910, Box 4, OWP.
20. Ibid., October 30, 1910, November 1, 1910, Box 4, October 27, 1910, Box 5, OWP.
21. MW to OW, telegram, October 31, 1910, OW to MW, November 3, 9, 1910, Box 4, OWP.
22. OW to MW, November 10, 1910, Box 4, OWP.
23. Ibid., November 15, 23, 1910, Box 4, OWP.
24. Ibid., December 1, 6, 1910, November 29, 1910, Box 4, OWP; Wister, *Roosevelt*, p. 294, *Philadelphia Evening Bulletin*, October 13, 1911, clipping, Box 48, OWP; OW to J. J. Chapman, December 29, 1910, HL; Wister, *Members of the Family*.
25. *Salt Lake City Herald*, June 22, 1911, clipping, Box 44, OWP; OW to J. J. Chapman, September 24, 1911, HL; Wister, ed., *Owen Wister Out West*, pp. xvi-xvii.
26. Wister, ed., *Owen Wister Out West*, p. xviii; the outline for "The Star Gazers" is in Box 83, OWP.
27. "Owen Wister Here After Long Rest on Loved Plains," interview in unnamed Denver newspaper, n.d., Box 86, OWP.
28. Ibid.
29. Wister, *Roosevelt*, p. 296; *Franklin* (Pa.) *News*, October 13, 1911, clipping, Box 48, OWP; a large collection of clippings detailing Wister's supposed death is in Box 48, OWP; "Owen Wister Is Dead," *Boston Transcript*, October 13, 1911, as quoted in Marovitz, "Owen Wister: An Annotated Bibliography," p. 39; *Findlay* (Ohio) *Courier*, October 13, 1911, *Philadelphia Evening Bulletin*, October 13, 1911, clippings, Box 48, OWP.
30. *Philadelphia Evening Bulletin*, October 13, 1911, *Sacramento Star*, October 13, 1911, clippings, Box 48, OWP; "Who's Dead?" *Waynesburg* (Pa.) *Messenger*, October 14, 1911, as quoted in Marovitz, "Owen Wister: An Annotated Bibliography," p. 40.
31. Wister, *Roosevelt*, p. 296.
32. Associated Press story, n.d., Box 48, OWP.
33. *Philadelphia Bulletin*, November 2, 1911, clipping, Box 44, OWP; Wister, *Roosevelt*, p. 296.
34. "High Prices Paid to Authors," *New York Sun*, December 2, 1911, clipping, Box 44, OWP.
35. Document dated November 7, 1911, Box 19, OWP.
36. Wister, ed., *Owen Wister Out West*, p. xiv; Wister, *Roosevelt*, p. 306; Wister's introduction is reproduced in a notebook in Box 90, OWP.
37. Wister, *Roosevelt*, pp. 316, 318.
38. OW to A. H. Morton, June 6, 1912, OW's reply is copied on the original letter from Morton to OW, June 6, 1913, Box 30, OWP.
39. *San Diego Union*, July 15, 1912, clipping, Box 40, OWP.

40. Wister, ed., *Owen Wister Out West*, p. xviii; OW to J. J. Chapman, October 29, 1912, HL.

41. Wister, *Roosevelt*, pp. 318-19.

42. OW to Howe, January 29, 1913, HL; a copy of the incomplete manuscript is in Box 83, OWP.

43. OW to J. J. Chapman, September 13, 1912, HL; manuscript of January 1913 speech is in Box 50, OWP.

44. OW to Henry James, August 25, 1913, HL; clippings in Box 5, OWP.

45. OW to Henry James, August 25, 1913, HL.

46. "Sallie Wistar Says," *Philadelphia Public Ledger*, August 26, 1913, Box 5, OWP.

47. Roosevelt to OW, October 1, 1913, Box 33, OWP.

48. *Philadelphia Evening Bulletin*, October 14, 1913, clipping, Box 5, OWP; J. J. Chapman to OW, December 3, 1922, Box 16, OWP; *Civic Club Bulletin* 8 (May 1914), pp. 1-55.

49. OW to J. J. Chapman, October 28, 1913, HL; *Boston Globe*, March 15, 1914, clipping, Box 44; Owen Wister, "Address at the Julia Ward Howe School," November 14, 1914, Box 49; *Philadelphia Evening Bulletin*, November 27, 1914, clipping, Box 48; Henry James to OW, February 23, 1914, Box 25; OWP.

50. Cecil B. DeMille, *The Autobiography of Cecil B. DeMille* (New York: Prentice-Hall, 1959), pp. 101-2.

51. Brett to OW, April 28, 1914, Box 28, OWP.

52. OW to Robert Grant, June 16, 1914, HL; Owen Wister, *Pentecost of Calamity* (New York: Macmillan Co., 1916), pp. 18-19. Wister's calendar lists the operas he attended, Box 84, OWP.

53. Wister, *Roosevelt*, pp. 321-22.

54. Henry James to OW, September 4, 1914, Box 25, OWP.

Chapter XV. The Curmudgeon Unveiled (1914–1923)

1. Wister, *Roosevelt*, pp. 329-30; Roosevelt's quotation is from Mark Sullivan, *Our Times*, 6 vols. (New York: Charles Scribner's Sons, 1926–35), 5: 202.

2. W. P. Few to OW, January 26, 1912, OW to Few, February 4, 1915, Box 19, OWP.

3. Wister *Pentecost of Calamity*, pp. 61, 73; Brett to OW, January 4, 1916, Box 28, OWP; Owen Wister, "Preface—Pro-British!" *The Writings of Owen Wister: The Pentecost of Calamity and A Straight Deal* (New York: Macmillan Co., 1928), pp. 140-41.

4. Wister, *Pentecost of Calamity*, pp. 140-41.

5. Henry Cabot Lodge to OW, October 27, 1915, Box 27, OWP; Howells to OW, August 13, 1915, Box 24, OWP; *New York Times Book Review*, September 5, 1915, p. 317, and *Review of Reviews* 52 (October 1915), p. 507, both quoted in Marovitz, "Owen Wister: An Annotated Bibliography," p. 43; Roosevelt to OW, July 7, 1915, Box 41, OWP; also quoted in Wister, *Roosevelt*, pp. 349-50; Eliot to OW, September 29, 1915, OW to Eliot, December 6, 1915, Box 19, OWP.

6. Wister, *Pentecost of Calamity*, p. 55; OW to Frederick W. Kahn, August 4, 1915, Box 26, OWP; "Writers and Books," *Boston Evening Transcript*, August 28, 1915, p. 8, as quoted in Marovitz, "Owen Wister: An Annotated Bibliography," p. 43.

7. Wister, *Pentecost of Calamity*, p. 135; James R. Angell to OW, October 14, 1915, Box 13; Albion Small to OW, October 24, 1915, Box 36; OW to Small, October 26, 1915, Box 36; Small to OW, November 1, 1915, Box 35; Brett to OW, January 11, 1916, Box 28; OWP.

8. Howard Mumford Jones and Richard M. Ludwig, *Guide to American Literature and Its Backgrounds since 1890*, 4th ed. (Cambridge: Harvard University Press, 1972),

p. 178; Walter Millis, *Road to War: America 1914–1917* (Boston: Houghton Mifflin Co., 1935), p. 154.

9. Wister, "Quack-Novels and Democracy," *Atlantic Monthly* 115 (June 1915), pp. 721-34.

10. Sedgwick to OW, March 29, 1915, Box 13, OWP; Howells to OW, June 17, 1915, Box 24, OWP; Meredith Nicholson, "The Open Season for American Novelists," *Atlantic Monthly* 116 (October 1915), pp. 456-66, as quoted in Marovitz, "Owen Wister: An Annotated Bibliography," p. 43.

11. Upton Sinclair to OW, June 14, 1915, Box 34, OWP.

12. Marina Wister, "Listening," *Night in the Valley* (New York: Macmillan Co., 1930); OW to J. J. Chapman, January 1, 1916, HL.

13. J. J. Chapman to OW, August 29, 1915, September 3, 25, 1916, Box 16, OWP.

14. Wister, *Roosevelt*, p. 332; the poem was reprinted in the *New York Times*, February 24, 1916, p. 3, among other places.

15. *New York Times*, February 24, 1916, p. 3.

16. The poem, by Arthur Hinds, appeared in the *Boston Transcript*, February 26, 1916. J. Hampton Brown to OW, February 23, 1916, Box 15; John Trent to OW, March 7, 1916, Box 37; John Roberts to OW, February 24, 1916, Box 34; Henry D. Sedgwick on OW, February 25, 1916, Box 34; Roosevelt to OW, April 11, 1916, Box 41; OWP.

17. OW to J. B. Bishop, March 25, 1920, Box 15, OWP.

18. "500 Americans Declare for Allies," *Boston Advertiser*, April 17, 1916.

19. *Louisville Courier-Journal*, June 3, 1916, clipping, Box 37, OWP.

20. "Men of Letters in Politics," *Louisville Courier-Journal*, June 3, 1916, Box 37; OW to Henry Watterson, June 5, 1916, Box 37; telegram from OW to Watterson, June 9, 1916, Box 37; Watterson to OW, June 9, 1916, Box 37; Watterson to OW, April 16, 1917, Box 40; OWP.

21. Owen Wister, "If We Elect Mr. Wilson," *Colliers* 58 (November 4, 1916), pp. 5-6, 22-23; Wister, *Roosevelt*, p. 362.

22. Lady Musgrave to OW, February 10, March 19, April 4, 1917, Box 30, OWP.

23. Ernest Poole to OW, August 16, 1918, September 9, 1918, Box 40; E. F. Harvey to OW, April 1, 1918, Box 31; Lee F. Hanmer to OW, March 12, 1919, Box 40; OW to Robert Grant, October 5, 1918, John M. Siddell to OW, July 5, 1918, Box 13; OWP.

24. Perry, *Henry Lee Higginson*, pp. 462-502.

25. Higginson to OW, November 1, 3, 7, 1917, Mrs. H. L. Higginson to OW, May 28, 1918, Box 23, OWP.

26. Higginson to OW, November 15, 20, 1917, Box 23, OWP; Perry, *Henry Lee Higginson*, pp. 500-501.

27. *Harvard Alumni Bulletin* 22 (November 27, 1919), pp. 222-23.

28. Statement of income, Box 87; Jeanie Lucinda Fields to OW, August 11, 1918, February 9, 1918, December 25, 1919, Box 30; OWP.

29. "Wister's Boy Valet in Prison," *Boston Post*, November 11, 1917; *Boston Advertiser*, August 10, 1917, clipping, Box 44, OWP.

30. OW to Robert Grant, October 5, 1918, HL.

31. Notebook entry, January 5, 1921, in "Journal, 1920–21," Box 1; OW to J. B. Bishop, March 25, 1920, Box 20; the poem is in OW's notebook, Box 90; OWP.

32. Roosevelt to OW, October 27, 1918, Box 41, OWP.

33. Notation in calendar book for November 7, 1918, Box 84, OWP; OW to Howe, November 13, 1918, HL.

34. Duke to OW, February 9, 1919, Box 18, OWP.

35. West to OW, August 11, 1920, Box 38, OWP.

36. Brett to OW, December 30, 1919, Box 28; Wister was to get twenty percent of the net profits for *Red Men and White* and *Members of the Family* as indicated

NOTES

by an undated document and a document of December 2, 1919, Box 89; memo dated December 21, 1920, Box 89; OWP.

37. OW telegram to *New York World*, March 10, 1919, Box 31, OWP; OW to Barrett Wendell, March 22, 1919, HL.

38. Owen Wister, "The Ancient Grudge," *American Magazine* 86 (November 1918), pp. 14-15, 88, 90, 92, 94; Wister, "Preface," *Writings of Owen Wister: The Pentecost of Calamity and A Straight Deal*, pp. vi-vii; calendar in Box 84, OWP; notebook entries, May 7, 15, [1919], Box 1, OWP.

39. "Preface," *Writings of Owen Wister: The Pentecost of Calamity and A Straight Deal*, p. ix.

40. Owen Wister, *A Straight Deal or The Ancient Grudge* (New York: Macmillan Co., 1920); the pamphlet was published in 1920 in Washington, D.C.; Mrs. Bertha Jones Arnold to OW, January 15, 1922, Box 13, OWP; "An Effusive Friend," *Athenaeum* No. 4704 (June 25, 1920), p. 825; Robert Livingston Schuyler, "New Grudges for Old," *Bookman* 51 (July 1920), p. 568; Francis B. Biddle to OW, May 17, 1920, Box 14, OWP.

41. Owen Wister, Introductory note, *Neighbors Henceforth* (New York: Macmillan Co., 1922).

42. Henry Cabot Lodge to OW, May 6, 1920, Box 27, OWP.

43. Ibid., June 14, 1920, Box 27, OWP; "Harding and Foreign Affairs," *New York Times*, October 9, 1920, p. 14.

44. Notebook entries, December 28, 1920, January 5, 1921, in "Journal, 1920–21," Box 1; June 6, 1921, entry in calendar, Box 84; entry, December 23, 1920, in "Journal, 1920–21," Box 1; entry, April 24, 1921, in "Journal, 1920–21," Box 1; Ellery Sedgwick to OW, June 11, 1921, Box 34; entry, April 22, 1921, in "Journal, 1920–21," Box 1; OWP.

45. Entry, March 1, 1921, in "Journal, 1920–21," Box 1, OWP.

46. Notebook dated 1905 but which includes details of later years, including 1921, Box 89, OWP.

47. "Plead for Our Dead in France," *New York Times*, April 15, 1921, p. 1.

48. "Only 2 Unclaimed Soldier Dead Here," *New York Times*, April 16, 1921, p. 1; "Writers Disagree on Soldier Dead," ibid., April 17, 1921, p. 20; Secretary of War Newton Baker said that 74,770 questionnaires had been mailed, and of the 63,708 returned, 43,909 wanted their soldiers' bodies returned home. ("Government Is Bound by the Wish of Families," *New York Times*, April 16, 1921, p. 5.)

49. "Our Dead in France," *New York Times*, April 17, 1921, p. 2, Section 2.

50. Notebook entry, August 21, 1921, Box 84, OWP.

51. *Rochester Herald*, August 24, 1921, September 25, 1921, clippings, Box 85, OWP.

52. Russell McFarland to OW, November 19, 1916, Box 28, OWP.

53. *New York Times*, June 9, 1921, clipping, Box 85, OWP.

54. "Wister on France and America," *New York Times Book Review*, January 7, 1923, p. 8; Owen Wister, "Preface—A Piece of Extravagance," *The Writings of Owen Wister: Neighbors Henceforth* (New York: Macmillan Co., 1928), p. vii.

CHAPTER XVI. ENTANGLEMENTS (1923–1938)

1. Julie B. Kimball to OW, June, n.d., 1928, Box 26; Beulah Overman to OW, October 19, 1925, Box 31; OWP.

2. J. J. Chapman to OW, December 3, 1922, Box 16, OWP.

3. Ibid.; notation dated January 20, 1933, Box 49; program dated December 12, 1922, Box 96; OWP.

4. A copy of the March 1923 speech is in Box 49, OWP.

5. Ibid.

6. *Washington Post*, November 24, 1923, clipping, Box 86, OWP; *Philadelphia*

Public Ledger, June 2, 1923, clipping, Box 64, OWP; the script for *Watch Your Thirst* was printed in a limited edition in 1923 by Macmillan Co., and a revised version was privately printed in 1933; Owen Wister II to OW, March 17, 1924, Box 7, OWP; H. G. Vaughan to OW, March 24, Box 37, OWP.

7. *Boston Herald*, June 4, 1923, clipping, Box 86, OWP.

8. *Philadelphia Bulletin*, April 12, 1924, clipping, Box 86; *Philadelphia Inquirer*, April 17, 1924, clipping, Box 87; OWP.

9. OW to General Henry T. Allen, February 19, 1924, Box 13, OWP.

10. Allen to OW, February 23, 1924, OW to Allen, March 3, 1924, Box 13, OWP; G. S. Viereck to OW, February 25, 1924, Box 37, OWP; correspondence published in *American Monthly* 16 (April 1924), p. 56.

11. E. R. Burroughs to OW, January 31, 1923, Box 14; "Famous Living Writers," undated clipping, Box 41; OWP.

12. Owen Wister, "Padre Ignazio," *Harper's Monthly* 100 (April 1900), pp. 692-703, reprinted as a book by Harper and Brothers in 1911 as *Padre Ignacio.*

13. Owen Wister, *Philosophy 4: A Story of Harvard University* (Philadelphia: Lippincott, 1901); Wister, "Preface," *Writings of Owen Wister: Safe in the Arms of Croesus*; OW to SBW, August 11, 1901, Box 11, OWP.

14. Owen Wister, "The Right Honorable the Strawberries," *Cosmopolitan* (November 1926), pp. 34-41, collected in *When West Was West* (New York: Macmillan Co., 1928).

15. Philip A. Rollins to OW, January 7, 1923, Box 34, OWP.

16. W. R. Spalding to OW, November 21, 1923, Box 35; Mrs. Jansen Haines to OW, March 9, 1923, Box 3; OWP.

17. *Richmond Times-Despatch*, December 2, 1923, *Green Bay Press Gazette*, November 30, 1923, clippings, Box 80, OWP.

18. Douglas Fairbanks to OW, May 31, 1924, Box 19; OW to Marina Wister, May 21, 1926, Box 5; OWP.

19. Untitled newspaper obituary on Trafton, n.d., Box 80, OWP.

20. E. Montgomery Reily to OW, April 24, 1924, Box 33, OWP; Frank Lynch, "Seattle Scene: 'The Virginian' Family Grows and Grows," *Seattle Times*, column, n.d. [1950 or 1951], in possession of George M. West.

21. J. B. Choate to OW, December 29, 1924, Box 17, OWP.

22. OW to John Krohne, January 13, 1922, Box 26, OWP.

23. OW to Mary Channing Wister, September 28, 1920, Box 5, OWP.

24. OW to William I. Nichols, March 10, 1928, William I. Nichols Papers, Box 2, Library of Congress; OW to Rosa Mordecai, July 15, 1934, Alfred Mordecai Papers, Vol. G, Library of Congress.

25. Frances Wister to OW, November 15, 1924, Box 3; Anne Mitchell to OW, September 20, 1925, October 13, 1925, Box 29; OWP.

26. Note, July 4, 1924, Box 49; Wister's itinerary, Box 84; note, September 19, 1924, Box 40; OWP; OW to J. J. Chapman, July 6, 193[?], HL.

27. Quoted in *Detroit News*, November 23, 1924, clipping, Box 96, OWP.

28. Henry Cabot Lodge to OW, January 16, 1924, Box 27, OWP.

29. Wister's feature was released in July 1925 by Johnson Features, Inc.—a copy of it is in Box 96, OWP; "A Tribute from Owen Wister," *New York Times*, December 15, 1925, p. 24.

30. Owen Wister, Preface, "The St. Paul's School War Memorial," March 1927, Box 59, OWP.

31. "At the Sign of the Last Chance" first appeared in *Cosmopolitan* (February 1928), pp. 66-75; Lambert, "Western Writings of Owen Wister," pp. 190-97.

32. Wister, "Preface," *Writings of Owen Wister: The Virginian*, p. vii.

33. William Curtis, *Town & Country*, March 15, 1929, pp. 78, 120; OW to Marina Wister, August 18, 1928, Box 5, OWP.

NOTES

34. W. B. Cameron to OW, April 3, 1930, Box 41; Burton Emmett to OW, December 5, 1930, Box 78; OWP.

35. R. N. Hancock to OW, September 18, 1933, Box 24; "Map of the History and Romance of Wyoming," Laramie, Wyo., 1928, Box 40; F. M. Fryxell to OW, October 31, 1929, Box 40; OWP; *New York Times*, February 24, 1939, p. 21; *Every Evening* (Wilmington, Delaware), July 13, 1929, clipping, Box 86, OWP.

36. The entire poem is in Box 40; Wister's speech, "The Creed of a Charter Member," is in Box 52; OWP.

37. George Waring to OW, July 13, 1928, Ellery Sedgwick to OW, July 31, 1928, Box 40, OWP.

38. Oliver Wendell Holmes to OW, July 16, 1928, Box 23, OWP; Carlos Baker, ed., *Ernest Hemingway: Selected Letters, 1917–1961* (New York: Charles Scribner's Sons, 1981), pp. 254-55, 284; Carlos Baker, *Ernest Hemingway: A Life Story* (New York: Charles Scribner's Sons, 1969), p. 196.

39. Hemingway to OW, March 1, 1929, Box 23, OWP; Wister, *Roosevelt*, p. 152; Hemingway to OW, March 11, 1929, September 27, 1928, February 20, 1929, June 4, 1929, July 26, 1930, December 26, 1931, January 30, 1932, February 9, 1933, Box 23, OWP; Baker, ed., *Hemingway: Selected Letters*, pp. 272, 301.

40. Hemingway to OW, March 1, 1929, Box 23, OWP; Baker, *Ernest Hemingway*, p. 201; Maxwell Perkins to OW, May 1, 1929, Box 31, OWP; A. Scott Berg, *Max Perkins: Editor of Genius* (New York: Pocket Books, 1978), p. 180; Baker, ed., *Hemingway: Selected Letters*, p. 299.

41. Hemingway to OW, February 9, 1933, Box 23, OWP.

42. Mrs. Theodore Roosevelt to OW, March 26, 1920, Box 33; George Roosevelt to OW, November 7, 1929, Box 41; OWP; OW to J. J. Chapman, September 10, 1930, HL; OW to Edward S. Martin, September 14, 1930, HL.

43. George H. Lorimer to OW, January 21, 1930, Box 41, OWP.

44. General correspondence concerning the threatened suit appears in Boxes 28 and 29, OWP.

45. Wister, *Roosevelt*, pp. 103-5.

46. Brett to OW, July 8, 1930, July 14, 1930, Box 28; John K. Mitchell to OW, June 27, 1930, Box 29; OWP.

47. Associated Press article, June 26, 1930, clipping, Box 29; Brett to OW, July 14, 1930, Box 28; OWP.

48. Wister, *Roosevelt*, p. 87.

49. OW to J. J. Chapman, September 10, 1930, HL.

50. "Former as a 'Might Still Be,'" *Fresno Republican*, August 23, p. 4; OW to editor of *Fresno Republican*, n.d., Box 32, OWP; Ben R. Walker to OW, October 9, 1930, Box 32, OWP.

51. OW to Elizabeth Chapman, October 19, 1930, HL.

52. H. F. Bowen to OW, January 3, 1931, June 7, 1931, Box 15, OWP.

53. Ibid.

54. Ernest S. Greene to OW, September 3, 1931, OW to Greene, September 6, 1931, Box 22; Sinclair to OW, October 22, 1931, Box 34; OWP.

55. OW to Sinclair, November 9, 1931, Box 34, OWP.

56. OW to Marina Wister, November 29, 1927, Box 5; OW to William I. Nichols, March 10, 1928, William I. Nichols Papers, Box 2, Library of Congress; Marina Wister, *Night in the Valley*; OW to Rose Mordecai, March 13, 1933, Papers of Alfred Mordecai, Vol. 6, Library of Congress; ibid., July 15, 1934.

57. OW to "Mr. Hancock," September 2, 1933, as quoted in N. Orwin Rush, *Fifty Years of The Virginian, 1902–1952* (Laramie: University of Wyoming Library Associates, 1952), pp. 2-3; OW to Edward S. Martin, December 21, 1933, HL.

58. Notations in Box 89, OWP.

59. Wister, "John Jay Chapman," *Atlantic Monthly* 153 (May 1934), pp. 524-

39; OW to Edward S. Martin, November 13, 1933, HL; Chanler Chapman to OW, December 25, 1933, Box 15, OWP.

60. The history's first draft is in Box 68; golfing dates are in OW's pocket calendar, Box 85; OWP.

61. OW to Howe, May 10, 1934, HL; OW's notation concerning the "supreme success" is in the section for November 1, 1934, pocket calendar, Box 85; Henry G. Vaughn to OW, November 7, 1934, Box 36; OWP.

62. Amos T. French to OW, November 19, 1933, Box 20, OWP; OW to J. J. Chapman, August 2, 1928, HL.

63. West to OW, August 11, 1920, July 26, 1934, Box 38, OWP.

64. OW to Lomax, January 12, 1933, Lomax to OW, February 14, 1933, Box 27, OWP.

65. Percy Goetschius to C. Engel, April 19, 1936, included in a letter from Engel to OW, April 21, 1936, Box 34; Engel to OW, July 24, 1935, Box 34; the terms offered Wister were a ten percent royalty on the net professional price per copy, thirty-three and one-third percent on performing fees, broadcasts, etc., and fifty percent on recordings and reproductions by mechanical processes; Engel to OW, September 19, 1935, Box 34; OWP; Wister, "Strictly Hereditary," pp. 1-7.

66. OW to Elizabeth Chapman, October 19, 1930, OW to J. J. Chapman, June 25, 1932, October 31, 1930, HL.

67. Edward Connery to OW, September 7, 1932, Box 16; OW to Amos T. French, October 31, 1932, Box 20; OWP.

68. "Arrest of Defenders of High Court Fails to Prevent Rally Here," *Philadelphia Inquirer,* May 11, 1937.

69. *Philadelphia Inquirer,* April 12, 1937.

70. Owen Wister, "In Homage to Mark Twain," *Harper's* 171 (October 1935), pp. 547-56; Wister, "Old Yellowstone Days," *Harper's* 172 (March 1936), pp. 471-80; Wister, "William Dean Howells," *Atlantic Monthly* 160 (December 1937), pp. 704-13.

71. The volume by Van Wyck Brooks was *New England Indian Summer, 1865–1915* (E. P. Dutton & Co., 1940); Van Wyck Brooks to OW, April 2, 11, 26, 1937, Box 14, OWP.

72. OW to Edward S. Martin, August 3, 1937, OW to Howe, September 27, 1937, May 21, 1938, OW to Robert Grant, October 9, 1937, HL; Henry D. Sedgwick to OW, May 5, 1938, Box 34, OWP.

Index

Boone and Crockett Club, 134, 137, 142

Boston, 61-65, 69-70, 103, 124, 249-50

Boston Symphony Orchestra, 185, 187-88, 249, 295-97

Boynton, H. W., 202-3

Bradley, James, 264

Bret, Charles, 297-98

Brett, George P., 165, 194, 215, 230, 236, 289, 322-23; encourages Wister's writing, 234, 239, 240, 284, 288, 299-300

Brian, Mary, 321

Brieux, Eugène, 283

Briggs, Le Baron Russell, 255-56

Brinton, John H., 168

Brooks, Lawrence, 117, 120

Brooks, Rev. Phillips, xv, 29, 31, 32-33, 44, 63, 70

Brooks, Van Wyck, 332

Brownsville, Texas, racial incident in, 244

"The Brushwood Boy" (R. Kipling), 163

Bryan, William Jennings, 160, 169

Bryce, Lord James, 303

Buchanan, James, 292

Burroughs, Edgar Rice, 311

Butler, Fanny (Mrs. James Leigh, OW's aunt), 7, 14, 26, 48, 214, 244, 274, 275

Butler, Nicholas Murray, 255

Butler, Pierce, xiii, 6, 7, 8, 10, 65-66, 172, 213, 263

Butler Place, 10, 17, 20, 25, 103, 145, 146, 165, 214, 263-64, 269, 273-74, 283, 291, 309-10, 315

Butt, Archie, 265

Cabot, Charles, 161, 163, 182

Cabot, Elliot, 36

Cabot, Mrs. Elliot, 88

Cabot, Henry, 45, 93, 182

Cabot, Ted, 93

Cabot, Mrs. Walter C., 95, 140, 160, 161

Cabot family, 30, 37, 62, 64, 88, 140, 160, 161, 163

Cadwallader, Sally, 99

Cameron, W. B., 232

Campeau, Frank, 221, 226, 244, 252

Cannon, Joe, 249

Canton, Frank, 125, 140

Carrigan, John B., 331

Carroll, Royal, 162

Century Magazine, 71, 74

Chanler, Elizabeth, 162

Chanler, William, 175

Chanler, Winthrop, 64, 134, 162, 172, 175, 243, 321

Channing, William Ellery, xvi, 7, 167, 173, 217, 268, 282

Chapman, Henry, 37, 39

Chapman, John Jay, xv, 161, 236, 293, 323, 328; and Boston society, 88; corresponds with Wister, 85, 86, 89, 170-71, 272, 275, 281, 291, 308, 321, 330; death of, 327; marries Minna Timmins, 111; meets Wister, 21; in New York, 174, 245; as a student at Harvard, 37-40, 43; as a student at Harvard Law School, 93, 95-96

Chapman, Mrs. (mother of Henry and John Jay), 86, 88

Charlemagne. See Wister, Owen: operas by

Charleston, South Carolina, 172-74, 195-96, 230-31, 234-35, 239-42, 322

Charleston Expedition, 195-96, 322

Cheyenne Club, 81, 152

Child, Francis James, 36

Churchill, Winston, 189, 239, 293

City Party of Philadelphia, 251, 257-61

Clemenceau, Georges, 303, 308

Clemens, Samuel L. See Twain, Mark

Cleveland, Grover, 146

154-55, 329-30; as a student, at Harvard, 29-45, 34-37; as a student, at Harvard law school, 93-94, 103-5; as a student, of music, 38-39, 51-55, 58-60; as a student, at St. Paul, 17-27; in theatricals, 41-43
—trips of: to Arizona, 142-44, 148-51; to Atlantic City, NJ, 233-34; to California, 144-45, 151-52, 155-56, 269, 280; to Charleston, SC, 172-74, 195-98, 234-35; to Europe, 47-48, 48-55, 58-60, 284-85, 300-301, 303-5, 315-16; to Hot Springs, Virginia, 235-36, 250-51; to Texas, 132-33; to the VR Ranch, 80-84; to Washington, 129-30, 174-77; to Wyoming, 77-90, 98-103, 105-8, 112-14, 117-21, 127-28, 140-41, 152, 270-76, 277-78, 280-81, 320
—views of: on American society, xvi, 84-85, 146-47, 229-30, 267-68, 330; on education, xvi, 67-68, 253-57; on minorities, 214, 237-38, 268, 308-9; on political issues, 290-95, 300-301, 302-5, 310, 330-32; on religion, 68-69; on the West, 84-85, 128-29, 160, 204-5
—works by, articles: "The Ancient Grudge," 300; "Down in a Diving Bell," 19, 20; "The Evolution of a Cow Puncher," 148, 165, 205, 207; "How Doth the Simple Spelling Bee," 246; "If We Elect Mr. Wilson," 294; "An Inquiry into the Future of the Opera" (not published), 44; "Keystone Crime; Philadelphia Corrupt and Contented," 257; "Quack Novels and Democracy," 290; "Republican Opera," 97; "Strictly Hereditary," 330; "What the Victory or Defeat of Germany Means to Every American," 295; "Your Child's Life—Or a Guinea Pig's?" 316
—works by, compositions: "Blow,

blow, thou winter wind," 330; "Dawn of Love," 222; "Emily," 222; Ivanhoe, 35; "Sigh No More, Ladies," 330; "Ten Thousand Cattle Straying," 222, 226, 264; "Winter's Song," 330
—works by, fiction, book-length: The Jimmyjohn Boss and Other Stories, 183, 193; Lady Baltimore, xv, 230-31, 233-44, 262, 268, 276, 301, 307, 322; Lin McLean, 168-69, 170, 171, 203, 209-10, 221, 300; Members of the Family, 278, 300; The New Swiss Family Robinson: A Tale for Children of All Ages, 44; Red Men and White, 156-57, 159, 160, 163, 164, 166, 300; The Virginian, xv, 135, 215, 301, 329, analysis of, 198-200, 202-6, critical reception of, 199-200, 201-3, 288, 306, 307, 313, 314, 318, 323-24, new edition of, 278-79, publication of, xiii, 198-200, sales of, xiv, 200-201, 213-14, 230, 232, 318, Wister's criticism of, 231, 311, writing of, 182, 193, 195-96, 197-98, 230; When West Was West, 317; "A Wise Man's Son" (not published), 71-72, 73-75, 110
—works by, non-fiction, book-length: Neighbors Henceforth, xv, 302, 306; The Pentecost of Calamity, xv, 288-89, 294, 300, 301, 306; Roosevelt: The Story of a Friendship, 277, 321-23, 324; The Seven Ages of Washington, 253, 262; A Straight Deal or The Ancient Grudge, 301-2, 303, 306; Ulysses S. Grant, xv, 182, 184, 185, 187, 188, 189, 190, 217, 253
—works by, operas: Charlemagne, 110, 111; Lady of the Lake, 41; La Sérénade, 54; Montezuma, 54, 111-12, 132, 168; Villon, 132, 168; Watch Your Thirst, 309, 328, 329